LUSTRATION AND
TRANSITIONAL JUSTICE

PENNSYLVANIA STUDIES
IN HUMAN RIGHTS

Bert B. Lockwood Jr., Series Editor

A complete list of books in the series
is available from the publisher.

LUSTRATION AND TRANSITIONAL JUSTICE

PERSONNEL SYSTEMS
IN THE CZECH REPUBLIC,
HUNGARY, AND POLAND

ROMAN DAVID

PENN

UNIVERSITY OF PENNSYLVANIA PRESS

PHILADELPHIA

Copyright © 2011 University of Pennsylvania Press

Published by
University of Pennsylvania Press
Philadelphia, Pennsylvania 19104-4112
www.upenn.edu/pennpress

Printed in the United States of America
on acid-free paper

10 9 8 7 6 5 4 3 2 1

A Cataloging-in-Publication record is available from the Library
of Congress
ISBN 978-0-8122-4331-4

To Susanne, Jan, and Antonin

CONTENTS

PREFACE

This book addresses one of the most pressing problems that new governments face in the aftermath of transition: the personnel they inherit from the previous regime. They may not be perpetrators of human rights abuses, but their prior role casts doubt on their loyalty to the new regime. For these states, a dilemma arises: should the old personnel be excluded from or incorporated in it? The new political elites have to consider whether the policies they adopt—for instance, the expulsion or retention of these tainted officials—would have a negative impact on their primary objective: democratization and establishing a stable administration. The consequences of the de-Baathification in post-Saddam Iraq have revealed the importance of effective personnel policies. Although it originally intended to establish trustworthy government by ridding the state apparatus of discredited Baathists, the policy augmented historical rifts in society as a whole. The negative social effects of de-Baathification may have undermined its primary political purpose.

Although transitional personnel policies are essential to successfully consolidate state structures and are important because of their spillover effect on social reconciliation, research in transitional justice and democratization has not given adequate attention to this topic. The variety of inclusive alternatives to dismissals that developed in Central and Eastern Europe have also been largely overlooked. While Czechoslovakia and other countries purged their administrations of the remnants of previous regimes, Hungary and Poland developed considerably more sophisticated methods for dealing with their discredited personnel. They adopted methods based on truth revelation and confession that were stipulated as conditions for inclusion. The personnel policies put into place may produce various results in terms of the people's trust in government and social reconciliation. Consequently, in contrast to the role of electoral systems and truth commissions in democratization, very little is known about the operation and consequences of transitional personnel policies.

To fill this gap, this book proposes the concept of *personnel systems* as a theoretical abstraction of transitional public employment measures that regulate access to non-elected positions in public administration. It classifies personnel systems as three types: exclusive, inclusive, and reconciliatory. The exclusive system is based on the dismissal of inherited personnel from the state apparatus, whereas the inclusive system is based on their exposure and the reconciliatory system on their confession of past wrongdoing. Although they have political-security objectives, personnel systems are viewed in the eyes of its protagonists as different purification measures that aim at cleansing society from the taint of the past. The acknowledgment of the symbolic role of personnel systems helps to explain both the demand for personnel systems and their effects. Each system reflects and conveys a different ideological message about the previous regime and its tainted officials. Consequently, each system has a particular propensity to generate direct (political) effects on trust in government, as well as indirect (social) effects on reconciliation with former adversaries and on the collective memory of the past. Thus, personnel systems appear at a critical juncture, which may affect a society's political culture for many years.

The utility of these systems is examined in Central Europe, which has implemented personnel systems by means of lustration laws. *Lustration* refers to the screening or vetting of public officials against the archives collected by the secret police under their socialist regimes. In order to deal with personnel inherited from the communist regimes, the Czech Republic, Hungary, and Poland have developed three archetypal models: exclusive, inclusive, and reconciliatory systems, respectively. This book interprets the different meanings of these systems, demonstrates their operation, analyzes their origins, assesses their implementation, and examines their effects. To examine their origin, we analyzed a number of historical surveys conducted in these countries in the early 1990s and scrutinized parliamentary debates on lustration laws. In order to examine the political and social effects of different systems, we have devised an original and uniquely tailored experimental vignette, which was embedded in nationwide surveys in the Czech Republic, Hungary, and Poland. The survey experiment tested the effect of dismissal, exposure, and confession on trust in government and on social reconciliation at the level of individual and their effect on collective memory at the country level.

A word about terminology used in this book. Part II of the book uses the concept of *lustration systems* as a regional variant of personnel systems. We use *lustrations* to honor the widespread terminology for the transitional personnel process in Central and Eastern Europe. Although Hungarians—unlike Czechs, Slovaks, and Poles—do not use the term *lustration*, a number of Hungarian scholars and scholars writing on Hungary use *lustration* or *lustrations* (*lustration*, like *examination*, may be used in a singular form or as a plural depending on the context). Many scholars writing on the Baltic states, Albania, Georgia, the former Yugoslavia, Bulgaria, or Romania also use *lustrations*. The word *lustration* is used because it is widely accepted in the academic literature and because no other word, such as *vetting* or *screening*, can capture the dual meanings of the different personnel processes as vividly as *lustration*. At the same time, we cannot use *lustration systems* to encompass personnel systems in all transitional countries because not all personnel systems used lustration procedure: a screening against secret police archives. On the other hand, the different meanings of lustrations in common parlance in different countries in Central and Eastern Europe required that we avoid using the word *lustration* in our survey experiment. The experimental part of the book, Part III, therefore primarily uses *personnel systems*, and their methods of dismissals, exposures, and confessions, instead of *lustration systems*.

We use the term *reconciliatory system* to describe the lustration process in Poland, although the message of reconciliation was not communicated to the public there. In previous publications I have called the lustration system *semi-reconciliatory*. There are a number of reasons why my opinion has evolved. The reconciliatory system is derived from theoretical considerations of major perpetrator-centered strategies of transitional justice: retribution, revelation, and reconciliation. It has hallmarks of the reconciliation process, similar to that of the South African Truth and Reconciliation Commission (TRC). The reconciliatory system is based on confession, similar to that of the TRC's amnesty committee; in contrast, the inclusive system is based on external exposure, similar to the TRC's human rights violation committee. Like the TRC in South Africa, the reconciliatory system in Poland has been conceived in protracted political negotiations, which included a wide range of political parties on the right, the center, and the left. Although the coalition did not include the successor Communist Party, President Aleksander Kwaśniewski, a former communist, signed it into law. With the blessing of the Constitutional Tribunal, the system has been implemented for more than a decade in spite a number of challenges and amendments to it. Finally, the reconciliatory system deserves its name because it is the only system which can lead to reconciliation.

Unlike the word *nomenclature*, which refers to terminology or classification, the word *nomenklatura* refers to the stratum of communist party cadres, each of whom was selected to occupy senior positions in all areas of public and quasi-public spheres based on their loyalty to socialist regimes. *Nomenklatura*, tainted officials, wrongdoers, people associated with former regimes, former communist party leaders, members of the repressive apparatus, and secret informers are all used interchangeably to refer to persons whose deeds have led to breaches of an interpersonal trust but who did not commit a criminal offense under the socialist regime. Although gross human rights violations, including extrajudicial and judicial killings, concentration camps, torture, and imprisonments, did occur during socialism, this books deals with the "soft" nature of collaboration. The terms *socialist regimes* and *communist regimes* are used interchangeably to refer to the regimes in Czechoslovakia, Hungary, and Poland prior to 1989. We do not capitalize the "communist parties" in Central Europe unless we refer to the Communist Party of Czechoslovakia by name. Communist parties in Hungary and Poland did not call themselves "communist." Czechoslovakia refers to the federation of the Czech Republic and the Slovak Republic, which ceased to exist as of December 31, 1992. When referring to the Czech Republic before 1992, we refer to the territory of the Czech Republic within the Federation. The term *tainted official* is used to refer to both men and women in Parts I and II; however, in Part III we only use *masculinum* in line with the realistic nature of our experimental vignette because most collaborators in Eastern Europe were men. In the text, we try to spell the names of all authors correctly with diacritics (e.g., Vojtěch Cepl), but we cite them as they published their work (Vojtech Cepl). Similarly, we refer to historical actors by their names with diacritics (e.g., Lech Wałęsa), but we maintain the original titles of English publications and citations referring to them (Lech Walesa).

ABBREVIATIONS

ANC	African National Congress (South Africa)
ÁVH	State Security Authority (Hungarian secret police prior 1956)
AWS	Election Action Solidarity (Poland)
CBOS	Public Opinion Research Center (Poland)
CPA	Coalition Provisional Authority (Iraq)
ČSSD	Czech Social Democratic Party
ČSSR	Czechoslovak Socialist Republic
ČTK	Czech Press Agency
CVVM	Center for the Public Opinion Research (Czech Republic)
Fidesz	Alliance of Young Democrats (Hungary)
FKgP	Smallholder Party (Hungary)
HZDS	Movement for Democratic Slovakia
IFP	Inkatha Freedom Party (South Africa)
IPN	Institute of National Memory (Poland)
KDNP	Christian Democratic Party (Hungary)
KDS	Christian Democratic Party (Czech Republic)
KDU-ČSL	Christian Democratic Union–Czech People's Party
KLD	Liberal Democratic Congress (Poland)
KPN	Confederation of Independent Poland
KSČ	Communist Party of Czechoslovakia
KSČM	Communist Party of Bohemia and Moravia (Czech Republic)
LPR	League of Polish Families
MDF	Hungarian Democratic Forum
MIÉP	Hungarian Justice and Life Party
MSzMP	Hungarian Socialist Workers Party
MSzP	Hungarian Socialist Party
NKVD	People's Commissariat of Internal Affairs (Soviet Union)
NP	National Party (South Africa)

OBOP	Center for Research of Public Opinion (Poland)
ODA	Civic Democratic Alliance (Czech Republic)
ODS	Civic Democratic Party (Czech Republic)
OF	Civic Forum (Czech Republic)
OH	Civic Movement (Czech Republic)
PAP	Polish Press Agency
PC	Center Agreement (Poland)
PiS	Law and Justice Party (Poland)
PO	Citizens' Platform (Poland)
PSL	Polish Peasant Party
PZPR	Polish United Workers' Party
SB	Security Service (Poland's secret police)
SdRP	Social Democracy of the Republic of Poland
SIS	Slovak Information Service (Slovak counterintelligence agency)
SLD	Democratic Left Alliance (Poland)
SRP	Self-Defense (Poland)
SSM	Socialist Association of the Youth (Czechoslovakia)
StB	State Security (Czechoslovak secret police)
SzDSz	Alliance of Free Democrats (Hungary)
TRC	Truth and Reconciliation Commission (South Africa)
UB	Security Office (Poland's secret police)
UD	Democratic Union (Poland)
UP	Labor Union (Poland)
UW	Freedom Union (Poland)
VPN	Public Against Violence (Slovakia)
ZChN	Christian-National Union (Poland)

INTRODUCTION

We had free elections, . . . we elected a free parliament, we have
a free press, we have a democratic government. Yet we have not
managed to deal with the burdensome legacy of the totalitarian
system. Powerful structures of the former regime still exist and
remain at work. . . . Many places are governed by the same
people as before. . . . The old bureaucracy persists at all levels. . . .
It is not true that our revolution failed. It just has not been
finished yet.

> —Václav Havel, "Výročí okupace Československa
> vojsky Varšavského paktu"[1]

Should we revoke our de-Baathification policy, as some in
Washington now seemed to want? I wearily reminded the others
that Iraq was a zero-sum game. We needed to keep the Shia and
Kurds in mind too. Calling back former [Baathist, mostly Sunni]
senior army officers would not solve our problems.

> —L. Paul Bremer, *My Year in Iraq*[2]

This chapter introduces the issue of policies designed to deal with personnel
inherited in the apparatus of transitional states from previous regimes. The
puzzle is that transitional personnel policies as well as their absence may
negatively impact democratization. This is because these policies carry symbolic
meanings that may create social effects that contradict their original
political purpose of establishing trustworthy government. We identify
major institutional innovations in Central Europe, manifested in a variety
of alternative personnel policies, as plausible ways to address this conundrum.
The alternative policies may convey a message of inclusion and conversion
of inherited personnel and may produce different constellations of

political and social effects. The theoretical and empirical investigation of the effects of different personnel policies on trust in government and historical divides in society is the primary objective of this book.

The Personnel Problem and Its Problematic Solutions: Chile, South Africa, and Iraq

How can states undergoing the transition from authoritarianism to democracy deal with inherited state personnel complicit with abuses of prior regimes? Failure to acknowledge the problem of the inherited personnel, or an inability to effectively address it, may create considerable obstacles for the prospects for democratization. Whether open or clandestine, loyal to the past elite or seemingly "accommodating" to the new democracy, members of the anciens régimes who have retained their positions of influence have impaired democratic consolidation and undermined critical policies in many transitional countries. The so-called authoritarian enclaves, consisting of non-democratic institutions, unresolved human rights problems, and "social actors not fully willing to play by democratic rules," have for a long time been impediments to redemocratization in Chile and other countries of the Southern Cone.[3] The result has been an "incomplete democracy" that maintained itself via the inherited constitutional and judicial structures and prevented the democratically elected government from launching political and social reforms for more than a decade.[4]

In South Africa, the continuation of the former apparatus had even more ominous consequences. While Nelson Mandela and his African National Congress (ANC) were negotiating the handover of political power with the reformist president Frederick de Klerk and his not-yet-reformed National Party (NP), the remnants of the old elite, with vast experience in the technology of political and military power, were actively seeking to derail the process. Entrenched in the administration and armed forces, sections of the outgoing white minority government instigated and prolonged so-called black-on-black violence in the early 1990s.[5] The country found itself on the brink of civil war after the South African Ministry of Defense trained and armed the Inkatha Freedom Party (IFP) to stir violent clashes with the ANC and encourage the independence of the KwaZulu-Natal province.[6]

However, systematic solutions to the problem of inherited personnel may be difficult for transitional governments to implement: these governments may be relatively weak in the face of rigid legal, institutional, and structural constraints imposed by previous regimes and backed by their powerful security apparatuses. In South Africa, the "Inkathagate scandal" of 1991 led eventually to the demotion of the minister of defense, Magnus Malan, and the minister of police, Adriaan Vlok, to lower cabinet positions by President de Klerk.[7] Nonetheless, later negotiations between the outgoing NP government and the ANC at Kempton Park resulted in the approval of a so-called sunset clause.[8] According to this clause, the apartheid-era personnel would retain their positions until the second democratic elections in 1999. It was a compromise solution between the ANC's demand for immediate majority rule and the NP's demand for continuous power-sharing arrangements.[9]

In Chile, attempts to remove the personnel of the previous regime from state institutions provoked the threat of a new military takeover. The leader of the military junta, General Augusto Pinochet, exercised his power during the transition process in his position as both commander in chief and senator for life. In 1992, Chilean president Patricio Aylwin proposed a set of constitutional reforms that would allow presidents to appoint and remove military officers. After his proposals were politically defeated, he threatened to exercise his power to veto the promotion of army personnel through administrative inaction in order to renegotiate the time when General Pinochet would step down as the army's commander in chief.[10] Aylwin's actions provoked the so-called *boinazo*, during which soldiers in combat gear paraded in downtown Santiago to remind the civilian government about the real distribution of political power in Chilean society at that time. It took another six years (1998) for Pinochet to eventually step down as a military chief. He was stripped of his senatorial immunity only in 2000.[11]

Solutions to the problem of inherited personnel in the state apparatus may be at least as problematic as the dilemma itself. Since the Reconstruction era in the United States,[12] personnel policies have usually been one-dimensional, oscillating between greater and lesser exclusion of inherited personnel. The wave of post–World War II purges conducted under various banners, such as attempts at the denazification of Germany, defascification of Italy, and demilitarization of Japan, sought to completely rid state apparatuses of people associated with previous regimes and the propagators of their authoritarian ideologies.[13] However, the policies of wholesale dismissal, if implemented, are very problematic in terms of their contribution to successful political transformation. They may inhibit rather than facilitate democratization.

The de-Baathification of Iraq clearly manifested the deficiency of one-dimensional measures. After the defeat of the Saddam Hussein's regime in 2003, the occupying powers targeted structures, members, and assets of the ruling Baath Socialist Party and the Mukhabarat secret police. Paul Bremer, the head of the Coalition Provisional Authority (CPA), which administered governance in occupied Iraq, issued Order Number 1, which mandated the de-Baathification of Iraqi society.[14] Pursuant to the order, no member of the Baath Party was allowed to hold a senior government position, and no senior member of the Baath Party could work in the state apparatus. The de-Baathification and the disbanding of the Iraqi army have widely been considered as two of the major reasons for the insurgency that spread in Iraq after 2003. Excluded and marginalized Baathists had no other option but to resist the new system.[15] However, as the insurgency intensified throughout the following year, CPA attempted to moderate the application of this policy and allowed civil servants and members of the disbanded army to rejoin their original professions.[16] This, however, resulted in the infiltration of the state administration, the leaking of critical security information, and a near derailment of the democratization process.

Thus, the choice of a personnel policy seems to be an important factor in political transition. In South Africa, problems arose as a consequence of the new government's inability to make any meaningful changes to the state apparatus. In Chile, the initial attempts to solve the complex personnel situation almost undermined the very democratic transition that they sought to strengthen. In Iraq, the solution of the personnel problem created new problems, which appeared more serious than those that they actually attempted to solve. Many transitional democracies find themselves faced with a dilemma that bears many similarities to the scenarios described above. How can transitional elites solve this conundrum? Why are personnel measures so controversial?

Governmental policies, even when pursuing a narrow political objective, may have unintended social consequences. The de-Baathification order had ignored the possibility that transitional policies, though intended to establish trustworthy administration and secure irreversible political changes, could have profound social implications that would affect historical divides in society. Thus, personnel policies may have dual effects.

1. Political effects. Personnel policies are designed to make political changes irreversible and to satisfy the social need for discontinuity with the past.[17] Thus, they may have direct political effects on the attributes of state apparatuses, including its trustworthiness, loyalty, efficiency, and impartiality. They may affect the objective dimension of these attributes as well as their subjective dimension, which rests in the perception of these attributes by the public. They may affect citizens' trust in government.

2. Social effects. In their effort to reform state apparatuses, personnel policies pass judgment on the persons involved. They may label former personnel as trustworthy or untrustworthy, and this may in turn determine whether any civic relationship with them is possible at a societal level. Personnel policies may convey ideological messages that redefine the social standing of former personnel and transform social relationships. In the past, the former political and security elites in Chile and South Africa were credited for their patriotic struggle against communists and terrorists. Transitional personnel policies may take these credentials away. Similarly, de-Baathification may have condemned the Baathists, but in doing so it imported, and preserved, the divisions of the past into, and in, the new order. The process, which was initially designed as a policy for the reform of governmental structures, subsequently augmented historical rifts in society as a whole.

The fact that personnel policies may produce dual effects could help explain their failures. The rejuvenation of trust in government through the political project of personnel policies is conditional on the situation within society. The attempt to secure political transition by establishing trustworthy administration may augment historical divides in society. Conversely, ignoring the problem of inherited personnel may not lead to the rejuvenation of trust in government.

The Variety of Personnel Policies in the Czech Republic, Hungary, and Poland

The question is: how can we solve the personnel conundrum? Is there any alternative treatment? Given the historical prevalence of purges and other one-dimensional exclusive policies, it is not surprising that all transitional public employment policies have been generally regarded as the same tools for political change. "Politicized public [employment] law," according to Ruti Teitel, "can effect radical change when it distributes power explicitly on the basis of the new ideology."[18] The importance of this view is that it acknowledges the instrumental nature of public law, through which these policies are implemented. Public law is seen as the handmaiden of transitional politics and ideology and, as such, a manifestation of the balance of political power between the government and the opposition. From the perspective of political realism, the focus is on hard power and tangible consequences manifested in lesser or larger exclusions.[19]

Consequently, viewing all personnel policies through the prism of political realism as a mechanism for redistribution of political power in transition treats all personnel policies as conceptually identical and reduces their variety to one dimension.[20] However, not all personnel policies are qualitatively the same. Exclusion and continuation of inherited personnel are not the only solutions to complex personnel problems. While it is true that some personnel policies do redistribute power, others maintain, legitimize, or transform the status quo. Alternative approaches aspire to achieve the political objectives of personnel policies in establishing trust in government by more nuanced and sometimes more lenient means than holus-bolus dismissal of all former state personnel. As we shall demonstrate, research in comparative democratization and transitional justice has largely overlooked the major institutional innovations manifested in the variety of lustration (screening, vetting) laws in post-communist countries. While some countries, such as Czechoslovakia, Germany, Bulgaria, and Albania, resorted to simple exclusions, others developed fairly sophisticated procedures to deal with personnel associated with former socialist regimes.[21] Hungary, Romania, Serbia, Lithuania, and Poland approved personnel measures that stipulated conditions for the inclusion and conversion of inherited personnel. People associated with former regimes were granted a second chance in exchange for the revelation of truth about their past conduct.

The personnel policies adopted in Hungary in 1994 and in Poland in 1997 stand out. The two countries decided not to emulate the Czechoslovak model of lustrations launched in 1991, which was based on dismissals. In Czechoslovakia, former Communist Party leaders, secret police officers, their collaborators, and other "wrongdoers" were excluded from senior posts in the state apparatus and barred from returning. In contrast, Hungary gave every high public official who was tainted by the past an option to either resign or face the public revelation of his or her past. It attempted to reform the state apparatus through transparency and deal with tainted officials through reintegrative shaming. Poland required that its high public officials submit an affidavit, through which they would confess their involvement in the past regime. Each affidavit was then judicially verified. If the confession was true, the tainted official—regardless of his or her past—was given a second chance. If it was incomplete or false, the official was dismissed and prohibited from holding public posts for ten years. In both cases, the past of the tainted official was made public.

Alternative personnel measures may aspire to address the same problem but may convey different social meanings. Methods based on exposure and confession, which were pursued as alternatives to dismissal, may send different ideological messages about the gravity of the crimes committed in the previous regime, the legitimacy of the new government, and the malleability of tainted officials. Consequently, owing to their different symbolic meanings, different personnel policies may affect the trustworthiness of the state apparatus, its loyalty and political neutrality, in different ways, as well as generate a variety of indirect effects, which may impact the public perception of the loyalty and identity of people associated with former regimes in different ways.

The impacts of different personnel policies may reflect the impacts of different methods of transitional justice. Indeed, the retributive nature of dismissals resembles criminal trials, exposure of tainted officials resembles truth commissions, and confessions in exchange for public offices resemble the process of qualified amnesties in South Africa's Truth and Reconciliation Commission. Each of the major methods of transitional justice has been argued to have different propensities to transform post-conflict societies. The dismissals, exposures, and confessions that have been implemented as cornerstones of public employment policies in the Czech Republic, Hungary, and Poland provide us with a great opportunity for their in-depth assessment.

Indeed, as scholars of transitional justice argue about the positive and negative impacts of criminal trials, truth commissions, and qualified amnesties, the utility of alternative policies may be questioned. Their perceived leniency may reflect a degree of unwarranted complacency. Forgiving public employees from the previous regime may put a nascent democracy with fragile institutions at risk politically and in terms of its security. It may also undermine the societal need for justice, especially in the eyes of victims: those who profited from the previous regime should not be allowed to continue in their posts under the new democracy. Thus, it seems at first glance that every personnel policy may have its difficulties and that one is not necessarily better than the others. Every personnel policy may carry its particular advantages and disadvantages, dangers and benefits, in terms of its specific contribution to democratic transformation. The utility of different personnel policies is primarily an empirical question that will be addressed in this book.

The unique institutional development in dealing with inherited personnel has prompted policymakers in different countries to express their desire to learn from the experiences in the Czech Republic, Hungary, and Poland and to avoid their problems. Although the TRC "decided not to recommend [exclusive] lustration because it was felt that it would be inappropriate in the South African context,"[22] the president of Chile, Eduardo Frei, successor to Aylwin, expressed an interest in lustrations and "stressed the need to thoroughly cleanse state and government institutions of people implicated with former totalitarian regimes."[23] The "Iraqi Opposition Report on the Transition to Democracy in Iraq," recognizing the importance of the personnel situation, recommended that the new transitional government examine the Eastern European experience with lustration.[24]

Objectives and the Main Argument of the Book

This book aspires to be a first step in substantiating the thesis that the importance of personnel systems in transforming states may be as significant as electoral systems or truth commissions. While elections determine the personnel who will take up elected positions, personnel systems concern individuals in non-elected positions within the new democracy. While truth commissions are generally viewed as mechanisms to achieve reconciliation, personnel systems have a significant bearing on both social reconciliation and trust in government. In this analysis *trust in government* refers to confidence in its institutional designs. *Social reconciliation* is multifaceted: it encompasses interpersonal trust, tolerance, and a decrease in social distance.

The Main Argument

Transitional personnel policies are not only political-security measures. They carry symbolic meanings that help explain their origin and shape their political and social effects. At the political level, they signify discontinuity with the past: the end of the old regime and the start of the new one. Personnel policies reflect the perception of inherited personnel as "tainted" but in their effort to purify government, they send ideological messages that affect the social standing of "tainted officials" in different ways. Policies based on dismissals may lead to the establishment of trust in government at the expense of social reconciliation. These policies augment a negative image of the tainted official and may fail as a result of the discord between political and social effects. In contrast, alternative policies may generate a different constellation of effects. Policies based on exposure may purify the government by increasing its transparency and shaming the tainted officials, but nevertheless these policies give them a second chance. Policies based on confession are forms of self-purification rituals, which, it is argued, promote both trust in government and reconciliation.

The Main Objective

The primary goal of this book is to examine the effects of various transitional personnel policies on trust in government and overcoming historical divisions in society. In order to achieve this objective, this book

- proposes the concept of personnel systems as a theoretical abstraction of transitional public employment laws and similar measures;
- classifies these personnel systems into exclusive, inclusive, and reconciliatory systems, which are defined by dismissals, exposures, and confessions, respectively, and represent three major methods of transitional justice: retribution, revelation, and reconciliation;
- theorizes that different personnel systems carry different symbolic meanings in the process of democratization, which dramatize the regime change in different ways and help explain their origin and hypothesize their effects;
- examines the operation, the origin, and the implementation of different personnel systems within the framework of lustrations in the Czech Republic, Hungary, and Poland; and

- empirically tests the effects of dismissals, exposures, and confessions by means of an original experimental vignette embedded in nation-wide representative surveys of 3,050 respondents in the three countries.[25]

The Research Site

The Czech Republic, Hungary, and Poland are a unique site for our research. On the one hand, the selection of the three countries for comparison is convenient for achieving theoretical parsimony: these three countries share similar histories, similar cultural roots, and since 2004 a common future in the European Union. However, they have adopted different personnel systems. The Czech Republic has pursued an exclusive system, Hungary has pursued an inclusive system, and Poland has pursued a reconciliatory system. This heterogeneity allowed us to assess the effects of different personnel systems on the country level and, more significant, to test the effects of methods upon which the systems were based, namely dismissal, exposure, and confession, on an individual-level analysis within the particular historical-political contexts that gave birth to each particular system. Thus, the effects of dismissal, exposure, and confession were tested within cultures of dismissal, exposure, and confession.

The Research Methods

The following resources have been instrumental in our analysis: parliamentary debates, lustration and other public employment laws, rulings of constitutional courts and other international bodies, governmental and non-governmental reports, newspaper articles, interviews, existing surveys, and original surveys designed specifically for this book. In principle, we found that authentic parliamentary debates were more reliable than ex post facto elite interviews. Likewise, survey experiments were preferred over traditional cross-sectional surveys.

In order to help explain the origin of lustrations, we used data from nineteen nationwide surveys that were conducted by a research team led by Gábor Tóka in the Czech Republic, Hungary, and Poland between 1992 and 1996.[26] The effects of lustration systems were examined using the statistical analysis of our survey data sources that were specially conducted for this book in the Czech Republic, Hungary, and Poland in 2007. Thanks to grant support from the United States Institute of Peace, our questionnaire was embedded in omnibus surveys conducted by three of the most internationally renowned survey agencies in the region: CVVM in the Czech Republic, Tárki in Hungary, and OBOP in Poland. The agencies completed 3,050 face-to-face interviews.

To effectively test the effects of personnel systems, we devised an experimental vignette that was embedded in these three surveys. This has allowed us to examine the effects of personnel systems on the country level and, more important, at the individual level. The switch between levels of analysis has enabled us to effectively study the complex macropolitical process and provide persuasive evidence of its effects at the micro level. Indeed, the problems caused by personnel systems, illustrated earlier in the discussion of the de-Baathification of Iraq, bear down at a micro level.

The experimental design has several other advantages in this research. Methodologically, survey experiments are powerful research tools. One of their major strengths is their ability to eliminate alternative explanations and establish causal relations,[27] thus reducing the problem of endogeneity that arises at the country-level analysis. Not only do survey experiments have high internal validity, that is, an ability to attribute consequences to a particular treatment, they also have substantial external validity.[28] Their findings apply to the entire society.[29]

Analytically, the experimental design also enabled us to capture different meanings of personnel systems in the three countries. Unlike previous surveys that failed to distinguish between different personnel policies, the survey experiment tested the effects of different personnel methods: dismissal, exposure, and confession. Moreover, this distinction is theoretically relevant for all scholars in transitional justice because the methods of personnel systems represent proxies for three major transitional justice methods—retribution, truth revelation, and reconciliation—which were experimentally tested side by side.

One practical advantage of the survey experiment is that it enables researchers to transcend the political controversies of the day, as well as other problems that may have arisen in the implementation of different personnel systems in the respective countries. Sometimes transitional countries have been unable to fully enforce their public employment laws, just as they were unable to fully implement many other laws. Another practical advantage of experimental surveys is their ability to facilitate comparisons between countries. Personnel systems in different countries vary in scope; they concern smaller or larger numbers of public officials. Moreover, parliaments and constitutional courts often modify the scope. The ability to overcome the difficulties makes survey experiments a fruitful method of conducting comparative research.

Plan of the Book

The book comprises seven substantive chapters and is divided into three parts. Part I conceptualizes personnel policies and theorizes their effects. Part II focuses on three archetypal personnel systems that were devised in the post-socialist Czech Republic, Hungary, and Poland and explains their operation, origin, and implementation. Part III examines their political and social effects by means of an experimental vignette.

Part I

In order to provide a more solid definition, Chapter 1 proposes the concept of personnel systems as denotative of transitional personnel policies and situates them into the context of democratization. This permits the classification of personnel systems into three major categories: exclusive, inclusive, and reconciliatory.[30] This classification forms the horizontal conceptual framework of this book. It provides a variation that facilitates the explanation of the origin of these systems, examines their multiple effects, and situates them in the context of other measures of transitional justice.

The effects and origins of personnel systems are theorized in Chapter 2. Why did measures that were devised to deal with inherited personnel generate effects that were so wide and deep? Why do people care about something that in the eyes of outside observers appears as mundane as transitional personnel measures? The chapter theorizes that in addition to their tangible purposes, each personnel system carries a particular symbolic meaning that affects its propensity to generate political and social effects. Similar to other methods of transitional justice, personnel systems signify different rituals of purification of society after transition. Their origins and effects can be explained by using the particular social constructions of tainted officials under a particular personnel system.

Part II

The next part examines the operation, the origin, and the constitutional context of personnel systems in Central Europe. It focuses on lustration systems, which are the regional variant of personnel systems. Chapter 3 first delineates the dual meaning of lustrations, their security and symbolic dimensions. Then it examines the operation of three archetypal lustration systems in the countries of their origin. Namely, it focuses on the exclusive, the inclusive, and the reconciliatory systems, which developed in the Czech Republic in 1991, Hungary in 1994, and Poland in 1997, respectively.

Any empirical examination of the effects of various personnel systems, which is the main focus of the book, begs questions about their historical origins. To what extent are the purported effects of different personnel systems endogenous to the countries in which these systems developed? In what sense and to what extent does the situation in these countries after the introduction of these systems differ from the situation beforehand? Chapter 4 thus examines the origin of lustration systems. It argues that the choice of personnel methods is a function of the perception of former adversaries as tainted and the perception of one's own role in the previous regime. This approach permits a reinterpretation of the existing theorizations that link lustration policies to the severity of the previous non-democratic regimes, particular modes of exit from these regimes, and the politics of the present. It also allows us to explain the following puzzle: Why didn't all three countries adopt exclusive personnel systems after each country's sweeping defeat of former communist parties in their first democratic elections?

It is possible that the implementation of personnel systems is influenced by the political context in which they were embedded. But once personnel systems begin to be implemented, they may also affect the political landscape. Politicians are objects as well as subjects of lustrations. This chapter explores the hypothesis that personnel systems are part of a political cycle: they continuously affect, and are affected by, political contexts. Chapter 5 explores the implementation of personnel systems in the political context in the Czech Republic, Hungary, and Poland.

Part III

The empirical assessment of the political and social effects of various personnel systems is central to this book. Which personnel system helps transform the state apparatus? Which personnel system best serves the interests of divided societies? Chapter 6 examines the political effects of personnel systems on trust in government. The effects of the exclusive system, the inclusive system, and the reconciliatory system are tested at the individual level of analysis by means of our survey experiment that manipulated central values upon which these systems were based, namely the effect of dismissal, exposure, and confession.

Which personnel policy helps overcome historical divisions in society? In transitional democracies, it is essential that people are able to overcome inimical relations and mutual distrust in order to coexist with each other as citizens, comply with the law, work together, and live as neighbors. Moreover, the inherited divisions are not exclusively political and social; they are borne by fundamental historical grounds. Personnel policies may represent a particular way of rewriting history. Chapter 7 examines the indirect effects of personnel systems on social reconciliation and the memory of the past. Namely, it examines the effect of dismissal, exposure, and confession on reconciliation with former adversaries at the individual level of analyses and the effect of the exclusive, inclusive, and reconciliatory systems on collective memory at the country level.

PART I

Personnel Systems
and Transitional Justice

1

Personnel Systems and Their Classification

Regierung vergeht, Verwaltung besteht.
(Government passes, bureaucracy remains.)

—German saying

In a country where offices are created solely for the benefit of the
people no one man has any more intrinsic right to official station
than another. Offices were not established to give support to
particular men at the public expense. No individual wrong is,
therefore, done by removal, since neither appointment to nor
continuance in office is a matter of right. . . . He who is removed
has the same means of obtaining a living that are enjoyed by the
millions who never held office.

—Andrew Jackson, First Annual Message to Congress[1]

Policies designed to deal with personnel inherited from previous regimes
in the apparatus of transitional states are not limited to dismissals. Dismissals are specific types of personnel policies which, owing to their low transformative value, have been referred to as one-dimensional. In contrast to
these policies, several Central European countries have developed alternative personnel policy models based on the inclusion of former personnel. It
is therefore useful to conceive a concept with a wider ambit in order to
encompass a variety of personnel policies within and outside the region
and to facilitate their classification.[2] The concept proposed here to denote

all transitional public employment policies is personnel systems. This chapter defines personnel systems, classifies them as exclusive, inclusive, or reconciliatory, and describes their characteristics.

Personnel Systems

Transitional countries address the problems surrounding the appointment and employment of personnel for their state institutions through a range of legal and quasi-legal measures. These measures have different origins and binding authority. They may be devised by the transitional states themselves, by occupying powers, by the United Nations, or by peace brokers; this distinguishes them from unofficial personnel methods that are implemented in non-state organizations or methods of exposure pursued, for instance, by non-governmental organizations that collect and release information about the abuses of the past. The measures may take the form of constitutions, laws, international treaties, UN resolutions, peace accords, or military orders.

There are many examples of such measures. The Constitution of Haiti, approved in 1987, mandated that a range of persons who had been involved in the previous dictatorship were ineligible for public office.[3] The German Unification Treaty of 1990 provided a legal background for vetting personnel in the former East Germany after its reunification with West Germany.[4] In 1991 Czechoslovakia approved the so-called lustration (screening, vetting) laws that disqualified Communist Party leaders, secret informers, and anyone associated with the former socialist regimes from public posts in new democratic institutions.[5] In El Salvador peace accords formed the legal basis for vetting personnel,[6] while a resolution passed by the UN Security Council in 1996 provided a mandate for restructuring police forces in Bosnia and Herzegovina.[7] In 2003 Order Number 1 on the de-Baathification of Iraq virtually excluded all the senior members of the Baath Party from the new Iraqi institutions and prevented all Baath members from accessing top state positions.[8] Although most of these measures are special transitional instruments, new governments may pursue personnel policies through available public employment laws, especially in the face of rigid structural and political constraints imposed by the former regimes. All of these diverse legal and quasi-legal measures, with their different origins and binding authority, fall within the ambit of personnel systems.

The concept of personnel systems reflects the logic behind these special public employment measures. It is an abstraction of all public employment law mechanisms in transitional states in the same way that *electoral systems* are abstractions of *electoral laws* and that *constitutional system* reflects a particular class of *constitutions*. Personnel systems therefore comprise the methods a transitional state uses to regulate the access that members of the former regime have to public positions in the aftermath of a regime change. It is a conceptual tool developed to classify various methods of dealing with inherited personnel in the state apparatus, to explain their origins, and to assess of their various effects. The concept is a theoretical construction that places most of the nitty-gritty substantive and procedural provisions of these special public employment laws in abeyance.

Using personnel systems enables us to subject the problem of personnel policies to a meaningful social and political inquiry. Previous discussion about these policies has often focused on particular aspects of them without offering an overall conceptual and analytical framework to study them systematically. For instance, scholars have examined who should and should not be subjected to these policies;[9] the alleged retrospective nature of the policies, which may violate tenets of criminal justice;[10] and the possible unreliability of background information obtained from archives of the previous regime.[11] Although most of these studies greatly contributed to the understanding of the procedural requirements, they focused on the problems of public employment laws per se rather than on the trustworthiness of government and the problem of personnel itself.

Discussion about legal nuances is not the main focus of this inquiry. In line with the political study of electoral systems, which is not primarily concerned with procedural details concerning electoral laws, such as the minimum age of candidates, procedures for recounts, and their judicial review, this study does not concern itself with the procedural aspects of personnel selection and appointment in the aftermath of regime change: these provisions can be found in the appropriate legal documents. Instead, this study seeks to go beyond the legal debate to draw attention to the essence of personnel systems and their defining features. From the vantage point of a more abstract perspective it is possible to theorize about patterns and general tendencies, to test their effects empirically, and to communicate them to a wider audience. This study aspires to remove the essence of transitional public employment laws from the field of law and return them to the realm of social sciences.

As mentioned earlier, *personnel systems* is a general concept. It is not primarily concerned with the procedural provisions of the public employment laws, nor is it concerned with their scope: it leaves out the consideration of the number of members of the repressive apparatus who may be affected by the personnel system. This number is usually derived from the statutory stipulation of a level within the hierarchy of the former state or from the statutory stipulation of a particular type of action committed. In addition, the concept does not consider the seniority of positions within the new state administration affected by a personnel policy. All personnel systems differ in their scope and may be classified according to this criterion. By determining which sectors and services are targeted by the law, one can distinguish between the depoliticization of the state administration, such as denazification, de-communization, and de-Baathification, and its "de-juntification," demilitarization, and "lustration" in its original meaning of a verification tool for sifting out secret collaborators. Indeed, some authors writing on the topic of lustration laws tend to classify transitional public employment laws on the basis of which posts in the past repressive apparatus are included in the law. Thus, they distinguish between lustration, which they relate to the former security apparatus, and de-communization.[12]

However, such a classification is not useful for our purposes because it does not allow us to draw conclusions from one country and apply them to another. For example, when former Chilean president Eduardo Frei visited the Czech Republic, he was more interested in the country's experiences with what is here termed its personnel system than how it dealt with particular segments of the administration and judiciary. He sought to discover a general method for dealing with members of previous regimes who had been deeply entrenched in the state institutions as a whole, not to discover a process for dealing with the leaders of the Communist Party and their collaborators.[13] The classification of personnel systems based on the types of posts targeted in the repressive apparatus, though possible, is not the major concern of this chapter.

Likewise, personnel systems go beyond the particular evidentiary procedures involved in determining whether a state official was a collaborator under a former regime. Accepting that a new government will establish substantive and procedural rules to identify individual members within the "old" public administration and security forces, personnel systems focus on *what happens* to those who are identified as collaborators, abusers, and so forth. They concern various methods of dealing with inherited personnel situations within the framework of public administration, security, and other positions in the state structure, regardless of the methods used to determine the position of the officials and their actions, or omissions, in the past. In other words, personnel systems concern mechanisms that determine what happens if a member of the past repressive apparatus wants to retain a particular public post rather than how the fact of his or her collaboration is determined, whether it involves screening against secret police records, public archives, cadre materials, witness testimonies, or public inquiries.

Different countries utilize various procedures to determine the extent of past collaborations. For instance, in the early 1990s El Salvador used a wide range of sources, including the findings of a truth commission, as well as information provided by private sources, non-governmental organizations, and foreign governments, to identify perpetrators of various kinds but pursued one personnel system for dealing with them all.[14] To implement the personnel reform of its police force, the UN Mission in Bosnia and Herzegovina utilized the databases of the International Criminal Tribunal for the Former Yugoslavia, statements of victims and witnesses, information from non-governmental organizations, and data in the registration forms completed by the police officers themselves.[15] While it is accepted that different background materials may have various levels of accuracy, the assessment of the reliability of different sources is a matter that falls within the ambit of the law of evidence.

Finally, the concept of personnel systems provides a means of focusing attention away from many controversies that surround the implementation of the process. The process of dealing with inherited personnel has been extremely controversial in practically all transitional countries, from postwar France to post-socialist Poland; it can be compared with the debates surrounding the pro-life versus pro-choice debates in the United States and the debates on taxation in any country in the world.[16] The evidentiary procedures, the scope of the systems, due process guarantees, and other important aspects of these processes are questioned by myriad political statements and contradictory decisions. The concept of personnel systems offers some protection against these debates by establishing a threshold of abstraction from which to review the fundamental features of the process first, and only then examine the details of each personnel system's purported deficiencies. At the same time, understanding personnel systems as instances of public rituals, which is discussed in the next chapter, will enable us to explain the controversies about the process.

Transitional Justice and the Classification
of Personnel Systems

Although scholars label personnel systems differently—as measures of non-criminal sanctions,[17] administrative justice,[18] vetting,[19] and purges[20]—they generally consider them part of the broader field of transitional justice. Transitional justice is an interdisciplinary area of study that examines various ways in which divided societies deal with the legacies of repressive regimes, wars, and other instances of mass human rights violations. Transitional justice starts with realizing the limits of traditional judicial responses to the past and with questioning their purported consequences. Addressing past injustices through criminal trials may not always be legally feasible or politically acceptable in national settings; punishing perpetrators may require large financial and human resources, which are limited in transitional countries; and the social needs for post-conflict reconstruction may go beyond the punishment of major perpetrators.[21] The study of transitional justice is inspired by the development of alternative, or complementary, measures to deal with historical injustice, especially international, mixed, and grassroots courts of justice and truth commissions. The debates surrounding these developments are intensified by claims from victims that perpetrators should acknowledge their wrongdoings and apologize.

Despite the variety of transitional justice measures that have flourished around the globe since the third wave of democratization,[22] their systematic classification in social science is still lacking. So far, measures of transitional justice have been conveniently classified in terms of areas of law. Legal scholarship has tended to distinguish among constitutional justice, criminal justice, administrative justice, reparatory justice, and other forms of justice.[23] The problem with this legal approach is that it downplays the social meaning of justice and measures taken in its pursuit, which may cut deep into the core of transitional society, affecting the norms of behavior, loyalties, identities, trustworthiness, social positions, fears, and reconciliation. Legal details are of less use to social scientists, who are more concerned with an assessment of their social meanings. The rich variety of methods of and perspectives on transitional justice provide many opportunities for their classification. But the purpose of this chapter is not to offer a comprehensive classification of all transitional justice measures; it focuses on perpetrator-centered measures of transitional justice,[24] which are salient for the classification of personnel systems.

The classification proposed here is largely derived from an analysis of the so-called dilemmas of transitional justice. In the initial period of theorization in the area, scholars considered the choices that successor elites had in order to deal with the past after transition. The debate on "what should be done about the guilty"[25] evolved around the so-called torturer problem: prosecute and punish versus forgive and forget.[26] The initial dilemma, which can be roughly described as prosecutions versus amnesty, was instrumental in furthering the debate on transitional justice and democratization. By the end of the 1990s, the debate, inspired by the rise of truth commissions, had become more nuanced and scholars considered a second dilemma of transitional justice: truth versus justice.[27]

However, the list of choices was still incomplete. It was formulated at a time when additional policy options had not yet been fully appreciated by transitional justice scholars.[28] In particular, the notion of a qualified amnesty as a specific process of truth revelation was only introduced by the Amnesty Committee of the Truth and Reconciliation Commission (TRC) in South Africa in 1995. Unlike other truth processes, and unlike the Human Rights Violation Committee of the same commission, which was based on the public exposure of perpetrators by their victims, the amnesty process was conceived as mainly perpetrator centered.[29] It was based on the confessions of perpetrators, who had to make full disclosure of all relevant facts concerning gross human rights violations in order to qualify for amnesty. Had scholars been aware of these options in the first place, they might have classified transitional justice mechanisms differently. They could have formulated another transitional justice choice, which would have distinguished between two different truth processes: exposure versus confession. The former is based on the disclosure of human rights violations and on "naming the guilty," which has been typically pursued by truth commissions, commissions of inquiry, and other forms of truth revelation.[30] The latter is based on the process of self-revelation through which perpetrators can "earn" a second chance. Thus, with the advantage of hindsight, it is possible to distinguish not three but four methods of transitional justice: *amnesia*, *truth*, and *confession*, which are alternatives to the traditional method of retributive *justice*.

The emergence of alternative measures for dealing with perpetrators on the criminal justice level runs in tandem with personnel systems put into place at the public employment level. There is congruence between the variation of criminal measures of transitional justice and the variation of personnel systems. The field of transitional justice was inspired by the development of *alternative* approaches to dealing with gross human rights violations and other historical injustices in situations where criminal trials were not feasible owing to political, legal, and institutional constraints accompanying transition. In this sense, the spread of personnel systems that are *alternatives* to wholesale dismissals coincides with the emergence and the development of transitional justice. One-dimensional policies that oscillate between dismissal and the continued employment of former personnel have been challenged by the spread of truth-based alternatives. In order to disclose the human rights violations committed in the past and to increase transparency within the new administration, transitional governments adopt various policies to promote exposure of former personnel. Moreover, in apparent conformity with the South African amnesty model, the use of confession was employed in the personnel system in Poland in 1997.[31]

These considerations suggest that the dilemmas of transitional justice at the level of criminal law also apply to public employment. Justice, truth, reconciliation, and amnesty may be pursued by personnel policies centered around dismissals, exposures, confession, and continuation, respectively. The major difference between the two perpetrator-centered strategies of transitional justice resides at the level on which the measures for dealing with wrongdoers take effect. Personnel systems are measures that concern public employment, while the perpetrator-centered measures of transitional justice belong at the criminal law level.

Thus, personnel systems can broadly be grouped into four major families. The key distinguishing characteristics among them are the particular consequences that each personnel system attaches to an official's association with the former regime. Persons associated with the past regime may be *dismissed* from their positions; their past may be *exposed* but they may be allowed to retain their posts; they may be given a second chance to stay in exchange for the *confession* of their past involvement; and no action may be taken against them, allowing them to *continue* in their posts without stipulating any other conditions.

A personnel system that is based on dismissal, that is, a system under which a person associated with the previous regime is not allowed to hold certain posts in the new administration, may be referred to as an *exclusive system*. The system is exclusive because it does not give tainted officials any chance to retain their positions. A personnel system that is based on exposure of tainted officials may be called an *inclusive system*. The system is inclusive because the official is allowed to hold a position of trust in spite of his or her past. The third type is a personnel system under which the wrongdoer has to demonstrate that he or she is worthy of receiving a fresh start through his or her confession of wrongdoing. Owing to its resemblance to the amnesty process of TRC in South Africa, in which amnesty applicants had to demonstrate their change of heart by making full disclosure of their human rights violations, the personnel system is referred to as *reconciliatory*. Although the official is allowed to hold a public position, this system is not a type of inclusive system because it is based on a different method: the inclusive system is based on government-based exposures, while the reconciliatory system is based on the wrongdoers' confessions. A personnel system that does not deal with the problem of former personnel, and thus may not even be labeled a personnel system, is referred to as a *system of continuance*.

These classifications are ideal types. In reality, countries may combine different solutions to the personnel dilemma, creating a *mixed system*. The outcomes of the mixed system most frequently oscillate between exclusion and continuation, but they may also blend elements of dismissal, exposure, and confession. But, as it will be demonstrated later, not all policies that result in dismissal, exposure, or confession are personnel systems.

The exclusive system correlates with criminal trials, while the inclusive system correlates with the naming of perpetrators at truth commissions (see Table 1.1). Similarly, continuation is tantamount to amnesty, but within public employment. The reconciliatory system is, roughly speaking, a public employment version of the Amnesty Committee of TRC in South Africa.[32] Consequently, transitional justice consists of four strategies. The first is *retribution*, which encompasses all forms of criminal trials, including domestic, international, and mixed tribunals on the criminal justice level, with an exclusive personnel system on the public employment level. The second is *amnesia*, which is represented by collective amnesties and passive policies that do not deal with the past and are devised to conceal the perpetrators with impunity for gross human rights violations. On the level of personnel systems amnesia is represented by systems of continuance, such as drawing a "thick line" between the present and the past.[33]

Table 1.1. The Classification of Perpetrator-Centered Strategies
of Transitional Justice

Strategy of Transitional Justice	Measures at the Criminal Justice Level	Personnel System	Means of Discontinuity
Retribution	Criminal Trials	Exclusive System Mixed System**	Punishment/ Dismissal
Amnesia	No Policy of Dealing with the Past, Amnesty	Systems of Continuance	None
Revelation	Truth Commission	Inclusive System	Exposure
Reconciliation	Reconciliation Commission*	Reconciliatory System	Confession

  * Denotes the Amnesty Committee of the Truth and Reconciliation Commission in South Africa.
  ** The mixed system typically oscillates between exclusive systems and systems of continuance. It can be applied exclusively or inclusively but it nevertheless assumes that some dismissals take place. Thus, it is conceptually closer to exclusive systems.

The third is *revelation*, which is represented by a variety of truth revelations and other government-sanctioned disclosures that are external to wrongdoers, including naming perpetrators by truth commissions. On the level of personnel systems, revelation is represented by the Hungarian inclusive system based on exposure. The fourth is *reconciliation*, which encompasses methods based on confession, during which a wrongdoer reveals his or her past. The mode was adopted in the amnesty process in South Africa and on the public employment level in the reconciliatory personnel system in Poland.[34]

   The variety of personnel measures adds to the number of institutional choices that transitional countries can and must make in order to pursue democratization. But while constitutional and electoral choices have been the subject of extensive discussion, the problem of choices involved in adopting a personnel system is a topic that has been neglected. The objective of the following sections is to characterize different personnel systems, outline their distinctive features, and distinguish them from other methods of dealing with the past. An in-depth examination of personnel systems in their context in the Czech Republic, Hungary, and Poland will be conducted in Part II.

Traditional Personnel Systems

Our investigation starts with traditional, or one-dimensional, personnel systems, namely the exclusive system, the system of continuance, and the mixed system. We then proceed to alternative personnel systems, namely the inclusive and the reconciliatory systems.

Exclusive Systems

Exclusive personnel systems are based on preventing persons associated with the past regime from holding certain positions in the state apparatus of the new regime. An exclusive system may authorize the dismissal of persons who were associated with the previous regime, a past conflict, or a foreign power. It may also disqualify certain people from positions of trust even though they did not previously hold any public office; they might have collaborated with the old regime or participated in paramilitaries and other organizations responsible for human rights abuses. Exclusive systems may be valid indefinitely or for a period of time sufficient for the new democracy to take root. The application of the exclusive system results in personnel discontinuity with the past via personnel changes in the state administration and the armed forces. As a result, crucial posts in state institutions of the new regime are disconnected from past practices.

Exclusive systems pass only one judgment: a judgment about the record of the official under investigation. A tainted record effectively disqualifies an official from participating in the new political dispensation. Once evidence about previous collaboration has been established, there is no discretion that can be exercised to mitigate the inevitability of dismissal. The automatic nature of dismissal distinguishes the exclusive system from discretionary dismissals pursued by the mixed system. Mixed systems usually pass two judgments: a judgment on the official's past and an assessment of his or her suitability for a particular position. Thus, in the mixed system, as shall be shown below, the past is not the only factor that determines the future of the official.

The automatic nature of dismissals has two important consequences for the functioning of exclusive systems. On the one hand, the new regime may be able to process a large number of cases within a short period of time, allowing for the dismissal of the discredited personnel as long as evidence can be established and adequate replacements can be found.[35] The fact that exclusive systems are not burdened by the rigorous procedural requirements of a criminal justice system, according to Neil Kritz, makes them less costly in comparison with criminal trials in terms of financial and human resources, which are often scarce in transitional countries.[36] On the other hand, without due process guarantees, exclusive systems are more likely to be abused by members of the new regime to pursue personal vendettas or to empty the old bureaucracies and install their own loyalists.[37] Thus, the major strength of exclusive systems may also be their major weakness. The need to conduct speedy dismissals of discredited members of the police force, pursued by the UN Mission in Bosnia and Herzegovina, led to the suspension of the right to be heard and to a relaxation of standards of proof.[38]

Exclusive systems are traditional and frequently used as methods for dealing with inherited personnel. History has witnessed numerous examples of wholesale dismissals that have followed changes of political regimes and civil wars or that were designed to prevent regime change.[39] They include the Reconstruction era in the United States and the dramatic purges that occurred in postwar Europe, including France, Belgium, and The Netherlands.[40] Somewhat gentler exclusive systems were pursued in post-socialist countries, such as Albania, Bulgaria, Czechoslovakia, Latvia, and Lithuania,[41] and in postwar Bosnia and Herzegovina.[42] In countries that face structural obstacles, governments try to utilize any available leverage to pursue "disqualification" through alternative methods, such as "promotion screenings" in Argentina.[43] The Greek post-junta government first tried to rid itself of tainted officers by placing them on inactive rosters, by forcing them to retire, by transferring them to insignificant posts, by annulling their promotions, or by temporarily suspending them from duty before embarking on more comprehensive vetting policies.[44]

Although initially designed as transitory measures, personnel systems may remain part of the legal order even after the transition is technically complete. For instance, as a result of seventeenth-century religious wars, only a Protestant can rule the United Kingdom. The Act of Settlement of 1701 effectively excludes Catholics from succeeding the throne in the United Kingdom.[45]

Not all measures that result in dismissals are exclusive systems. They may differ in their objectives, focus, and character. For the purposes of this book, a policy that results in dismissal is not considered an exclusive system if dismissal is a by-product of another measure. Dismissal may be a by-product of a policy of rehabilitation for victims of the previous regime or be a part of the wrongdoers' punishment. Exclusive systems have two essential features: they are perpetrator centered, and they do not impose any punishment other than dismissal. These features distinguish them from victim-centered and punitive measures.

For the purposes of this book, the perpetrator-centered approach to transitional justice involves the dismissal of people associated with the past regime from the state structures of the new regime. In contrast, a victim-centered approach treats dismissals as the by-product of a broader reparation program for the victims of human rights abuse.[46] A cooptation in the state apparatus is one means of redressing the wrongs done to victims of such injustices as discrimination and exclusion. Undemocratic regimes typically distribute public employment and state positions based on political criteria, loyalty to the regime, clientelism, or political corruption, leaving out the vast majority of people who did not associate with the regime. To redress these past inequities, the previously disadvantaged groups are given priority over the previously privileged groups in recruitment to positions in the new democratic order.

For instance, in Uruguay, Law 15.737 of 1985 provided for the reinstatement of those who were previously dismissed from positions of influence by the military regime on the basis of the Institutional Act.[47] The Act on Judicial Rehabilitation approved in Czechoslovakia in 1990 allowed a reinstatement of those who were dismissed in massive purges that followed the Soviet-led invasion of Czechoslovakia.[48] The Employment Equity Act approved in 1998 in South Africa stipulated provisions for affirmative action that aimed to redress discrimination in employment of previously disadvantaged racial groups.[49] These measures are not part of the exclusive personnel system as the concept is defined here, even though they may have caused dismissals.

Dismissals under the exclusive systems studied in this book differ from purely backward-looking punitive models of dealing with the past. Naturally, the exclusive personnel systems blend both perspectives: they are prospective and retrospective,[50] and they combine forward-looking justification and backward-looking justification.[51] In the forward-looking perspective, the primary objective of dismissals is, as officially claimed, the reform of the state apparatus. This reform may require that people associated with the past regime are prevented from accessing various positions of trust in the new state apparatus. Once people associated with the former regime are out of the state service, the exclusive system does not interfere with their lives, unless they hold or seek positions of trust. In the backward-looking perspective, the primary focus is on the punishment of those associated with the previous regime. In these situations, exclusion from public office typically constitutes one of several sanctions.

In referring to this distinction, Vojtěch Cepl, a former justice of the Czech Republic Constitutional Court, said, "if revenge had been our motivation, there are more effective ways of going about it that inflict a far greater sanction than symbolic acts of condemnation, lustration, and restitution."[52] Thus, for instance, in Hungary in 1990, the so-called Justitia plan was proposed by the Hungarian Democratic Forum (MDF), a parliamentary center-right political party, according to which those responsible for Hungary's critical situation at that time would face criminal proceedings, the regulation of wages, and the reduction of pensions.[53] Another version of backward-looking sanctions that intended to reach all persons associated with the previous regime was approved in Ethiopia, where members of the ousted Mengistu regime were deprived of their right to vote.[54]

Most of the legislation approved in Europe in the aftermath of World War II was backward looking with profound retributive features. Belgium, Czechoslovakia, Denmark, France, and Holland approved measures that had a primarily punitive character.[55] For instance, the Belgian Penal Code, approved by a legislative decree in 1944, stipulated additional penalties for convicted Nazi collaborators. In addition to prison terms, collaborators faced the loss of their civil and political rights, including the right to hold positions of trust in the public as well as the private sphere.[56] In Czechoslovakia, the so-called Minor Retributive Decree was approved in 1945 to retrospectively punish less serious criminal offenses by means of administrative justice.[57] In Denmark, an amendment to the Civil Penal Code stipulated that anyone who was found guilty was to forfeit eligibility for public office, public service, military service, and employment in the media and religious organizations.[58] Pursuant to the definition, such backward-looking retributive methods for exclusion cannot be classified as exclusive systems. However, some post-Reconstruction legislation in the United States would qualify as exclusive. For instance, section 3 of the Fourteenth

Amendment to the Constitution of the United States is primarily forward looking rather than backward looking: "No person shall be a Senator or Representative in Congress, or elector of President and Vice President, or hold any office, civil or military, under the United States, or under any State, who, having previously taken an oath, as a member of Congress, or as an officer of the United States, or as a member of any State legislature, or as an executive or judicial officer of any State, to support the Constitution of the United States, shall have engaged in insurrection or rebellion against the same, or given aid or comfort to the enemies thereof."[59] The amendment deals primarily with public positions. It affected those who took an oath and then engaged in rebellion if and only if they held or sought public positions. In reality, the distinctions between victim-centered and perpetrator-centered approaches and backward-looking and forward-looking perspectives may be blurred since they lead to the same outcome. However, these distinctions do matter for the assessment of different models of exclusion. They form different normative contexts under which the exclusions are implemented. People may judge perpetrator-centered and forward-looking dismissals differently from victim-centered and backward-looking exclusions because they are motivated by different concerns.

Systems of Continuance

Systems of continuance represent a null method of dealing with former personnel. People in positions of influence are allowed to continue in their posts under the new government. No exposure or confession is required to maintain the public posts.

Continuance can have various causes. Such systems may be a result of the balance of power in transition. For instance, as a result of political negotiations, the "sunset clause" was approved in South Africa, which resulted in continuation of the old bureaucracy under the ANC government until 1999.[60] Facing powerful forces of the outgoing regime, a new government may pursue a policy of not dealing with the past. Thus, the policy of drawing a thick line between the past and the present was declared by the first non-communist prime minister of Poland, Tadeusz Mazowiecki, in 1989 when the crucial posts in the police, the army, and the presidency were occupied by people associated with the past regime.[61] Sometimes the old elite may strengthen its influence by disqualifying the new elite from public posts. After the comeback of the post-communist bloc to power in Poland in 1993, its coalition approved a new public employment law in 1996, which required seven years of relevant working experience for senior public posts, making them available solely to old communist cadres.[62]

Another reason for continuance is that transitional government may be confronting an external threat at the time of a regime change. Facing the consequences of the breakdown of Yugoslavia, Slovenia, a nation of approximately 1.5 million citizens, could not afford to lose qualified professionals in many parts of its administration.[63] However, the continuance of former personnel may carry negative consequences. The collapse of Weimar democracy due to the continuance of the authoritarian Prussian-style bureaucracy is considered a paramount precedent.[64] Consequently, the need to prevent the lapse of German postwar democracy by approving stringent public employment laws has been recognized by the German as well as the European judiciary.[65]

Systems of continuance unconditionally allow people associated with former regimes to maintain a position of trust. They are not necessarily based on the continuity with the past in the literal sense. A situation in which a person associated with the past regime leaves a public office in order to hold another public administrative position is also a method of continuance. Hereafter we shall address the system of continuance only as it pertains to (the absence of) dismissals.

Mixed Systems

Mixed systems do not attach any automatic consequences to a public official's shadowy past; they are determined on a case-by-case basis, which provides leeway for different modes of dealing with the past. Past wrongdoing may or may not cause exclusion, and wrongdoers' confessions may or may not suffice to demonstrate their ability to hold a position of trust. Mixed systems may result in wholesale dismissals as well as wholesale indemnity of people associated with past regimes. Taking into account their past records, information gained during the interview process, the requirements of a particular post, and the position of the wrongdoers in comparison with other applicants, authorities can exercise discretion as to whether a second chance should be granted. The application of the mixed systems clears the way for partial discontinuity with the past.

Conceptually, mixed systems are similar to prosecutions and trials. Both deal with perpetrators on an individual basis and neither of necessity leads to condemnation of the wrongdoer.[66] However, the public employment aspect of the mixed system has to be distinguished from the criminal justice aspect. In the case of the former, the possible sanction is dismissal, while in the case of the latter the penalties are criminal. This distinction has not always been honored, although both require different legal procedures.[67] For instance, the denazification of Germany involved, among other things, not only the prosecution of Nazi criminality but also the removal of Nazis and their collaborators from positions of influence and responsibility.[68]

The flexibility of mixed systems seems politically pragmatic. It enables states to balance the wrongdoer's competence against his or her loyalty, or against the competence and loyalty of other applicants. Authorities may decide whether they want to fill posts with corrupt experts or loyal amateurs. They may consider the suitability of applicants against the pursuit of their political, security, economic, and regional interests. The flexibility of the mixed system also allows shifts in its application without changing the legal framework upon which it is based. For instance, the de-Baathification of Iraq was initially applied exclusively. But as the insurgency intensified, CPA tempered its radical stance and applied the same order on de-Baathification in a more moderate manner.[69] However, this flexibility can turn into a disadvantage by the system's inherent inconsistency in its application. The denazification of Germany is a case in point. According to John Herz, "[a] process that had begun with wholesale incriminations turned in the direction of wholesale exemptions and then ended in wholesale exonerations."[70]

Post-unification Germany faced another problem. The Unification Treaty provided a legal background for the introduction of a mixed personnel system in Germany.[71] The authorities required applicants for a public post to submit an agreement to be screened, along with a questionnaire on the extent of collaboration with the socialist-era secret services. Similar to the Polish reconciliatory model, the questionnaire was used as a test of loyalty. Those who concealed their involvement in past oppression were usually removed. However, unlike the Polish reconciliatory system, confession did not automatically grant collaborators a second chance. If a person admitted to being a collaborator, he or she was also asked for an explanation, followed by another interview and the possibility of further screening. The collaborator would then be permitted to keep the office and enjoy a second chance, transferred to a lower position, or dismissed.[72] The system could thus have inclusive or exclusive effects, depending on the particular case, the place where it was carried out, and who was in charge of the screening.

The inconsistent application of the mixed system in Germany was exacerbated by the country's federal structure. Different Länder within the federation adopted different public employment laws and applied different procedures. The mixed system was applied exclusively in some new German lands and inclusively in others. Berlin, Saxony, and Thuringia used their discretionary powers in a way that effectively caused personnel discontinuity. In contrast, Brandenburg was much more lenient toward its officials.[73] One of the reasons for a lenient application of the mixed system in Brandenburg may have been that its premier, Manfred Stolpe, was himself accused of being a Stasi secret informer.[74] Another reason was the presence of three senior members of the Lutheran Church of Brandenburg on the screening committee.[75] This contrasted with the situation in Berlin, where screening was conducted by officials from the Ministry of the Interior. In Brandenburg, the wrongdoers were given an opportunity to explain their past in detail. The underlying ethos of the committee was confessional: "[t]here was a conscious effort to not simply clean up the force, but to give individuals an opportunity to own up to their pasts."[76]

Since the outcomes of a mixed system depend on their application in different contexts, they cannot be conceptually considered an ideal typical category of personnel system. In spite of their potential to become a preferred method of dealing with inherited personnel in the state administration, mixed systems per se will not be empirically tested in this book.

Alternative Systems

Now we shall turn our attention to major institutional innovations in Central Europe. The following sections provide detailed characteristics of the inclusive and the reconciliatory systems that developed there. Similar to the previous sections, our objective here is to distinguish exposure and confession from exclusive methods.

Inclusive Systems

Inclusive systems are based on the exposure of persons associated with the past regime who hold or seek public positions. They effectively offer the tainted officials a second chance in exchange for greater transparency in public life. Inclusive systems may be motivated by the need to rectify the secrecy that usually surrounds undemocratic regimes. The exposure may enable the public to scrutinize the conduct of tainted officials and minimize the risk of blackmail, which could compromise national security.[77] In inclusive systems, the public is informed about the background of public officials in terms of their involvement in the past regime. Inclusive systems are based on discontinuity with the past: they do not allow personnel continuity but manifest changes from previous practices of governance.

The methods of dealing with the exposure of former personnel are fairly innovative. Under an inclusive system exposure does not imply exclusion. In fact, exactly the opposite is true: exposure provides a substitute for exclusion. Hungary, Romania, and Serbia were among the first countries that attempted to incorporate exposure into an inclusive personnel system. In Hungary, exposure largely concerned cases of secret informing. Public officials who had passed on information to the socialist-era secret police were confronted with evidence about their offenses and could either step down or face public exposure of their misconduct.[78] In Romania, the disclosure of the past concerned, among others, public officials, diplomats, journalists, and university professors.[79] In Serbia, exposure was combined with dismissals in a different way. It was applied to those in the lower echelons of the state administration, while those who held top positions were dismissed.[80]

Although exposure has frequently been applied in cases of covert informing in Eastern Europe, it can be applied in other contexts. All authoritarian regimes are typically surrounded by secrecy and lack transparency. The war records of some politicians in Germany, France, and other countries in Western Europe have also been exposed and publicly scrutinized. For instance, Kurt Waldheim, the former UN secretary-general (1972–82) and president of Austria (1986–92), was publicly exposed in the mid-1980s for having served in the Nazi SA forces. It was alleged that he had not been responsible for any war crime that would have made him liable for criminal prosecution but had served as a loyal servant of the Nazi regime.[81]

However, not all methods of exposure are classified as inclusive systems. A measure of exposure may emanate from institutions that are mandated to clarify the events of the past. Truth commissions, commissions of inquiry, other investigatory bodies, and all kinds of institutes of national memory in Eastern Europe have been established in more than three dozen countries and continue to spread.[82] Argentina, Chile, Uruguay, South Africa, Sierra Leone, and East Timor are among the most prominent examples of countries that used truth commissions. They largely address the truth deficit by focusing on the investigation of human rights violations and other controversial incidents of the past. Although such bodies contribute to greater transparency in public life, they do so as a by-product of their primarily historical function. This is the reason why, in parallel with truth commissions and other historical institutes, some countries such as El Salvador have pursued personnel policies through other means.[83] In sum, the focus of truth commissions is truth and not public administration. They operate on the criminal law level, not the public employment level. Therefore they are not classified as personnel systems in this study.

Similarly, inclusive systems are not the same as the opening of secret archives that allow historians access to files of former members of the repressive apparatus and the publication of their findings, which was pursued via various historical institutes in the Czech Republic, Germany, Hungary, Lithuania, Poland, and Slovakia.[84] Likewise, the effort of nongovernmental organizations in Argentina that gathered information about the role of certain individuals or institutions in the past regime is not part of an inclusive system.[85] Private revelations made by historians, nongovernmental organizations, and journalists lack the authority of the state's adjudication. The methods of exposure can be classified as inclusive systems if the investigations concerned former state employees or their collaborators and are pursued by the state for future employment considerations.

Reconciliatory Systems

Unlike other personnel systems, the reconciliatory system was implemented in only one case: Poland between 1999 and 2006. However, this does not diminish the conceptual significance of the reconciliatory system and its potential to become a personnel system that divided societies can successfully implement. Similar to the inclusive system, the reconciliatory system also institutionalizes a second chance, which is granted in exchange for truth. Under both systems, people associated with former regimes may hold positions of influence in the state administration of the transitional regime. However, the reconciliatory system differs from the inclusive system with respect to the conditions for obtaining the second chance. The inclusion is conditional upon the concerned individual's public revelation of past collaboration. Each official has to disclose prescribed relevant facts related to the past as stipulated by law. The truthfulness of these confessions is then verified. If persons were involved in the past regime but reveal this fact, they may retain their public position. However, their involvement is made public. If they conceal any relevant facts or if they are found to be dishonest, they are dismissed from their positions and their involvement is also made public.

This system is grounded in value-based discontinuity because the truth becomes publicly known. But, unlike inclusive systems, the primary revelation rests with the tainted official, not with the political system. The reconciliatory system demonstrates the change of the transgressor's attitude: a willingness to disclose the past serves as evidence of a change of heart. By disclosing their past, collaborationists renounce previous misconduct, which signifies a normative shift. The system therefore conducts value-normative discontinuity with the past. While inclusive systems merely require that collaboration is exposed, the reconciliatory system extends the message that the collaboration was also wrong and rejected by its very own perpetrators. In divided societies, in which former adversaries have their own interpretation of history, the illegitimacy of past wrongdoings is not self-evident to everyone.[86] The denouncement of past wrongdoings by collaborators of the past regime thus serves as a powerful statement about the nature of the past.

It is probably not accidental that this system developed in Poland in 1997 and was launched in 1999. It is a country that is deeply polarized about its past. Likewise, it may not be a coincidence that this system adopted the same mechanism of "truth exchange" as the Amnesty Committee of TRC in South Africa, another deeply divided country. Thus, both South Africa and Poland have developed fairly sophisticated and unprecedented procedures of transitional justice. Both the South African amnesty process and the Polish reconciliatory system have advanced the potential of the traditional value of "confession" to address vital sociopolitical needs in transitional societies. Both are based on the principle according to which wrongdoers are given a second chance in exchange for telling the truth about their deeds. The South African amnesty process makes the waiver of criminal charges conditional upon the revelation of truth, while the Polish lustration process provides access to high public office in exchange for candidates' truth revelation about their past.[87]

In addition to the fact that the amnesty process is conducted on the criminal justice level and the reconciliatory system on the public employment level, another feature that distinguishes the two is their different focus. Although both reconciliatory methods are based on an individual's active demonstration that he or she deserves a second chance, the Polish reconciliatory system remains one-sided and perpetrator centered. However, in South Africa, full reconciliation, it was argued, required perpetrators to face their victims, have a dialogue, and, ideally, apologize;[88] victims then had a right to learn more about the truth and to decide whether to forgive or not.[89]

The defining feature of a reconciliatory system is confession that is pursued as an alternative to dismissal. This alternative nature is stressed because not all personnel systems based on confession are reconciliatory. Confession that results in dismissals has been a traditional personnel method, which was implemented by means of loyalty oaths in the post-Reconstruction era in the United States, questionnaires in post-Nazi Germany, and screening interviews elsewhere.[90] In contrast, under the reconciliatory method wrongdoers are given incentives to confess, such as eligibility to hold public office in the personnel system in Poland in 1999–2006; amnesty in the Amnesty Committee in South Africa, thus allowing them access to public positions; or financial rewards for providing critical information about past human rights violations and the burial places of the disappeared in an attempt that turned out to be unsuccessful in El Salvador in the late 1970s.[91]

Confession under the Polish reconciliatory system serves as a loyalty test. Wrongdoers are "tested" to see whether they are able to dissociate themselves from the past and express loyalty to the new regime. Their wrongdoing is not an obstacle to holding public office. This distinguishes it from "confessions" in loyalty oaths, which are self-incriminating or self-disqualifying measures that do not give wrongdoers a second chance. They serve, under the threat of penalties, as a filter that does not allow the wrongdoer to continue in his or her position. For instance, in 1862 the Congress of the United States enacted legislation that prescribed an oath of office aimed at disqualifying former Confederate officials.

> [E]very person elected or appointed to any office of honor or profit under the government of the United States, either in the civil, military, or naval departments of the public service, . . . shall, before entering upon the duties of such office, take and subscribe the following oath or affirmation: "I, A. B., do solemnly swear (or affirm) that I have never voluntarily borne arms against the United States since I have been a citizen thereof; . . . that I have neither sought nor accepted, nor attempted to exercise the functions of any office whatever, under any authority or pretended authority in hostility to the United States; . . . that I take this obligation freely, without any mental reservation or purpose of evasion, and that I will well and faithfully discharge the duties of the office on which I am about to enter, so help me God.[92]

Any person who falsely took the oath was deemed to be "guilty of perjury; and, on conviction, in addition to the penalties now prescribed for that offence, [would] be deprived of his office, and rendered incapable forever after of holding any office or place under the United States."[93] Confessions under loyalty oaths are therefore not classified as reconciliatory systems.

The Scope of Personnel Systems

Until now major personnel systems have been classified according to their methods without considering their scope. The reason for this approach is that the scope of personnel systems is not a defining feature of their classification as exclusive, inclusive, or reconciliatory. However, each system may concern a smaller or a larger number of personnel, introducing another, albeit secondary, analytical dimension to our work.

Personnel systems may apply to different positions of trust under the new democracy, which may not be directly compatible with different kinds of involvement in the past regime. Thus, personnel systems usually have two dimensions: backward looking and forward looking. The forward-looking dimension defines positions and institutions in the new democracy, and the backward-looking dimension concerns institutions, positions, actions, or omissions in the past. The *scope* of personnel systems can then be defined as the magnitude of backward-looking and forward-looking provisions of the public employment laws upon which these systems are based. The backward-looking and forward-looking aspects may be pursued either institutionally by dissolving, or exposing, entire departments or individually by screening selected personnel of a particular department.

The total *dissolution* of institutions that had executed the repressive policies of former regimes was pursued, for instance, by disbanding the military police in post-junta Greece[94] and dissolving the army in post-invasion Iraq.[95] The *exposure* of the activities of entire institutions is usually conducted by investigatory commissions. For instance, the Goldstone Commission probed the role of post-apartheid security departments in fomenting political violence during transition in South Africa.[96] "Collective" *confession* was pursued, for instance, by TRC, which conducted special institutional hearings to disclose their role under apartheid.[97]

In the forward-looking perspective, prominent new institutions such as constitutional courts are established in transitional countries to remedy the personnel situation in the judiciary. First established in Czechoslovakia and Austria in 1918, constitutional courts served as remedies for the servile mentality of judges inherited from the Austro-Hungarian Empire.[98] Equipped with the power to review and annul judgments of general courts, as well as acts of parliaments or particular provisions within them, constitutional courts buttressed political transformation in most post-authoritarian states, including Germany, Spain, Portugal, Italy, Greece, South Africa, Chile, and almost all Central and east European countries.[99] Owing to the fact that only a handful of judges are appointed to these courts, the establishment of a constitutional judiciary is not an unaffordable alternative in societies with depleted human resources. It seems easier to establish a new institution that is superior to all other courts and staff it with fifteen or so jurists than challenge the tenure of all judges. However, staffing new government ministries or restructuring the entire security apparatus is considerably more difficult to implement. Thus, in South Africa, as is the case in many countries that have pursued extensive institutional reforms, old personnel have filtered through into new institutions.[100]

Similarly, selective screening has both backward- and forward-looking perspectives. In the forward-looking perspective, the individual screening of personnel may concern all the personnel in a state institution, only its senior members, or only its leadership. For instance, the screening of the Salvadorian army concerned only its officers.[101] On the other hand, the screening of the judiciary usually concerns all the judges. For instance, post-junta Greece approved constitutional acts to vet the entire judiciary, as well as to reinstate judges unfairly dismissed by the junta.[102]

In the backward-looking perspective, persons associated with the former regime may be defined either by the positions they held in the past or by their actions or omissions. Depending on the nature of backward-looking provisions, personnel systems may be classified as status-based or activities-based systems. In status-based systems, people are classified according to their association with repressive departments in the former regime, whether directly as employees or indirectly as collaborators. They may have been members of political organizations and paramilitary groups responsible for human rights violations. For instance, the Czechoslovak personnel system adopted status-based exclusions in 1991: it excluded persons who worked in, or collaborated with, the repressive apparatus of the socialist regime.[103] In activities-based systems, personnel systems deal with those who engaged in activities resulting in human rights violations. The Serbian personnel system adopted activity-based exclusions: it excluded all persons who previously participated in violations of human rights.[104] South Africa and the UN Mission in Bosnia and Herzegovina combined both approaches: the human rights record and status-based records.[105]

Similar to forward-looking provisions, the scope of the status-based backward-looking provisions of personnel systems may include all persons associated with particular departments and groups or only their top echelons. The variety offers an opportunity to classify status-based personnel systems into categories according to their scope. One can distinguish top-top systems, which prevent the top echelons in the past regime from unconditionally accessing the top positions in the new democracy; top-down systems, which prevent top echelons from unconditionally accessing all positions in the new democracy; or action-top systems, which prevent persons involved in illegitimate activities from accessing top positions. For instance, Order Number 1 on the de-Baathification of Iraqi society was based on both bottom-up and top-down exclusions. It prohibited all Baathists from holding government positions and top Baathists from holding any positions in the state apparatus, unless an exception had been granted.

Forward-looking provisions of transitional public employment laws and similar measures may expand to other branches of government: the legislature and the judiciary. For instance, the Fourteenth Amendment to the U.S. Constitution specifies exclusions that apply to members of Congress. However, personnel situations in the legislature are regulated by elections, and the personnel situation in the judiciary is subject to much stricter criteria than that of personnel systems. Introducing the exclusive system into the legislature is often considered a politically expedient means of eliminating political opponents from the electoral contest rather than a process of overcoming historical cleavages. By disqualifying opponents the new elite deprives itself of an opportunity to defeat them in elections.

Relatively less controversial is the exposure of tainted records of political candidates that was introduced by Romania after 1999 and the self-exposure of political candidates in Poland at approximately the same time.[106] Both methods give voters an opportunity to form their own judgments and make a more informed choice about candidates. Nevertheless, personnel systems that are examined in this book are limited to the non-elected branch of state power. They have been conceptualized as theoretically parallel to electoral systems. While electoral systems regulate the personnel situation in the legislature, personnel systems regulate the personnel situation in non-elected positions in the administrative branch in times of transition.

State-sanctioned personnel systems tend to expand to the corporate sphere in order to regulate state-owned companies and private businesses where pressing public interests, the protection of national security and public safety, and the protection of the rights of citizens are at stake. The expansion of personnel systems may also be attributed to the circumstances of a transitional country emerging from a situation of total state control. Under socialist regimes, all enterprises—schools, the media, unions, theaters, and other institutions, which were elsewhere considered independent institutions of civil society—were completely owned and controlled by the state. Although special public employment laws and other transitional measures, upon which personnel systems are based, may extend to the private sphere and to other branches of government, they predominantly concern public employment. This book therefore examines the effects of personnel systems on the state administration and their spillover effects on reconciliation in divided societies and does not address, for instance, the effects of the regulation of security-sensitive trades on regional security.

2

The Symbolic Meaning of Personnel Systems

[I]mpressive international conferences were mounted on the
moral and legal problems associated with disqualification from
office, police dossiers, "truth commissions," and screening
laws. . . . Worried liberals from the West, McCarthyism in mind,
discoursed earnestly on the folly of score-settling and the wisdom
of amnesties and active forgetfulness. Local moderates urged
compatriots to "draw a thick line," to quit rummaging around in
the past, and to take up more creative and less prosecutorial tasks.
          —Steven Holmes, "The End of Decommunization"[1]

Chapter 1 classified personnel systems as exclusive, inclusive, and reconciliatory. Different personnel systems can have different origins and produce
various effects. The main objective of this chapter is therefore to hypothesize the origin and the effects of personnel systems. We situate personnel
systems into the context of the transformation of political culture and
observe that personnel systems carry symbolic meanings that signify a purification of society in the aftermath of regime change. Although they were
conceived as administrative-security measures, different personnel systems
may be seen by the public as carriers of symbolic meanings that signify
different methods of purification from the taint of the previous regime. The
dual nature of these systems enables us to draw hypotheses about their
origin and effects.

Democratization and the Transformation of Political Culture

How shall we assess the effects of personnel systems? Where shall we look
for the variables of interest to explain their origin? Should we survey people
and examine their opinions instead of just looking at political institutions,
operational abilities of government departments, and their efficiency in
enforcing law, collecting taxes, and apprehending thieves? To answer these
questions, this section will shift our attention from the study of political
institutions to the study of political culture as a critical dimension of
democratization.

As with other policies of transitional justice, personnel systems are usually invoked in the aftermath of profound political change. In contrast to
changes in government that result from uncontroversial elections in democratic countries,[2] personnel systems are applied in the aftermath of the
demise of undemocratic political regimes, civil wars, and other radical
political changes, such as decolonization, the establishment of new states,
or military occupation or protectorate. Not all of these political transitions
are necessarily bound to result in democracy.[3] In some instances, emerging
regimes may be dictatorships that are as ruthless as their predecessors. In
this context, personnel systems may serve the narrow power interests of
one ruling elite over another and strengthen its grip on power.

However, this book does not adhere to a value-neutral approach, which
would generally assess the utility of personnel systems against their contribution to the consolidation of a new regime regardless of its character.
Instead, it accepts a normative component of democratization[4] and evalu-
ates various personnel systems against their potential for transforming and
fostering political culture, which is one of the major preconditions for
democracy. The "democratic transformation" provides a normative background for the assessment of various strategies of transitional justice in
general and personnel systems in particular. The critical question here is:
what does democratic transformation mean? What are its major features?

The need to systematically and empirically study democracy has led
many scholars to adopt a minimalistic conception of democracy. Following
Joseph Schumpeter, who has defined "democratic method" simply as a
"hunt for votes" and "dealing in votes,"[5] they tend to reduce democracy to
free elections. For instance, according to Samuel Huntington, a political
system is democratic when the "most powerful collective decision makers
are selected through fair, honest, and periodic elections in which candidates

freely compete for votes and in which virtually all the adult population is eligible to vote."[6] Although such definitions are easy to operationalize for the purposes of empirical research,[7] they have failed to satisfy many scholars in the field of democratization studies. Observing "reverse transitions," Linz and Stepan contend that reducing the notion of democracy to an election process is an "electoralist fallacy."[8] This has led some political scientists to postulate more substantive definitions of democracy and adopt indices that capture the civil rights scores of specific countries, while others have expanded the taxonomy of basic democratic attributes. Schumpeter considered democracy as having one feature. Robert Dahl, on the other hand, in his work listed seven features,[9] while Philippe Schmitter and Terry L. Karl listed nine.[10] One wonders whether there are still any democracies in the world.

In tandem with developments in political science, modern European constitutional law has traveled along the same intellectual trajectory. Constitutional experts have also discovered that democracies that were legitimized by electoral procedures have proved to be weak in the face of their undemocratic majorities. The collapse of the Weimar democracy, established in Germany after World War I, is an oft-cited example. Weimer democracy adopted the principle of the so-called formal Rechtsstaat, a legal principle that upheld the fundamental importance of formal electoral and parliamentary procedures.[11] The democracy was unable to prevent the rise of Adolf Hitler, who effectively destroyed it by employing parliamentary means to approve laws that eliminated his political opponents. Consequently, postwar Germany and most Central European democracies have approved constitutions based on Der Materieller Rechtsstaat, which adds a value-based content of justice and human rights to the formal procedures.[12] They believed that the substantive content of their constitutions would prevent undemocratic majorities from legislating against the rights of individuals.

The advocates of procedural definitions of democracy, and their counterparts in constitutional law, continue to rely predominantly on external institutional and macropolitical arrangements instead of the internalized norms of behavior and political culture. In defending their approach, Schmitter and Karl refer to theorizations that stress the need for civic culture as "misleading": "The principles we have suggested here rest on rules of prudence, not on deeply ingrained habits of tolerance, moderation, mutual respect, fair play, readiness to compromise, or trust in public

authorities. Waiting for such habits to sink deep and lasting roots implies a
very slow process of regime consolidation—one that takes generations."[13]
They assume that transitional political culture starts in negative values and
gradually improves as time passes. But the very fact of what many transitol-
ogists, including Schmitter and Karl, refer to as "pacted transitions"[14]
already assumes mutual respect, moderation, and readiness to political
compromise as the political elites have to deliver "the pact." It does not
take a generation to observe the fluctuation, the malleability, and the
changes in political cultures in transitional countries. The level of civic culture may dramatically deteriorate in political transitions as the enclaves
and residuals of trust are destroyed. In fact, personnel policies, such as
the exclusion of ethnic Albanians from the Kosovo parliament, the state
bureaucracy, and state-owned industries by Slobodan Milošević in 1989,
dismissals of ethnic Serbs from the Croatian administration by Franjo Tudjman in 1991, and de-Baathification in Iraq in 2003 seemed to instantly
produce negative impacts on political culture, deepening inimical relationships and effectively triggering ethnic conflict[15] even among those who previously lived as neighbors.[16]

Similarly, constitutionalists have attributed the blame for the collapse
of Weimar democracy and other similar collapses in Central Europe to the
weakness of formal constitutional structures rather than to the behavior of
the undemocratic majorities. It is widely accepted that the institutions of
the formal Rechtsstaat, not the majority of the German people or the
Czechoslovak people, failed to prevent Nazism and communism, respectively.[17] However, the opposite seems to be true: constitutional engineering
and post-conflict intervention strategies themselves are unlikely to sustain
democracy. Indeed, history tends to repeat itself. In spite of the rapid development in institutional designs in new democracies since the end of World
War II, concerns about the rise of "illiberal democracies" through liberal
means have not waned. Fareed Zakaria observed in the 1990s that in many
democracies elections were "declared free and fair and that those elected
were racists, fascists, separatists, who were publicly opposed to peace."[18]
Thus, every refinement to the definition of democracy and its formal infrastructure has been tested, and challenged, by a particular historical condition that exposed weaknesses in the nature of human characters.

Inspired by Alexis de Tocqueville, scholars such as Gabriel Almond and
Sidney Verba, Robert Putnam, and others therefore directed attention at
political culture. They have recognized that people's historical experiences,

habits, beliefs, attitudes, behaviors, and perceptions are as important to a successful democracy as the institutional frameworks that govern them.[19] Almond has defined political culture as "consisting of cognitive, affective, and evaluative orientations to political phenomena, distributed in national populations or in subgroups."[20] The concept was "adapted to the analysis of the cultural properties assumed to be associated with democratic stability."[21] It was conceived as a reflection of "the tragic collapse of Italian and particularly German democracy and their subversion into participant-destructive manias, and the instability of the French Third Republic."[22]

Likewise, the fragility of some third wave democracies caused scholars to realize that constitutions, human rights charters, and international treaties, no matter how sophisticated, are nothing more than legal documents that in reality may not be accepted and internalized by the people to whom they pertain.[23] For these reasons, James L. Gibson, Amanda Gouws, and many other scholars in transitional justice routinely refer to the need for the transformation of human rights culture, facilitating a shift from regimes that systematically violate human rights to regimes based on human rights and tolerance.[24] Transitional justice originates in transition, but it is deeper and lasts longer than the handover of political power and institutional reform. It epitomizes the urgency to end the violent conflict and a long-term commitment to reconciliation.

The often-cited "post-amble" of the Constitution of South Africa titled "National Unity and Reconciliation," which provides a normative framework for the country's experiment with transitional justice, is an example of the need to transform human rights culture in practice. It portrays the political transition as "a historic bridge between the past of a deeply divided society characterised by strife, conflict, untold suffering and injustice, and a future founded on the recognition of human rights, democracy and peaceful co-existence and development opportunities for all South Africans, irrespective of colour, race, class, belief or sex."[25] The pursuit of this transition requires reconciliation and reconstruction, which according to its drafters can be threatened by revenge and can only be advanced by means of amnesty for political crimes of the past. True, this section of the constitution is an ideological text that itself guarantees nothing. But unlike other constitutional guarantees it captures the need for a value-normative change in the new South Africa. It highlights the significance of the subjective dimension of democratization that requires changes in peoples' behaviors, norms, values, and beliefs.[26]

Scholars who have experience with undemocratic regimes routinely argue that effective transformation comes about as a result of personal and cultural change rather than institutional change. With a measure of idealism the South African philosopher Hennie Lötter claims that every citizen must "transform into a true democrat" by accepting the underlying values of democracy and new forms of responsibility.[27] Similarly, in "The Transformation of Hearts and Minds in Central Europe," the Czech lawyer Vojtěch Cepl and Mark Gillis are concerned about the transformation of moral culture.[28] According to Zevedei Barbu, a Romanian-born political psychologist, democracy and totalitarianism are ways of life that include both specific social and political structures and specific types of behavior and personality.[29] In Barbu's view, democracy is defined by flexibility in the macropolitical context, which is mirrored by flexibility on the individual level.[30]

Purification from the Taints of the Past

Now we have descended from political institutions to political culture. The vertical approach to our analysis, however, needs to be accompanied by the dynamic component that underpins the *process* of transition at the micro level. If political culture is a significant component of stable democracy, democratization assumes a transformation of political culture. How do people experience and perceive such dramatic social and political transformation? In this section, we shall demonstrate that the complex transformation of political culture is underpinned by a relatively simple process of purging society of its previous sins or sinners. The outcomes of this process in turn affect the basic evaluative perceptions that people have about others and about political institutions in the aftermath of regime change.[31]

One of the common features that underpin the work by Lötter, Cepl, and Barbu is that people who live for prolonged periods of time under authoritarian regimes may not have the same perceptions about the same phenomenon as citizens who live with the rhetoric and practices of democratic societies. The same act may have different meanings in different contexts. The personal security of citizens under dictatorships is a function of their loyalty to the regime, while citizens in liberal democracies are guaranteed security that is independent of their political views. In a democratic state, professional success and promotion may be attributed to personal achievement and individual accomplishment, while in a non-democratic regime it may signify collaboration with the ruling elite. Every action taken under an undemocratic regime may be viewed as political manifestation of affiliation with the regime. Consequently, value systems that shape perceptions of people in dictatorships may be rigid, dualistic, and hierarchical: distinctions are drawn between "they" and "we," between those who are involved with the regime and those who are not.

However, the dualistic vocabulary seldom reflects any rigid distinctions in the reality of authoritarian regimes in which distinctions are imprecise and obscured in shades of gray. The murky reflection of reality spans the continuum between two poles of society: perpetrators and victims. By taking certain actions everyone may be placed on the continuum between these extremes. But hardly anyone sees oneself in this way. Everyone aspires to justify his or her behavior in a particular way, which makes the notion of "they" very subjective. First, "they" may refer to those who have a higher rank in society than oneself. People who may have engaged with the previous regime in one way or another are likely to portray themselves in a more favorable light as "we," as innocent victims. Only victims may be seen as pure thanks to their innocence, the injustice that they experienced, and the sacrifice they made.[32] Second, the ideological content of the repressive regime and its propaganda tools may obstruct a clear vision. "They" may refer to the opposition to the regime, to dissidents who are portrayed as subverting the system. This may help justify wrongdoings, but it will likely not change the perspectives of their victims.

The following extracts from Václav Havel's play *Audience* illustrate these points. The play is situated in a brewery under the former socialist regime. The brewery employs a dissident playwright, Ferdinand Vaněk, who is apparently under surveillance by the secret police. A secret police officer, Tonda Mašek, who is not present in the play, asks the brewery foreman to write regular reports about Vaněk. The foreman is apparently more interested in drinking and in a celebrity actress than in writing regular reports for the secret police. The foreman meets Vaněk, whose daily task is to roll barrels, and offers him a better job in a warehouse.

Foreman: (*He lowers his voice.*) They come here and ask about you . . .
Vaněk: Who do?
F: Who do? What d'you mean "who do"? *They* do, of course.
V: Really? . . .

F: I'm damned if I know what to tell 'em every bloody week. . . .

V: I'm sorry, but I hardly think I can help you there. . . .

F: But that's just it—you can. . . . Listen, Ferdinand, in that warehouse you'll have plenty of time to spare—what harm would it do if you put it on paper for me once a week. . . . Writing comes natural to you, it'll be child's play. That Tonda Mašek is a decent sort. . . . I've known him since we were boys . . . and he really needs it. Can't leave him in the lurch, can we. Didn't we say we'd stick together? . . .

V: I'm truly most grateful to you for everything you've done for me . . . but I just can't . . . I can't inform on myself . . .

F: Inform . . . inform? Who's talking about informing?

V: It's not myself I am worried about . . . it wouldn't do *me* any harm . . . but there's a principle involved. How can I be expected to participate in . . .

F: In what? Go on, just say it! What can't you participate in?

V: In something I have always found repugnant . . . *(A short, tense silence.)*

F: I see. So you can't, eh. You can't. I like that. Now you've really shown your true colors, haven't you? A fine pal *you've* turned out to be. (*He gets up and starts to pace the room in great agitation.*) And what about me? Going to drop me right in it, aren't you? Let me stew in my own juice. Doesn't matter about *me* being a right bugger. Never mind about me, *I* can be allowed to wallow in the slime, I'm just an ordinary brewery yokel—but a fine gentleman like you can't participate. I can soil my hands as much as I like, as long as the gentleman stays clean. The gentleman has principles. Everything else go hang. Just so he keeps his lilywhite soul. Putting principles before people. That's you lot all over.[33]

By rejecting the foreman's request to write reports about himself, Vaněk is holding a mirror that shows the foreman his character and his role in the system. Vaněk gives a negative meaning to the actions, which until now the foreman considered normal. His involvement with the regime was not collaboration in his eyes but was framed as reciprocity to a "fair" secret policeman, Mašek. When the foreman realizes that Vaněk clearly sees him as collaborating with the regime, he angrily responds. The foreman who, until that moment, seemed to be politically clueless and who was not burdened by guilt suddenly aspires to be portrayed as innocent in Vaněk's eyes.

The three persons may be viewed as representatives of three sections of undemocratic society: Vaněk is the victim, Mašek is the perpetrator, and the foreman is in the gray zone in between. Now imagine what would happen with our heroes after transition. Vaněk is inculpable. He is innocent, in the foreman's words, "lilywhite," purified by his victimhood. The foreman, however, is tainted because of his complicity with Mašek. This gives him two options for purifying himself. He could make excuses by accusing Mašek, who forced him to collaboration in the first place. Alternatively, he could admit his role in the past, confess, and/or apologize to Vaněk and thus purify himself. It is not difficult to imagine other scenarios: the foreman could accuse Mašek, who would be likely to exculpate himself on the grounds that he followed orders, thus shifting the blame to his political masters.[34] Thus, owing to blurred distinctions about culpability and cooperation, the positions of individuals who might have been involved in the nefarious activities of previous regimes remain undefined before transition. Political transition exposes these activities and redefines their meaning.

Thus, citizens may not necessarily be burdened with feelings of guilt for their complicity in the past regime. Wrongdoing is inherent in such regimes, but before transition no negative meaning has been assigned to it. The fuzzy nature of authoritarian regimes is likely to be aggravated when otherwise abusive or wrongful conduct has been officially justified by impersonal laws of historical necessity and committed in the name of the vanguard party, the superior race, the nation, and the people.[35] As a result of regime change, the demand of the victims for justice may assign political meaning to the past behavior of those who persecuted them or violated their rights. The role of the abusers becomes explicit, their culpability clear, and they are seen as tainted. Appeals of moral leaders, such as "we are all responsible" for the totalitarian machinery, which was raised by Václav Havel on the eve of political changes in Czechoslovakia, do not have lasting resonance with the public.[36] At the onset of democracy, everyone may have made his or her petty political compromise, but nobody wants to be seen as tainted. Accusations and the identification of internal enemies are likely to become convenient escapes for all who do not want to acknowledge any role in the past. These actions alleviate them from the burden of collective guilt.

Foreign occupation and colonization are different sources of taint. According to Ian Buruma, occupation is always a humiliating business.[37] Persons who were dominated by a foreign power found themselves in positions that were lower in the social hierarchy than they would normally expect. Like political crimes, occupation carries an expressive dimension through which the occupier, or the colonizer, projects its political dominance: the occupier communicates the insignificance of its victims, telling them that they, their nation, race, ethnicity, or religion, do not count.[38] Consequently, dealing with the "foreign elements" and their domestic collaborators after transition is not only a process of channeling the collective guilt but also an empowering experience for the victims and a way to purify the rest of society. Shaving the heads of French women who were linked to Germans served as a shaming ritual that sought to purify not only the women but also other French citizens who were complicit with the Vichy regime.[39]

The individual and social need for purification may have moral, social, psychological, and historical causes. Our moral worth, according to Jeffrie Murphy, is largely derived from how others perceive us.[40] People naturally aspire to being perceived in a good light, says Erving Goffman, especially in situations that challenge their social status and aspirations.[41] Regime change is a situation that redefines the social status of people and establishes new social hierarchies, or social ranks, according to the degree of complicity with the past regime. Nobody wants to be associated with circumstances from the past that are perceived as unethical in the present.

Various purification rituals can be found in many religions and cultures. Robert Parker documents several roles that purification played in ancient Greece: purification operated as a divider, separating higher from lower, better from worse, the disgraced from communal life; it was an expression of horror and rejection by separating citizens from abhorrent events; it provided access to the sacred and perhaps to civic sacredness, and, conversely, it imbued profane events, acts, and venues with sanctity; and it united individuals into groups (e.g., the purification of the army expressed repentance, change of heart, rejection of anarchy, and reassertion of the army's corporate identity).[42] Referring to lustration rituals in ancient Rome, Parker has noted that "Purification, which removes dirt from the past and so makes ready for the future, is ideally suited as a ritual to mark transition. . . . As well as marking change in a neutral sense, purification is also, of course, well suited to satisfy the urge periodically felt by most people to make a new start, and feel a tainted environment grow fresh again."[43]

The dual meanings of purification, cleaning, and washing have been acknowledged by anthropologists and psychologists. For instance, spring cleaning not only gets rid of dirt but it also marks a seasonal transition, serves as a renewal rite, makes a house a home, and creates boundaries inside the home.[44] Similarly, in their psychological experiments on "clean hands," Chen-Bo Zhong and Katie Liljenquist have established the existence of the "Macbeth effect": an empirical link between physical and moral purity.[45] The need for ritual cleansing may derive from human experience. The observation that curing rituals in some societies assume an intuitive understanding of microbiology has led René Girard to conclude that rituals are grounded in fact.[46] The need for purification may be firmly based in past experiences of betrayals, and the memories of their consequences, especially in countries experiencing frequent regime changes. In Central Europe, each regime change in the twentieth century, including the establishment of the independent states in the aftermath of World War I, the Nazi takeover, the Nazi defeat, the communist takeover, and military takeover or invasion, was accompanied by the ideological negation of the previous regime, the destruction of monuments, and wholesale dismissals.[47]

To escape from their role in the past, individuals have two options for purifying themselves after transition: externally by "finger-pointing," proclaiming one's innocence, making excuses, and raising accusations against others; or internally by self-purifying through confession, apologies, or other admissions of guilt that enable them to present themselves as reformed persons. Social theories have anticipated both methods of purification for some time. The possibility of external purification has been assumed, for instance, as one of the arguments for criminal trials in transitional justice: to avoid collective guilt. The original intention of the Allies in setting up both the Nuremberg and Tokyo trials was that they provided the opportunity to assign the guilt to the military leadership,[48] thus wiping the rest of the nation clean of its "sins." Conversely, Martin Buber argued against the execution of Adolf Eichmann, seeing it as a "mistake of historical dimensions" that might "serve to expiate the guilt felt by many young persons in Germany."[49] Likewise, in the process of the "collectivization of guilt," Susanne Choi and I have argued that an inability of a new democracy to prosecute individual perpetrators turned former political prisoners in the Czech Republic against the Communist Party as the collective entity responsible for their suffering.[50]

Similarly, the second method, self-purification, has existed in various forms of "personal change" for quite some time. The oft-proclaimed needs for *metanoia* (confession, inner change, and moral development) are older

than the notion of confession in Christianity.[51] Although these concepts
have been viewed as normative in the literature, the connotation of personal transformation with religious conversion does not undermine the
need for the empirical study of personal change in a political context.[52]
Another ancient concept that has been associated with personal purification
is that of catharsis. The original medical term for the purification of the
body and emptying the digestive tract[53] was reinvented by Aristotle, who
suggested that drama may produce catharsis by purging the audience of
pity and terror.[54] However, the emotional abreaction that is at the core of
catharsis suggests that catharsis is narrower than purification. According to
Freud and Breuer, catharsis included "the whole class of voluntary and
involuntary reflexes—from tears to acts of revenge—in which . . . the affects
are discharged."[55] Modern psychology has further reduced catharsis to the
release of pent-up frustration and revenge.[56] Although catharsis is relevant
to our discussion here, transitional justice is usually evoked months, if not
years, after the demise of undemocratic regimes when the impact of negative affects may be diminishing. It also offers a variety of methods that may
have different cathartic effects with a different dynamic than a release of
aggressive behavior.[57]

Because of its ability to redistribute guilt, transitional justice can be
viewed as a cleansing process that seeks to formally put the past behind and
provide a fresh start—with "clean hands." The role of transitional justice is
to provide "discontinuity with the past," purify the body politic, rejuvenate
its existence, and sign a new social contract by excluding, or purifying, the
tainted elements in its core. The purification of government and society by
various means for the redistribution of guilt after transition works as a
social compass by which people navigate establishing a relationship of trust
and evaluating political institutions. The question is, How can political and
legal measures taken in transition be seen as trivial processes of purification? Are they features that are specific to transitional countries? Can all
personnel systems be seen as purification rituals?

Purification by Personnel Systems

The dual meaning of political, legal, and security measures has long be
recognized in the social sciences. The instruments of sociology are particularly useful in interpreting the meaning of personnel systems. In the pursuit

of political objectives, government policies often send ideological messages to civil society that either reproduce or transform social relationships.[58] To understand the social importance of law, one therefore needs to go beyond consideration of the concrete manifestations of legal institutions to the understanding of law "in connection with the patterns of belief evoked by legal symbols."[59] The distinction between "expressive properties of social behavior" and their "instrumental purposes" brings an important analytic dimension to our study, directing our attention from what Goffman calls "intended messages" to "unintended or latent forms of communication."[60] This approach, according to Robert Wuthnow, emphasizes "the capacity of rituals, ideologies, and other symbolic acts to *dramatize* the nature of social relations."[61] The insights from cultural sociology about the symbolic expressive aspect of social behavior[62] enable us to understand the dual meanings of personnel systems.

Indeed, every tangible political act, law, policy, or process carries an expressive dimension, which communicates its meaning to its citizens.[63] The expressive power of political processes is particularly strong in times of transition, which are highly politicized and thus have repercussions for future social relations. Criminal tribunals are traditionally argued to have a "deterrence effect"[64] and truth commissions are mandated to promote reconciliation.[65] Although they concern a limited number of perpetrators and victims, they are expected to affect reconciliation in the entire society. For instance, an empirical study of the TRC in South Africa has demonstrated that it was able to buttress reconciliation across many sections of the society.[66] The process of democratization, as Laurence Whitehead has pointed out, can be studied through its performative and dramatic features.[67] Consequently, personnel systems in democratic transitions, which are highly politicized and ritualized,[68] carry profound symbolic meanings. Understanding these meanings may be a key to explaining the origins of these systems and understanding their effects. In light of these considerations, personnel systems may be viewed as instances of ritual purification of a society in transition.

The symbolic and ritual nature of personnel systems should not be overestimated or underestimated. It should not be overestimated because we do not suggest here that personnel systems are a form of religious ceremony. It should not be underestimated because the process—as attested by speeches of political leaders—does signify purification and discontinuity with the past: a symbolic end of the oppressive rule and a symbolic start of a new era. Personnel systems may be viewed as instances of "negative rites" in a Durkheimean sense, which purify the state apparatus by dealing with, or re-creating, subversives and internal enemies.[69] Different personnel systems carry inherent social meanings that signify different methods of the ritual purification of society.

1. The exclusive system is based on dismissal. The symbolic meaning of dismissal suggests the purification by sacrifice and exclusion of the tainted individual. According to Albert Bergesen, "[t]he discovery of 'wreckers' in factories, 'hostile elements' in the Party bureaucracy, 'bourgeois thoughts' in literature, and 'anti-state' activity in government is the ritual activity which functions to reaffirm the presence of the sacred struggle . . . within the fabric of everyday life."[70] The need to discover the enemies in one's own ranks may stem from the need to reaffirm the collective existence of social groups and the historical purposes of the nation. Finding enemies may then provide a convenient escape from the burden of collective guilt and from admitting one's own responsibility for the traumatic past that challenged the existence of the nation. Societies undergoing transition are in need of "ritual cleansing," according to Stanley Cohen, and "lustration is one such method—to remove impure elements or ways of thinking so that they will lose their power."[71]

2. Likewise, an inclusive system can be a type of cleansing ritual. Through increasing transparency, the political body cleanses itself by exposing and stigmatizing particular individuals. Exposure signifies the shaming of the individual in the eyes of the public, friends, and relatives,[72] thus negatively impacting the shamed individual. It is an instance of a "degradation ceremony" which, according to Harold Garfinkel, transforms the public identity of the individual from a higher to a lower social position.[73] On the other hand, exposures that are not accompanied by dismissals, as in the inclusive systems, may also signify a "reintegration ceremony," which proponents of restorative justice such as John Braithwaite and Stephen Mugford believe provides a shaming of the offenders but also gives them a voice that may facilitate their eventual social acceptance.[74]

3. A reconciliatory system that revolves around confession signifies a ritual of self-purification, which carries profound religious connotations. Although Dan Kahan has suggested that public confessions

may signify self-debasement and contrition penalties,[75] confession has a reformative nature, suggesting the moral transformation of the individual. Such views are strengthened when confession, unlike the confessions under Stalinism or McCarthyism, does not result in self-incrimination. By confessing his or her behavior the offender requests to be reassessed as a moral agent capable of personal change.[76] Similar to apologies, confessions may be viewed as expressions of embarrassment and chagrin,[77] which enable the offender to distance himself from his or her past sins. Consequently, confession may be viewed as a ritual of social inclusion.[78]

The view of personnel systems as ritualized instruments for the purification of society helps us explain their origins and hypothesize their effects. Each personnel system may be motivated by the perception of others as "clean" or "tainted." Each personnel system also conveys ideological messages about the reliability of the new government, the severity of the previous regime, and the malleability of tainted officials. These considerations also assume that transitional justice and personnel systems are not exclusive facilitators of purification from the taint of the past. There are many other transitional factors that affect perceptions about former adversaries: their behavior as experienced on a daily basis at the interpersonal or political level; evidence of their involvement in criminal activity during transition; the public image of their former political masters, such as the dogmatic style of their electoral programs; their attitudes toward others; their attitudes toward the past generally; and others.

Personnel Systems in Transition

Transitional justice, as Teitel has observed, is constituted by and constitutive of political transition.[79] Political transitions affect transitional justice, which in turn affects political transition. The same dynamic applies to personnel systems as instances of transitional justice. In situations in which political transition is not tied by structural constraints imposed by previous regimes, the critical moment of choosing among different personnel systems resides in the realm of perceptions. The choice is a function of perceptions about former adversaries as clean or tainted. Although the current perceptions may be affected by the severity of the infractions of the previous regime, they are largely derived from current observations of former adversaries.

Perceptions of adversaries as tainted and untransformed increase the need for a personnel system that facilitates their exclusion from public life. Likewise, perceptions of adversaries as transformed increase the need for an alternative personnel system. In other words, the demand for an exclusive personnel system may be affected by the strength of the perceptions of adversaries as not only a security threat to the new regime but also a moral threat to its citizens and their leaders. The word *untransformed* may include a number of other vices that are broader than the notion of security threat: inherited personnel may be perceived as corrupt, loyal to the previous regime, inefficient, and so forth. These features may not necessarily lead to the perception of threat, but they may lead to the dismissal of inherited personnel. The weaker, the more likely the possibility of choosing among alternative (non-exclusive) personnel systems.

While the origin of the security threat may be rooted in the past experience and in the perceptions of its current protagonists, the origin of moral threat has a two-way social dynamic. First, the public may find the presence of tainted officials in the government repugnant. People may not trust government that is tainted by its association with the former regime. Second, the moral threat may stem from the anxiety and insecurity that people have about themselves because their moral standing may be threatened by the perceptions that other people have about them. Such fears may arise among the people from the so-called gray zone—those who are in between the perpetrators and victims of the former regime on the societal continuum. They are susceptible to being perceived as complicit with the former regime. Thus, they may need to demonstrate that they are clean. Earlier we suggested that finger-pointing and taking a radical stand against the other tainted are convenient methods of purifying oneself externally.

The dual role of transitional justice indicates its propensity and that of personnel systems to produce effects on political transformation. We have mentioned that personnel systems may be viewed as a set of different methods that aspire to purify government. The perceptions of government as purified may be essential prerequisites of trust in government. However, their effect may be much wider. In their role of cleansing government, personnel systems send ideological messages that affect the social standing of tainted officials, highlighting or absolving their sins, licensing their untrustworthiness or trustworthiness, and reassessing their role in the past as inexcusable or excusable. Thus, personnel systems may affect trust in government and perceptions about people associated with the past.

1. Trust in government. Since the groundbreaking work by Almond and Verba, Niklas Luhmann, Anthony Giddens, and Robert Putnam, trust in government has been viewed as an essential feature of democratic order[80] and, according to Francis Fukuyama, of a market economy.[81] Trust enables governments to implement their policies, collect taxes, enforce law, and foster citizens' compliance and ethical reciprocity, thus helping to sustain democracy. Even those, such as Eric Uslaner, who disagree with the link between democracy and trust acknowledge that the authoritarian government may destroy trust.[82] In the context of regime transition, the culture of rampant distrust may spill over to shape the attitudes of citizens toward the new democratic state.[83] Rebuilding trust in government is thus an important issue confronting transitional societies. Personnel systems that signify means of discontinuity with the past are invoked as rituals for the purification of government from the taint of the past. Although they use different means that may vary in the degree of their efficiency, their primary goal is to establish a trustworthy government that has been eroded by an authoritarian regime. We therefore hypothesize that *the application of all personnel systems increases trust in government.*

2. Reconciliation. According to Dahl, democracy assumes inclusiveness,[84] and it seems obvious that inclusiveness requires social reconciliation. It is essential that people in democracy are able to establish a minimal relationship of trust, tolerate each other's opinions, and work together. In their research on the TRC in South Africa, Gibson and Gouws clearly demonstrate the relevance of transitional justice policies for overcoming intolerance and fostering reconciliation.[85] Owing to their expressive power, each strategy of transitional justice generally, and more specifically its personnel system, has the propensity to foster either a flexible or a rigid view of former adversaries. In their effort to reform state administration, each personnel system processes, or recreates, the tainted by either officially certifying their taint and solidifying the existing perceptions, similarly as other measures of transitional justice give some victims an official status of a victim; or acting as a purifying agent and altering the perceptions. In

doing so, each method makes certain assumptions about the malleability of "human nature." We hypothesize that owing to the ritual of exclusion, *the exclusive system inhibits reconciliation* because it strengthens adversarial perceptions; depending on the nature of the shaming ritual, *the inclusive system facilitates reconciliation* in cases of reintegrative shaming but inhibits reconciliation in derogatory shaming rituals; and owing to the ritual of confession, *the reconciliatory system facilitates reconciliation.*

To sum up, personnel systems can help transform perceptions of tainted officials as fellow citizens or at least passively not inhibit more flexible views that arise when personal transformation does occur. This approach permits recognition of the autonomy of people to make independent moral judgments and at the same time allows for the possibility of governmental action to shape public perceptions. When unrestrained by powerful forces of the old regime, personnel systems appear at a critical juncture, which may facilitate a

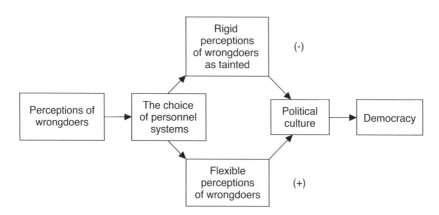

Figure 2.1. Personnel systems in transition. Personnel systems are theorized to rest in the critical juncture of democratization. Their choice is affected by the perceptions of wrongdoers as tainted but (like other institutional choices) the elite decision does not need to follow popular preferences. Non-exclusive systems may mollify the negative perception about wrongdoers as tainted by replacing it with a more flexible view, while exclusive systems may perpetuate, or worsen, their perceptions by creating an official status of wrongdoers as tainted for life. The resulting perceptions affect trust, tolerance, and other components of political culture, which are preconditions of liberal democracy.

Table 2.1. The Symbolic Meaning of Personnel Systems

Personnel System	Means of Discontinuity	Type of Ritual	Transformative Measure
Exclusive	Dismissal	Exclusion	No
Inclusive	Exposure	Shaming	Yes/No
Reconciliatory	Self-exposure	Confession	Yes

Note: The exclusive system is hypothesized to be an untransformative measure of transitional justice because it perpetuates, or even strengthens, the rigid view of tainted officials as unchangeable. The inclusive system is hypothesized to be a transformative measure because it redefines tainted officials as victims of the previous regime. Exposure may shame the tainted officials but the message of shaming may be reintegrative given their non-dismissal. The reconciliatory system pursues transformation by allowing the tainted to disassociate themselves from the past.

change in the path toward successful democracy. The choice of a personnel system may be able to transform perceptions about adversaries as tainted by replacing them with more flexible attitudes, or they may solidify historical divides by preserving and strengthening inimical perceptions.[86] Figure 2.1 illustrates the place of personnel systems in democratization, and Table 2.1 gives an overview of the symbolic meaning of personnel systems.

PART II

Lustration Systems
in Central Europe

3

Lustration Systems and Their Operation

Czechoslovakia also had an interest in ensuring the morality of its government officials. The country could boast the world's most professionally moral head of state; why staff the government with finks? Democracy requires confidence in government institutions, and Czechoslovaks were not going to trust a government staffed with old Communists. While they debated lustrace, Czechoslovaks heard the [1992] U.S. presidential election. Americans were passionately interested in Bill Clinton's alleged affair with Gennifer Flowers; many felt that the episode said a lot about Bill Clinton's character and qualification to be president.

—Tina Rosenberg, *The Haunted Land*[1]

This chapter explains how personnel systems operate in practice. It focuses on three archetypal versions of personnel systems: the exclusive, the inclusive, and the reconciliatory systems, which developed in the Czech Republic, Hungary, and Poland, respectively, in the 1990s. In Central Europe, these personnel systems were governed by transitional public employment laws known as lustration laws because they incorporated a lustration procedure: a method of screening inherited personnel against the socialist-era secret police archives. *Lustration system* is a regional variant of *personnel system*, which is theoretically derived from these lustration laws. It is a subset of personnel systems; both lustration systems and personnel systems may be classified as exclusive, inclusive, or reconciliatory. The need for two concepts that both denote processes for dealing with inherited personnel who may have been perpetrators of human rights violations may seem unnecessary. However, the term *personnel system* does not honor the widely accepted regional nomenclature of lustration laws that spread across Central and Eastern Europe in the 1990s. Conversely, the term *lustration system* is not an appropriate label for personnel systems, which did not incorporate lustration procedures per se.

The Dual Meaning of Lustration

Lustration has been viewed by some scholars as a process of purge,[2] vetting,[3] non-criminal sanctions,[4] or administrative justice,[5] while others see it as the process of a ritual sacrifice.[6] In view of the symbolic meaning of political and legal processes (Chapter 2), we argue that lustration encompasses both meanings: it is a political-security process, which signifies the purification of society. No other term can capture these meanings as vividly as lustration. The dual perspective on lustrations can be traced back to the Latin origin of the English word. *Lustration* derives from the noun *lustratio* and the verb *lustrare*, which has two meanings: to review, survey, observe, examine; and "purify by means of a propitiatory offering," "purifications by sacrifice," "ritual sacrifices."[7]

Lustration was barely used in English before 1990,[8] when it was revitalized by its Czech-language equivalent, *lustrace*, which alluded to the first meaning.[9] *Lustrace* was a technical term used by Slavophone archivists for searching an inventory, registry, or database for a particular name[10] or other relevant information.[11] The word *lustrum* then means the result of this search, an excerpt from an official registry or a catalogue, such as a land registry.[12] Lustration as a means of examination in order to gain information (e.g., to check on a person's background) has been used by the police as well as other government agencies. For example, "property lustration" refers to the disclosure of the property situation of politicians in Poland,[13] and "lustration of second-hand cars" in the Czech Republic means the verification of data about a vehicle in the databases of stolen vehicles.[14] "Lustration" as screening has been colloquially used outside the political sphere as well, for instance, to determine the suitability of parents who wish to adopt a child.[15]

Prior to 1989, *lustrace* was also used by the socialist-era Czechoslovak secret police to determine whether any information existed about a person of interest is its databases.[16] According to the Czech historian Jiří Žáček, the

term *lustration* as used by the police referred to the process of inquiry initiated by an operative or a leading member of the Czechoslovak Corps of
National Security directed at the statistical evidence department to determine whether any data existed about a particular person.[17] Two kinds of
data were gathered: information about persons who were considered inimical to the socialist regime, and information about secret police informers.[18]
Following the collapse of socialist regimes, lustration has maintained the
same meaning, but its context has changed. It has come to mean "the
examination of certain groups of people, especially politicians, public officials, and judges, to determine whether they had been members or collaborators of the secret police, or held any other positions in the repressive
apparatus of the totalitarian regime."[19] Such examinations were conducted
under the so-called lustration laws.

Lustration law is a special public employment law that stipulates conditions for the access of persons who worked for or collaborated with the
political or repressive apparatus of socialist regimes to certain public positions in new democracies.[20] The special character of lustration laws signifies
their transitory nature. Their role is to facilitate a shift from one political
regime to another or, more generally, to bridge two distinctive states of
affairs.[21] These laws may be in effect for limited periods of time or become
incorporated into standard public employment laws. Their public employment character distinguishes them from other measures taken against
members of the former repressive apparatus on the level of criminal law,
that is, prosecutions. Lustration laws may make some positions in new
democracies directly incompatible with positions under preceding authoritarian systems or specify a method of inclusion of the old personnel into the
new system. The law usually defines who can and who must be subjected to
examination and who is in charge of the examination. It delineates the
purpose of the lustration process and defines how the lustration procedure
should work. It also specifies the consequences of an eventual "positive
lustration." A finding of "positive lustration" means that the examination
uncovers evidence that a person worked for the repressive apparatus of the
previous regime.[22]

Interestingly enough, none of the lustration laws has the word *lustration*
in its title. The first lustration law, which was approved in Czechoslovakia
in 1991, was entitled the act "That Prescribes Certain Additional Prerequisites for the Exercise of Certain Positions Filled by Election, Appointment,
or Assignment in State Organs and Organizations."[23] The Hungarian

lustration law of 1994 was officially known as the "Law on Background Checks for Individuals Holding Certain Key Offices."[24] Similarly, the Polish Lustration Act was entitled "On the Revealing of Work or Service in State Security Organs or of Collaboration with Them Between 1944 and 1990 by Persons Holding Public Positions."[25] Why then do we use lustrations here? These laws are recognized as lustration laws in the common as well as official language in the Czech Republic and Poland. The use of the word *lustration* continues to grow. In 2001, the search engine Google returned 2,190 hits for the Czech word *lustrace*, 2,790 for the Polish word *lustracja*, and 4,010 for the English word *lustration*.[26] In May 2009, there were 61,900 matches for *lustrace* at Google's Czech site, 1,360,000 for *lustracja* at the Polish site, and 144,000 for *lustration* at Google.com.[27] Although the Hungarian language has not accepted a word with the Latin roots of *lustration*—the Hungarian equivalent for lustration is *átvilágítás*, which approximately means "screening"[28]—a number of scholars writing on Hungary use *lustration*.[29] Indeed, the word *lustration* is widely accepted in the academic literature.[30]

As indicated above, the Latin roots of *lustration* imply another meaning that has been attributed to the lustration process in Eastern Europe: ritual sacrifices.[31] It referred to the ceremony *lustrum condere*, which was practiced in ancient Rome. According to R. M. Ogilvie, *lustrum condere* was a circular procession with sacrificial animals and purifying fire; its function was to purify and at the same time insulate the Roman people.[32] The dual meaning of lustration, or *lustrare*, and the question of their common or separate origin preoccupied Latin scholars.[33] It is apparent that lustration was associated with a technical process of census and gradually gained a religious meaning of purification: "[S]ince the most important of the censors' duties was the listing and classification of the members of the society, 'lustrum condere' denotes the composition of that list which might be regarded as an instrument of purification in so far as its composition involved the expulsion of alien elements. The exclusion of 'foreign bodies' was an essential part of ritual."[34]

The link between lustration and census seems to be a persuasive argument in support of its dual meaning. The very idea of census is exclusionary: counting somebody in inevitably means leaving somebody out. Likewise, the officials responsible for census, *censors*, seem to be those entrusted with conducting technical inclusion as well as social exclusion. Censor, according to the *Etymological Dictionary*, means a "Roman magistrate who took censuses and oversaw public morals."[35] This may also explain the common link between census and censorship—censorship of books, newspapers, and films. *Censure,* from the Latin *censura,* means "judgment" or "assessment,"[36] which brings us back to *census* as "the enrollment of the names and property assessments of all Roman citizens."[37] Census then implies that a list had to be composed, effectively determining who is included and who is excluded. Lustrations, then and now, have had a dual meaning.

When introducing lustrations, some authors have emphasized the ritual meaning, suggesting that lustration means "the purification of state organizations from their 'sins' under the communist regimes."[38] Although east European lustration did not primarily mean ritual sacrifice, it could be construed in that way. The Czechoslovak lustration law, for instance, disqualified high-ranking communist cadres, secret police members, and their collaborators from senior posts in the new administration and security forces and barred them from regaining their positions. For its supporters, the law did *symbolize* purification: personnel discontinuity with the past and a new beginning stripped of the tainted officials.[39] For others the law *signified* a politically expedient purge through which the new elite used the old methods of exclusion to create new injustices. Journalists depicted the process as a "witch hunt,"[40] suggesting a situation of moral panic.[41] Both proponents and opponents of lustrations viewed the process of dismissal as symbolic: a symbolic departure from old practices in the eyes of the supporters and a symbolic continuation of old practices of exclusion in the eyes of critics.[42]

The concepts of *sacrifice* and *purification* have deep cultural and religious meanings, which go beyond mere observable aspects of politics. Many if not all political institutions, processes, and policies carry symbolic meanings that may have profound social consequences.[43] In a highly politicized environment, even seemingly minor laws, speeches, and actions may convey deep symbolic meaning that affects people's perceptions, norms of behavior, and the prestige of social positions. In political transitions, which are characterized by uncertainty and unpredictability, the expressive power of political processes is particularly strong as people look for guidance on the new modes of behavior. Symbols help people understand complex processes and serve as a benchmark for their assessment. In the previous chapter it was acknowledged that a symbolic perspective of politics offers a useful explanatory framework for understanding the import of this relatively new and complex process. For instance, the transitory role of lustration laws signifies the need to purify society, to rejuvenate its collective existence, and to reaffirm the sacred purposes of the nation after traumatic events.[44] The list of positions, or actions, in the past that are incompatible with positions in the new democracy clearly resemble the enrollment of names and properties in the ancient census; although both are material processes, they carry symbolic meanings that signify exclusion and censure.

The titles of lustration laws suggest that the methods of lustrations were country specific. In all countries, lustration means "examination," but this meaning is affected by the operation of lustration laws themselves. In the Czech Republic, lustration refers specifically to "disqualification": it determines whether a person is qualified to hold public office, purchase a second-hand car, or adopt a child. In Poland and Hungary, lustration refers to the revelation of previously unknown information about the past of politicians. Furthermore, the revelation in Hungary is conducted by means of "exposure," while in Poland it is done by means of "self-exposure." In Polish, "lustro" in common language means "mirror."

Consequently, the symbolic meaning of lustration laws differs in these countries. The different methods of different lustration laws signify different rituals that convey different meanings: disqualification from office signifies the purification of the state by excluding the tainted elements; exposure symbolizes a shaming ritual; and self-exposure is a clear manifestation of a confession ritual. The following sections will use the symbolic apparatus to examine the technical operation of three paradigmatic personnel lustration systems in three Central European countries: the Czech Republic, Hungary, and Poland.

The Exclusive System in the Czech Republic

Czechoslovakia was the first post-socialist country to approve lustration law.[45] The law was approved on October 4, 1991, and set "additional qualification prerequisites" for holders of certain positions in the new democratic system. The prerequisite was that they did not hold certain positions under the previous regime. Persons who had been working in particular positions in the repressive apparatus of the socialist regime had to be dismissed from leading positions in the new regime. Thus, Czechoslovak lustration law provided a legal background for the exclusive system. It symbolized personnel discontinuity with the past. It sent an ideological message that effectively negated and condemned the previous communist regime and its protagonists. The symbolic meaning of the law helps us explain its disproportionate criticism, its excessive implementation, and its duration.

The law generated a great deal of criticism domestically as well as internationally. President Václav Havel criticized the law but signed it despite his reservations.[46] As a former dissident who was imprisoned and worked in a brewery, he was not tainted by the regime. But the chairman of the Federal Assembly, Alexander Dubček, was in a different position. He was regarded as an iconic figure of the communist reformist movement known as the Prague Spring, which might have led to the abandonment of authoritarian ways of governance and to the building of "socialism with a human face" if it had not been halted by the military intervention of the Warsaw Pact armies in 1968. Dubček was absent during the voting on the original lustration bill, which symbolized the condemnation of communism. Defying the constitution, he then refused to sign the lustration law.[47] In fact, he provided the International Labour Organization with the misleading information that one million people would lose their jobs due to the application of the lustration law.[48]

Similarly, at the international level, many seemed to be more concerned about the ideological message of the law rather than about its content. The law was criticized by the International Labour Organization,[49] the Parliamentary Assembly of the Council of Europe,[50] the U.S. Department of State human rights reports,[51] and human rights organizations.[52] Some Western journalists and activists depicted lustrations as a "witch-hunt in Prague," "hunts for reds in Eastern Europe" or the "velvet purge."[53] Many exerted pressure on the Czechoslovak Constitutional Court to nullify the law. Pursuant to the petition of ninety-nine deputies, on November 26, 1992, the Constitutional Court of the Federation abrogated several provisions but upheld the act in its substance.[54]

After the breakdown of Czechoslovakia on December 31, 1992, the lustration law was incorporated into the legal system of its successor states: the Czech Republic and Slovakia. Owing to the association of some Slovak leaders with secret police, the law was not enforced in Slovakia and formally expired there in 1996.[55] Although the law was initially designed as a transitory measure, which was supposed to be valid for five years, it was extended for another five years in September 1995 and indefinitely extended in October 2000 in the Czech Republic.[56] In both cases, President Havel tried to veto the law to exert pressure on the Parliament—to approve a comprehensive civil service act—but both vetoes were overruled by the Parliament.[57] The law solidified the picture of persons associated with the previous regime as tainted. In such situations, the need for lustration laws remains urgent. In 2000, more than 36 percent of Czechs supported the extension of the lustration law, and 33 percent were against it.[58] On December 5, 2001, pursuant to the petition of a group of deputies, the Constitutional Court of the Czech Republic upheld the law and its extension.[59]

The Exclusive Method

There were two methods for determining previous involvement in the former communist regime. A person who held, or applied for, a particular public position had to submit two documents: a lustration certificate and an affidavit. The certificate and affidavit were not required for citizens born after December 1, 1971; they were considered too young to sin in the past because they had not reached eighteen years of age during the Velvet Revolution in November 1989. Everybody older than that was eligible to apply for a lustration certificate at any time. The option enabled applicants and other candidates for public positions to verify their status in advance of facing embarrassment in front of bosses.[60] The lustration certificate was issued by the Ministry of the Interior at a candidate's or incumbent's written request. The ministry examined recorded evidence of secret collaboration or work for certain security departments of the former regime. If no record of collaboration could be found, the person received a negative lustration certificate, which was a prerequisite for holding certain public positions. Conversely, a positive lustration certificate provided verification about the person's past involvement. It officially certified the taint of the past. Everybody else was declared clean.

The second document that had to be submitted was an affidavit testifying that the candidate did not belong to other groups specified in the lustration act. The affidavit concerned the kinds of involvement in the socialist regime that were not secret but were difficult to certify. In the Czech case, it included, for instance, members of the paramilitary People's Militia and external sources of taint, such as students and trainees at the KGB and other Soviet political-security universities. The affidavit signified a self-incriminating confession. If an individual belonged to any group specified in the act, his or her superior was required to terminate his or her employment contract or transfer him or her to a position not specified by the act.

The publication of the lustration certificate was not permitted without the written consent of the lustrated person. Thus, positively lustrated persons would leave their positions without any public knowledge of their collaboration. The dilemma of the truth versus the protection of the privacy of former informers was solved for the benefit of the latter. The reason for this difference originated at the beginning of the lustration process. The Czechoslovak government, which prepared the lustration bill, took a radical stand in protecting those who collaborated with the previous regime at the expense of truth. It proposed a provision to the bill that prohibits the publication of the names of collaborators. Offenders could have faced up to three years of imprisonment. Several deputies responded critically to the provision.[61] The provision has not been approved, but the spirit of incriminating journalists for publicly revealing collaborators has persisted.[62]

Rituals, by their very nature, are public. It is not surprising that the secrecy of the official lustration process soon ended when the names of secret informers were leaked to the media. In 1992, an incomplete list of secret police collaborators was published by a former dissident, Petr Cibulka, in his "uncensored newspaper" called *Rudé krávo* (The Red Cow), a title that ridiculed the Communist Party mouthpiece *Rudé právo* (The Red Right).[63] The entire secret police file of the prominent Czech politician Jan Kavan was published as a book in 2000, documenting his alleged contacts with the secret police and the remuneration he was alleged to have received although—or because—a court had cleared him of being an informer.[64] It is possible that the leaked information was not correct. President Havel condemned the leakages,[65] but he did not express trust in Kavan when he initially hesitated to appoint him as a minister in the social democratic government after the 1998 parliamentary elections.[66] The official secretiveness of the process ended in 2001 when the Parliament authorized the Ministry of the Interior to publish all the names of secret police informers.[67]

In order to counterbalance its sweeping ambit, the lustration act provided a high degree of legal protection for lustrated persons. Any person could object to the termination of his or her employment at a second-tier regional court instead of a first-tier district court and then appeal the decision to the High Court.[68] Beyond that an aggrieved person could submit a constitutional complaint if his or her rights had been encroached.[69] According to a Czechoslovak Supreme Court's lustration decision of 1992, the truthfulness of the certificate issued by the ministry could also be challenged on the basis of civil procedures.[70] Other legal protection in this area was guaranteed by the civil code's clauses that protect personal privacy.[71] Many who received positive certificates and applied for the judicial review of these decisions won their cases. The Ministry of the Interior was often unable to assemble judicially acceptable evidence, since most of the secret files were transferred to microfiches, which were not permitted as evidence in court. However, the taint of the past was likely to stay with the person regardless of the court's decision.

The Scope of the Exclusive System

Which institutions had to be purified? The list of democratic positions requiring lustration certificates and affidavits included elected, appointed, and assigned positions in the state administration and high-ranking officers in the army and the Ministry of Defense, the Security and Information Service, the police, and the Corps of the Castle Police. The act applied only to the managerial ranks in the listed organizations and did not affect ordinary employees.[72] Elected members of legislative assemblies and local governments were not affected. The list also included leading positions in the offices that support the presidency, the Chambers, the government, the Constitutional Court, the Supreme Court, the public media, and the management of enterprises in which the majority shareholder was the state. In academic institutions, the list included officials in management positions, judges, assessors, prosecutors, investigators, state notaries, and in some security-sensitive concession-based trades involving firearms, weapons, ammunition, and so forth. Strictly speaking, tainted officials in leading positions did not need to leave their institutions. They could be transferred to a lower position. However, this seldom happened, and the ambit of the lustration law expanded with its application. Once the tainted elements were defined, the institution was not purified by their mere demotion.[73]

What was seen as the source of "pollution"? Backward-looking provisions, that is, provisions relating to positions that had been held in the former regime, concerned the parts of the repressive apparatus that were proclaimed incompatible with the above-specified positions in state organs and organizations.[74] The list included members of the State Security (StB, secret police) and its collaborators at the specified levels, as well as the top echelons of the Communist Party except those who held these positions during the period between January 1, 1968, and May 1, 1969. This exemption protected the protagonists of the Prague Spring, including Alexander Dubček, who tried to launch social and political reforms of the totalitarian system. The scope of this exemption was nonetheless too narrow to save the legacy of 1968 because many reformists did not climb to their top posts during that short period. This effectively meant that once the communist regime was condemned by lustration law, all communists—the Stalinists and the reformists—were viewed the same.

The backward-looking provisions also included the political management of the Corps of National Security and the members of the paramilitary People's Militia.[75] Among other incompatible positions were those held by members of the purge committees, which were ad hoc bodies established after the communist takeover in 1948 and after the Soviet invasion into Czechoslovakia in 1968 to facilitate broad arbitrary exclusions of hundreds of thousands of people from their posts for political reasons. Students, scholars, or visitors at the KGB and other specified Soviet political-security universities between 1948 and 1989 were also among those excluded by the lustration act.

It is difficult to quantify with any precision how many people were affected by the exclusive system. Separate estimates would have to include the number of backward-looking posts and the number of forward-looking posts. These numbers are necessary but still not sufficient to determine the number of disqualified personnel. Former dissident Václav Benda, one of the key supporters of the law, estimated that there were 60,000 to 80,000 former agents of state security, about the same number in the People's Militia, and 50,000 members of the purge committees established after the 1968 revolt, which together with other categories totaled at least 300,000 people in the Czechoslovak Federation.[76] The total number of the high communist echelons affected by the law might reach several hundred. For instance, the category of party secretaries at the district level was one of the widest but it encompassed seventy-two districts that existed before 1989 in the territory of the Czech Republic.[77] However, these numbers referred to the scope of backward-looking provisions. It included all those who fell in these categories regardless of their age: not only had many of them retired before 1991 but many were no longer alive.

The scope of forward-looking provisions is also difficult to estimate. Its upper limit can be determined by using the total number of applications for lustration certificates. By November 1992, the Federal Ministry of the Interior issued 168,928 lustration certificates.[78] According to information provided by the successor Czech Ministry of the Interior in March 2001, approximately 345,000 lustration certificates had been issued since the law took effect.[79] This number was not expected to increase dramatically as the era of building new institutional infrastructure had been completed. However, the actual number of affected people would have been considerably lower for several reasons. First, since the law had taken effect in 1991, the number of issued certificates included personnel who were employed in state apparatuses of "three states": the Czech Republic, the Slovak Republic, and the Czech and Slovak Federative Republic. Although not all institutions were tripled, the federal structure meant that three governments operated in Czechoslovakia until 1992. Second, it included persons for whom certificates were not mandatory, namely election candidates who had applied for lustration certificates as a condition for running for Parliament as stipulated by their parties, and members of organizations that had made membership conditional upon the production of negative lustration certificates, for example, the Confederation of Political Prisoners.[80] Third, the number included those who had applied for the certificate without applying for any post in order to ensure that they had a clean record.

It is therefore difficult to estimate the number of personnel dismissed.[81] By March 2009, the total number of lustration certificates issued was 473,398. Of these 10,325 (2.18 percent) were positive.[82] It can be concluded from this that no more than 10,500 people could have been dismissed due to their membership or collaboration with the secret police. But the actual number of those dismissed may be lower because it does not take into account those who received positive certificates without applying for any public positions. It might be higher due to the fact that the number does not capture, for example, the members of the purge committees and the People's Militia.

The certification of tainted elements by the lustration law also implies that anyone who was involved with the previous regime in another capacity was purified. These categories included, for instance, the members of the Communist Party (KSČ), the members of the Socialist Youth Union (SSM), which was a communistic alternative of Hitler-Jugend without the paramilitary drill, the cadre secretaries of the Communist Party who were responsible for writing regular personal reports about each individual from primary school to retirement, and the street trustees of the party who typically provided information to the authorities about the situation in their neighborhood. It is not surprising that according to a poll conducted in 1991, 50 percent of Czechoslovak respondents thought the lustration act would be beneficial to personnel situations in (state) enterprises and offices.[83]

The Inclusive System in Hungary

The Hungarian inclusive system was implemented by the lustration law passed on March 8, 1994.[84] Praised as a model of lustrations that was compliant with human rights,[85] the system did not lead to exclusion of compromised officials from positions of trust as the Czech model had. But neither did it ignore their presence in public life. "In order to promote the integrity of government business," stipulated its preamble,[86] the inclusive system was based on the public disclosure of identities of senior officials in various positions of trust who previously worked as specific types of secret agents, secret informers, or certain government officials under the previous socialist regime or who were members of the Nazi Arrow Cross Party. Personnel who fell into these categories were confronted with evidence against them and offered a chance to resign from their posts without being exposed. If they refused to resign, their names were made public in an official government gazette. The government was supposed to be purified by exposing the tainted officials or forcing them to resign.

The use of truth revelation as a major means of transitional justice was not surprising. According to Heino Nyyssönen, the Hungarian process of dealing with the past has evolved around the word *igazságtétel*, which means doing justice. The Hungarian word consists of two parts: *igazság*, which means both truth and justice, and *tétel*, which means the act of making.[87] After the initial attempts to pursue justice had failed,[88] Hungary started to explore alternative options for dealing with the past. Thus, the lustration law signified value-based discontinuity with the past. By exposing the tainted officials to the public, it aspired to end the secrecy of the previous regime.

The law was challenged before the Constitutional Court, which abrogated some of its provisions concerning its scope on December 24, 1994.[89] The Court ordered the Parliament dominated by former communists to prepare a revised version of the law, but it did not stop the process of the exposure of tainted officials.[90] The new version of the law came into force in 1996 and was amended in 2000 and 2001 without changing the method of inclusion based on exposure.[91] The method of exposure was nevertheless modified in 2002 by the gradual introduction of a backward-looking perspective: the objective of establishing transparent administration was superseded by the need to disclose the truth about all people who had compromised themselves in the past. The process was regulated by the lustration law and its amendments, the relevant decisions the Constitutional Court made in 1994, 1999, 2003, and 2005, the administrative procedures, and the civil procedures.[92]

The Inclusive Method

The Hungarian lustration system provided for two different methods of exposure in two stages. In the first stage, the method of exposure was explicitly pursued as an alternative to dismissal. The second chance was conditional upon the exposure of tainted officials, although they could, at their own election, step down without facing exposure. The right to privacy was pitted against the right of the public to be informed. In the second stage, the method of exposure was not tied to dismissal. It was assumed that tainted officials had already received sufficient time to step down.

In the first stage, the system was implemented by special judicial committees consisting of three members. The professional judges, appointed by the Parliament and approved by the Chief Justice of the Supreme Court, were released from their regular duties to conduct the screening of the prescribed public officials. The first three judges were elected on April 7, 1994, just before the parliamentary elections.[93] The judges had to sign written statements that they had not been involved in the prescribed activities and were themselves subject to screening conducted by the National Security Committee of the Parliament to ensure the purification process was not contaminated by the presence of the tainted. However, the appointment of two of the first three judges became controversial after their past involvement in the "show trials" of the 1950s had been revealed.[94] But they did not see themselves as tainted, refused to step down, and, following public outrage, they had to be relieved of their appointments eighteen months later.[95] The second judicial committee was established in 1995 and the third committee in 2000.[96] Five judges elected in 1995 served during three different parliamentary sessions, which revealed a certain level of consensus in the process.[97] Compared to other methods of transitional justice, such as criminal tribunals or truth commissions, the apparatus of these committees was fairly modest: each screening committee had one professional registrar and one administrator.[98]

The system was implemented in several steps. Upon commencement of the screening procedure, the judicial committee informed those whose backgrounds were being checked that they were under scrutiny. The committee then informed them about the results of its investigation as to whether data existed about them or whether no evidence had been found. The persons could appear before the committee to clarify their past or to submit clarifications by a set deadline. The screened persons were permitted to obtain legal representation. To prevent any media speculation about officials under investigation, every screened person was initially called to appear in front of the committee, regardless of whether any relevant facts had been found.[99]

To carry out their work, the committees were authorized to have access to relevant documentation from the Ministry of the Interior and the Ministry of Defense, and after 1997 from the Historical Archive.[100] The committees were mandated to use any lawful means to obtain evidence; they were not limited to relying exclusively on the lustration procedure. The committees called witnesses, screened personnel files, and read vitae of the public officials concerned.[101] After this process was complete, the committee established whether the concerned individual had been involved in legally "tainted" activities as laid down in the lustration laws and informed him or her about its decision. The committee then requested that he or she resign from his or her position within thirty days, "otherwise the decision will be made public" in the government journal *Magyar Közlöny* and the Hungarian News Service.[102] Individuals had the right to appeal their decision before a court of law. The filing of a claim had the effect of delaying the public release of a committee's decision.

Although the purpose of the law was to establish transparency of government, the screening process was conducted in camera and the decisions of the committees were reached by majority in secret vote. The secrecy meant that the public was precluded from engaging in meaningful discussion about the past; from formulating social consensus on the nature of collaboration with the past regime; and from overseeing the steps taken by the lustration committees. The public could only rely on the short official statements by the committees, which were often contradicted by the responses of the screened officials, who typically denied their involvement in the past or made excuses for their involvement.[103]

The secrecy of the process was motivated by the consideration that public disclosures would cause the tainted officials great embarrassment. The objective of the legislators was to maintain political stability and avoid harassment.[104] The drafters of the original inclusive method, initially proposed in the Hack and Demszky bill in October 1990, did not anticipate that screened persons would not resign in the face of evidence against them.[105] Cases in which individuals denied wrongdoing made legislators realize that the benefit of holding a position of trust outweighed the eventual social cost of the shame associated with exposure and the loss of social prestige. The second chance granted by the inclusive system did not need to be conditional on the secrecy of its process. The appreciation of this fact was an important consideration in later revisions of the law.

The original inclusive method was not altered by the 1996 amendment to the law. The 1996 amendment nevertheless created conditions that led to its modification at later stages. It created the Historical Archive Office, a special institution that handled the files of the former secret police and allowed all citizens to access these files by applying for information that had been collected about themselves.[106] The 2002 amendment allowed disclosure of information about the past of anyone holding public office.[107] It allowed individuals to access their own file and allowed third parties limited access to the files of persons who were, or who had been, holding public office.[108] The files of public officials initially had their names blacked out, allowing only the code name of an agent to appear.[109]

The delicate nature of conducting lustration rituals could not be entrusted to just anyone. Thus, access to code names remained limited to persons who were either recognized by the secret services or acknowledged to be historians.[110] This effectively meant the introduction of a backward-looking perspective to the process: the purification of government by exposing a few tainted officials was supposed to be gradually replaced by the purification of society through exposing tainted (public) individuals. This change was a response to the original inclusive method: owing to the secretiveness of the screening procedure, people wanted to make their own independent judgments; and owing to the exposures, they knew that "secret informers were around." At the same time, an opposite tendency emerged: exposures led to denials, and denials diluted the abhorrence against the tainted. Which tendency prevailed?

In 2003, the Parliament passed a law titled "Disclosure of the Secret Service Activities of the Communist Regime and on the Establishment of the Historical Archives of the Hungarian State Security."[111] Inspired by widespread disclosures that had already been under way in Germany and the Czech Republic, the Parliament was effectively pressing to make all the information in the archives accessible to the public. According to its 2005 proposed amendment, all documents not stipulated as "anonymous" on the archive's Web site were supposed to be accessible.[112] However, the Constitutional Court struck the amendment down in October 2005.[113] At the government level, there was an apparent desire to end the lustration rituals.

However, the work of young historians resulted in an increase in the number of disclosures. Two groups of persons were newly exposed. The first group consisted of officials who had been previously screened and were found not to have worked with the repressive apparatus. However, they were later exposed for working for a section of the apparatus that had not been regulated by the initial lustration law, such as Prime Minister Péter Medgyessy, who had collaborated with the communist-era intelligence.[114] The second group of persons included public figures outside the realm of politics. Thus, one of the iconic figures of Hungarian and world cinema, the director István Szabó, was exposed as an alleged former secret informer. However, such private revelations are not adjudicated by the authority of the state and cannot be considered personnel systems.

The Scope of the Inclusive System

According to the original law, the institutions determined as requiring purification encompassed a range of public posts, including members of the government, secretaries of state, their deputies, and other high state officials, high-ranking members of the army and the police, judges and district attorneys, mayors and their deputies, the leadership of the Hungarian National Bank, and all individuals elected by the Parliament who were required to take an oath.[115] Similar to the Czech Republic, the Hungarian system also included the managers of banks and enterprises with majority state ownership, senior employees in the public media, and academic officials holding positions as heads of departments or other senior positions in state universities. Their inclusion may have been justifiable owing to the nature of the society that was undergoing transformation from total state control. Managers were to be exposed to prevent privatization scams, the media to prevent the twisting of public opinion, and the universities to end the era of manipulating students and damaging the careers of colleagues. On the other hand, their inclusion extended the scope of the system into areas that would not help achieve the system's purported objectives of purifying government.[116] It was not surprising that the Constitutional Court in its 1994 ruling struck down these provisions.[117] Curiously enough, the Court allowed legislators to either introduce a narrower definition of those to be checked or extend the background checks to include other subjects who played a role in shaping public opinion. Thus, the private media, political parties, churches, and trade unions, which fall outside the realm of the state, were in principle allowed to become subject to exposure, if legislators deemed it necessary.

Unlike the Czech exclusive system, the forward-looking positions of the Hungarian system included elected members of Parliament.[118] This decision, though it had not precluded discredited candidates from being elected, proved to be quite controversial. The controversies arose because of the timing of the exposures rather than from substantive concern about the alleged interference into the private lives of elected officials. Exposure of the private lives of public officials had previously been considered legitimate in European jurisprudence, which recognized that the scope of the privacy for public officials is narrower than that of ordinary citizens.[119] The controversy arose because the exposure took place on the eve of the election campaign of 1994 when the incumbent parties were facing imminent defeat.

Similar to gerrymandering, the limited political consensus behind the law has led to frequent changes in its scope. The lustration law of 1994 and its amendments of 2000 and 2001 were approved by the center-right parties, while the 1996 amendment was also approved by the post-communist party, which was forced by the Constitutional Court to legislate it. The original 1994 law included judges and district attorneys, its 1996 revision dropped them, and the 2000 amendment reinstated them.[120] Likewise, the public media were initially subject to screening, the screening was subsequently narrowed to include the leadership of public radio, TV, and news agencies, and then it was expanded to include all who influenced public opinion directly or indirectly.[121]

The original version of the law targeted career officers of the secret services, their informers, and all those who held offices in which they received secret information; it also included all members of the state security units in 1956 and 1957, when the revolutionary attempt to overthrow the communist regime was thwarted by Soviet intervention, and members of the Nazi Arrow Cross Party. The secret services targeted by the law included political police and other departments that were assigned to deal with domestic opposition. This left aside departments of intelligence and counterintelligence and their informers, creating a loophole that allowed Prime Minister Medgyessy to avoid exposure under the initial lustration law.

The nature of secret informing and collaboration was a sensitive topic. Many secret dossiers were destroyed, and the reliability of the remaining ones was often questioned. Although to a lesser extent and intensity than in Poland, Hungary also engaged in a debate concerning so-called dead souls. *Dead Souls* is a satire written by the Russian novelist Nikolai Gogol in 1842; its main character goes from house to house to buy the names of servants who had died since the previous census in order to claim a higher social status.[122] In the context of political transition, it was alleged that the members of the secret police were recruiting "dead souls" as their informers in order to meet the quota. The problem was that the souls recruited by the secret police were often quite alive. People who were listed in Department III of the Third Directorate of the Interior Ministry may not have been aware of the fact that they were supposed to collaborate with the secret police. For this reason, legislators applied strict criteria to determine whether a person collaborated with the secret police. It effectively required evidence regarding the status of the informer *and* evidence regarding his or her activities.[123]

As with other countries in the region, the incomplete nature of the archives was another reason why a person who was involved in the past regime could avoid the screening process. According to the first head of the Historical Archive Office, György Markó, about 42 percent of all materials were taken to the archives, 50 percent were destroyed, and about 8 percent went to the successor security organizations.[124] The relatively limited scope of the process affected its outcomes. According to Elizabeth Barrett, Péter Hack, and Ágnes Munkácsi, 7,872 persons were screened and incriminating data were found in 126 cases by December 2003. Pursuant to the nature of the inclusive system, the decision was published in 15 cases, 24 individuals resigned from office during investigation, 14 investigations were terminated because the term of the office of the official ended, 42 cases were dropped due to insufficient evidence, and other cases were under investigation or in court.[125] The limited number of cases was partly caused by the strict evidence procedure and by citizens' awareness that materials existed about their past. According to Markó, during his term in the Historical Archive Office between 1997 and 2003, more than 11,000 citizens turned to it, of which almost 3,800 received materials; more than 1,000 requests from researchers were also served.[126]

The law also concerned the members of the paramilitary units that participated in the suppression of the 1956 uprising. The former prime minister, Gyula Horn (1994–98), a leader of the post-communist Hungarian Socialist Party, was a potential target of the law, but his involvement in the pro-Soviet squads had been known prior to the approval of the law.[127] The system did not include political officials of the previous regime unless they received information gathered by the secret services as a basis for their decision-making. Neither did the system include high echelons of the Hungarian Socialist Worker's Party, as the Czech system did. According to critics, the Hungarian lustration law made a scapegoat out of just one department of the Ministry of the Interior while ignoring the responsibility of the previous political elite for the dictatorship.[128] Curiously enough it included the members of the Nazi Arrow Cross Party. No one could seriously expect that former Nazis would be able to hold any public position. Their inclusion may have served to divert the blame from ex-communist officials to uncontroversial scapegoats. Everyone could condemn Nazism, but not everyone was ready to condemn socialism.

The Reconciliatory System in Poland

The Polish lustration act went into effect on August 3, 1997, and was amended several times.[129] However, the law was not implemented until 1999 owing to difficulties in establishing the lustration court. The law was challenged at the Constitutional Tribunal, which upheld the act on October 21, 1998,[130] although in a subsequent decision of November 10, 1998, it found two of its provisions unconstitutional.[131] Meanwhile, the center-right government promulgated an amendment to the law, extending its scope and overcoming the difficulty of creating a lustration court. In 1999, 56 percent of Poles supported lustrations, while 31 percent were against them.[132]

It is certainly ironic to refer to the process as reconciliatory; Polish society is far from being reconciled with its past. But, similar to the South African truth and reconciliation process, the system was based on the ritual of confession. It pursued a value-normative discontinuity with the past: it revealed the truth about the past and signaled that the past was wrong. It is a matter of empirical research to establish whether the system in itself failed to achieve reconciliation because of the inherent deficiencies, due to its improper enforcement, or due to politicians on both the left and the right who were unable to uphold the agreed-upon compromises and reopened the debate whenever possible.[133] It is clear, nonetheless, that the coalition dominated by the former communists that won the 2001 elections amended the lustration law in February 2002, narrowed its scope and modified its procedures but did not abandon it. Center-right deputies asked the Constitutional Tribunal for review of the lustration law.[134] After the Constitutional Tribunal repealed this amendment, the coalition pushed another amendment through Parliament in September of the same year in order to avoid screening some of its prominent politicians.[135] In 2005, a conservative center-right coalition won the elections in Poland. In 2006, it approved a sweeping lustration system in an effort that was eventually halted by the Constitutional Court in 2007 before it could be implemented. After that Poland reversed to the previous confessionary method.

One of the reasons for the complicated situation surrounding lustration debates may have been the lengthy, unregulated, wild lustration stage in Poland. The period between 1989 and 1999 made a significant impact on the character of the law and the needs that it attempted to meet. On the one hand, the period offered Poland time to learn from the experiences of other countries and from international criticisms against them. On the other hand, the unresolved problems of the past penetrated top politics to a much greater extent than in Hungary and would have been unimaginable in the Czech Republic. In total, at least three Polish prime ministers, including Włodzimierz Cimoszewicz, Józef Oleksy and Jerzy Buzek, and two presidents, Lech Wałęsa and Aleksander Kwaśniewski, were publicly denounced for having tainted pasts before the law was enacted.[136] As a result, Polish lustration law had a complex procedure, narrow scope, and minimal sanctions. This contrasted with the broader and more simplistic Czech lustration law, which was based on the disqualification of former political elites and security networks from leading public posts.

The Reconciliatory Method

In describing the method of the Polish lustration system, this section shall mainly focus on the version that began to be implemented in January 1999. The main feature of the system was submission of affidavits by persons who applied for public positions specified by the act. In the affidavits, some senior public officials and other public figures had to disclose whether they had worked or collaborated with security services of the socialist regime between 1944 and 1989. The candidates or incumbents had to complete two documents, both of which were annexes to the lustration laws.

Annex A, the affidavit proper, requested that the persons identify themselves, acknowledge that they were aware of the penalty for submitting an untrue statement, and state that they did (not) work, did (not) serve, and were (not) a conscious and secret collaborator of state security organs. Persons who collaborated with the security organs had to also complete Annex B in order to identify the particular organ, their position, and the duration of collaboration. Annex B was treated as confidential. The substance of Annex A, if it revealed collaboration, was published in the *Monitor Polski* (Polish Monitor), the official government gazette. However, the disclosure of the past did not lead to automatic dismissal. Only in cases in which officials were found to have been dishonest (they concealed relevant facts about their past) did they lose "moral qualification" for ten years, which meant losing the right of access to any public positions for that duration. In addition, the names of such persons were published in the *Monitor Polski*.[137]

The affidavits represented a form of confession and the non-dismissal of confessors signified public employment forgiveness. By confessing, the tainted official was officially declared to be purified. In cases of denial, the official was certified as tainted, ineligible to hold public office, and thus effectively banished from the community for ten years.

The problem was that the output of the process was very narrow. The only "truth" that was revealed through the process was the identity of "the confessor" or "the liar." The essence of the affidavit published in the *Monitor Polski* was limited to a brief official statement that the person revealed his or her collaboration or that he or she did not submit a true affidavit. As an example of the first instance, the announcement stated: "On the basis of [the lustration act] the following is presented to the public knowledge: [name surname], son of [name], born on Nov. 16, 1930 in Warsaw, resident in Warsaw, has stated that he worked in security organs within the meaning of the [lustration act]."[138] In the second instance, the announcement stated: "The Lustration Court of Appeal in Warsaw, Department of Lustrations, informs that in its decision from Sep. 15, 1999, No. V AL. 6/99, it confirmed that [name surname], [maiden surname], daughter of [name] and [name], born on June 13, 1929 in [place], submitted a lustration affidavit [that was found to be] not in accordance with truth as required by the [lustration act], because she concealed the fact of conscious and secret collaboration with security organs according to the [act]."[139] With this information the public could ascertain whether a state official had worked, served, or collaborated with security organs but not the nature of that collaboration, its motives, or whether it had harmed anyone. The process only gave limited information about the status of an informer in terms of his or her position in the repressive apparatus. The lustration process effectively prevented society from engaging in meaningful debates about its past. Instead, the past reappeared in the form of speculations and rumors.

The act established a special lustration prosecutor, the Spokesperson of the Public Interest (RIP), and authorized the Warsaw Court of Appeal to serve as the Lustration Court after an initial attempt to create a separate lustration court failed. Many judges were originally reluctant to serve at the Court for various reasons. Some objected to inadequate pay, while others viewed the law as flawed, did not want to screen their colleagues, and perhaps were afraid that the politicization of the process would affect the perception of their independence.[140] In other words, they could become tainted when facing accusations of releasing the deniers from the sacrificial ritual. The process was hampered until the law was changed. According to the 1998 amendment, the Chair of the Supreme Court appointed the lustration prosecutor and the Warsaw Court of Appeal served as the Lustration Court.

While the credibility of the lustration tribunal escaped scrutiny, the appointment of the first Spokesperson of the Public Interest sparked yet another controversy. On his last day of service as the Chair of the Supreme

Court, Adam Strzembosz appointed Bogusław Nizieński, a former judge of
the Supreme Court, the Spokesperson of the Public Interest. Both Strzembosz and Nizieński were activists of the opposition Solidarity movement at
the Ministry of Justice in the beginning of the 1980s and Nizieński's task at
the Supreme Court prior to his 1998 retirement was the rehabilitation of
communist victims. These would have been excellent qualifications for the
posts in countries such as the Czech Republic or Germany, but not in
divided Poland. It was no surprise that the new head of the Supreme Court,
appointed by the ex-communist president Kwaśniewski, was against Nizieński.[141]

The act established a special judicial procedure that was directly connected to the regular criminal law. If there was evidence that the official
was dishonest, the spokesperson initiated the verification procedure at the
court. However, the lustration procedure could also be launched by the
members of Parliament in order to stop the spread of unwarranted denun-
ciations of political opponents; at the request of a publicly active person
who had been denounced; or by a person who demanded an official statement that he or she had been forced into such collaboration. The Court
decided whether the affidavit was true or false or ordered a suspension of
the case. The situation of lustrated persons was similar to that of accused
persons in criminal law, and they could appeal the judgments handed down
against them. The judicial procedures ensured fairness of the process at the
expense of speed and the number of resolved cases. Although about 23,000
affidavits of senior public servants and judges were screened within four
initial years, the hearing of suspected cases was a very lengthy process.[142]

The procedures, however, failed to ensure the openness of the process.
Judicial hearings at the Lustration Court could be closed to the public if
lustrated persons requested it. In practice, the doors usually remained
closed. Such arrangements were unusual because the power to close the
courtrooms normally resides with judges. This practice also conflicted with
the essential democratic principle of transparency. Poles were deprived of
the right to question the integrity of lustration decisions. This has led to
continuing accusations from competing politicians and media speculations,
and has contributed to an atmosphere of overall mistrust.[143] Certifying
truthfulness of confessions without public scrutiny lasted until 2006. After
the electoral victory of the Law and Justice Party (PiS), which aspired to
launch moral revolution and purify society from pervasive corruption, the
law was supposed to be replaced by a lustration bill that partially modified

its method and considerably expanded its scope. The new bill gave authorities discretion to determine whether a second chance would be granted in cases of honest confessions, while the dismissal for dishonesty remained mandatory as in the original law. The method effectively transformed a reconciliatory system into a mixed system. The method of the bill was invalidated by the Polish Constitutional Tribunal in May 2007.[144]

Since 2007, Poland's lustration system has reverted to its reconciliatory method. It implemented the same method of confessions as had been previously implemented. The affidavits of public officials had to be submitted to the vetting office of the Institute of National Remembrance instead of the Spokesperson for Public Interest.[145] Similarly, the eventual disputes were handled by ordinary district courts instead of the High Court in Warsaw.

The Scope of the Reconciliatory System

Like gerrymandering, the magnitude of lustration systems is a very controversial issue. In Poland, in particular, the issues of who should be included in the law and what constitutes a sin of secret collaboration were reopened again and again. The lustration law changed many times, and any eventual benefits from capturing all these changes would be outweighed by the description of too many nuances. For this reason, this text focuses on the ambit of the lustration system in its original version. In 1999, the public positions affected by the act's forward-looking provisions included the highest constitutional officials, namely the president of Poland; deputies and senators; and persons assigned, elected, or appointed by the president and other constitutional organs. The provisions also included senior public officials, judges, prosecutors, and advocates and those who occupy leading positions in public media.

The sources of taint were positions held in several security organs between 1944 and 1990, such as the Ministry of Public Security, the Committee for Public Security Affairs, and their subordinated units; and the security services (secret police), army intelligence, army counterintelligence, and other services of the military forces. The lustration act also covered civil and military organs and the institutions of foreign states that engaged in tasks similar to the aforementioned organs. The most contested issues were the attempts to exempt the intelligence and counterintelligence units. The rationale for their exemption was that even the socialist state was a sovereign state and that those who helped pursue national interests should not be disadvantaged. The rationale against their exemption was that these units violated human rights like any other unit of the repressive apparatus. The motivation of supporters for exemption was to clear political allies, while the opposition sought their inclusion. Unlike the Czech lustration system, and similar to the Hungarian system, the Polish system did not include the leaders of the former communist party, implicitly acknowledging their purity.

In total, over 25,000 public officials were required to submit affidavits about their work or collaboration with secret services. This number was supposed to reach 220,000 with the implementation of the lustration law of 2006.[146] According to information available from the annual reports of the Spokesperson of the Public Interest between 1999 and 2005, 212 persons confessed that they had collaborated with secret services in the past, and 65 persons made false or incomplete confessions.[147] The largest positively lustrated sector were lawyers,[148] although the possibility of retaining public office in exchange for truth has been a powerful incentive in compelling many public officials to confess. In the verification of the first wave of affidavits submitted by the end of 2001, the spokesperson found that among the 315 positive affidavits submitted, 165 were unwarranted. Thus, only 150 of them were published in the *Monitor Polski.*[149] The spokesperson had probably been motivated by a need to balance the truth-centered approach of the system with the right to privacy.

Discussion

In this chapter, we have reviewed the dual meaning of lustrations. In ancient Rome as well as in post-communist Central Europe, the tangible process of lustrations had a profound symbolic dimension. Similar to the way in which the Roman census turned into purification rituals, lustration systems turned from the tangible process of dealing with tainted personnel in the apparatus of transitional states into a process of purifying public life. The Czech lustration law, which stipulates "additional qualification prerequisites" for holding a public office and effectively provides for dismissal from the office, signifies the purification of government by excluding tainted officials. The "background checks" of government officials in Hungary, which lead to the exposure of tainted officials, signify a shaming ritual.

The affidavit in the Polish lustration law signifies a form of public confession, which is accompanied by public employment forgiveness.

Although all personnel systems were devised to purify government, they also enabled an external purification of society. By defining "tainted officials" in the law they exonerated the rest of society. Who was not on the list was off the hook. They redefined society into "we" and "they," "the innocent" and "the tainted," in a way that did not correspond with the reality of the past regime. Consequently, members of various socialist associations who were not on the list were declared as clean as former dissidents in all countries.

Our analysis in this chapter focused predominantly on the operational side of the process. It revealed that the lustration systems were shaped by a number of variables: decisions of the constitutional courts, elections that signified a swing from the right to the left, and the secretive nature of the process. We nevertheless observe apparent differences in the stability of these lustration processes. Apart from the 1992 decision of the Constitutional Court, the exclusive lustration system has been unchanged and continuously implemented in Czechoslovakia and the Czech Republic since 1991. The system survived several governments led by social democrats, although the Czech Communist Party was never part of any ruling coalition. In Hungary, the process survived the ex-communist-dominated coalition government (1994–98), thanks to the decision of the Constitutional Court and perhaps also its junior coalition partner with a dissident pedigree. In Poland, the ex-communists attempted to significantly narrow the lustration process after their electoral victory in 2001, but their first attempt was halted by the Constitutional Tribunal. In 2006, the right attempted to expand the scope and alter the method of lustration from reconciliatory to mixed, but the tribunal nullified many parts of the law in 2007.

The common problem of lustration systems in the three countries was their secretive nature. Initially, the Czechs did not know who was dismissed, while the Hungarians and the Poles were deprived of an opportunity to scrutinize decisions of lustration organs. This led to a number of leaks of confidential information about secret collaborators and to uncertainty about the fairness of the lustration decisions. The secretiveness of the lustration in all three countries prevented the citizens from engaging in meaningful dialogue about "the banality of the evil" and resulted in demands for widespread revelations and open archives. The increasing transparency in all three countries had an uneven effect on the process. It did not affect the implementation of the Czech and Polish lustration systems, but it may have made the Hungarian inclusive system redundant.

The three countries attached different consequences to doubts arising from incomplete archival records, which had been partially burned by the secret police at the end of the communist regimes. In Czechoslovakia, a consensus emerged that the country could not afford to tolerate the presence of tainted personnel in the state apparatus. Once their names had been listed at particular higher levels of collaboration, the persons were excluded even if their files had been destroyed.[150] Consequently, the Czech lustration process is administrative in nature and provides comprehensive legal protection only ex post facto. In contrast, Poland and Hungary placed an emphasis on determining who was and who was not a tainted official using strict judicial mechanisms. The observance of criminal law standards in a non-criminal administrative procedure prolonged the lustration process and resulted in a low number of processed cases in Hungary and Poland.

4

The Origin of Lustration Systems

You don't want to hurt genuine talent. It's enough to scare them.
In the end, they will work with us. . . . Every new regime demands
betrayal until it consolidates its power, and uses traitors, and then
gets rid of them.

—István Szabó[1]

I of course agree—I underline that—that it is absolutely necessary
to make the purification of this state, which however must be done
in a way that a true agent will be uncovered in an open legal way.
—Jan Kavan, Speech to the Federal Assembly[2]

The purpose of this chapter is to explain the origin of and differences
among lustration systems approved in Czechoslovakia in 1991, Hungary in
1994, and Poland in 1997. It addresses the following puzzle: All three countries had overwhelming non-communist majorities in their parliaments
after their first democratic elections. But only Czechoslovakia adopted an
exclusive system. Why did they each develop a different lustration system?
Pursuant to our discussion in Chapter 2, we examine two hypotheses: (1)
the variation in the choice of a lustration system is a function of differing
perceptions about whether former adversaries have been transformed; and
(2) the variation in the choice of a lustration system is a function of the
role that people themselves had in the previous regime. We tested these two
hypotheses at both the grassroots and macro levels. In our analyses we used
data from historical surveys that were conducted in the three countries at
the time they had non-communist majorities and from the parliamentary

debates and other public debates concerning lustrations in the three countries.

The Perceptions of the Tainted

Scholars have different views about the factors that give rise to transitional
justice in general and about the origin of lustration systems in particular.
Lustrations are seen as a function of factors including the balance of political power; the severity of the previous regime; the politics of the present;
interplay between the beliefs of political leaders, retributive emotions, and
different political interests; and various combinations of these factors.[3] For
instance, Huntington argues that the balance of power during transition
affects the choice of a transitional justice strategy: "Officials of strong
authoritarian regimes that voluntarily ended themselves were not prosecuted; officials of weak authoritarian regimes that collapsed were punished."[4] The convincing logic of the realistic approach has inspired other
scholars in transitional justice. Luc Huyse argues that the conclusions elites
reach about transitional justice are functions of the circumstances of each
regime's passage to democracy.[5] Similarly, Eric Posner and Adrian Vermeule observe that "the kind of transition affects the kind of transitional
justice that will occur."[6]

However, the development of lustration systems in the three Central
European countries under study here is richer than trajectories of political
power in transition. In the Central European cases, the realistic approach
is unable to fully explain the path stretching from the exit of an authoritarian regime to the choice of a particular system. These paths were trammeled
by democratic elections that shifted the balance of political power. After
the first democratic elections, the non-communist elite in each country
gained a sufficient number of seats to make sweeping personnel changes,
which could have included the adoption of exclusive personnel systems.
The election results in Central Europe in 1990–91 were similar: approximately the same proportion of voters rejected communism in each of the
countries examined here, leaving their successor parties with 13.24 percent
support in the Czech Republic (the Czech National Council), 10.89 percent
in Hungary (List Votes), and 11.99 percent in Poland (Sejm).[7] In spite of
the large non-communist majorities, which allowed them to further expand
their power and pursue their interests, only Czechoslovakia approved an

exclusive personnel system; Hungary approved an inclusive system and Poland belatedly approved its reconciliatory system in 1997. In other words, the case of Central Europe poses a challenge to the validity of the realistic perspective.

In response to the lack of a causal link in Huntington's study, John Moran explains the origin of different strategies of transitional justice using Hirschman's psychological theory of exit, voice, and loyalty, which were experienced differently by people under the different regimes.[8] According to this theory, individual loyalty exhibits itself in "voice" that verbally attempts to reverse the decline in a system; when the voice option is absent, politically active individuals may exit from the system. "[T]he tendency to forgive and forget," according to Moran, "may be found in those countries . . . where either exit and/or voice were allowed."[9] Building on Moran and Huntington, Helga Welsh argues that the choice of lustration systems is a result of the interplay among various factors, including the weight of the past, the mode of transition, the politics of the present, and contextual factors.[10] However, if Welsh were right, the lustration debate would become irrelevant as transition progresses[11] and desires for retribution weaken. Reviewing her arguments in light of the case of Poland, Aleks Szczerbiak argues that the choice of a lustration system is influenced by the politics of the present, such as using lustrations to undermine the credibility of political opponents.[12] This may explain lustration in Poland, but it fails to explain the exclusive system in the Czech Republic, which was conceived as secret.

Nadya Nedelsky used the natural experiment of the Czecho-Slovak separation to explain the continuation of lustrations in the Czech Republic and their breakdown in Slovakia. She argued that lustrations are functions of the legitimacy of the previous regime: the more legitimate the previous regime appears under current conditions, the lower the likelihood of lustrations.[13] In accord with Nedelsky, Lavinia Stan concludes that transitional justice has been more stringent where communist rule was enforced through repression and ideological rigidity (the Czech Republic, East Germany, the Baltic States) than it has been in countries that allowed some level of reforms (Hungary and Poland).[14] Monika Nalepa then used game theory to explain why post-communists voted for lustrations in Poland and Hungary.[15] Nalepa's premises clearly contradict the findings by Stan, who concluded that "[i]n a clear pattern throughout Eastern Europe, former communists voted against lustration and file access law, while their opposition provided the impetus for them."[16]

We argue that the factors used by most of these scholars to explain the origin of lustration systems are not invalid, although they may have played a different role than suggested: the severity of the past regime, its ideological rigidity, and legitimacy; the mode of exit and the distribution of political power during transition; and the politics of the present were important indicators of the perception of former adversaries. They provided the former communist parties with opportunities to demonstrate that they were, or were not, transforming. At the same time, these factors shaped the gray zone of people in between the victims and the transgressors. In more repressive regimes, more people may need to make petty political compromises on daily basis than do people in less repressive regimes. The sudden revolutionary change of a repressive regime may expose their taints and prompt them to engage in finger-pointing and to hold others responsible for the past.

Pursuant to our theorizations in Chapter 2, there are two possible dynamics that can affect which personnel system a new regime adopts. First, the perception of others as pure or tainted may lead to different demands for the purification of public life by means of personnel systems. Second, the need of people from the gray zone to avoid responsibility for the past may lead to assigning responsibility to tainted officials by means of personnel systems. The "perceptions of the tainted" are critical in both hypotheses although its objects and subjects differ: in the first case, the determining factor is the "perceptions about the tainted" while in the second it is "the perception by the tainted." Each dynamic provides us with theoretical guidance to explain the need for the exclusive system at the grassroots level as well as the political level.

Hypothesis I. The Perceptions About the Tainted: Is the Communist Party Transforming?

The role of the former communist party in all three countries was critical in shaping public perception about all persons associated with the former regimes. The parties had, in their own words, held "the leading role in the state and society."[17] They stood at the top of the repressive apparatuses, and their tentacles penetrated and controlled each unit of the three societies.[18] In contrast, secret collaborators did not have an opportunity to demonstrate their transformation. They were perceived and treated differently in these countries although they engaged in the same activities in the past.

While Czechoslovaks did not have any illusions about the repressive nature of the secret police (StB), Hungarians and Poles were in a different situation owing to the changing façade of their regimes. Although "the goulash communism" created an impression of the Hungarian communist party as a harmless transforming force, the secret police operating under the Ministry of the Interior pursued its surveillance activity even after the end of the regime.[19] Similarly in Poland, the number of people employed in the repressive apparatus dramatically increased during the period of liberalization.[20] The secret police operated in the same way in the three countries, but owing to the perception of their masters only Czechoslovaks saw them differently and excluded them from public posts.[21]

To be sure, the presence of secret collaborators in public life was a motive for the approval of lustration laws in all three countries. But their different treatment can only be explained by the different transformations of their communist party superiors: they were excluded along with leaders of the communist party in the Czech Republic, while they merely had to be exposed in order to satisfy the need for truth in Hungary. They were no longer considered harmful because of the reforms that had taken place in the Hungarian communist party. Although the role of former secret collaborators during political and economic transformation raised serious concerns in Poland,[22] the post-communist Social Democracy of the Republic of Poland (SdRP) was increasingly considered as a transformed, perhaps even progressive, pro-Western political force.[23] The uncertainty as to whether a secret informer had been purified was resolved through a system that verified the truthfulness of his or her confessions in Poland.

Thus, the factors that have been used by scholars to explain the origin of lustration systems may be reinterpreted in light of this hypothesis. Factors such as (1) the different records of communist parties in launching political reforms prior to 1989, (2) their different attitudes toward their opposition during transition, and (3) their willingness to reform their programmatic orientation by adopting modern left-democratic policies may have played a major role in shaping public perceptions about whether these parties had transformed.

1. Although the three countries experienced massive human rights abuses and military interventions during four decades of socialism, they each experienced the final year of communist party rule very

differently. In fact, 1989 was full of contrasts and paradoxes in Central Europe. In the winter of 1989, the Czech communists repeatedly suppressed demonstrations that commemorated the twentieth anniversary of the death of Jan Palach, who had immolated himself in protest against Soviet occupation.[24] At approximately the same time, Imre Poszgay, a leader of the reformist faction within the Hungarian communist party, rehabilitated Imre Nagy, the prime minister who was executed in the aftermath of the Soviet intervention in 1956; and the Polish communists invited the opposition Solidarity trade union movement to the negotiating table.[25] While semi-democratic elections were being held on June 4, 1989, in Poland as a result of the roundtable talks, and Nagy was being buried in an official state funeral attended by 250,000 people and watched on television by millions on June 16, 1989, the Czechoslovak Communist Party stood firm and continued to suppress the signatories of the so-called Several Sentences petition that requested the government have a dialogue with the opposition.[26]

While the Polish communists allowed Tadeusz Mazowiecki to become the first non-communist prime minister in Poland in August 1989 and the Hungarian communists embraced political reforms, a multiparty parliamentary system, the protection of civil rights, and a mixed economy in October 1989, Czechoslovak communists suppressed opposition demonstrators until the final days of the regime in November 1989, after the fall of the Berlin wall.[27] Despite the fact that all three communist parties had poor human rights records, one can expect that perceptions about them would have differed because some had resorted to violence until the very end, while others had favored peaceful solutions or had initiated political negotiations.

2. The mode of exit of the authoritarian regimes provided the former communist parties with another opportunity to demonstrate the extent of their transformation or lack thereof. In a sudden revolutionary change, in Huntington's terms "replacement," the Communist Party of Czechoslovakia was defeated, "ran away" from power, and was weakened to such an extent that it was not even able to nominate its own people to a government of "national understanding."[28] In Hungary, the political "transformation" was launched from above and enabled the party to gain more favor than the Czech communists had enjoyed. The same was true during the so-called

transplacement in Poland, which resulted in institutional power sharing and accommodation.

3. The level of transformation of the communist parties has proceeded differently in the three countries during the post-transitional stage. The communist parties in Hungary and Poland were able to change their names, pursue internal reforms, and reorient their policies. The Hungarian Socialist Workers Party (MSzMP) was renamed the Hungarian Socialist Party (MSzP) in 1989, and the Polish United Workers Party (PZPR) transformed itself into the Social Democracy of the Republic of Poland (SdRP) in 1990 and formed a social democratic coalition, the Democratic Left Alliance (SLD).[29] The name changes and new programs probably enabled both parties to dissociate themselves from their pasts to a greater extent than their Czech counterpart. The Communist Party of Bohemia and Moravia (KSČM) insisted on retaining the word *Komunistická* in its title, identified itself with the past, and maintained its dogmatic approach to previous policies.[30] In view of this, no one in the Czech Republic expected KSČM to ever subscribe to the same pro-EU and pro-NATO foreign policies that ex-communist parties in Hungary and Poland adopted.[31] Despite being previously defeated, post-communist parties in Hungary and Poland were voted back into power in the second democratic elections. They became dominant parts of governing coalitions, and their leaders assumed posts as prime ministers. This contrasted with the situation of the KSČM, which has been marginalized by the elite ever since the collapse of socialism.[32]

Thus, we can hypothesize that the choice of a particular lustration system is a function of the perception of the transformation status of former adversaries: the perception of the former communist party as aligned with the old regime—hence untransformed, tainted—led to the approval of the exclusive system in the Czech Republic; and the perception of the former communist party as a transforming, self-purifying force led to non-exclusive systems in Hungary and Poland.

The perception of former adversaries as transforming or untransformed is wider than the perception of threat. A political adversary may seem untransformed by being associated with the past, which may include a variety of characteristics such as ideological dogmas, contempt for human rights, corruption, inefficiency, power abuses, threat, internal change, programmatic reorientation, and so forth. These characteristics may be considered not only dangerous but also repugnant, outdated, or generally undesirable in the eyes of those who strive to start anew. They may constitute a reason for dismissal. These perceptions are derived from the perception of the former communist parties instead of the perception of secret informers because secret police and its informers operated as a subordinate, executive unit of the communist party. Secret police were not as visible.

In sum, the end of socialist rule, the dynamic of regime change, and the post-transitional situation gave former communist parties the opportunity to demonstrate whether they were transforming. However, outward transformation does not automatically signify a change in perceptions. Whether the successor parties were perceived as transformed in Hungary and Poland and untransformed in the Czech Republic is an empirical issue that will be investigated after we formulate our second hypothesis.

Hypothesis II. The Perceptions by the Tainted: The Gray Zone

In extreme conditions people develop various coping and survival strategies. In the context of undemocratic regimes, they may have different motives for engaging with their political structures and repressive units. Some may have been motivated by the desire for personal gain, while others may have sought to protect their families. Some may have been heroes playing a dangerous game of double agency, while others only thought they were heroes.[33] They may be considered perpetrators as well as victims of the undemocratic regime. They become trapped in the historical, political, and moral ambiguity of not being either entirely tainted or entirely spotless. They become part of the so-called gray zone.

According to David Luban, the "gray zone" is Primo Levi's "label for the demimonde of Lager and ghetto inmates who imitated, collaborated with, or assisted the Nazis in return for marginally better treatment for themselves or others."[34] While Levi points to the ambiguous role that members of the gray zones played, Hannah Arendt accuses the Jewish gray zone of facilitating the Holocaust.[35] As history challenged the very survival of the Jewish community, modern history has challenged the existence of small European nations. The gray zone may be blamed for the loss of their independence and credited for their survival. Jiřina Šiklová, a Czech sociologist who applied the concept of the gray zone to the situation of the communist regimes, defined it, somewhat strictly, as "people who did not lose their qualifications because they were not dismissed by the communists from their positions, nor did they become disqualified because of opportunism or immorality, which are the problems that plagued the so-called [*nomenklatura*] class."[36] Naturally, there are many shades of gray. In his historical study of transitional justice, Elster distinguishes several sections of divided societies: beneficiaries, helpers, neutrals, wrongdoers, victims, and resisters.[37] For the purposes of our research, the gray zone encompasses anyone who actively engaged with the former regime. This effectively includes anyone who is not, or has not become, a perpetrator, a victim, or a resister, and it does not include neutrals because remaining neutral in the context of authoritarian regime requires a degree of courage. Therefore it includes "beneficiaries" and "helpers" as defined by Elster.

The nature of the gray zone suggests that its members are trapped in this historical and moral ambiguity and face uncertainty in political transition. They may be held responsible for being indirect beneficiaries of human rights violations of the previous regimes and for being ignorant bystanders while others were experiencing hardships, but they are seldom lauded as heroes who contributed to the survival of the nation in a difficult historical period. In Chapter 2 we illustrated that a regime change exposes the taint of the people in the gray zone. To escape from the gray zone, its members may take one of two exit routes to "purify" themselves after transition: the first is the easier route of finger-pointing and making excuses that exonerate them and proclaim their innocence. The second route is the more difficult and uncertain route that involves self-purification through confession, apology, and other forms of admitting guilt, which enable members of the gray zone to present themselves as reformed persons.

Postwar France provides an example of this social dynamic. From 1943 to 1946 about twenty thousand French women of all ages were accused of having collaborated with the occupying Germans and had their heads shaved.[38] Many of them were paraded on the streets in what was tantamount to a public purification ritual. Together with other methods of *épuration*, such as purges, punishments, and executions, the ritual possibly served to exonerate the complicity of many French people with the Vichy regime. According to Fabrice Virgili, "[a]mong those who carried it out can be found members of the Resistance, those who took part in fighting at the time of the Liberation, neighbours who came down into the streets once the Germans had left and men whose authority depended on the police and courts."[39] Although some of these actions were carried out illegally and others as lawful measures of administrative justice, they were all social actions, marking "the beginning of a new age."[40]

In this exercise, we are not passing moral judgment on members of the gray zone. We are merely considering their responses to a situation that typically calls for passing moral judgments. In fact, we suggest that the call to pass such judgments—to prosecute and dismiss the officials tainted by the former regime—comes from the gray zone itself in order to purify its own complicity with the previous regime. We hypothesize that the demand for the exclusive system comes from the gray zone, which is striving to purify itself, and that the absence of a large gray zone may explain the absence of the demand for dismissals of tainted officials. We anticipate that the size of the gray zone helps explain the choice of an exclusive system at the grassroots level as well as at the elite level. Sudden revolutionary change in a political regime may expose the taint of the gray zone and set off finger-pointing at the micro level. Simultaneously, a sudden political change could catapult the gray zone into higher political positions in the new system in which they are required to explain their past conduct. In an effort to do so they may resort to attributing blame to others.

The Grassroots Perceptions

The former communist parties, although politically discredited and marginalized after the first elections, remained major political players in all three countries. Their perception as transformed or retrogressive political forces may have been also determined by public perception of their attitudes toward major policy issues. The three countries inherited difficult legacies of the former regimes and had to launch political, social, and economic reforms that were critical for the success of transformation toward liberal democracy and market economy. The different perceived level of transformation of former communist parties at the grassroots level may be illustrated by data from surveys conducted by a team led by Gábor Tóka,[41] which provide unique historical insight into the political and policy preferences in the Czech Republic, Hungary, and Poland between 1992 and 1996.[42]

Predictor I. The Perceptions About the Former Communist Parties

In order to capture the view of the former communist parties, ten major policies have been selected for this analysis.[43] Table 4.1 demonstrates the perception of former communist parties as the most likely and the least likely supporters of particular policies. The successor parties were perceived as parties that were the least likely to support a market economy and to speed up privatization in all three countries, although the negative perception was considerably stronger in the Czech Republic than in Hungary and Poland. All three parties were perceived as likely to reduce unemployment. As to the differences, KSČM was perceived as the least likely party to deliver competent managers, human rights, health care and education, and environmental protection to the Czechs. In contrast, SdRP was one of two parties to be considered most likely to deliver better health care and education in Poland. Similarly, MSzP and SdRP were the most likely to increase pensions and social benefits in Hungary and Poland, respectively. The Polish SdRP was also seen as a party that would be the most likely to allow women to make their own choice about abortion.

The KSČM and SdRP were perceived as the most likely to reduce unjust inequalities. But KSČM was at the same time perceived as the least likely to reduce unjust inequalities. This paradox can be explained by the dual nature of "unjust inequalities" in the Czech Republic. For some "unjust inequalities" referred to an individual's position in a particular social stratum, which may have been affected by the newly emerging market economy, while for others it referred to the inequalities inherited from the previous regime under which "the new class" of apparatchiks and *nomenklatura* cadres used their privileged position at the expense of the rest of society.[44] To summarize, the Czech KSČM had the least transformative profile, followed by the Polish SdRP and the Hungarian MSzP. KSČM was perceived as the least likely to pursue seven policies, MSzP two, and SdRP also two. On the other hand, the potential utility of the successor parties was also perceived differently across the three countries: KSČM was perceived as a party that was the most likely to deliver two policies, MSzP also two, and SdRP five.

Predictor II. The Gray Zone

For the purposes of this analysis, the gray zone is defined as a group of communist party members before 1989 who switched their allegiances

Table 4.1. The Perceptions of the Former Communist Parties as the Most/Least Likely Advocates of Selected Policies in the Czech Republic, Hungary, and Poland in 1992 (Percentage of all respondents; respondents could choose any political party)

	Czech Republic		Hungary		Poland	
	Most Likely	Least Likely	Most Likely	Least Likely	Most Likely	Least Likely
Guarantee that competent people are in charge of the economy	3.1	34.4*	8.6	1.4	4.3	1.7
Defend human rights and individual freedom in <country>	5.4	26.3*	5.4	3.2	5.5	3.7
Provide better health care and education	8.5	11.3*	8.0	2.3	11.8*†	0.3
Take more effective steps toward environmental protection	0.6	15.1*	1.6	2.3	1.4	0.8
Increase pensions and social benefits	15.1	4.9	18.1*	1.4	13.8*	0.3
Help the development of private enterprises and a free market economy in <country>	0.1	58.3*	2.4	13.2*	0.9	15.4*
Guarantee that women can have an abortion if they decide to do so	8.5	2.7	7.0	0.4	26.3*	0.6
Reduce unemployment	24.3*	6.3	17.2*	0.8	14.4*	0.4
Speed up privatization of state-owned companies	0.1	59.8*	2.2	15.4*	0.3	15.6*
Reduce unjust inequalities between people	18.9*	16.1*	13.8	3.1	13.1*	1.9

Source: CEU, *The Development of Party Systems and Electoral Alignments in East Central Europe*.
Note: The survey question was formulated as follows: "I am going to read these political goals again. Please, tell me after each, which party or parties you think really wish to reach that objective. . . . Then I am going to ask you which party you think is the least likely to pursue that goal."
* The party was seen as the most/least likely to pursue a policy.
† Two parties were seen as the most likely providers.

Table 4.2. The Gray Zone in the Czech Republic, Hungary, and Poland

	Czech Republic		Hungary		Poland	
	N	%	N	%	N	%
Pre-1989 non-party members	652	80.0	1,021	85.9	1,026	90.4
Pre-1989 party members	159	19.5	167	14.0	108	9.5
Of them gray zone	113	13.9	128	10.7	93	8.2

Source: CEU, *The Development of Party Systems and Electoral Alignments in East Central Europe*.
Note: For the purposes of this analysis, the gray zone consists of pre-1989 party members who voted for non-communist parties in the first democratic elections.

during the regime change and voted for non-communist parties in the first democratic elections. Tóka's surveys asked respondents about their membership in the communist party before 1989 and about their voting in the first elections. This allowed us to create a variable of gray zone pursuant to our definition. Table 4.2 describes the magnitude of the gray zone in the Czech Republic, Hungary, and Poland.

In the first survey conducted in 1992, 652 respondents in the Czech Republic indicated that they were not members of the communist party (80 percent), while 159 respondents (19.5 percent) said that they were party members. Among them, 113 respondents (13.9 percent) represented the gray zone: they said that they did not vote for the communist party in the first elections. In Hungary, 1,021 (85.9 percent) respondents said they were not party members, 167 (14 percent) were party members, and 128 were classified as a gray zone (10.7 percent). In Poland, 1,026 respondents (90.4 percent) were non-party members, 108 were party members (9.5 percent), and 93 of them (8.2 percent) represented the gray zone. Thus, the Czech Republic had the largest gray zone, followed by Hungary and then by Poland.

Dependent Variable: Demand for the Dismissals of Party Members

Different attitudes toward policies and different magnitudes of the gray zone may have affected the removal of former party members from positions of influence.[45] In accordance with our considerations about the crucial role of the perceptions about the communist parties in choosing a personnel system, the removal of party leaders serves here as a proxy for the exclusive system. It allows us to test whether the effects of the perception about the party as a transforming force and the magnitude of the gray zone played any role in selecting an exclusive system in the Czech Republic and in not selecting an exclusive system in Hungary and Poland in spite of strong support for non-communist parties in the first democratic elections in all three countries.

Descriptive Statistics: Support for the removal of former party members from positions of influence was considerably higher in the Czech Republic than in Hungary and Poland (see Figure 4.1). The support reduced slightly in subsequent surveys in the Czech Republic but fluctuated in Hungary and Poland. The mean support for the policy was 55.1 percent in the Czech Republic, 38.8 percent in Hungary, and 36.6 percent in Poland between 1992 and 1995 (see Table 4.3). In the Czech Republic, support for the policy peaked in the second half of 1993, a year in which the act against the lawlessness of the communist regime was passed, challenged, reviewed, and upheld by the Constitutional Court. Opposition to policy about the removal of party members from positions of influence was similar across the three countries in that period. The mean of the opposition to the policy across the different surveys ranged from 24.2 percent in the Czech Republic to 28.6 percent in Hungary to 27.6 percent in Poland.

The results of the descriptive statistics are in line with our hypotheses. Both the perception about the Communist Party as untransformed and the large gray zone seem to increase the demands for the removal of its leaders in the Czech Republic. On the other hand, more favorable perceptions about the ex-communists and a smaller gray zone in Hungary and Poland may explain the reluctance of the majority to remove former communists from positions of influence. However, these results concern only the macro level. They do not provide us with evidence that people from the gray zone engaged in finger-pointing by supporting the removal of their lookalikes from the position of influence.

Multivariate Analyses: In order to effectively test our hypotheses about the origin of lustration systems, we now turn to the multivariate analyses. We shall use the perception about the communist party as the most likely force that would protect human rights as an indicator of its ongoing transformation. There are two reasons for selecting the policy of human rights. First, it may be unfair to judge former communist parties as embracing pro-market economic policies or abandoning their social policies even

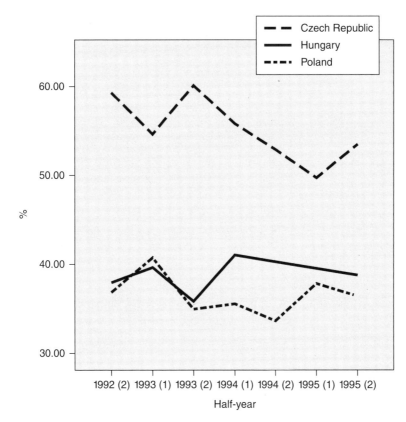

Figure 4.1. Support for the removal of the members of former communist parties from positions of influence in the Czech Republic, Hungary, and Poland (1992–95). Source: CEU, *The Development of Party Systems and Electoral Alignments in East Central Europe.*

though their welfare policies may be seen as unsustainable in the aftermath of the collapse of the centrally planned economies. Second, the policy of human rights is of universal value. Human rights generate a clear distinction between liberal and illiberal regimes. While in the past human rights violations occurred on a mass scale, there is no guarantee that the new regime—regardless of the ideological color of its political representation— would subscribe to human rights. Thus, our first hypothesis can be revised in the following way: the greater the perception about former communist

Table 4.3. Support (Percentage) for the Removal of Former Communist Party Members from Positions of Influence in the Czech Republic, Hungary, and Poland (1992–95)

	Czech Republic		Hungary		Poland	
Half-Year	Support	Oppose	Support	Oppose	Support	Oppose
(2) 1992	59.30	20.20	37.90	28.70	36.80	34.60
(1) 1993	54.60	24.80	39.60	23.80	40.70	23.30
(2) 1993	60.10	21.90	35.80	29.60	34.90	28.70
(1) 1994	55.80	22.90	41.00	33.80	35.50	24.50
(2) 1994	52.90	25.70	—	—	33.60	30.60
(1) 1995	49.70	26.40	39.50	27.30	37.80	24.20
(2) 1995*	53.50	27.30	—	—	36.40	27.50
Mean	55.13	24.17	38.76	28.64	36.53	27.63

Source: CEU, *The Development of Party Systems and Electoral Alignments in East Central Europe.*
*The survey in the Czech Republic was conducted in early 1996.

parties as champions of human rights, the lower the demand for their dismissal.[46] Conversely, the perception of the party as an untransformed force may increase the demand for the exclusion of its members from the public positions.

Our second hypothesis requires including the members of the gray zone and controlling for the former members of communist parties. We shall also control for other sociodemographic factors, including sex, age, education, and the frequency of church attendance. Our dependent variable ranged from 0, indicating an opposition to the removal of party members from positions of influence, to 4, indicating a strong support for removal. The results of the OLS linear regression analyses are presented in Table 4.4.

The perception of the former communist parties as the most likely guarantors of human rights generates highly significant negative effects in the Czech Republic and Poland. It means that those who see the successor parties as a transformed force that guarantees human rights tend to oppose the removal of former party members from public life, and those who do not see the successor parties as a transformed force support their removal from office. The perception is stronger in the Czech Republic than in Poland. Other things being equal, the lack of perception of the party as transformed increases the demand for the removal of its members by almost 1.2 points in the Czech Republic and by 0.7 points in Poland. However, they fail to reach a statistical level of significance in Hungary. These

Table 4.4. Predictors of Support for the Removal of Communist Party Members from Positions of Influence

	Czech Republic		Hungary		Poland	
	B	SE	B	SE	B	SE
The former communist party is the most likely to protect human rights	− 1.17***	(.23)	− 0.04	(.18)	− 0.70***	(.20)
Gray zone	0.80***	(.25)	0.29	(.25)	− 0.24	(.41)
Member of the communist party before 1989	− 1.31***	(.23)	− 0.82***	(.23)	− 0.56	(.39)
Sex (female)	− 0.49***	(.10)	− 0.21**	(.08)	− 0.18*	(.09)
Age (four categories)	0.02	(.05)	− 0.02	(.04)	0.04	(.04)
Education	− 0.04	(.05)	− 0.09**	(.03)	0.03	(.04)
Frequency of church attendance	0.07^	(.04)	0.11***	(.03)	0.09*	(.04)
(Constant)	3.71	(.29)	2.79	(.20)	1.99	(.26)
R^2	0.154		0.060		0.052	
Adj. R^2	0.146		0.053		0.046	
N	796		1082		1055	

Source: CEU, The Development of Party Systems and Electoral Alignments in East Central Europe.

^p < .1   *p < .05   **p < .01   ***p < .001

findings can be interpreted in accordance with our first hypothesis. In the Czech Republic, they show a strong link between the perceptions about the communist party and the demand for the exclusive system. In Poland, they show a moderate link between the perceptions about the former communists and demand for dismissal. Any meaningful conclusions about Hungary can only be drawn from its comparison to the Czech Republic and Poland. They may signify that the successor party in Hungary was more transformed than its counterparts in the Czech Republic and Poland.

Turning to the perception by the gray zone, we observe that being a member of the gray zone is a significant predictor of the removal of party members in the Czech Republic but fails to generate significant effects in Hungary and Poland, other things being equal. Thus, the analysis at the micro level only gives support to our second hypothesis in the Czech Republic, where membership in the gray zone appears to be a significant predictor of the support for the dismissal of tainted officials. In the situation of a sudden implosion of a rigid undemocratic regime, which only happened in the Czech Republic, the gray zone seeks to purify itself externally by excluding former members of communist parties from their positions of influence. The historical irony is that the gray zone members are themselves former members of the party. How can we explain this paradox?

Qualitative Analysis: In addition to finger-pointing and the need to present oneself in a better light, which we have described in Chapter 2, there may be other reasons why moral judgments passed on others may be stricter than moral judgments passed on oneself. Naturally, finger-pointing may be rooted in mere scant perceptions about others that contrast with detailed knowledge of difficult situations one faced in the past. It is our nature that we can better observe spots on other people's cloths than on ours. Another possible explanation may be that the gray zone is—like politics, church, school, and parenting—another instance of institutionalized hypocrisy. Its members may apply stricter criteria to judge others not as disguise of their own failures in the past but as an effort to meet social expectations or as an expression of their genuine striving for the better.

The following example of a woman in her late thirties who participated in a focus group session with other ordinary members of the center-right ODS in the Czech Republic is illustrative of this point.[47] She and her party may be considered representatives of the gray zone (although a light-gray zone because she was not a communist in the past) who advocated the removal of party members from public life. When the group was asked whether they had participated in the events that glorified the previous regime, she volunteered with a positive response. If she had not participated, she would not have been allowed to complete secondary school. Her answer did not signify excuses or embarrassment. She did not feel any pressing need to support the removal of party members *in order* to be seen as innocent. Instead, she just judged the similar thing differently in the past from the way she judged it now. The discrepancy appeared again later during that session, when she categorically excluded any possibility of allowing her daughter to engage in any capacity with the communistic regime if it returned. In her eyes she was quite consistent: she did not wish the communists to rule her country, so she demanded exclusion of former communists and her daughter not to collaborate. No one can expect that she wished anything bad for her daughter, although her daughter would have eventually failed to complete her education if she followed her advice in the same grim political situation that her mother had faced in the past. Clearly, the mother applied a double standard here without realizing it, and perhaps she would eventually face her daughter accusing her of hypocrisy. The mother genuinely strived for the better without considering her own moral record in the past. She is an instance of the banality of the gray zone.

This case invalidates the assumption of the homogeneity of motives within the gray zone. The use of finger-pointing as a means of external purification, though plausible, is conditional on certain internal transformations, self-reflection accompanied by concern felt by the people of the gray zone that someone may see them as complicit with the former regime. Consequently, the results of our statistical analyses should not be overestimated. First, the members of the gray zone may not see themselves as tainted. Second, we cannot exclude the possibility that this may be because some of them may have already purified themselves internally by acknowledging their role in the past in their personal circle or that they won their status of innocence by accusing someone else at the time of transition. Third, membership in the communist party is the largest predictor of opposition to the process of dismissal of party members in the Czech Republic, other things being equal. It means that non-membership in the party is still a stronger predictor of the removal of former party members than is membership in the gray zone. We also note that the past membership in the communist party is a strong predictor of the opposition to the removal of party members in Hungary, other things being equal. It does not make any impact in Poland, where many party members were also members of the Solidarity Unions.[48]

Elite Perceptions

In spite of the popular perceptions, the decision on lustration was made by the elites, who may have overruled the popular will in a manner similar to the way in which they made many other unpopular decisions to facilitate political transformation. In order to examine the origin of lustration systems on the elite level, the following section utilizes political statements made during parliamentary and other political debates about lustration laws. In contrast to elite interviews, or elite surveys, conducted years after the laws were approved, opinions expressed in parliamentary debates and other public statements provide us with a more authentic source of information about *doing* the purification of public life after transition than do retouched testimonies of local politicians given ex post facto to Western researchers.

We Are (Not) Like Them: The Origin of the Exclusive System in Czechoslovakia

Czechoslovakia was one of the last countries in the region to overthrow communism but the first one to enact a lustration law. Faced with unexpectedly massive demonstrations and the collapse of socialism in neighboring countries, the Communist Party of Czechoslovakia (KSČ) gave up its monopolistic power in November 1989. The message of the Velvet Revolution was non-retributive, characterized by the slogan "we are not like them."[49] Chanted by demonstrators in town squares across the country, the leadership of the newly formed mass opposition movement Civic Forum (OF) successfully quelled the vengeful emotions of the masses with an appeal for a moral high ground. A long history of purges in Czechoslovakia indicated that the elite's concerns were not entirely unwarranted.[50]

However, the inability to make visible changes in the administration and armed services within two years of the Velvet Revolution and increasing international security concerns prompted the newly elected Federal Assembly of the Czech and Slovak Federative Republic to pass the lustration law.

Being approved just a few weeks after the failed attempt at a coup d'état in the disintegrating Soviet Union in August 1991, the Czechoslovak leaders were aware of the security risk that hard-line communist forces in Russia posed and turned against persons who had been associated with them. The perception about the hard-liners in Moscow may have shaped the perception about domestic hard-liners and their henchmen and resulted in a call for their removal from public life. This gives some preliminary support to our first hypothesis concerning the negative perceptions about adversaries.

Among the 300 deputies of the Federal Assembly, 148 voted for the act, 31 voted against it, and 22 abstained; the rest were absent.[51] The voting pattern also indicates a preliminary support for our hypothesis about the gray zone. Although the voting did not exactly split the assembly along party lines, it was supported by the center-right parties Civic Democratic Party (ODS), Christian Democratic Party (KDS), Public Against Violence (VPN), and Civic Democratic Alliance (ODA), and also included centrist, independent, and ethnic minority deputies; while the deputies of KSČM, nationalists, and a majority of former dissidents in the Civic Movement (OH) voted against it or abstained.[52] In the following sections, we shall therefore examine both hypotheses in detail.

The old communist cadres and their secret collaborators were perceived as "untransformed," and indeed as "intractable," by the new Czechoslovak political elite. The inherited apparatus was seen as inimical to the new democracy because its posts were filled on the basis of the unfair ideological criteria of the previous regime, for example, on the basis of "political maturity, a creative Marxist-Leninist approach to the solution of problems, and the determination to consistently bring the party's policies to life."[53] Under the Czechoslovak communist regime, once a person had been dismissed from his or her position for political reasons, there was hardly any way to regain the post under the omnipresent surveillance of cadre secretaries. One of the legislature's post-1989 objectives might have been to accomplish a form of redress, to provide opportunities for those who had previously been excluded from office for political reasons. But the effort of achieving certain minimal standards of justice, of de-legitimizing past injustices, and of denouncing those who had profited from those injustices was voiced by only a few deputies of the assembly.[54] At that time, the Federal Assembly had already passed the Act on Extra-Judicial Rehabilitation, which among other things reinstated those who had been unfairly dismissed for political reasons to their former positions.[55]

The enactment of a special public employment law was considered necessary because people holding important public positions were usually reluctant to leave and it was nearly impossible to dismiss them under inherited communist employment law. Unlike the situation in Poland, where initial personnel changes were subject to limits set out during roundtable negotiations, Czechoslovak "revolutionaries" anticipated that former members of the old regime would leave voluntarily. They were soon disappointed and discovered that their policy of unconditional forgiveness had been unrealistic and that members of the former repressive apparatus would not leave their posts voluntarily: "[W]e could not get rid of the head of the international department [of the Federal Assembly], who was proved to be a [former] member of [the communist] intelligence and . . . [the speaker] Mr. Dubček took him for international visits. For example, our American counterpart alerted us that it did not contribute to the honor of our state when such a person accompanied the speaker of the highest legislative assembly."[56]

Clearly, the "honor" of the nascent democracy was seen as being compromised by the presence of tainted officials. These officials, however, may not have seen themselves as compromised. Similarly to the Foreman in Havel's *Audience*, quoted in Chapter 2, they may have been from the gray zone and attributed the responsibility for the past to some other "they." Thus, two contradictory interpretations of the Velvet Revolution coexisted: the new elite sought peaceful personnel change, and the old elite wanted to preserve its status. Deputy Ján Mlynárik (VPN), a Slovak historian, aptly pointed out: "It was certainly right that we implemented the principle 'we are not like them', that we refrained from witch-hunt, from vengeance, but we underestimated our rival. He interpreted the generosity and decency in his own term and he used his unbroken and partly kept positions to the destruction and destabilization of our democratic efforts."[57] Similar disappointment was expressed in the speeches of ten other deputies.[58] According to the leader of KDS, Deputy Václav Benda, "We are on the very complicated way from the totalitarian regime to democracy. . . . The way is not irreversible and it is far from its accomplishment. In this situation we cannot afford that representatives who without any doubt participated in crimes of the Communist Party . . . will continue their conspiracy against the democratic regime. . . . We gave them the opportunity [to leave], there was more or less a silence about these things within the first year after November [1989] and the results are catastrophic and we can see them everywhere around us."[59]

Initially, the pressure for change and the effort to preserve the status quo were combined: former *nomenklatura* cadres moved to different positions but did not leave. This was called "the rotation of cadres."[60] Therefore, for some deputies the lustration act was essentially "a second revolution," a quest for dismissals coined by President Havel on August 21, 1990.[61] Hence, the law reflected the congested political situation following the fall of communism and the actions of the former networks. It was a response to certain defective features of the political transition rather than to the totalitarian regime; it was a response to current perceptions about past networks. It reflected the frustration of the new elite in its naïve belief that the old elite would just give up their privileges after the transition and in the *metanoia* of former oppressors after external factors of the old regime had disappeared.

The support for exclusive lustration law contradicted the principle of a second chance. It arose from the disappointment of thwarted expectations that people associated with the past regime would leave voluntarily and the realization that they were not to be trusted in the new government. The risks associated with giving them another chance were considered too high. According to Štefan Bačinský (VPN), the director of the new Czechoslovak security service at the time, "networks that destabilize all the spheres of our public life are everywhere: in the television, in the radio, in printed media, in the public administration and the self-government, in enterprises and also trade unions."[62] While debating whether these people should be disqualified from senior public offices Bačinský added that they "certainly have the right to go with us to build the democratic society. But I am convinced that they should not lead us."[63]

The legislature also sought to avoid blackmail against public officials that could spread during the democratization process. Those who, as members of or collaborators with the secret police, had informed on their fellow citizens were regarded as vulnerable in this respect. Those who may have been involved in yet unreported criminal activities of the secret police and communist *nomenklatura* that were typical in regimes lacking the rule of law were also seen as vulnerable to blackmail. According to the Czechoslovak Parliamentary Commission of November 17 the "only way to prevent blackmail, the continued activity of StB collaborators, and a series of political cal scandals that could surface at crucial moments is to clear the government and legislative bodies of these collaborators."[64] Similarly, Federal Vice-Minister of the Interior Jan Ruml (later ODS) suggestively asked: "[I]f KGB has the [copies of Czechoslovak secret police] files, it can blackmail whenever it wants. Can anyone who can be blackmailed be a representative at any level? There is a parallel here with the situation in Czechoslovakia after the [second world] war. Lists of Gestapo collaborators were given to the communist police. Hence, it was the beginning of its enormous power, which depended also on blackmail."[65] Some scholars believe the fear of threats arising from blackmail was exaggerated for the sake of implementing lustration policy.[66] However, the affiliation with the repressive apparatus was used as a means of blackmail, for example, by the Slovak leader Vladimír Mečiar. On several occasions he publicly mentioned that he had just found the secret police files of various people on his desk.[67] A possible explanation for these mysterious findings may be the fact that after his appointment as the first non-communist Slovak minister of the interior in January 1990, Mečiar led a nighttime police raid of the secret police archives, allegedly taking his own file and those of his political rivals.[68] He then used the materials in a successful bid to become the head of the ruling movement in Slovakia, VPN, and eventually the prime minister of Czechoslovakia's Slovak Republic in June 1990.[69]

A number of left-wing deputies, such as Petr Uhl, Ivan Fišera, and Jan Kavan, cautioned about the implementation of lustrations. The representatives of the former Communist Party (KSČM) had different views. Deputy Ivan Rynda, for instance, called the lustration bill "legal violence,"[70] Deputy Miloslav Ransdorf labeled it "inquisition and McCarthyism,"[71] and Deputy Jiří Černý saw it as "a proxy for the inability to prosecute communist crimes."[72] Some deputies argued that the bill was an expression of collective guilt and caused unjust punishment.[73] Advocates of lustrations dismissed these concerns. According to Deputy Marián Farkaš (VPN), a rapporteur on the lustration law for the Chamber of the People, "during the debate of the bill in the [parliamentary] committees, deputies of some political groups deliberately brought in an impression of the criminal character of the proposed norm."[74] Another deputy, Jana Petrová (ODS), argued that the bill's sole concern was employment law relationships.[75] The difference in views was highlighted by Deputy Daniel Kroupa (ODA): "[O]n the one

hand, many of us are motivated by the spirit of vengeance against representatives of the old regime, and on the other hand, there is hysterical fear of
the spirit of vengeance."[76] The allegations of institutionalized revenge and
its denial were raised by seventeen deputies in the Czechoslovak lustration
debate.[77]

This overview demonstrates support for our first hypothesis: the
demand for dismissals is largely derived from the perception of former
adversaries as untransformed, and in this case mainly as a security threat,
although deputies have also seen *nomenklatura* as ideological loyalists of
the previous regime. There is mixed support for our second hypothesis.
While former dissidents in the Civic Movement (OH) did not support the
final lustration law, many members of ODS, ODA, VPN, and KDS did.
Could they be considered a gray zone? The answer is not straightforward.
On the one hand, the parties had several high-profile dissidents such as
Václav Benda, Zdeněk Kessler, Daniel Kroupa, Jana Petrová, and Jan Ruml;
on the other hand, these dissidents were a minority in their parliamentary
clubs.

Nothing But the Truth: The Origin
of the Inclusive System in Hungary

The perceptions of the Hungarian elite about the former communist party
were apparently not as negative as those the new Czech elites had held
about its Czech counterpart. It is therefore not surprising that the Hungarian political elites handled the process of dealing with the past in a non-
exclusive manner. In fact, there is almost no evidence to suggest that exclusion of people associated with the former regime was ever taken seriously
in Hungary. The first democratically elected government of Prime Minister
Jószef Antall had de-communization and "political spring cleaning" in the
1990 government program but instead of exclusion the ruling coalition
proposed an inclusive lustration system.[78] There was not even one viable
parliamentary initiative that put forward a proposal for personnel changes.
However, there was a bill, proposed by Zsolt Zétényi and Péter Takácz,
which allowed for the prosecution of criminal offenses committed during
the previous regime.[79] In order to avoid breaching the prohibition against
retroactivity, the bill took the communist penal code as a legal benchmark;

despite its moderate nature it was struck down by the Constitutional Court.[80]

One of the most "radical" lustration bills was proposed by Péter Hack and Gábor Demszky from the Alliance of Free Democrats (SzDSz) in October 1990.[81] SzDSz was a party of former anti-Kádár dissidents, which became an opposition party after 1990 elections. Their consistent human rights concerns may explain both the party's interest in dealing with the past and its caution in not creating new human rights violations. Their bill sought to pursue three objectives: to promote the purity of public office, to restrain those who had collaborated with the former regime, and to forestall leaks of confidential information.[82] While these objectives did not significantly differ from those of the Czech lustration law, they differed in the method by which they were achieved. In terms of the Hack-Demszky bill, a list of persons who had unambiguously collaborated with the former regime would be compiled and entrusted to the president, the prime minister, and the head of Parliament's National Security Committee; the president would disclose the names of persons if they had occupied public positions and had opted not to step down without being exposed.[83] Although its proponents hoped that the public officials would choose to step down without being exposed, the Hack and Demszky bill was effectively based on the inclusive lustration method. The bill was eventually defeated in the Parliament, but the method of exposure became part of subsequent proposals.

In order to promote "the transparency of the democratic state," the government first tried to introduce the lustration bill in May 1991.[84] After excessive amendments to the bill were proposed by the deputies, the government withdrew it for revision in 1992 and reintroduced it in 1993.[85] The Parliament approved the lustration law by a vote of 177 to 12 with fifty abstentions on March 8, 1994.[86] As with Czechoslovak lustration, the law was supported by the center-right parties, namely the Hungarian Democratic Forum (MDF), the Smallholder Party (FKgP), and the Christian Democratic Party (KDNP), which formed the governing coalition. The Alliance of Young Democrats (Fidesz), independent deputies, and the xenophobic Hungarian Justice and Life Party (MIÉP) also supported the bill while the (former) Hungarian Socialist Party (MSzP) voted against it. Most of the deputies for the Alliance of Free Democrats (SzDSz), the former dissident party, abstained.[87] This suggests an influence of the gray zone in the pursuit of lustration in Hungary.

Despite the relatively high degree of political consensus in Hungary, the law was undermined by the timing of the process. The law was approved two months before the second democratic elections were conducted in May, which made it a subject of the electoral campaign, thus increasing the politicization of an already sensitive topic and diverting the debate from its substantive issues to ad hominem accusations among politicians who quarreled about their pasts. The timing of the process led some observers to conclude that attempts to increase the scope of the lustration laws were motivated by intentions to use it against political rivals: to counter the growing political competition posed by candidates of the socialist party.[88] But neither MSzP nor its predecessor was targeted by the law (see Chapter 3). The law primarily exposed secret police members and informers who remained in public office. Although it gave the newly reformed MSzP an opportunity to further distance itself from the past by attributing blame to secret collaborators, the party did not utilize this opportunity.

The transcript of the parliamentary debate that started on October 27, 1993, is nearly seventy-five pages long.[89] But none of the major speeches given by the minister of the interior, the rapporteurs of parliamentary committees, or the leaders of parliamentary factions considered exclusion as a major feature of the lustration law. The bill was introduced by Péter Boross (MDF), who still acted in his capacity as minister of the interior before he assumed the post of the prime minister after the death of József Antall. In his agenda-setting speech, Boross stated that the aim of the revised bill was not to implement coercive measures against those who had collaborated with the socialist regime and who had maintained positions of trust or positions in which they could influence public life: "If one voluntarily gave up her position, the information about her past activity would be encrypted for 30 years in order to prevent publicizing such information."[90] Speaking on behalf of the center-right governing coalition, Minister Boross reiterated that the objective of the bill was to achieve "the purity of public life" and eliminate unsubstantiated accusations.

The speaker of the National Security Committee of the Parliament, Zoltán Kátay (MDF), agreed with "the moral sanction" of exposure introduced by the government bill. He considered the bill ready for the plenary parliamentary session but noted that many reservations against the bill concerned human rights.[91] Indeed, the speaker of the Committee for Human Rights, Minority and Religious Affairs, Vilmos Horváth (SzDSz), conveyed the majority opinion, which did not find the bill suitable for parliamentary debate. Seeing the bill as politically expedient, Horváth pointed out that the lack of procedural guarantees in the bill undermined its aspiration to purify public life, and its belated introduction could not justify society's need for justice.[92] According to the minority opinion of the same committee, persons should not be allowed to participate in public life if their present and their past could not be reconciled.[93] The spokesman for the minority, Zsolt Zétényi (MDF), admitted that there were some problems with the bill but agreed with the lustration method: "the option of exit from public life [given to a positively screened person in order to avoid his or her exposure] should be upheld to ensure human dignity and human rights of the person under scrutiny."[94]

The speech on behalf of the ruling MDF parliamentary faction came closest to an argument for an exclusive system. According to its spokesman, Balázs Horváth, historical justice requires that "People who impeded democratic development in the past and spread the atmosphere of fear, terror, and mistrust should be filtered out from public life. Therefore such people could not be considered the champions of transition and strongly committed adherents of the transition because of their past life. . . . This bill does not start from the past, but from the present, and does not try to condemn the past but tries to protect our future."[95] These considerations have been typical in the Czechoslovak Federal Assembly. The past record of the person under scrutiny determined perceptions about him or her in the present. But in direct contradiction with this perspective, Horváth acknowledged the absence of any legal consequences for stepping down. This means that, in accordance with our first hypothesis, those associated with the past regime were perceived as tainted but not too tainted to warrant their dismissal.

Similar dissonance between aspirations and the reality of the situation was apparent in the speech of Antal Kocsenda, who spoke on behalf of the conservative Smallholder Party (FKgP): "Open and honest [process of] facing the past, truth revelation and dealing with the past are unavoidable to assure the purity of public life and politics and to leave behind burdens of the past. Without them the rule of law and democratic decision making cannot be accomplished. It is also clear that people in connection with III/III directorate of the Ministry of the Interior are those who did everything to serve the past regime. This is where real oppressors can be found."[96] Kocsenda aspired to find them and expose them, not dismiss them. In the main speech of the opposition Free Democrats (SzDSz), Ferenc Köszeg criticized the government for being late with the submission of the proposal. He stressed that people should know "who did what in the past" if a person from the old regime ran for office.[97] Such transparency was achieved in Hack-Demszky bill, which was proposed by their faction in 1991. The Free Democrats expressed concerns that any eventual exclusion from public life would violate labor law. They nevertheless found the government bill to be almost identical to the Hack-Demszky blueprint.[98] Another critical voice against the bill was that of Béla Katona of MSzP. Speaking on behalf of the club, Katona stated that the bill served the interests of the government and did not satisfactorily solve the problem of collaboration. He questioned the completeness of the secret archives and said the bill would create an atmosphere of suspicion during its proposed duration of six years.[99] Thus, like their Czechoslovak counterparts, Hungarian post-communists were concerned that instead of promoting trust the bill would generate public mistrust.

The Hungarian inclusive method could be interpreted either as institutionalized blackmail or as a second chance. But neither of these two views seemed to reside in the minds of the bill's opponents and proponents. They simply saw the truth deficit regarding the past behavior of public officials as an obstacle to transparent and trustworthy public life. The officials themselves were not seen as obstacles to democratization, but the failure to publicly disclose the information about their past activities was. In accordance with our second hypothesis, Hungarians' view about tainted officials was very moderate. This was dramatically different from the perception of former officials in Czechoslovakia, where a person's past was an integral part of his of her profile and as such could not be rectified by exposure. The Czechoslovak lustration system therefore concerned the exclusion of all personnel whose past conduct had been considered problematic, including former leaders of the Communist Party, secret police members, and their informers. The Hungarian lustration system did not directly target the leadership of the party and only exposed the previous activities of clandestine collaborators.

The method of exposure was not questioned by parliamentary factions. There was, however, one notable exception: one parliamentary club proposed an amendment to the method of the inclusive lustration system. Speaking on behalf of the Christian Democratic People's Party (KDNP),

Miklós Gáspár stated: "Our major disagreement concerns the issue of proving the harm done to others. The lack of information and that of clarity and accuracy of the lustration procedure will bring about its malfunction. We have a suggestion. A person holding a position of trust should sign a statement about her 'innocence' which could be later checked. If evidence would be found afterwards her credibility would be questioned."[100] In other words, KDNP proposed a lustration system that replaced exposure with confession. Although this attempt was not successful, confession as a method of lustration was later implemented in the reconciliatory system in Poland.

Negotiating Scandals: The Origin of the Reconciliatory System in Poland

Poland was the first country in the region to find its way out of socialism but the last to approve a lustration law. Polish transformation was negotiated through roundtable talks from February through April 1989. At that time, communists who remained confident conceded only semi-democratic elections, making only 35 percent of the seats in the Sejm (the Lower Chamber; the power of the newly established Senate was marginal) open to contest. Although Tadeusz Mazowiecki was appointed the first non-communist prime minister after the sweeping "victory" of Solidarity in the election held in June 1989, General Czesław Kiszczak remained the minister of the interior until July 1990, and General Wojciech Jaruzelski occupied the Polish presidency until December 1990.[101] Facing a communist clique that was viewed as powerful at that time, the Mazowiecki government announced a policy of drawing "a thick line after the past."[102]

In spite of political changes ushered in by the 1991 elections, the bulk of former communist *nomenklatura* remained in control in both formal and informal ways during the first decade of Poland's transition. Approximately one-quarter occupied senior public posts in the mid-1990s,[103] while the majority of cadres capitalized on their positions during the privatization process.[104] A survey conducted among Polish business, political, and administrative elites in 1998, one year after the electoral defeat of post-communist SdRP and one year before the Polish lustration system went into effect, confirmed that no single sphere could be characterized as dominated by the former anti-communist opposition and that the claim that the origin of the business elite was in the communist world was well founded.[105]

The non-communist political parties elected in 1991 strived to approve a lustration law. In September 1992, the Sejm debated six lustration bills, which differed in terms of their scope and duration but also in their methods.[106] The Senate and the Confederation of Independent Poland (KPN) proposed that tainted officials in elected posts should be exposed and excluded from administrative posts; the Christian-National Union (ZChN) and the Solidarity proposed various exclusive systems; the Liberal Democratic Congress (KLD) suggested an inclusive system based on exposure with an option for the official to resign without being exposed; and the Center Agreement (PC) proposed a method of self-incriminating confessions: every official would submit an affidavit which, if positive, would lead to exclusions; if an official concealed any relevant facts, he or she would face a sanction for dishonesty.[107] None of these proposals was approved.

The sudden surge of lustration initiatives was a response to a previous attempt to determine the nature of the past activities of high state officials. In May 1992, the Sejm, dominated by non-communists, passed a resolution that requested Minister of the Interior Antoni Macierewicz (ZChN) to prepare a list of all state officials from the rank of chief administrator of the region and above who collaborated with the secret police between 1945 and 1990. "Macierewicz's list," which was delivered to the Sejm, contained the names of thirty-nine deputies, including the Speaker of the House, eleven senators, eight deputy ministers, three ministers, three officers from the President's Office, and the newly elected president Lech Wałęsa.[108] What followed was a hysterical parliamentary quarrel that lasted nearly sixteen hours and became known as the "Night of Files." It resulted in public statements made by each of the opposing camps that the democracy in Poland was under threat and led to a motion of non-confidence and the fall of the government of Jan Olszewski (PC).[109]

The parliamentary debate was a defining moment for the future of lustrations in Poland. Many could not simply believe that the national hero of anti-communist resistance and the democratically elected president, Lech Wałęsa, had agreed to collaborate with the secret services.[110] Although a number of lustration scandals were reported in each of the Central European countries before the law was enacted, the topic of lustration in Poland became more controversial than anywhere else. The Poles tried to shelve lustration, but dealing with its issues could hardly be avoided. After the appointment of former dissident Andrzej Milczanowski as the minister of the interior in the government of Waldemar Pawlak (Polish Peasant Party

[PSL]), access to secret files was forbidden.[111] But the prohibition of lustration was not a solution. It deepened unsubstantiated gossip and false accusations, leaving people without an opportunity to defend themselves. As Wałęsa stated, a "human being is defenseless against defamation. . . . The defamed person does not have any chance to clear himself from suspicions."[112]

The new political elite faced a dilemma: carrying lustrations out may have solved some problems but deepened others, while not carrying lustrations threatened to destabilize public life. The continuing scandals in Poland demonstrated that the problem of collaboration would not disappear. The previous chapter mentioned that at least three Polish prime ministers, including Józef Oleksy (SLD), Włodzimierz Cimoszewicz (SLD), and Jerzy Buzek (AWS), and two presidents, Lech Wałęsa and Aleksander Kwaśniewski, were publicly denounced. The issue would continue being raised until it was resolved, said Vice Premier Janusz Tomaszewski (AWS),[113] who was later accused of collaboration. As Klaus Bachmann, a German scholar living in Poland, pointed out, East Germany "chose a horror ending—lustrations, opening files. . . . Poland chose a horror without an end and therefore the secret police files will create fear for many years."[114]

Analyzing the lustration debate in the Polish Senate in 1991, Maria Łoś identified three affirmative lustration discourses that reflected the three main pro-lustration themes: state security, historical truth, and minimal justice.[115] Among the affirmative lustration discourses, security topics were mentioned by 52 percent of the senators, truth revelation by 20 percent, and minimal justice by 16 percent. But in the mid-1990s, after the Poles voted the ex-communists back to power, it became apparent that solving the personnel problem was possible only through revealing the true identity of the tainted officials. The disclosure of truth about the past became a priority.

Learning the truth about the past seems to have been a powerful notion in many emerging democracies. People desired to have access to information that had been withheld from them by the former regime, which maintained a monopoly on truth and used censorship, misinformation, and the secret police. Immediately after the fall of communism, people could learn a good deal about human rights violations, border killings, torture, and concentration camps. Many victims shared their personal stories in newspapers, on television, and on the radio. However, materials that were collected about them and their relatives by former cadres and security services (Security Office [UB] and Security Service [SB]) remained a secret. Public interest in learning the truth led to a need to open the archives and publicize the list of those who had gathered information and reported about the members of the public. Even the Polish president, Aleksander Kwaśniewski, a former communist, wanted the lustration law to grant all citizens unimpeded access to their secret files.[116] According to the former prime minister, Jan Olszewski (PC), "Anybody who runs for a high office has to be prepared for the lustration process and for the questions about his own past. There are no legal limitations that a [secret police] agent cannot become a president. I think, though, it will not happen."[117]

On the other hand, opposition to public exposure by means of a lustration process came from the deputies in the coalition led by the former communist party (SLD) and from the liberal dissident Adam Michnik, who was the editor of the daily *Gazeta Wyborcza*. They stressed that secret archives are not reliable sources of information for the purpose of lustrations. The myth of the "Dead Souls," according to which rank-and-file secret policemen falsified their archives in order to deceive their superiors and to meet recruitment quotas, was considerably more widespread in Poland than in Hungary.[118]

The ongoing quarrels indicate that the center-right and center-left parties held conflicting perceptions of people associated with the past regime. The Polish center-right parties saw former *nomenklatura* cadres and their alleged alliance with former secret police members and their informers as a threat to democratization, national security, and economic transformation, while the Polish left dismissed such claims as conspiracy theories.[119] Center-right politicians advocated exclusion of leading members of the former communist party and their secret collaborators from important positions of public life in a manner similar to that of Czech lustration law. Center-left politicians were either entirely against lustrations or advocated mere exposure of secret collaboration.[120]

Lustration law was formed as a result of a political compromise forged between major ideological camps in the commission headed by Deputy Bogdan Pęk from the PSL.[121] The resolution of the deadlock was based on three premises:

1. Persons to be lustrated would be obliged to submit a declaration concerning their work or service in the security organs of the socialist regime or collaboration with them.
2. This information would become public knowledge.

3. Confession of collaboration would not bear any legal consequences, except that any attempt to conceal this fact would lead to the suspension of the right to hold public office for ten years.[122]

The Polish Sejm adopted the lustration bill based on these premises on April 11, 1997. Among its 460 members, 214 voted in favor, 162 against, and 16 abstained.[123] The Polish Senate approved the bill in May 1997. Among 100 senators, 47 voted in favor while 33 voted against it.[124] The bill was supported mainly by the Solidarity Election Action (AWS), the Freedom Union (UW), and the Polish Peasant Party (PSL). Only the role of the PSL, a party that was officially tolerated by the communist regime and which defected its ex-communist coalition partner on the eve of the 1997 elections, supports our hypothesis about the gray zone. Opposition to the bill came mainly from the Democratic Left Alliance (SLD), which was led by the ex-communists (SdRP). In fact, SLD deputies Jerzy Jaskiernia, Kazimierz Pańtak, and Jerzy Dziewulski used various obstructions to derail the approval of the lustration law.[125] President Kwaśniewski, a former communist who had previously criticized the bill for a lack of clarity concerning the term *secret collaboration*, signed the bill in June 1997. Nevertheless, he also requested that the Constitutional Tribunal abrogate some of its provisions.[126]

The perception of the transformation of the former communist party and its members went through two stages in Poland. First, many centrist and liberal politicians did not perceive the former PZPR as a carrier of immediate threat because it handed over political power to the democratic opposition. According to Adam Czarnota, "This position, expressed quite often by Adam Michnik and his newspaper *Gazeta Wyborcza*, stressed the transfer of power through round-table talks as a decisive moment. The former communists had recognized the opposition, and, as a result, the political agreements achieved at the round-table talks between the two sides (the communists and the opposition) were translated into constitutional and legal language."[127] In other words, lustrations were redundant in the view of Michnik and centrist political parties, such as the Democratic Union (UD), because of the initial transformative effort of ex-communists. Second, the advancing political transformation furthered personal transformation of those associated with the former regime who were able to present themselves as purified. In a stark contrast with the Czech situation where the communists upheld their dogmas, the people associated with the past regime in Poland reinvented themselves and rewrote their biographies. According to Maria Łoś and Andrzej Zybertowicz,

> By steadfastly denying that they had ever believed in the communist ideology . . . or had had anything to do with it, the Party succes-sors—the SdRP leaders—disconnected themselves discursively from totalitarianism. . . . [T]he malleability and swift makeover of former *apparatchiks* into smart mannequins for the latest fashions . . . defined the psychological landscape. By 1993 the refurbished Com-munists had come to symbolize, at least to a part of the population, the consumption- and choice-oriented future, while their former opponents were identified with a past dominated by martyrdom and difficult moral dilemmas.[128]

This observation is in line with the reality. The former communist leaders transformed into progressive pro-Western-oriented politicians. Most nota-bly, the former member of the politburo of PZPR at the end of the commu-nist regime, Leszek Miller, became the prime minister of Poland in 2001–4,[129] and a former minister in the last communist government, Aleksander Kwaś-niewski, served as the country's president during 1995–2005.[130] In 1999, Kwaśniewski signed the North Atlantic Treaty; together with Miller they oversaw the EU referendum in 2003 and the integration of Poland with the EU in 2004, and joined the U.S.-led coalition to depose the regime of Sad-dam Hussein.[131] The option of dismissing former communist leaders from positions of influence was seriously advocated but has not been available in Poland. The attempt to make a stricter lustration law, proposed by the conservative parties in 2005 and advocated by later President Lech Kaczyński and his brother Jarosław, who was the prime minister (both PiS), was per-ceived as moral entrepreneurship[132] and eventually failed in 2007.[133]

Consequently, the two conflicting views about the former communists shaped perceptions about the secret police. The center-right saw former members of the secret services (SB and UB) connected to all levels of power within the post-communist state. Operating on an informal basis as net-works or being employed in new state and security departments, they were seen being associated with many unfortunate decisions of the state organs in the process of transition.[134] Those who believed that the party had changed typically dismissed the allegations of subversive activities by the network between former secret police members and their former masters as conspiracy theories.

Discussion

In this chapter, we have tried to explain the paradox of non-communist majorities: why only Czechoslovaks adopted the exclusive system if non-communists parties dominated parliaments after the first democratic elections in all three countries. We have hypothesized that the choice of the exclusive system is a function of two factors: the perceptions about the former communist parties as transformed and the support coming from the gray zone that seeks to exonerate itself from its complicity in the past. We have examined both hypotheses at the grassroots level and at the elite level.

The brief overview of the historical development of the successor parties before, during, and after transition indicated a low level of transformation in the Czech Republic and a high degree of transformation in Hungary and Poland. We used survey data to examine the perceived transformation of these parties at the grassroots level. The first indicator of the perceived transformation, which measured their perceptions as a provider or inhibitor of ten major policies, showed that crucial differences existed across the region: the perception of Czech KSČM as a potentially most likely provider of ten major policies received a score of 2:7, which indicated a negative perception, while MSzP received 2:3 in Hungary, and SdRP 5:2 in Poland. SdRP clearly established its policy profile as an advocate of social issues, including abortion. In contrast, KSČM was perceived as an inhibitor of all policies that were considered significant for political, economic, and social transformation. The perceived transformation of successor parties was reflected in their electoral performance. Electoral campaigns provided these parties with an opportunity to demonstrate to voters the level of their transformation. Thus, both SdRP and MSzP won the second democratic elections and led their respective governments. Unlike KSČM in the Czech Republic, the successor parties in Hungary and Poland rehabilitated themselves as a plausible democratic alternative.

Consequently, the survey question evaluating the feature "removal of former party members," which reflects the demand for the exclusive system, confirmed that the Czech Republic was on a completely different trajectory from that of Hungary and Poland. A significantly higher proportion of the Czech general population supported the removal of former party members from positions of influence compared to the support in Hungary and Poland. The results of the multivariate analyses suggest that the perception of the former communist party as a proponent of human rights was negatively associated with the demands for removal of its members from public positions in the Czech Republic. The results were also highly significant in Poland, although the effect was weaker. The results were insignificant in Hungary. This may explain why Hungarians did not have any need for exclusive measures.

The perceptions about the former communist parties by the elites did not differ significantly from popular perceptions. In 1991 many Czechoslovak deputies perceived the members of the former *nomenklatura* class and their informers as untransformed: dangerous, corrupt, inefficient, and incapable of holding a position of trust. Such definitive views were seldom voiced during the parliamentary debate of the inclusive lustration system in Hungary. Hungarian deputies were more concerned about reducing the truth deficit and never seriously considered dismissals. In Poland, different perceptions about the former adversaries have led to quarrels and scandals, which were unprecedented in Central Europe. The case of Poland requires refining our first hypothesis that the choice of a particular lustration system is a function of the perception of the transformation status of former adversaries. While the perception of the former communist party as aligned with the old regime led to the approval of the exclusive system in Czechoslovakia and the perception of the former communist party as a transforming force led to the inclusive system in Hungary, conflicting perceptions about the former communist party led to the reconciliatory system in Poland: views of the party that was behind the martial law and human rights violations in the early 1980s clashed with the views that saw the party as a progressive force that handed over political power.

As to the second hypothesis, membership in the gray zone is a significant predictor of the support for the dismissal of tainted officials in the Czech Republic, while it fails to generate any significant effect in Hungary or Poland. It is a historical irony that a group of former communist party members tends to support dismissal of former communist party members from public posts in the Czech Republic. On the other hand, qualitative evidence from the Czech Republic suggests that this support may not be a result of socio-psychological needs to present oneself in a better light by accusing others of wrongdoing. Instead it is an instance of the banality of the gray zone that does not have needs for finger-pointing because its members lack any self-reflection. On the elite level, there may be a weak effect in support of lustration attributed to the gray zone in the Czech Republic and Hungary, where former dissidents either opposed the lustration system or tried to mollify its impacts. On the other hand, politicians of the gray zone in both countries were well aware of their moral deficit and sought public support of victims' organizations. Our results do not indicate any conclusion about the gray zone in Poland, where the mass opposition against the communist regime did not allow much space for people in-between.

5

The Politics of Lustration Systems

I was [a member of the Communist Party], of course. But first,
from an ideological point of view, I was never a Communist. In
Poland I've seen very few Communists, especially since the 1970's.
I met a lot of technocrats, opportunists, reformers, liberals.
— Aleksander Kwaśniewski[1]

Who is actually a communist? The one who was at some time in
the communist party? All sorts of people surely joined it; just
during the past decades seven million people went through its
ranks [in Czechoslovakia]. There were obviously not many
worshipping and enthusiastic communists or genuine servants of
the [former] regime, yet at the time [of transition] it was
impossible to separate ones from others by a wave of a magic stick.
It had to be a long and difficult process, especially when we wanted
to be not only just but also practical.
— Václav Havel, *Prosím stručně*[2]

The implementation of lustration systems was inevitably affected by the
political context in which these systems were embedded. However, once the
implementation of lustration systems began, the systems in turn started
affecting the political landscape. For many scholars, lustration systems orig-
inate in political scandals and create new political scandals. This chapter
concurs, and it proposes a hypothesis of virtual cycles according to which
the implementation of lustration systems is affected by the perceptions of

former adversaries that these very systems shape. Pursuant to our theorization in Chapter 2, the exclusive system fosters a rigid view of former adversaries, which increases demands for the exclusive system. Alternative systems foster a flexible view that allows the possibility of decreasing demand for lustrations. This chapter explores these hypotheses in the political contexts in which these systems were embedded.

The Lustration Cycles

Political realists tend to see transitional law and justice as a function of politics.[3] Personnel systems are no exceptions, given their propensity to be used, or misused, for political purposes. An exclusive system may be viewed as a means to redistribute political influence in transitional administration; an inclusive system as a means to shame political opponents; and a reconciliatory system as a means to demonstrate the dishonesty of political rivals. Indeed, a number of political leaders in Central Europe have been accused of using lustrations in order to strengthen their grip on power and to discredit their political opponents.[4] Others may have had an interest in shelving or circumventing lustration systems in order to avoid disclosing their own pasts or the pasts of their political allies. Reflecting on this process, Cynthia Horne and Margaret Levi conceptualize "a lustration cycle" to explain why lustrations damage the credibility of government: "politicians have an incentive to use lustration against their opposition as a means of discrediting their opponents. Once this is done, the opposition, when it obtains power, retaliates."[5] The propensity of lustrations to create political scandals and the abuse of lustrations for political purposes have led Csilla Kiss to consider the entire process a failure.[6]

Indeed, if we were guided only by the results of common population surveys, the implementation of lustrations in the Czech Republic, Hungary, and Poland would be considered a failure. In our survey on the effects of lustration systems conducted in these three countries in 2007, we asked respondents to assess the objectives of the three lustration systems: personnel discontinuity, transparency, and confessions of tainted officials.[7] The mean score for perceptions of personnel changes in the Czech Republic, which implemented an exclusive system (at 1.26 on the scale ranging from 0 to 4), is almost identical to that of Poland (at 1.28), which pursued a reconciliatory system (Figure 5.1). The level of transparency in Hungary was the lowest among the three countries in spite of the exposures-based

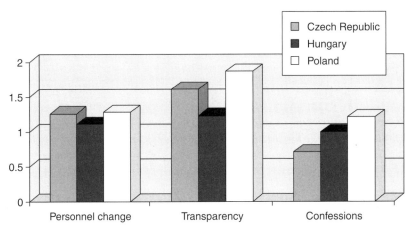

Figure 5.1. Personnel change, transparency, and confessions in the Czech Republic, Hungary, and Poland in 2007. The figure presents the mean scores for questions about the major objectives of the three lustration systems. The wording of the survey questions was as follows: (1) personnel change: "Most of those who in the past evidently informed the secret police about their fellow citizens have left the state apparatus"; (2) transparency: "There is enough available information to determine whether in the past a state official informed the secret police about his fellow citizens"; (3) confessions: "Most of those state officials who evidently informed the secret police about their fellow citizens confessed their secret collaboration." Respondents could choose from five response categories, ranging from the most positive (coded as 4) to most negative (0), allowing a neutral response (2) but excluding indecisive answers ("don't know"). Source: David, Lustration Systems, Trust in Government, and Reconciliation.

inclusive system. Poland was seen as a leader in public confessions, which was the method of its lustration system. But even in Poland, the results were still in negative values.

There are a number of reasons why a government's policy may be considered a failure. To be sure, a lack of political consensus can make any policy a target of partisan and ideological struggles and that may, in turn, undermine its implementation and the assessment of its results. The policy may have been poorly designed in the first place, its objectives may have been unattainable, and its implementation may have been affected by another policy. There may be discrepancies between high social expectations and low political will to address a burning social issue. But in addition to typical policy failures, lustration systems may fail due to their political nature: lustrations and other personnel systems affect not only the anonymous mass of government bureaucrats but also the top positions in the state apparatus. This makes personnel systems as politically sensitive as changes in electoral systems and gerrymandering of voting districts. While the former affects the personnel composition in non-elected positions, the latter affect the personnel situation in the legislature. However, in contrast to elections, the stakes in lustrations may rise even higher owing to their profound symbolic meanings. Lustrations may affect not only the political lives of candidates for public posts but also their ideological and moral standing in society vis-à-vis the wrongdoings in the past. While elections create losers, lustrations may create losers of history.

These considerations suggest that lustration systems may play a dual role during transition. Similar to other methods of transitional justice, as Teitel argues, they are constituted by, and constitutive of, political transition.[8] Political leaders shape lustration systems as lawmakers, law enforcers, political campaigners, and opinion makers, but they are subjects as well as objects of lustrations. Not only does the political context affect the implementation of lustration systems but lustration systems also affect the political landscape and memories of the past. Consequently, lustration systems may create a new value-normative reality that may in turn affect the implementation of lustration systems and their assessment. The virtual value-normative reality consists of people's perceptions shaped by the media's reflections on the process. The continuous interplay between the evolving perceptions of people associated with past regimes and the lustration system is a cyclical process, although its dynamics differ from the small tit-for-tat cycle hypothesized by Horne and Levi. Here lustration systems affect people's perceptions, which in turn affect views of lustration systems.

Different lustration systems may move in different virtual cycles. The need for exclusive lustration may not only stem from the perception about the tainted officials owing to their actions in the past but the perceptions of them as tainted may be strengthened by the implementation of lustration law. On the other hand, pursuant to our considerations in Chapter 2, we expect that the lustration cycles would decelerate in Poland and Hungary. In particular, continuing exposures and confessions may make lustration processes gradually redundant. If exposures are followed by denials, excuses, and blaming the previous system, then everyone may become a victim of the totalitarian machinery; nobody will be perceived as tainted, and lustrations would be abandoned. This may explain the low demand for opening secret archives in Hungary where the public's access to them is considerably more restricted than in the Czech Republic and Poland. If confessions signify a moral transformation of wrongdoers, one cannot exclude the possibility that individual transformation would inspire social transformation and demand for lustrations would drop. On the other hand, each lustration cycle may—at least temporarily—accelerate. Any new discovery of a tainted official in the administration may be evidence of an inefficiency of the system of exposures in Hungary, which may lead to new discoveries and new claims of inefficiency. Likewise the conviction of a dishonest official in Poland may lead to rechecking of confessions and new discoveries of lustration liars.

The conflicting theorizations suggest that the question of lustration cycles is an empirical question, which is explored in the following sections. We explore whether the hypothesis of virtual lustration cycles has any substance by looking at the broader context of the politics of overcoming the past in the Czech Republic, Hungary, and Poland. In doing so, we explore the hypothesis about small lustration cycles: the lustration process is a function of political power which is in turn affected by the lustration process. We also explore a number of more prosaic hypotheses that may affect a delivery of any public policy: its scope, its procedures, the implementation of other policies, and other factors (Figure 5.2 summarizes their interplay).

The hypotheses of virtual lustration cycles are highly relevant to the study of transitional justice and its psychological assumptions. Accelerating cycles would signify a difficulty of overcoming the past by means of transitional justice. Instead of purging the past, releasing pent-up frustration, and "purifying public life," the periodic recall of the past through lustration rituals would revive the past. Vice versa, an eventual deceleration of any of the lustration cycles—through the rituals of dismissal, revelation, or confession—would signify a promising avenue for the application of a particular lustration model. Deceleration would indicate that the flame of the past has been extinguished[9] and that purification has been completed, marking the end of transition.

From Dismissals to Ritual Sacrifices: The Politics of the Exclusive System in the Czech Republic

Background: The implementation of the exclusive lustration system in the Czech Republic did not appear to give rise to more problems than were experienced with the implementation of any other law. Dismissals were

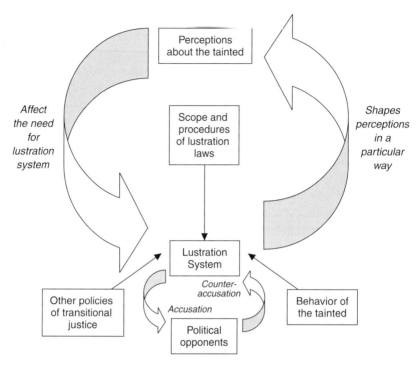

Figure 5.2. Lustration cycles. The implementation and assessment of lustration systems may be affected by (i) perceptions that these very systems shape, creating virtual lustration cycles; (ii) their use and misuse in political struggle, as hypothesized by Horne and Levi; and (iii) general factors that can affect lustration systems like any other policy, such as its design (e.g., scope and procedures), existence of other policies, and the adaptability of the addressees of the policy.

carried out relatively efficiently and decisively. During the initial stages of transition in Czechoslovakia, the exclusive system enabled the new non-communist elite to secure control over the leading posts in the state administration, to launch crucial reforms, and to catch up with Poland and Hungary, where political and economic transformation started earlier.[10] Although the exclusive system was relatively successfully implemented, instances of circumvention were also reported: the system was by-passed in some cases by means of informal "authorization."[11] This enabled people who were not eligible to occupy certain specified posts because they did not meet the lustration criteria to temporarily fill positions they would not otherwise have been authorized to hold.[12]

Backed by ODS during the first four years of its existence, the government, led by the Social Democratic Party (ČSSD) from 1998 to 2006, strengthened its ties with old *nomenklatura* cadres.[13] Because the country's lustration system prevented many of the previous vanguard from officially holding public posts, they became part of a team of advisors to the prime minister, Miloš Zeman (ČSSD).[14] Many of them had held positions either within the secretariats of KSČ or the Socialist Association of the Youth (SSM), had graduated from the Communist Party's University of Politics, or had engaged in business activities with Miroslav Šlouf, a former apparatchik and Zeman's chief advisor who was considered by the Czech press as possessing almost supernatural powers.[15]

The appointment of Stanislav Gross (ČSSD) to the seat of the minister of the interior (2000–2004) and the prime minister of the Czech Republic (2004–5) was also marked by the return of compromised officials to public life. Gross became a minister at the age of thirty and later the youngest prime minister in Central Europe. He had no previous administrative experience and had only recently completed his education at the time of his appointment.[16] Thus, he was compelled to rely on more experienced cadres. Perhaps the most visible of them was Pavel Přibyl, who was appointed as the head of the prime minister's office, despite the fact that he had previously been in charge of suppressing opposition demonstrations that took place before 1989.[17] It is likely that to divert attention away from the return of personnel from the past regime Gross pointed to the failures of his predecessors: he announced in 2001 that negative lustration certificates had been illegally issued to many former members of the army intelligence.[18] As a result, 150,000 lustration certificates that had already been issued were rechecked. Of these, 117 were found to be illegal, nearly all of which had been issued in 1992 as a result of the "incorrect analysis" of documents.[19] Although the Czech press reported that the revelation unsettled NATO officials,[20] this number represented less than 0.08 percent of those that were rechecked.

No serious abuses of state power that would have constituted human rights violations committed by personnel associated with the past regime were reported in the Czech Republic after the lustration law was approved.[21] However, the abuses of power were restored in Slovakia after the new regime had halted the implementation of the Czechoslovak lustration law.[22] During the years 1994–98, Slovakia was ruled by the semi-democratic regime of Prime Minister Vladimír Mečiar of the Movement for Democratic Slovakia (HZDS). The country's counterintelligence agency, the

Slovak Information Service (SIS), allegedly employed a large number of former secret police agents, including its first deputy, Jaroslav Svěchota.[23] SIS was involved in several incidents that seriously violated essential democratic principles. It placed its opposition parties and politicians under surveillance; monitored churches, trade unions, and journalists critical of the Mečiar government; organized the abduction of the son of Mečiar's rival, Slovak president Michal Kováč; sabotaged public meetings; and blew up the cars of journalists.[24] These illegal activities were carried out by the 52nd Department, which was under the direct command of Svěchota.[25] Consequently, Slovakia was temporarily suspended from the negotiations concerning its membership in NATO and the EU.

Had the law been in force, Mečiar himself might not have been eligible to hold the appointed post of prime minister, depending on the nature of his alleged collaboration with the secret police.[26] This also raises a question about the extent to which the exclusive system was a factor in the "conversion" of Mečiar, formerly a federalist, into a Slovak separatist, thereby contributing indirectly to the breakup of Czechoslovakia. The lustration law went into effect in November 1991 and the fate of the Federation was sealed seven months later.[27] It also begs the question as to what Mečiar's motive was: was it because he feared that the lustration law would deprive him of the eligibility to become prime minister or because it would prevent him from blackmailing his political opponents?

Nevertheless, the Czech lustration system was unable to stop government officials from authorizing the suspicious arms trade. At the official level, economic slowdown and increasing unemployment at the end of the 1990s forced the social-democratic government to implement a more lenient licensing policy. For example, the Ministry of Foreign Affairs, led by Jan Kavan, was alleged to have agreed to the export of arms to Sri Lanka and Iran; at an unofficial level, by the end of the 1990s, some companies had been allegedly supplying countries like Algeria, Libya, Iran, and North Korea for a number of years:[28] "In a way, it is a tradition. The Czech Republic has from the past had very good relations with these countries. [It] has a number of receivables from the communist era there. It is still trying to have them repaid. Czech businessmen have really 'special' relations with local politicians and authorities. Because of its risky nature, any deal with such a country, both legal and illegal, increases the value of the bid. The amount of money involved is able to shut the eyes of politicians, officials, or businessmen in Prague over problems that may arise."[29]

Although the system substantially helped reduce political tensions, suspicions, and unwarranted accusations, scandals typical of the pre-lustration stage were also reported. The system did not entirely stop the leak of material, often published selectively, which led to further political intrigue. In most cases such materials attracted media attention because they concerned persons who had held high public office. For instance, news items concerning Jan Kavan have continued to be released because of his high position as the minister of foreign affairs (1998–2002) and as president of the UN General Assembly (2002–3). They included a broadcast on a Czech private TV program showing him meeting with alleged secret police members on his arrival to the Czech Republic in 1989, despite a court's 1996 ruling that he had not intentionally collaborated with the secret police; and an article about his 1996 Senate campaign, in which two alleged former secret police members had participated.[30] In his dispute with the daily *Mladá fronta Dnes* in 1998, the High Court in Prague ordered the daily to apologize to Kavan for falsely claiming that he was persona non grata in the UK but according to press it did agree with the daily that Kavan was "a convicted liar" there.[31] In 2002, Havel asked Kavan to resign after his aide, a former member of communist intelligence services, attempted to solicit a murder of an investigative journalist.[32] Jan Kavan denied his conscious collaboration with StB and a number of progressive intellectuals wrote in his defense.[33]

The system also suffered as a result of its narrow scope, which dissatisfied the expectations of a large part of the public who had anticipated a more comprehensive process for dealing with the past. As was the case in Hungary and Poland, the Czech lustration system was narrowly drawn. In its forward-looking dimension, it did not concern the entire public service. It only applied to leading positions in the administration, and it did not regulate the economic sector. This meant that members of the former repressive apparatus were allowed to run "their" businesses in many areas.[34] Unfortunately, their enterprises were often associated with *tunneling*, which reflected mismanagement, lack of transparency, fraud, and bankruptcy, which were highlighted by the press. For example, an alleged former secret police agent, Václav Junek, who was said to have been involved in industrial espionage in the French chemical industry, became the general manager of the Chemapol Group, and an alleged former *nomenklatura* cadre, Lubomír Soudek, became the general manager of Škoda Plzeň. The enterprises managed by them were almost all declared bankrupt.[35] Moreover, Soudek tried to supply weapons to regimes under the UN embargo.[36] It is therefore not surprising that the lustration process was perceived as inefficient in the eyes of the public, who were not aware of its narrow scope. According to a poll conducted in the Czech Republic in 2000, 32 percent of respondents thought that the lustration law was beneficial to democracy, while 27 percent held the opposite view; 29 percent thought that it was beneficial to the personnel situation in enterprises and offices, while 30 percent held the opposite view.[37]

In spite of its narrow scope, there is evidence to suggest that the Czech lustration system was fairly effective in decreasing the influence of tainted officials on political and economic transformation within a few years of its enactment. The law made it difficult to keep or redeploy old personnel in crucial decision-making positions in the privatization process. The business class of *nomenklatura* cadres could no longer rely on their connections with the Communist Party (KSČM), whose political influence also diminished due to its repeated electoral defeats and political isolation. The old power networks had to find other ways of pursuing their objectives: they exercised their influence over parties that were committed to privatization by means of liberal provisions on the financing of political parties.[38]

Assessment: The politics seemed to be closely associated with the implementation of the exclusive system as suggested by the hypothesis of small lustration cycles. Selective leaks intended to discredit Kavan may be seen as evidence. Conversely, the case of social democratic advisors and the case of Mečiar may reveal the potential of lustration in preventing abuses of public office. Nevertheless, these situations may be reinterpreted in terms of virtual circles. The lustration system fostered an image—sometimes true, sometimes inaccurate, but always the same—of people associated with former regimes as tainted. For instance, the demand for the use of lustration in areas in private sector may be attributed to the perception—fostered by its application in the public sphere, which concerned different individuals—that all people associated with the past regime are officially tainted and intractable as a class.

The exclusive system has also strengthened the negative image of KSČM. The party was politically isolated before the approval of the lustration law and remained marginalized thereafter because the political costs of any public contacts with KSČM increased. It was never part of any governing coalition; President Havel never invited KSČM to political consultations, and even its potential ally, the Czech Social Democratic Party

(ČSSD), approved a statement of non-cooperation with KSČM at the central level in 1997.[39] Nobody wanted to be tainted by the association with former communists. True, the main reason why KSČM remains in political isolation arises from its lack of effort to pursue discontinuity with its past. In Chapter 4, we showed how the party was perceived and how this perception led to the exclusive system. On the other hand, being forced into a corner, the communist leaders may have found it difficult to persuade their voters that democracy is for everyone.

In this environment, the confessions and apologies given by the people associated with former regimes were costly and seldom resonated with the public, which tended to see them as insincere. Typical responses to allegations of secret collaboration therefore included the denial of conscious collaboration, admissions concerning the interests of the secret police, and at best explanations of such contacts.[40] Confessions by people who had collaborated with the secret services in the past were rare, although one of the leading members of KSČM even issued an apology for injustices committed in the name of communism.[41]

If exclusive lustration seemed unable to heal historical divisions, it may have initially created new ones between former elites previously associated under the banner of the Civic Forum (OF). Although all non-communist parties originally supported lustrations,[42] the former dissidents held ideological positions that differed from the newly emerging center-right parties (ODS and ODA). Although some former dissidents used lustrations when it was convenient to do so,[43] those associated with the Prague Spring of 1968 felt threatened by the right-wing interpretation fostered by lustration that could summarily be depicted under the rubric: "there is no *former* communist." This interpretation effectively applied a biological perspective on political opinions because "a former communist" would be like a "former Black man."[44] The right claimed that everyone who had joined the communist party but later changed his political views and left the party or was expelled would always be considered tainted by the communist past. A person could never be separated from his or her past, he or she was not capable of changing opinions, and any eventual demonstration of such a change could never be considered credible. In rewriting the country's history, the center-right tried to discredit the generation of "sixty-eighters," previously held as heroes by many, by denouncing them as naïve builders of "the third way" that would bring the country to the "third world."[45] No serious consideration was given to the fact that twenty years of persecution might have changed the worldview of many of the so-called reform communists.

On the other hand, some former dissidents expected that after experiencing years in underground opposition to the previous regime they were purified of their communist past and were the only ones who could legitimately make moral judgments about the past. Unlike the Polish dissidents, who founded the Committee for the Protection of Workers (KOR) and participated in the Solidarity movement, the elitist views of Prague dissident-intellectuals prevented them from effectively communicating their ideas to what they denigrated as "the gray zone," the rest of society. Writing in 1996, Jiřina Šiklová, a former member of the Czechoslovak Communist Party and later a political prisoner of the communist regime, apparently felt unsettled when the problem of lustration became a matter for the whole society, not just the dissidents' elite: "Young people, not yet 'invited' [to join the party], and people who would have liked to have joined but could not (perhaps [because] their sister had emigrated), were placed on a waiting list [for party membership]. Such people are among those who now take credit for never [having] been members of the Communist Party. Such people were among those who clamored for the Screening Law's five-year extension."[46]

Šiklová's ideological position, typical of the Civic Movement (OH), the dissidents' party, irritated the center-right ODS for several reasons. She questioned the credibility of people who demanded the extension of lustration law because their past non-partisanship could be attributed either to their age or to the communist party's perception of them as untrustworthy for minor reasons. She did not mention dissidents who supported the extension of the lustration law, such as Václav Benda and Jan Ruml (both ODS in the mid 1990s) and the entire Confederation of Political Prisoners.[47] Consequently, ODS may have been under the impression that OH did not consider the problem of trustworthy government a political problem that concerned everyone but a moral problem that could be exclusively entrusted to people with dissident pedigrees of the 1970s and 1980s, not the 1950s and the 1960s. Although this ideological platform largely disappeared from the mainstream discourse after the electoral defeat of OH in 1992, it significantly weakened the moral credentials of Václav Klaus and his ODS.

Thus, the exclusive lustration system created three different sets of interpretations of the past in the Czech Republic. Former communists, being defiant, insisted on the legitimacy of the previous regime and illegiti-macy of any measure devised to deal with it. Former dissidents associated with the centrist OH nurtured their moral purity and intellectual superior-ity, suggesting that any lustration process that had not been pursued by them could not be considered credible. The center-right ODS and Václav Klaus, whose adoption of the moral discourse put him on the defensive, saw virtue in moral poverty: the genuine heroes of the past were ordinary people because they resisted the system by "their inefficiency."[48] Thus, while the communists locked dissidents in jail and "the ordinary people" drove their faulty Škodas to spend the weekend at their cottages in the Krkonoše Mountains, a decade or two later all three groups claimed the moral high ground as the righteous masters of the past.

Different interpretations of history that arose from the lustration laws have in turn affected the lustration politics. In contrast to the interpreta-tions of former dissidents and communistic interpretations of the past, mainstream political discourse has emerged as strongly anti-communistic. Initiatives to outlaw the Communist Party in the Parliament, the condem-nations of the communist regime, and anti-communist petitions, such as "Communists Should Not Be Talked To," became part of the national folk-lore in post-transition Czech Republic.[49] The Communist Party was said to be "waiting for power in the shadow,"[50] according to the title of a book by two young journalists who argued against communists and communism, not for the prosecution of crimes committed under the communist regime.[51] The former members of the secret police and their alleged collab-orators have been routinely subjected to public ridicule by using, for instance, their cover names, such as Germ, which described the front man of a rock band, the Germs, who was allegedly a secret informer.[52] In 2000, an exhibition organized by the Pode Bal art group, which displayed a num-ber of politicians who allegedly collaborated with StB, was entitled "Malík urvi: Galerie etablované nomenklatury" (Little as Holes: The Gallery of the Established Nomenklatura).[53] But the title of the exhibition provided for a second interpretation: "Malí kurvi" (Little Assholes).[54]

In the years since the collapse of socialism, it has been increasingly difficult to discover new traitors. To reaffirm its corporate identity, Czech society had to find soft targets or to restage the rituals. As to the former, the celebrity actress Jiřina Bohdalová was accused of secret collaboration although nothing in the file suggested that; in fact she was psychologically tortured while her father was a political prisoner but she had to struggle for years to have her name removed from the official list of informers.[55] As to the latter, in 2008, an exhibition on Prague's Wenceslas Square displayed pictures of twenty-eight former secret police officers.[56] The lack of tangible purposes for such exhibitions makes it hard to avoid the impression that their meaning was merely symbolic and cultural: a ritual sacrifice.

The continuing presence of Jan Kavan in top politics, and the contradictory court decisions, turned his lustration into public ridicule. In 2000, Kavan's entire file was published as a book with his alleged cover name, Kato, in the title: *Kato: Příběh opravdového člověka* (Kato: A Story of a Genuine Person).[57] Owing to its frequent use in crosswords, Kato is known to most Czechs as "the Roman moral censor."[58] The subtitle referred to the Soviet war novel *A Story of a Genuine Person* by Boris Polevoy, which was compulsory reading in Czech schools. In 2003, another book published the analysis of his file and outlined some of Kavan's controversial activities after 1989.[59] Thus, lustration that started as a secular process with the examination of secret police archives was eclipsed by its second meaning: it became a means of ritual sacrifice that was periodically repeated to purge the body of politics of the tainted officials in conformity with the new anti-communist religion.

Becoming a dominant part of the modern Czech culture, the ideological clichés of anti-communist rhetoric fostered by the lustration system not only affected politics but in turn affected the country's lustration system: they could explain the continuation of the lustration system, the informal expansion of its scope, and the indiscriminate treatment of persons affected by it. First, although the system was originally devised as a process of dealing with personnel in the state administration that would last for five years, it was extended in 1995 and indefinitely extended in 2000. The prominent status of lustration in the national mythology prevented it from being abandoned, despite the fact that the risk of the relapse of the communist regime had waned even before the country joined NATO and the EU. Threats to security came from other quarters, and corruption became associated with bureaucrats and politicians across the political spectrum.

Second, the lustration system started to be implemented in administrative positions that went beyond the scope of the lustration system, including the posts of ordinary rank-and-file bureaucrats. The presence of any personnel associated with the past typically led the press to demand their resignation.[60] Third, the memory of the past fostered by the lustration system led to the indiscriminate social construction of people associated with the former regime. In the initial stages, the exclusion was also justified by mistrust of people who were seen as the vulnerable ones, those who, for whatever reason, could not sustain the pressure created by the former regime. The second decade of the application of the lustration system eclipsed that interpretation. The collaborators were held to be accountable for the acts of the previous regime. All of them were considered its protagonists; none of them was its victim. There were no "former" communists or collaborators; anyone who had ever associated with the communist regime acquired the official status of "a former communist" or "a former collaborator," being tainted for life.

Shame and Denial: The Politics and Implementation of the Inclusive System in Hungary

Background: The implementation of the inclusive system in Hungary contrasted with the country's ongoing transformation of its historical divisions. The negotiation on handing over political power in the summer of 1989, initiated by MSzMP (the ruling communist party), enabled the party to strengthen its image as a pragmatic democratic left party after transition, one that was not bound by its ideological dogmas but defined by its malleability in reaching out to its enemies.[61] The Hungarian transition received another strong transformative impulse when the Alliance of Free Democrats (SzDSz), a party of former dissidents, gave moral weight to the exoneration of its former persecutors in the Socialist Party (MSzP) after the elections in 1994. At the time when the lustration system went into effect, SzDSz accepted an invitation to join the coalition government with MSzP, a deal that allowed both parties to rule unchallenged between 1994 and 1998, and again between 2002 and 2006.[62]

In stark contrast with the situation in the Czech Republic and Poland where dissidents never formed a ruling coalition with former communists, in Hungary both parties were able to relinquish their diverging pedigrees, transforming themselves into modern reformist parties that worked toward the country's accession to NATO and the EU. When the coalition eventually restarted the lustration process at the request of the Constitutional Court, both parties benefited from what may be seen as the legitimization of the status quo: some tainted officials were exposed in exchange for their continuation in power.[63] Contrary to what had taken place in Czechoslovakia, it was not that difficult to reach a relatively wide social consensus on the continuance of the personnel that had implemented "goulash socialism" under the rule of János Kádár.

Many agree that the process of dealing with the past in Hungary, given its moderate nature, cannot be considered a success. Hungarian scholars, however, tend to see the failure in different ways. According to János Kis, a Hungarian political philosopher, former dissident, and a leader of SzDSz in 1990–91, dealing with the past would not be ideal in any society. Hungary in his view was not an exception in making progress in some domains while failing in others.[64] In assessing the impact of the inclusive system, Kis did not see the role of exposure as contributing directly to enhancing the general public's trust of the new government; he thought that revelations of relevant information about the past conduct of public figures was likely to decrease the level of mistrust in government.[65]

On the other hand, Sebestyén Gorka, a former member of the parliamentary committee that investigated the alleged collaboration of Prime Minister Medgyessy with secret services, considered the same element of exposure without dismissal as a major deficiency of the lustration process in Hungary.[66] In direct opposition to Kis's view, Gorka hailed the Czech model of exclusive lustrations as doing "a relatively good job of excising the cancer of post-dictatorship networks."[67] Indeed, Medgyessy and many other politicians whose pasts were exposed defied popular demands and refused to resign from their posts. But exposure without dismissal was precisely the principle that has been adopted as a cornerstone of the inclusive system in Hungary.

Instead of "increasing the transparency of government," the role of exposure has been seen as creating political scandals in Hungary. Earlier we mentioned Horne and Levi's claim that lustrations created political scandals that undermined trustworthy government.[68] Gábor Halmai, a prominent Hungarian lawyer, has partly confirmed their diagnosis: "The whole process [of lustrations] was unfortunately very much discredited by the politics, so it does not mean very much to the people but is merely a political means for fighting the political enemies."[69] But he has diagnosed the origin of the symptom in the fact that the Parliament "very late enacted a soft law on lustration of very few public officials, without dealing with the access of both the victims and the general public to the files."[70] In other words, it was not a lustration system based on exposure but the lack of exposure of a wide range of officials conducted strictly according to law since the beginning of the transition that created the difficult situation.

In 2002, one of the largest scandals in the history of post-communist Hungary broke out after the newspaper *Magyar Nemzet* revealed that the country's newly elected prime minister and ten ministers in post-1989 governments were associated with the secret police.[71] Péter Medgyessy of the Socialist Party (MSzP), alleged cover name D-209, eventually admitted that he was a communist counterintelligence officer from 1977 to 1982.[72] Defying the demand of the media and the opposition for resignation, Medgyessy maintained that he had not violated the lustration law. However, the opposition and his coalition partners from SzDSz pushed socialists to propose a bill to broaden access to the secret archives and to establish a parliamentary commission to investigate the pasts of government officials.[73]

The commission, headed by Imre Mécs, was mandated to investigate the links between post-1990 government officials and secret services. Although the commission was established by a unanimous vote,[74] it did not have an easy life. Hungarian president Ferenc Mádl called the commission "illegitimate and unconstitutional" and charged it with interfering in the country's lustration system.[75] The members of Fidesz and the Hungarian Democratic Forum (MDF) walked out of the commission session on August 5, 2002, protesting the way in which the commission chairman handled classified documents and suggesting that the commission served to exonerate Medgyessy;[76] the socialist members of the commission led by its deputy, László Toller, submitted a separate report on its activities, claiming that Medgyessy's links had not violated any legal regulations at that time.[77] The attitude of those under investigation toward the commission differed: all members of the Medgyessy government, former prime minister Gyula Horn, two members of his 1990–94 cabinet, István Balsai and Balázs Horváth, and two members of Viktor Orbán's government (1998–2002), Ibolya Dávid and György Matolcsy, as well as parliamentary speaker Katalin Szili gave their consent to have the commission make public its findings on them, while the National Bank (MNB) governor Zsigmond Járai and László Kövér, who in 1998–2000 was in charge of the secret services in the cabinet headed by Orbán, did not.[78] The press reported that the commission ended its work in acrimony.[79]

When it became clear that the public would not be allowed to learn the commission's results, its findings started to leak to the press. First, the daily *Népszabadság* published allegations that a former minister in Orbán's government, Imre Boros, alleged cover name Comrade D 8, served previously as a chief secret officer in the III/II counterintelligence department in 1989.[80] A few days later, the daily *Magyar Hírlap* published a list of eleven ministers and state secretaries, five of them from the Orbán's center-right government, who allegedly had ties to the secret police.[81] Orbán's Fidesz responded with a press statement that the Mécs commission was running "politically amok."[82]

The exposures, revelations, and speculations had a twofold effect. First, it signaled that people associated with the former regime belonged to all major political parties. This confirmed the initial allegations that former secret collaborators had been employed across the political spectrum.[83] Second, the revelations created media turbulence and sharpened the political contest to a level that was more typical of confrontational Poland than of consensual Hungary. Consequently, 75 percent of the Hungarian public thought that the parliamentary commission headed by Mécs should wind up its work.[84]

The reason why Medgyessy's secret collaboration with security services in the past had not been discovered earlier could be attributed to the narrow scope of its lustration system. The system concerned only department III/III of the Interior Ministry, which was mandated to deal with internal enemies, leaving out departments III/I (foreign intelligence) and III/II (counterintelligence) because they were deemed necessary to protect national interests.[85] However, according to Miklós Haraszti (SzDSz), a former dissident, "all departments—not only 3/3—were involved in acts of political repression."[86] Another problem related to the inclusive system in Hungary was probably due to the strict evidentiary procedures that were followed before the official exposures could take place; this made it likely that some former informers could slip through the legal net.[87] György Markó, the first head of the Historical Archive Office, which served as a data provider for the judicial lustration committees, did not exclude this possibility: "We sent materials concerning more persons than who were later condemned [exposed]. The act was strict. . . . Several conditions needed to be satisfied in order to be able to condemn someone, i.e., she collaborated with the secret police. Nota bene, we had more hits than condemnations. But in this process, we served as data providers: I only had a formal role in the judgment procedure; we only sent materials. Judges were there to decide."[88] In social science methodology, this situation is described as a Type II error: a failure to reject the null hypothesis although it is not true. The presumption of innocence is upheld although a defendant committed the crime. In the political context of the Hungarian transition, the past of public officials may not have been exposed because there was not enough evidence required by the lustration law to prove that they had actually collaborated with the secret police. This has caused politicians and the media to question some lustration decisions.

Assessment: At first glance, the above narrative supports the hypothesis that political scandals and lustrations are intertwined. Politicians seemed to use lustration to discredit their opponents. In line with more prosaic hypotheses about the inherent problems of particular policies, we can also observe that owing to it is narrow scope and strict procedures the Hungarian lustration system allowed more scandals to erupt, which intensified demands for additional lustration procedures. However, the lustration system also created a virtual reality that affected both the politics and the assessment of its implementation in a more nuanced way. The inclusive lustration systems sent an ideological message about tainted officials, which affected their perception and the perception of the past. However, this message was different than the message of the exclusive system in the Czech Republic. The shaming message of exposure was moderated by the message of non-dismissal.

In this environment, denial remained the typical response of officials to revelations about their tainted pasts, although some admitted partial responsibility, some apologized, and some prominent politicians confessed. Medgyessy, for instance, initially avoided any clear statement on his past, but he later admitted that he had been a counterintelligence officer from 1977 to 1982.[89] He explained that his role as a secret agent in the Finance Ministry had been to keep the country's preparations for joining the International Monetary Fund secret from the Soviet Union.[90] As the scandal accelerated, Medgyessy, in an interview on Hungarian television on June 23, 2002, even apologized to the electorate for not having revealed his past as a communist counterintelligence agent before the April 2002 elections: "I admit making a mistake in not telling voters about my past. I am sorry and I ask forgiveness."[91] No such admissions ever happened within the culture of the exclusive system in the Czech Republic.

The previous socialist prime minister, Guyla Horn (1994–98), also admitted, at least partially, his role in the past. In his biography published before the 1994 election campaign, Horn confessed that he had been a member of the militia that worked on the suppression of the uprising in

1956,[92] Another prominent example of confession was that of the populist politician István Csurka in the initial stages of transition when lustrations were not yet regulated by the lustration law. Csurka clashed with then prime minister József Antall (1990–93), demanding his resignation. Antall retaliated by hinting that he had evidence about Csurka's involvement with the socialist secret services. According to Gil Eyal, Iván Szelényi and Eleanor Townsley, "Csurka's (rather savvy) response was to publish a 'self-lustration,' in which he described how he was recruited and what he did as an informer. Public reaction to this confession was telling: many people were moved by his 'courage' in confessing—it was evidence that his soul was 'saved.' After this confession, not even his most bitter enemies could use his informer past against him. The confession purified Csurka."[93] Confessions typically occurred in situations in which the individuals had nothing to lose (e.g., retired informants), they had much to gain (e.g., top officials), or they could not reasonably continue their denial in the face of mounting evidence against them. Although hailed by intellectuals as manifestations of human courage, cases of confession were still relatively rare in Hungary. Even before the Medgyessy case started to occupy the front pages of all major dailies, any case of exposure was typically accompanied by the exposed person's denial. Sanctions for denials were extremely rare. In one case, Imre Boros said he had been blackmailed into working with state security organizations during the communist era[94] before he was accused of lying and eventually forced out of MDF.[95]

The spread of denials has made the Hungarian public receptive to the excuses of people who were exposed. The public that witnessed this drama may have been sympathetic to the plight of those who attributed their collaboration to forces beyond their control in one political regime only to be punished for it by another. Why should a person who fell "victim" under communism continue to be victimized in a free society? Denial effectively transferred people's human agency and individual responsibility for their actions in the past to the abstract structural forces of the former regime. As a result, the role of transgressors as victims was given empathetic consideration in Hungary. A survey conducted at the end of 2002 found that 26 percent of Hungarians viewed former collaborators as victims of the dictatorship.[96] If the culture of denials prevailed, the lustrations would be redundant.

The Hungarian center-right was concerned that it had lost the ideological battle over the memory of the socialist era. The inclusive lustration system led to denials or confessions, which did not condemn the previous regime and its protagonists as vividly as dismissals. The center-right launched a counteroffensive. In 2002, a few months before the elections, Hungary opened the so-called House of Terror, a museum that was backed by Prime Minister Orbán and his Fidesz.[97] Being symbolically located in a building that had been used by the Nazi Arrow Cross Party and in the 1950s by the communist secret police The State Protection Authority (ÁVH) as their headquarters, the museum was seen as meeting both historical and political goals: equating communism with fascism may have served as a means of discrediting the past of MSzP.[98] Although the political architects of the museum lost the elections in 2002 and again in 2006,[99] the museum survived and has been widely attended by Hungarians of whom one million visited the museum by 2005.[100] However, the symbolic message of the museum only reinforced the message of the inclusive system, which attributed the responsibility for the past to the abstract state structure.

Fidesz's feelings about losing to ex-communists were not entirely unwarranted for another reason. The interconnectedness between the social class system and its purported political advocates was upended in Hungary. While the center-right engaged in populist rhetoric, the nominally leftist MSzP continued to represent the interests of large businesses and to pursue policies that were considered antisocial by the international left.[101] In interviews with ordinary members of Fidesz in 2006, a man in his sixties lamented a lack of discontinuity with the past and the continuation of "the new class" of communist apparatchiks in the new system:

Before 1990 there was a ruling class, the political elite. Now the forty- to forty-five-year-old, well-educated speakers of foreign languages are the descendants of the old elite of the cadres. . . . One only has to glance at the recent Hungarian government and the one hundred wealthiest people of Hungary. These two groups are full of millionaires who were brought up in the former regime. Among the members of the [socialist] government there are at least four or five billionaires. These billionaires strongly opposed capitalism twenty years ago, and they fought for overthrowing capitalism. Here one sees a schizoid thing: people who claimed that communism and socialism were the only true way and opposed rotting capitalism are those who are spreading the message of the market right now. How can this be?[102]

In 2006 another socialist prime minister, Ferenc Gyurcsány, admitted that he had lied to the electorate about the true scale of the country's budget deficit.[103] Riots and massive demonstrations broke out in September and continued until October when the country commemorated the fiftieth anniversary of Soviet military intervention and the Budapest uprising in 1956. The event served as a platform to release pent-up frustration with what many had seen as ongoing socialist rule. In contrast with the memory of the military intervention in Czechoslovakia, which has been portrayed in mainstream discourse there as an internal struggle within the communist party that teaches the Czechs to "never trust the communists," ordinary Hungarians embraced a similar cleavage within its communist party and its then hero-leader Imre Nagy—previously an informer of the Soviet secret police NKVD under the code name Volodya[104]—to vent their frustration with the country's socialist government.

While the right has increasingly used nationalistic rhetoric to mobilize anti-government protests, young intellectuals and historians have pursued their private investigations into the past of all public figures, not only government officials. In 2005 a consultancy group, Political Capital, published the names of the mostly known informers of the secret police among the political and business elite.[105] Another list of informers was published under the pseudonym Szakérto '90 (Expert '90) on a U.S.-based Web site.[106] In 2006, the weekly *Élet és Irodalom* published the findings of Krisztián Ungváry, a historian, who asserted that the film director István Szabó, Cardinal László Paskai, and five bishops had previously been informants for the secret police.[107] But only a few in Hungary felt the need to find subversives and purify society. Lustration cycles eventually decelerated in Hungary over years of its implementation. The responses to revelations, as turbulent as they may have been in the short term, nurtured the flexible construction of former adversaries, which made the inclusive system redundant.

Poles Apart: The Politics of the Reconciliatory
System in Poland

Background: The launch of the reconciliatory system in Poland was marred by controversies, political disputes, and doubts over its implementation. It took some time for the center-right government that oversaw its launch to realize that the method of confession was supposed to lead to a second chance. Not all of those who initially submitted affidavits to reveal their collaboration were allowed to retain their positions. After confessing collaboration with the communist repressive apparatus, those involved were in a few cases dismissed or there was pressure for their dismissal.[108] For example, on March 2, 1999, after publication of the first list of affidavits revealing collaboration with security forces, Hanna Suchocka (UW), the minister of justice at the time, "reacted swiftly, demoting two district procurators who had acknowledged their collaboration. At the same time, she recommended that the presidents of courts dismiss those judges whose names had been published [as secret collaborators]."[109] However, these dismissals soon became exceptions to the norm, which were highlighted and criticized by the media. Some anti-lustration-oriented Polish media interpreted them as "punishment for truth,"[110] whereas some pro-lustration media considered the lack of continuity as the main shortcoming of the process.[111]

The scope of the Polish lustration system was narrow. As with the lustration systems in the Czech Republic and Hungary, the Polish lustration system was not designed to reach the business sphere. Although the public demanded it, the lustration of the business sphere was hard to justify and was never seriously considered. But even if the lustration law had covered the business sphere, it was enacted too late to prevent old cadres from taking advantage of their social capital during the massive privatization process.[112] In what Łoś and Zybertowicz have called the "capital conversion process," a section of former *nomenklatura* and their network swapped political capital for economic capital, which it later utilized to regain political power.[113] The system also did not extend to high communist echelons as the possible instigators of the human rights violations. Unlike the Czech system, it included only members of, and collaborators with, the secret police and other security branches. In Poland, even some of the opponents of lustration criticized this lack of de-communization, which was tantamount to a request to widen the system.[114]

The impact of the process on the relaxation of tension wrought by mistrust and denunciation was mixed. On the positive side, the process increased the transparency of public officials and offered a way out of political scandals and mutual mistrust. For example, after the lustration act was passed, Deputy Tomasz Karwowski publicly accused Prime Minister Jerzy Buzek of collaboration. Buzek responded by asking the Spokesperson of the Public Interest, Judge Boguslaw Nizieński, to examine his affidavit first. Nizieński agreed and announced that he had found no

grounds for requesting the lustration court to examine the prime minister's affidavit.[115] The contaminated lustration discourse probably arose
from the lengthy pre-lustration period during which the theme was used
quite arbitrarily to discredit political opponents. In spite of this atmosphere of mistrust and manipulation, the Polish Constitutional Tribunal,
in delivering its first lustration decision, expressed optimism that the situation would settle down with the passage of time: "In the present political
life, we can observe . . . allegations of politicians regarding the fact of
collaboration of particular persons with security organs as well as questioning the truthfulness of already submitted affidavits. This is a very bad
habit. [However,] looking from this point of view . . . the carriage of the
lustration proceeding . . . will without doubt contribute to the recovery
of the situation."[116] Indeed, the analysis of the Polish lustration process
seems to give some support to the tribunal's belief. Lustration has helped
reduce instances of defamation between opposing politicians as well as
clear the names of those who had been accused in the past, such as those
whose names had appeared on the Macierewicz list.[117]

In spite of this, the media has never embraced the reconciliatory system.
Instead, every single step of the lustration process was interpreted as a political scandal, and much of the criticism appeared to be negatively biased.
Some journalists sought to discredit the conclusions that were ultimately
reached about particular people even before their lustration process had
ended or even when it had only just begun. The provision that every member of Parliament could propose an initiation of the verification of "confessions" submitted by people holding state offices was considered a tool of
political struggle,[118] although without the provision, politicians would continue to denounce their rivals at their press conferences. A proposal to
initiate the lustration process was considered an orchestrated accusation,[119]
and a decision of the lustration court was treated as final though pending
an appeal.[120] The lustration of candidates for high state offices, namely the
presence of the presidential candidates at the lustration court, was interpreted as their discrediting,[121] despite the fact that both Lech Wałęsa and Aleksander Kwaśniewski had a chance to clear themselves from allegations that
they were secret informers.[122] They would not have had a chance to do so
if the lustration system had not provided them with the opportunity.

Media biases led to media wars. A reprint of the officially published
names of those who had revealed their collaboration in one newspaper
was portrayed as a scandal by another newspaper.[123] The newspaper *Gazeta*

Wyborcza and the weekly *Polityka* routinely attacked the daily *Życie Warszawy* and *Rzeczpospolita*, while the latter retaliated against their criticisms.[124] As a result, some of the public appeared to mistrust decisions delivered by the lustration court. The office of the Spokesperson had difficulty clarifying these misapprehensions.[125] Each media camp added its own meaning to the lustrations. For instance, cover names Bolek and Alek, which allegedly belonged to former presidents Lech Wałęsa and Aleksander Kwaśniewski, clearly resembled the Polish pre-1989 cartoon entitled *Bolek and Lolek*. For readers of the center-right press, the cover names ridiculed the two politicians, while for the leftist press it ridiculed the process of lustrations.

Bronisław Wildstein and Adam Michnik, who may be considered the most vocal supporter and opponent of lustrations among journalists, respectively, did not hesitate to use personal profiling to discredit or uphold the past credentials of their political rivals or allies.[126] For instance, Judge Krzysztof Kauba, the deputy of the Spokesperson of the Public Interest, issued a press statement that pointed out a misrepresentation of a lustration case by *Gazeta Wyborcza*.[127] In response, *Gazeta* suggested that Kauba's action amounted to censorship and was an example of lasting communist stereotypes among people who had worked for too long at the communist apparatus of justice.[128] Disagreeing with Michnik, Wildstein defended Kauba as a person of "unquestionable moral credentials" who never joined the communist party and after founding a judicial "Solidarity" had been expelled from his job for political reasons during the period of martial law.[129] Wildstein added that Michnik was a person who issued moral testimonials to General Wojciech Jaruzelski and General Czesław Kiszczak for their responsibility for political repressions and massacres.[130]

Michnik's case was rather more complicated than that of any other dissidents and a comparison with Nelson Mandela would be more revealing. Both opposed their respective previous regimes and negotiated their exits. Michnik was able to reach out to his former enemies as Mandela did, but unlike Mandela, Michnik was never able to inspire and lead his former fellow dissidents from the Solidarity movement to lasting reconciliation. Michnik never embraced the Polish reconciliatory system, although it was based on the same premises of the institutional compromise as the South African truth and reconciliation process and although it offered a solution to the personnel problem that was considerably more elegant than the Czech or the Hungarian lustration system. It is not surprising that Michnik lost many of his Solidarity mates even before he was tainted by what Robert Brier called his "somewhat suspicious role" in the Rywin case, one of the largest corruption scandals in post-communist Poland.[131]

Assessment: Similar to the Czech Republic, the two competing camps relied on their exclusive versions of history. The conflicting perceptions originated in the protracted pre-lustration stage. In contrast to our hypothesis about virtual lustration cycles, the lustration system did not transform the perceptions about persons associated with former regimes. On the other hand, the political controversies seemed to be most severe only at the launch of the lustration process in 1999. The media wars over lustrations culminated at the same time but both relatively decreased afterward as the system has been implemented. Nevertheless, they never stopped.

The lustration debate in Poland was typically contaminated by ad hominem accusations between its opponents and proponents. The supporters' side included all sorts of "moral persons," ranging from those who truly possessed moral integrity to political entrepreneurs who used the moral arguments to advance their political ambitions. It included the democratic center-right around the Law and Justice Party (PiS), the populists in Self-Defense (SRP), the Catholic fundamentalists around the League of Polish Families (LPR), and Radio Maryja. The center-right Civic Platform (PO), which won elections in 2007, "did not have time for lustration."[132] The opponents' side was also heterogonous and brought together a variety of characters ranging from the populist left, non-ideological pragmatists who did "business" with the West as well as the East, those who had a background in the former state apparatus, members of SLD, spokespersons for the postmodern generation, and a variety of intellectual critics of the right.

While supporters of lustration lamented moral decline as the fundamental mistake of political transformation, opponents of lustration claimed that Poland was being drawn back to the Middle Ages. The language of the first group was "national security," "justice," "morality," "law and truth," "evil," and "network."[133] The ridiculing term *ubekistan*, which was derived from the acronym for one of the secret services, the Security Office (UB), suggested "a country of secret agents."[134] The discourse of the second group used phrases such as "conspiracy theory," "can of worms," "Pandora's box," "affair-mania," "anti-communist Bolsheviks," "smear campaign," "game in files," and "hatred."[135] Both discourses had much in common. According to Paweł Śpiewak, a sociologist and a member of Parliament for

PO in 2005–7, authors of these competing discourses did not speak for themselves but attempted to act as voices of the national or democratic consciousness, as if they knew what was good and bad or as if they had found a deeper, but hidden, moral dimension to obvious problems.[136]

It may not be easy in any country—and it may have been particularly difficult in Catholic Poland—to contemplate the attributes of a trustworthy administration without employing moral categories such as the personal integrity of state officials, their impartiality, and neutrality. But morality, by definition a subjective and exclusive weapon, can hardly persuade, not to mention defeat, political adversaries. The advocates of the lustration system could have avoided moral arguments by framing the debate in the vocabulary of reliable state administration. But instead of arguing against inefficiency, campaigning against corruption, and combating abuses of power, which were associated with the past regime and which encouraged the formation of social consensus in support of the country's lustration system, supporters of lustration tailored the debate in what others viewed and disliked as the old-fashioned veil of morality. The political dispute about lustration became a moral crusade against opportunists, careerists, turncoats, and enemies. The right assumed that communism had not ceased to exist but only changed its nature.

The lengthy pre-lustration stage in Poland and the relentless bickering of political leaders over lustrations created doubt among the public about the utility of the lustration system. The question that arose in their minds was to what extent could they trust institutions occupied by those who had revealed their collaboration? Conventional wisdom about truth commissions is that disclosure may lead to reconciliation, but it may also exacerbate historical divisions. Thus, the reconciliatory system may paradoxically produce certain countereffects by increasing the level of dissatisfaction in society. However, empirical evidence has indicated that the approach did not necessarily have these consequences. According to a poll conducted in 2000, 52 percent of Poles considered lustration of presidential candidates necessary; 72 percent of them said it was necessary to know the past of candidates; and 10 percent stated that lustration proves the trustworthiness of a candidate.[137] One interpretation of these results suggests that supporters of lustrations were interested in the disclosure of truth as a general rule rather than in the outcome of the lustration process, that is, lustration supporters were more interested in the truth about whether a candidate had collaborated with the former security services than in his punishment.

These results may restore the image of lustration supporters as people who are willing to trust those who worked for the secret service once they have revealed this fact. The image of lustration supporters as a vengeful mass, hungry for popular justice, may therefore be unwarranted. The findings of this poll show that the majority of lustration supporters might be willing to give their discredited leaders a second chance as Poland's lustration system presupposes.

After a difficult start, the reconciliatory system eventually took off and was relatively well implemented between 2000 and 2004—since 2001 under the government led by ex-communists; they tried to narrow the law, but their major attempt was halted by the Constitutional Tribunal (see Chapter 3). However, continuing quarrels over it had led to thirteen changes in the system's scope and institutional framework after the major amendment to the lustration law was passed in 1999.[138] By 2004, the reconciliatory system appeared to be at its end after its operation had been seriously undermined by the publication of "Wildstein's List." In response to the continuing secrecy surrounding the process, Bronisław Wildstein copied an index of people who had had any previous contact with the secret services. The list originated in the Institute of National Memory (IPN), a government body that had been mandated to be in charge of the secret archives in Poland after its inception in 1998. According to its author, the list was publicly available and contained about 240,000 names of secret police members, their collaborators, their consultants, and those who were merely considered as potential targets for secret collaboration.[139] The list was circulated to other journalists and eventually published on the Internet. Although some of its hosting sites warned that persons included on the list may be "agents of the [secret] services as well as the heroes of the underground [resistance],"[140] *Gazeta Wyborcza* suggested that it was the list of the secret informers.[141] Consequently, both the revelation and the labeling caused the rapid rise in applications for lustration from people who feared the implications of having been listed. One of the applicants who was refused access to his or her file by IPN after finding his or her name on Wildstein's List pursued his or her case at the European Court on Human Rights in Strasbourg.[142]

The historical divisions over the past in Poland deepened further after the 2005 election victory of the Law and Justice Party (PiS). The party, in the words of one of its deputies, branded the reconciliatory system as "a myth, fiction, and satrap of lustrations, whose task was to deceive the public

opinion that everything was being taken care of."[143] Prime Minister Jarosław Kaczyński (2006–7) and President Lech Kaczyński (2005–10, both PiS)
advocated a new lustration system, which gave the government discretion
to dismiss officials even if they had confessed their collaboration. Criticizing
their effort, Adam Michnik saw the new system as an attempt by the losers
of transition to take on the winners of transition.[144] Given the persisting
dominance of the post-communist elites in Poland, it seems that this time
Michnik's diagnosis was not out of line with that of his major political
rivals on the right.

The bill effectively changed the reconciliatory method into the mixed
method, and the change was eventually halted by the Constitutional Tribunal
in 2007.[145] After that Poland maintained the same method of confession
implemented under a different institutional framework (Chapter 3). IPN was
authorized to compile a catalogue of persons associated with the past and
made the search publicly available.[146] This diverted public attention away
from forward-looking to backward-looking perspectives. As was the case in
the Czech Republic and Hungary, young historians searched the secret
archives in pursuit of the past of prominent politicians. In 2008, Sławomir
Cenckiewicz and Piotr Gontarczyk from IPN published a book that investigated the alleged contacts of Lech Wałęsa with the Security Service (SB).[147]
However, unlike the situation in Hungary and the Czech Republic, the revelation ended in a way that was reminiscent of previous experience with lustration in Poland. Wałęsa's request for access to part of his files from 1970
to 1978 was declined by IPN in 2009. In response, Wałęsa on his blog issued
an attack against one of the authors for being the grandson of an alleged
collaborator with the Security Office (UB).[148] Thus, the unprofessional attitude of IPN may have effectively exonerated Wałęsa. But he launched the
same profiling method against his opponent for being a third-generation
tainted writer. In response, two more books on what seems to be a popular
topic were published in 2008 and 2009, alleging a link between the Nobel
Peace Prize Laureate and the communist secret police.[149]

Thus, it seems that the case of Poland is in line with the hypothesis of
small lustration circles. The dynamic of the lustration process suggests its
role as a tool of political struggle. On the other hand, one cannot exclude a
possibility of virtual lustration cycles. How can we otherwise explain that
the lustration system was continuously implemented for a number of years
and that after an attempt to alter it in 2007 the process returned to its
original method based on confession?

Discussion

The political context in which lustration systems were embedded affected their implementation, which in turn affected the political context. In all three countries, the implementation of lustration systems has created deep political and moral dilemmas and has launched a dramatic contest between protagonists of different interpretations of the past. Our assessment of lustration politics in the Czech Republic and Hungary provide some evidence for the existence of virtual lustration cycles: the perceptions of tainted officials—in addition to evidence of their behavior—may have been shaped by lustration systems, which in turn affected the implementation of these systems. The lustration process in Poland follows the cycle hypothesized by Horne and Levi: one political bloc attacks while the other retaliates. A number of other differences affected the implementation of lustration systems in the three countries.

It is apparent that the lustration systems fostered, if not created, divergent recollections about the past within each country and that different memories of the past in turn affected the existence of each lustration system. In the Czech Republic, the system of exclusions became so deeply entrenched in the country's mainstream political culture that it fostered a view of all persons of the past as tainted. To be sure, collaborators did exist in the Czech Republic, and many of them did participate in illegal activities after transition. However, the notion that there is no "former communist" created a situation in which the taint of one's past would remain regardless of the person's change or a real engagement in the past. Consequently, it became impossible to end the system or to suggest its change without being accused of heresy against the new anti-communist religion. Thus, the Czech exclusive system has been continuously implemented since 1991 and the opening of secret archives has led to its informal expansion.

In Hungary, the system of exposures seemed to facilitate inclusion by fostering a culture of denial rather than transparency. It allowed a redefinition of one's own role in the past, portraying many collaborators as victims. Since there were no real transgressors in the past, the system lost its meaning. Thus, the Hungarian system ended quietly and was gradually replaced by the process of opening files. The changing recollections about the past affect not only the standing of tainted officials but also views of historical events. Both Czechoslovakia and Hungary were invaded by the Soviets, but they have different recollections of these invasions. Czechs do not particularly commemorate the invasion; the lustration law taught Czechs to never trust communists because "they are all the same" and consequently consider the leaders of the Prague Spring as losers of history. In contrast the Hungarians, including the right, vehemently celebrate the events of 1956, and they do so despite the previous collaboration of the leader of the revolution with the Soviet secret police.

In Poland, the reconciliatory system, crafted in protracted political negotiations, was targeted by the left because it condemned the past and by the right because the institution of a second chance signified that "communism only changed its nature" and created a "fiction" about a common future. The reemerged conflict of moralists on the right and the pragmatists on the left eventually led to an attempt to introduce a mixed system in Poland. An attempt of the leaders on the right to expand the scope of the system and alter its method based on discretionary dismissals was halted by the Constitutional Tribunal, and Poland had to revert to a new reconciliatory system. The duration and the reversal of the lustration system to its reconciliatory form amid heated political debates nevertheless indicate a possibility that the system did create particular perceptions about tainted officials.

In view of these lustration cycles, the survey results shown in Figure 5.1 in the introduction to this chapter are not surprising. Similarly, the views about the best possible ways of dealing with secret informers (Figure 5.3) may not surprise many either: in 2007, 55.5 percent of Czechs, in contrast to 39.3 percent of Hungarians and 33.2 percent of Poles, would bar them from holding public positions, while 51.4 percent of Hungarians, in contrast to 36.1 percent of Czechs and 40.1 percent of Poles, would consider barring them only if they lied about their past.[150] The inclusive system in Hungary and the reconciliatory system in Poland, together with continuing political quarrels, may have contributed to more flexible perceptions of people associated with the past regimes. However, no present evidence of dishonesty is needed for the majority of Czechs to determine that an official with a tainted past is unsuitable for a public office. The rigid view fostered by the lustration system prevented the Czechs from converging to their Central European counterparts although communism had been over for more than eighteen years at the time of the survey. Like a puppy that chases its tail, the Czechs need more lustrations in order to deal with the tainted elements re-created by the lustration law.[151]

In all three countries, the expansion of the program to open secret archives affected the implementation of lustration systems. However, owing

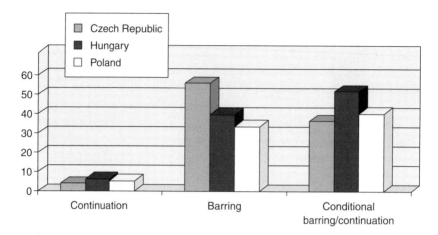

Figure 5.3. A preferred solution for dealing with secret collaborators in the Czech Republic, Hungary, and Poland (2007). The figure summarizes respondents' preferences (as percentages) for one of the three possible answers to the following question: "I will read you three different ways of how the issue of persons who evidently informed on their fellow citizens to the secret police was resolved in other countries. Which way would you prefer?" The three possible answers were: (1) "These persons should be allowed to hold government positions" (continuation); (2) "These persons should not be allowed to hold government positions" (barring); (3) "These persons should not be allowed to hold government positions if they lied about their past" (a failure to use a second chance). Source: David, Lustration Systems, Trust in Government, and Reconciliation.

to the particular constellation of perceptions fostered by a particular lustration system, these exposures produced different effects in the three countries. In Hungary, additional exposures have led to denials, or in some cases to confessions, but seldom to dismissals. In Poland, additional exposures have been motivated by the need to challenge the truthfulness of submitted affidavits through which officials did not reveal any link with the past. New information would signify incomplete confessions and result in dismissals. In contrast, the vast majority of the Czech press dismissed denials in the same way that they dismissed confession and apology as deceitful and insincere. Exposures typically resulted in dismissals if the tainted person held any public position. Thus, if additional exposures represented barking and dismissals biting of lustration dogs, then the Czech dog would almost always bite, the Hungarian dog would only bark, and the Polish dog's response would depend on his master of the day.

PART III

Experimental Evidence

6

Political Effects: Trust in Government

[W]hile there exists equal justice to all and alike in their private
disputes, the claim of excellence is also recognized; and when a
citizen is in any way distinguished, he is preferred to the public
service, not as a matter of privilege, but as the reward of merit.
Neither is poverty an obstacle, but a man may benefit his country
whatever the obscurity of his condition. There is no exclusiveness
in our public life, and in our private business we are not suspicious
of one another, nor angry with our neighbor if he does what he
likes.

—Pericles' Funeral Oration[1]

This chapter examines the effects of personnel systems on trust in government. The first section considers the role of trust in government in democratization and hypothesizes the effects that dismissal, exposure, confession, and other variables may have on trust in government. In order to test these effects, we devised an original experimental vignette that manipulated the methods upon which personnel systems were based, namely, dismissal, exposure, and confession. The experimental vignette was embedded in nationwide representative surveys conducted in the Czech Republic, Hungary, and Poland in 2007. The experimental setting of the survey is described in the second section. The third section presents the results of the statistical analyses of our survey experiment. The final section discusses our research findings.

Personnel Systems and Trust in Government

The establishment of loyal, efficient, and trustworthy administration is critical for the operation of any democratic system. The objective attributes of the state apparatus as well as their subjective perceptions by citizens affect law enforcement, public safety, tax collection, public service delivery, and other government functions. A degree of trust in the political regime and its representatives fosters citizens' compliance and ethical reciprocity, thus helping sustain democracy.[2] As trust has been associated with democracy, autocratic regimes have been associated with widespread mistrust.[3] Autocracies are typically characterized by abuses of power, pervasive secrecy, lack of accountability, and other attributes, which are generally considered as impediments to trust.[4] In the context of regime transition, a number of scholars have warned that the culture of endemic distrust may spill over to shape the attitudes of citizens toward the new democratic state.[5] How to rebuild trust in government is thus an important issue confronting transitional societies.

Trust is one of the most hotly debated topics in the social sciences. Although scholars disagree about its origin and the degree of its relevance, they usually distinguish between trust in government and interpersonal trust.[6] The former describes a vertical relationship of trust in abstract institutions, while the latter is horizontal and captures relations among people. Here we are interested in trust in government, which according to Hetherington has been broadly defined as "a basic evaluative orientation toward the government founded on how well the government is operating according to people's normative expectations."[7] According to Ken Newton, political trust is "the belief that those in authority and with power will not deliberately or willingly do us harm, if they can avoid it, and will look after our interests, if this is possible."[8] The minimalistic nature of the second definition captures the problem of trust in transitional countries, in which citizens have experienced the abuse of power that was deliberately committed by previous regimes. At the same time, the conditionality allows a certain degree of mistrust that may be healthy for the operation of every society because, as Russell Hardin reminds us, complete trust is not always a good thing.[9]

There has been limited consensus in the literature about the political effects that personnel systems have on trust in government. Owing to the relative novelty of transitional justice and the paucity of empirical research in the field during its first decade, different theories, which often contradict each other, have been developed. For each personnel system, one can find a large body of academic literature that theorizes its positive effects and another, equally plausible literature that theorizes its negative effects. Although scholars in principle agree on the need to assess the utility of personnel systems in terms of their prospects for achieving democracy, they often reach contradictory conclusions about the political effects of each system.

The theoretical perspective proposed in Chapter 2 enables us to review existing theorizations on personnel systems and theorize their impact more effectively. According to this perspective, personnel systems are instances of different purification rituals, which signify different methods of discontinuity with the past. Personnel systems seek to transform state administrations, and the perceptions that citizens had about them, from administrations that were instruments of oppression, discrimination, and abuse into administrations that would not act against their interests. Different systems adopt different means to symbolize the end of undemocratic rule. Dismissal suggests the purification by sacrifice and exclusion of the tainted official; exposure is alluded to a shaming ritual; and confession signifies a ritual of self-purification.

Hypothesis I. The Effects of Dismissal

An exclusive system provides for the discontinuation of the former state's structures by means of changes in personnel. Two analyses of Czechoslovak parliamentary debates showed that a clear break with the old system and its practices, security concerns, and the trustworthiness of the state apparatus were major considerations for members of Parliament in approving the exclusive lustration law.[10] Teitel noted that people associated with the former regime were perceived as corrupt, inefficient, and loyal to the previous regime.[11] They were originally appointed pursuant to the ideological criteria of the former regime, and their continued presence was considered a major threat to political-economic reforms by the new elite as indicated by Havel's anniversary-of-occupation speech.[12] Other scholars, however, have considered these dismissals as lacking the essential element of discontinuity because they signify the same methods of exclusion as those pursued by the previous regime. Schwarz has argued that exclusive lustrations were politically motivated methods that served the power interests of the new political elite similar to purges frequently used by the previous regime to eliminate its enemies.[13] Horne and Levi have contended that resorting to the old methods undermined the credibility of the new state apparatus.[14]

We argue that exclusive systems seek to establish trustworthy government by means of changes in personnel. Officials associated with the past regime are perceived as tainted, intractable, and incapable of personal change. Their continuing presence in the state apparatus undermines the trustworthiness of the new government. For these reasons, establishing trustworthy government requires their *dismissal* from any public position of trust. Their dismissals dramatize the regime change, draw a clear line between past and present, and enable the new government to distance itself from the old system and its practices. They signal that the new state is not an instrument of oppression but a trustworthy administration that will serve the interests of society. The effect of dismissal on trust in government is therefore hypothesized to be positive: the dismissal of tainted officials increases trust in government.

Hypothesis II. The Effects of Exposure

An inclusive system aims at establishing the trustworthiness of the state apparatus through pursuing its transparency and the exposure of persons associated with former regimes. According to Łoś, proponents of exposure believed that it should enable the public to view the conduct of tainted officials and minimize the risk of blackmail, which could prejudice national security.[15] In parallel with other truth processes, "naming perpetrators" is a form of truth revelation that, according to Hayner, manifests a change in political practices.[16] Exposure may not increase trust in government but it may, according to Kis, decrease mistrust in government.[17] In other words, scandals resulting from the policy of transparency may be less damaging for government than scandals resulting from its secretiveness and withholding information about the past of public officials.

Teitel, on the other hand, has argued that exposure perpetuates continuity with the past owing to its reliance on the materials collected under the old regime.[18] According to Havel and Michnik, these archives may not be reliable for the purpose of screening.[19] Whether or not exposures manifest continuity or discontinuity with the past is an empirical rather than a theoretical question. We formulate our hypothesis pursuant to the transformative perspective. We argue that by *exposing* the past of tainted officials to the public, the system aspires to establish trust in government. It demonstrates a change in practices that were previously secret. The effect of exposure on trust in government is therefore hypothesized to be positive.

Hypothesis III. The Effects of Confession

A reconciliatory method of transitional justice has been theorized to generate positive effects in most cases. According to Posner and Vermeule, such a system may lead to the rehabilitation of the wrongdoer.[20] *Confessions*, though given publicly, may, according to Tutu, Michnik and Havel, and other scholars, facilitate forgiveness.[21] According to Eyal, Szelényi, and Townsley, "The ritual nature of confession . . . serves to forge a moral community. . . . [It] dramatizes the message of collective guilt, but also indicates the means of atonement and reintegration. It is proof of the generosity, leniency, and forgiveness of the post-communist inquisition. Persuading individuals to confess is not an act of revenge. Rather, it serves to demystify the evil nature of the previous regime, and provides a way of saving the souls of sinners, enabling them to rejoin the community of saints. Even if there are only a few public confessions, the result is likely to be cathartic."[22]

There are also negative effects of confessions. They may represent self-debasement, or contrition, penalties that may generate stigmatizing effects.[23] However, our theorization is closer to the first perspective. The confessions of wrongdoers not only demonstrate their loyalty to the new system, but they also delegitimize the past regime and provide discontinuity with the past on the macro level.[24] Unlike simple exposure, confession gives "truth" a normative meaning. It not only discloses what happened in the past, it also signals, in a powerful dramatic voice, that what happened was wrong. In confessing, the wrongdoer accepts the terms offered by the society, enhancing its legitimacy or at the very least decreasing the number of those who consider the new system illegitimate. The transformation of the state apparatus that goes hand in hand with the personal conversion of wrongdoers may be acceptable to both parts of the divided society. The effect of confession on trust in government is therefore hypothesized to be positive.

Hypothesis IV. The Effects of Position, Motives, and Agency

People associated with the human rights violations committed under previous regimes had different levels of involvement. Some may have given orders, while others may have followed them. Some may have been ideologically motivated, while others may have pursued their self-interest. Some may have volunteered to engage in repressive activities, while others may have been forced to do so. Thus, decisions about who should be targeted by measures of transitional justice pose one of the major moral-political dilemmas after transition. These decisions require selecting those who are tainted by their involvements in the past, which inevitably means that others are exonerated.

The policy dilemma of transitional justice has been examined by Gibson and Gouws, who tested the assumptions of the South African amnesty process.[25] They found that an actor's role in the past (i.e., an apartheid security branch) and giving orders were significant predictors of blame attributions. On the other hand, consequences and motives were not found to be significant.[26] Similar to other methods of transitional justice, personnel systems assign blame for the past regime. They deal with tainted officials at various levels of the pyramid of the repressive apparatus; some officials may have been motivated ideologically or by their self-interest, and in the context of Central and Eastern Europe, many informers of the secret police claimed that they were forced to collaborate. For this reason, we have also tested the impact of the previous position of tainted officials (i.e., low or high), their motives (i.e., ideological or self-interest), and their agency (i.e., being forced to collaborate or acting as an independent social agent). We hypothesize that high position, self-interest, and independent agency of the tainted official each have a negative impact on trust in government.

Hypothesis V. The Effects of Historical Divisions

Trustworthiness, impartiality, political neutrality, and other basic attributes commonly required for state administration are desperately lacking in transitional countries not only because of the abuses in the past but also because each side of the historical conflict usually maintains its own view of these attributes. While one side may view them, and indeed experience them, as abuses of power, the opposite side may see them as part of a legitimate patriotic struggle against subversives, terrorists, guerrillas, and so forth and concede a few unfortunate aberrations of power at best.

Our research is conducted in divided societies in which a minority still sympathizes with the previous regime and the majority opposes it. For instance, the hypothesis that the dismissal of a tainted official from government increases trust in government may be valid only in the eyes of the majority. But the minority that is sympathetic with the previous regime may not appreciate that dismissal at all; instead, they may favor the continuation of his or her employment. If the survey was conducted in Iraq, one could conclude that dismissals of Saddam's loyalists from the government increase its trustworthiness among the Iraqi public, although the finding would be attributed only to the majority Shiites; or we would not find any effect, although the process of de-Baathification affected the entire society. The results of our experiment may reflect responses that are attributable only to the majority; or a large minority may statistically cancel the effect of the majority. Consequently, we would have imprecise evidence in support of the hypothesis.

In order to capture the historical divisions today, we controlled for the degree of historical animosity resulting from the wrongdoing. We have defined historical animosity as a set of moral attitudes held by a respondent with respect to the wrongdoing. For instance, those respondents who do not see the wrongdoer as tainted because they belong to the same historical side may have different responses to his dismissal from those who see him as tainted. Should the wrongdoer be morally condemned? Should we deal with the wrongdoer at all? The question of whether a society should deal with injustices of the past has been raised in the context of the first dilemma of transitional justice. This dilemma has been outlined by Huntington and by Moran in the so-called "torturer's problem," which may be formulated as "prosecute and punish versus forgive and forget" (see Chapter 1). Since condemnation, punishment, forgiving, and forgetting represent the plurality of attitudes that capture the degree of disapproval and condemnation of the wrongdoer caused by his past, we construct a *historical animosity scale* that consists of (i) moral condemnation, (ii) punishment, (iii) not forgetting, and (iv) not forgiving.

The Survey Experiment with Dismissal, Exposure, and Confession

The need to determine whether the different lustration systems are inherently retrogressive or potentially beneficial to political transformation provided the impetus for the experimental design utilized in this research. Experiments in general have gained prominence in political science for their ability to eliminate alternative explanations and establish causal relations.[27] Experiments embedded in surveys have been used in attitudinal research and were successfully applied to test similar aspects of transitional justice, for instance, the assumptions of TRC in South Africa by Gibson and Gouws.[28] According to Paul Sniderman and Douglas Grob, survey experiments are a revolutionary methodological tool that combines the internal validity of experiments with the external validity of cross-sectional surveys.[29]

The experiment pursued in our research manipulated the three methods upon which the personnel systems, or lustration systems, are based, namely dismissal, exposure, and confession. By using the three methods, we were able to overcome the lack of congruence in the precise meaning of lustrations, which is country specific and was a common problem in previous comparative research.[30] Each method was contrasted with the corresponding orthogonal version: dismissal from public office was contrasted with continuation in office, exposure of the past of a public official with no exposure, and confession of his or her past with denial. The manipulation of orthogonal versions was possible owing to the occasional difficulties of enforcing lustration systems, as discussed in the previous chapter. For instance, it allowed for an examination of the effects of the dismissal of tainted public officials in the Czech Republic despite the fact that some officials had succeeded in circumventing the system and had in this way avoided dismissal. Alternatively, it also provided a means of testing the effects of the dismissal of officials who had confessed their collaboration in Poland and should have been awarded a second chance. In Hungary, the original inclusive system has been inactive for a long time, which opened the possibility for various scenarios. Thus, the problems with implementation that lustration systems raised had practical advantages in this research.

Our research would normally require three experimental vignettes embedded in three surveys in each country, bringing the total number of surveys to nine. In order to reduce costs, the survey experiment was pursued through a 2 x 2 x 2 complete factorial design.[31] The factorial designs effectively tested the effects of various combinations of "dismissal," "exposure," and "confession" and their orthogonal versions at the same time. The surveyed population was divided into eight groups. Each group heard a story with a particular combination of dismissal and continuation, exposure and non-exposure, and confession and denial.

However, confession after exposure may not have the same effect as confession before exposure: confession after exposure may not be considered genuine. Likewise, exposure after confession may not be the same as exposure before confession: in the latter case, exposure may be considered redundant. For these reasons, the sequencing of the two factors was also manipulated. In the first sequence, the vignette started either with "confession" or with "denial." In the second sequence, the vignette started either with "exposure" or "no exposure." This led to a 2 x 2 x 2 x 2 factorial design, which required sixteen versions of the questionnaire in total. Each respondent heard only one combination of the factors. Vignette 1 manipulated confession, exposure, and dismissal. Vignette 16 manipulated the absence of exposure, denial, and the continuation of employment.

The experimental vignette had two parts. The first part was situated in the prior socialist regime and described the wrongdoing of a particular person (see Appendix B). The second part of the vignette was situated in the present and offered various solutions to the problem of the wrongdoing. The respondents followed a story about Mr. Novák, which is one of the most common Czech surnames. The corresponding common surnames in Polish and Hungarian were originally Kowalski and Szabó, respectively. After consulting local researchers to ensure that these names do not have any other particular meaning and did not resemble the names of anyone involved in a high-profile lustration case, the surname Kowalski was replaced with Nowak in Poland, and the surname Szabó was replaced with Kovács in Hungary. Hereafter in this book, the anglicized surname Novak will be used. The choice of Novak's gender was motivated by the need to provide a vignette that is as realistic as possible and conforms to the typical profile of public figures who were involved in wrongdoing. The majority of revelations concerned male public figures in all three countries (see Chapter 5).

The first part of the vignette described Mr. Novak as an expert who had worked in an enterprise in the past. The reference to his "expertise" eliminated the possibility that he had been a *nomenklatura* cadre who had held his position without being properly qualified. This in itself could constitute a reason for dismissal. Then, a typical wrongdoing committed in the past was described. Since lustration laws always targeted members of the socialist-era secret police and their collaborators but did not always target the officials of the former communist parties, Mr. Novak was described as someone who had secretly reported on his colleagues in his former workplace.[32] This provided respondents with an opportunity to assess the methods of dealing with the *fact* of collaboration. Mere rumors, politically exploited allegations, and unconvincing evidence would influence respondents' assessment of the effect of any lustration measure on trust in government as well as reconciliation. The method of determining collaboration is a matter for the law of evidence and is not a constitutive part of personnel systems.[33]

The vignette did not describe the motives of Mr. Novak and did not attach any particular consequences of them to the lives of his colleagues. Most lustration laws assessed neither the informers' motives nor the consequences of their actions, which could have become the subject of criminal investigation if they had given rise to gross human rights violations. Thus, the only consequence of Mr. Novak's actions was a breach of interpersonal trust. Our research has nevertheless determined the respondent's perception of Mr. Novak's past. After the first part of the vignette, respondents were asked questions about his position, motives, and agency, as well as their moral attitudes toward him. The answers to questions about moral attitudes provided a very useful tool for interpreting differences in perceptions among the three countries. These questions will be discussed in the next chapter.

The second part of the vignette announced that Mr. Novak had recently been employed at a government ministry. For the purpose of the experiment it was crucial that he had been affiliated with a ministry in order to test perceptions about the trustworthiness of the government. Moreover, it was necessary to mention that his employment had been recent because it would have been unrealistic to expect that anyone would continue his employment at that level due to the changes that have usually occurred in ministries after elections.

Each of the three experimental variables, or their absence, were operationalized in one sentence and summarized at the end of the vignette. The operationalization of "dismissal" and "confession" was quite straightforward (see Appendix B). However, the operationalization of "exposure" had to overcome the fact that respondents were already aware of Mr. Novak's past. Truth revelation in this situation would have been redundant. For this reason, "exposure" was conceptualized as a revelation that adds a new piece of information that may have a shaming effect on the wrongdoer. Since it was demonstrated that most informers chose or were assigned a "cover name," the additional information related to the publication of the informer's cover name. Alleged cover names such as Kato in the Czech Republic, D-209 in Hungary, and Bolek and Alek in Poland were often ridiculed in the press. Thus, the affirmative version stated that all the information about Mr. Novak's past, including his cover name, had been published. The negative version only stated that no information had been published. Thus, instead of transparency versus non-transparency, we were only able to compare the effects of shaming information versus no information. This nevertheless still served our purpose because it allowed us to test whether the government is viewed less trustworthy if it releases information about its official or if it upholds information embargo.

These sixteen scenarios enabled us to test the effect of central values upon which these systems were based, not the effects of personnel systems per se. They allowed us to test the ideal typical categories of dismissal, exposure, and confession within the surreality of post-communist politics. Each scenario represented a real-life situation that could have happened at any time during these transitions. Indeed, many cases described in Chapter 5 reveal that the lustration process was often accompanied by a mixture of dismissal and continuation, exposure and non-exposure, and confession and denial. If we simulated lustration systems strictly as described in Chapter 3, we would be criticized for being unduly legalistic because these systems were often applied inconsistently. We believe that the advantages of our realistic vignette outweigh the advantages of a legalistic vignette.

Moreover, our approach allowed us to reach comparative conclusions. First, dismissal, exposure, and confession are individual-level categories, while the lustration systems were country-specific. We could not be strictly legalistic anyway because these countries implemented different systems. Comparison of the effects of the exclusive system in the Czech Republic and the reconciliatory system in Poland would be ineffective because any difference in results could be attributed to the system or to the country. Second, we want to test the effect of dismissal, exposure, and confession within three political cultures that gave birth to three different lustration systems. We want to be able to compare, for instance, the effect of confession within the culture of confession and within the culture of dismissals.

To ensure that the experimental manipulation was successful, manipulation checks were included in the questionnaire. The purpose of these checks was to confirm that respondents understood the experimental treatment. However, a check that was intended to test the success of manipulation indirectly by testing perceptions proved to be contentious during the pre-piloting of the questionnaire. Questions that referred to the experimental vignette implicitly were challenged because their answers were "already known" to the respondents. Respondents started to become suspicious about the study and felt deceived. Thus, taking into account ethical issues, painful historical experiences in the three countries, and the sensitivity of the topic of secret collaboration, the manipulation check openly asked whether it was true or untrue that the person had confessed, was exposed, or had been dismissed. Respondents were given four response categories on the Likert scale. Incorrect answers to the manipulation check concerning dismissal were given by 17.1 percent respondents; concerning exposure, by 18.5 percent; and concerning confession, by 21.4 percent. Judging by standards set in research using the same methodology in similar contexts, the experimental manipulation was very successful.[34]

The fieldwork for the experimental part of the research was conducted in the Czech Republic, Hungary, and Poland in 2006–7. In its preparatory stage, twelve focus group sessions or interviews with ordinary members of major political parties and former political prisoners were conducted in each country to ensure that the topics of the past were still considered important and to understand how people described and interpreted them. They revealed that the topics remain quite divisive and that interpretations of the past vary within each of the three countries. The objective of the second stage was to prepare the questionnaire. Various drafts of the questionnaire were evaluated by fellow academics, students, and student assistants inside and outside the three countries. Sixteen interviews were conducted to prepare the first version of the questionnaire before double-blind reverse translations of the questionnaire were solicited. The questionnaire was translated into Czech, Hungarian, and Polish, and independent reverse translations were made from the three languages into English to reconcile differences in the questionnaire wording resulting from differences among the three languages. Thus, three bilingual speakers from each country participated in the translation. The questionnaire was piloted in all three countries in the spring of 2007 by means of sixty face-to-face interviews in total with twenty participants from each country. After analyzing the results of the pilot, a second round of reconciling differences among the three versions of the questionnaire was conducted.

Thanks to grant support from the United States Institute of Peace, the questionnaire was embedded in omnibus surveys conducted by three of the most internationally renowned survey agencies in the region: CVVM in the Czech Republic, Tárki in Hungary, and OBOP in Poland. These agencies used nationwide stratified random samples. CVVM completed 1,013 face-to-face interviews with persons older than fifteen years with a response rate of 48 percent; Tárki completed 1,033 face-to-face interviews with persons older than eighteen years with a response rate of 60 percent; and OBOP completed 1,004 face-to-face interviews with persons older than fifteen years with a response rate of 26.2 percent. To ensure the comparative aspect of this research, we have excluded respondents younger than eighteen from our analyses. We ensured that each of the agencies understood the nature of survey experiments in general and the need for random assignment in particular. Furthermore, we double-checked that all vignette versions were manipulated correctly in the sixteen versions of the questionnaire in each of the languages. The surveys were simultaneously conducted in the three countries in May–June 2007.

Measurement of Trust in Government

Owing to the nature of experimental research, this project could not rely on existing operationalizations of trust in government. For instance, the first of four questions routinely used in most surveys, including the American National Election Studies and World Values Surveys, asks, "How much of the time do you think you can trust the government in Washington [Prague, Budapest, Warsaw] to do what is right?"[35] However, the question is too general to be applicable to the concrete, real-life situation simulated by the experimental vignette. Governments may have "hundreds of thousands employees" and one could readily "distrust all these people as a class" and therefore distrust the government because only a few of them may take one's interests seriously.[36] This research therefore investigates real-life scenarios simulated by the experimental vignette: it seeks to situate the problem of personnel systems into the context of political transition and limits the scope of government to a government ministry.[37]

In order to measure the political effects of dismissal, exposure, and confession, a new scale that captures trust in government had to be developed. To ensure its theoretical relevance, the scale had to take into account the definition of trust that had previously served as a prerequisite for the above-quoted classic survey questions.[38] Trust in government had been defined as "a basic evaluative orientation toward the government founded on how well the government is operating according to people's normative expectations."[39] According to Donald Stokes, the original survey questions were developed to capture such evaluations: "The criteria of judgment implicit in these questions were partly ethical, that is, the honesty and other ethical qualities of public officials. . . . But the criteria extended to other qualities as well, including the ability and efficiency of government officials and the correctness of their policy decisions."[40] Recent reviews of the topic of trust adopt similar characteristics of competence, integrity, and motivation and thus do not dramatically depart from the original intention,[41] although they build on a different definition of trust.[42]

In constructing a scale for trust in government, several measures that are representative of its conceptual definition and its characteristics were taken. Pursuant to the theoretical interests of conducting research on the role of personnel systems in transitional countries, a trust in government scale was developed to capture discontinuity in the practices of governance. Respondents were therefore asked questions about their trust in the government ministry in general and about three specific items: their belief that the ministry would act efficiently in implementing government programs; their belief that the ministry would operate in accordance with law; and their belief that the ministry would be loyal to democracy (see Appendix B).[43] These attributes capture the transformation of state administration, which had been characterized under the previous regime as untrustworthy, inefficient, corrupt, and undemocratic.

Each question had five response categories, one of which allowed for a neutral response: "neither agree, nor disagree."[44] The responses were coded from the most negative value, "strongly disagree" (0), to the most positive value, "strongly agree" (4).[45] The scale was highly reliable.[45] Thus, a scale of four items was computed by adding the four items; the scale ranged from 0 to 16. The mean score of the scale was 7.15 (standard deviation, S.D. = 4.64) in the merged data set (see Table 6.1).

Measurement of Position, Motives, and Agency

Since trust in government may be affected by the past of the wrongdoer, especially by his position in the hierarchy of the state apparatus and his motives, this research also controlled for the *perception* of Mr. Novak's past. Manipulating too many items in experimental designs would run the risk that respondents would not be able to comprehend them. Our questionnaire therefore contained questions about the "position," "motives," and "agency" of Mr. Novak, which were included after the first part of the vignette. Since the position, motives, and agency were not clearly specified in the experimental vignette, we expected that most respondents would use a neutral category on the Likert scale. To prevent this from happening and to gain the critical information about the perceptions, our questionnaire did not offer respondents a neutral category and the Likert scale had only four items.

Thus, after respondents heard about the wrongdoing of Mr. Novak they were asked whether Mr. Novak in their view held a high or low position (coded from 0 to 3); was motivated by ideology or self-interest (coded from 0 to 3); and was forced by the system or acted independently (coded from 0 to 3). The mean position score was 1.76 (S.D. = 0.82); the mean motive score was 1.97 (S.D. = 0.82); and the mean agency score was 1.40 (S.D. = 0.80) in the merged data set (see Table 6.1).

Measurement of the Degree of Historical Divisions

Survey experiments have not always been able to fully satisfy theoretical interests without compromising their internal validity.[46] Internal validity means the ability to eliminate alternative explanations of the dependent variable.[47] Experimental designs without random assignment pose a threat to internal validity by their inability to eliminate selection bias. In such situations, measurements of dependent variables may not be attributed to the experimental treatment but to some preexisting condition. Instances such as experimental testing of political tolerance[48] and the legitimacy of state institutions[49] therefore normally require the incorporation of an "objection precondition,"[50] as both the concepts of "tolerance" and "legitimacy" are based on the acceptance of something "objectionable." It is of little theoretical relevance to study "tolerance of a friendly group" or "acceptance of a beneficial government policy." However, since different respondents have different objections, which predetermine their treatment, their assignment to the experimental treatment is not random. Thus, researchers often faced a dilemma: to satisfy theoretical interests by including the objection precondition at the expense of internal validity, or to satisfy the experimental requirements by forgoing the objection precondition at the expense of theoretical interests.

In order to satisfy the theoretical interests of conducting research in divided societies and at the same time to satisfy the requirement of random assignment, we determine the degree of a respondent's objection vis-à-vis the wrongdoer at the end of the first part of the vignette. The first part is non-experimental as it is common to all respondents. Thus, respondents hear the first part of the vignette, which is followed by the *historical animosity scale* that captures the respondent's objections to the wrongdoer. After this, the experimental part of the vignette continues. The historical animosity scale measured in the first step then serves as a control variable for the effects of experimental manipulations measured in the second step. In other

Table 6.1. Description of Major Scales

Scale	Range	Merged Data Set		Czech Republic		Hungary		Poland	
		Mean	S.D.	Mean	S.D.	Mean	S.D.	Mean	S.D.
Trust in government	(0; 16)	7.15	(4.64)	7.68	(4.58)	7.17	(4.74)	6. 65	(4.52)
Position	(0; 3)	1.76	(0.82)	1.78	(0.83)	1.77	(0.85)	1.72	(0.76)
Motives	(0; 3)	1.97	(0.82)	1.97	(0.81)	1.97	(0.79)	2.04	(0.78)
Agency	(0; 3)	1.40	(0.80)	1.53	(0.81)	1.19	(0.83)	1.49	(0.76)
Historical animosity	(−8; 8)	1.12	(4.03)	2.72	(3.61)	0.26	(4.14)	0.49	(3.83)
Reconciliation	(0; 32)	11.14	(7.25)	11.41	(6.86)	11.50	(7.42)	10.41	(7.30)

Source: David, Lustration Systems, Trust in Government, and Reconciliation.

words, the historical animosity scale is a covariate that is exogenous to the random assignment. Although the notion of control may sound redundant in experimental research, even experiments may produce biased results in divided societies as long as historical divisions are a subject of inquiry.[51] This design enables all respondents to be randomly assigned to different experimental manipulations, and it gains crucial information about each respondent's objection to the wrongdoer.

Since "condemnation," "punishment," "forgiveness," and "forgetting" represent the plurality of attitudes that capture the degree of disapproval of the wrongdoer caused by his past, a historical animosity scale was constructed by adding moral condemnation, punishment, the negative of forgetting, and the negative of forgiving (see Appendix B). Each question had five response categories, allowing a neutral response. The responses were coded from the most negative (0) to the most positive (4) in order to effectively present our analysis concerning the memory of the past in Chapter 7. Thus, the scale ranged from −8 to 8. The scale had a high level of reliability, with Cronbach's alpha at 0.85 in the merged data set, 0.88 in the Czech Republic, 0.83 in Hungary, and 0.83 in Poland (see Table 6.1).

Results

The results of our analyses are presented in two steps: (1) analysis of the data set from all three countries merged together, including the descriptive statistics and the multivariate analyses, which provide us with evidence

Table 6.2. Mean Scores of Trust in Government Scale for Dismissal, Exposure, and Confession in the Merged Data Set

	Mean	S.D.	N
Dismissal	8.60***	(4.41)	1,203
Continuation	5.73	(4.42)	1,223
Exposure	7.30	(4.66)	1,202
No exposure	7.01	(4.48)	1,224
Confession	7.63***	(4.58)	1,216
Denial	6.68	(4.49)	1,210
Sequence 1	7.16	(4.62)	1,183
Sequence 2	7.15	(4.66)	1,243

Source: David, Lustration Systems, Trust in Government, and Reconciliation.

Note: The table presents the mean scores of trust in government for each experimental treatment and their absence in the merged data set and the results of Anova tests that determine whether the difference between the means of experimental treatments and their orthogonal version is significant (*** $p < .001$).

about the effect of dismissal, exposure, and confession on trust in government and enable us to control for the effects of historical animosities and the perception of the wrongdoer's position, motives, and agency; and (2) separate country analyses, also including the descriptive statistics and the multivariate analyses, which provide us with evidence of the effects of dismissal, exposure, and confession within three different political cultures in the Czech Republic, Hungary, and Poland.

The Overall Effects of Dismissal, Exposure, and Confession on Trust in Government

A first look at the results indicates that none of the experimental variables decreased the perception of the government as being trustworthy. As expected, dismissal, exposure, and confession were all able to generate positive effects on trust in government in the merged data set.

Table 6.2 and Figure 6.1 summarize the mean scores of trust in government for each experimental treatment and their contrasts. The preliminary results indicate that dismissal produces the largest effect on trust in government, followed by confession, and then by exposure. The mean score of trust in government scale for dismissal of the tainted official is 8.60, while

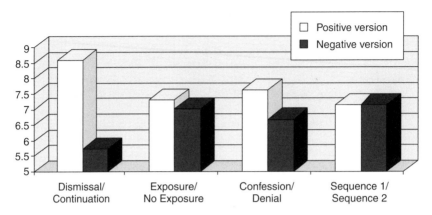

Figure 6.1. Mean scores of the trust in government scale for dismissal, exposure, and confession and their absence in the merged data set. The trust in government scale ranged from 0 to 16. Source: David, Lustration Systems, Trust in Government, and Reconciliation.

the mean score for his continuation is 5.73. Thus, the effect of dismissal on trust in government is 2.87 points. In comparison, the mean score of the trust in government for the confession of the tainted official is 7.63, while the mean for his denial is 6.68. The mean difference of 0.95 points makes the effect of confession on trust in government about three times smaller than that of dismissal. The mean for exposure of the tainted official is 7.30, while the mean for no exposure is 7.01. Consequently, the mean difference of 0.29 points suggests that exposure is about three times less efficient than confession and about nine times less efficient than dismissal. Our results also indicate that it is irrelevant whether the experimental vignette starts with exposure or with confession. There seems to be no difference in mean scores for the two vignette sequences. However, this description does not say anything about the significance of these effects, nor is it able to control for the effects of other variables. We therefore turn to our multivariate analyses of the merged data set.

Table 6.3 presents the results of three OLS linear regression models.[52] We have used the Czech Republic as a backdrop for our comparison in order to compare any country differences between the exclusive and non-exclusive

Table 6.3. Predictors of Trust in Government in the Merged Data Set

	Model 1		Model 2		Model 3	
	B	SE	B	SE	B	SE
Dismissal	2.87***	(.18)	3.07***	(.19)	3.13***	(.19)
Exposure	0.27	(.18)	0.20	(.19)	0.14	(.19)
Confession	0.93***	(.18)	0.79***	(.19)	0.76***	(.20)
Sequence	−0.03	(.18)	0.08	(.19)	0.09	(.19)
High position			−0.28*	(.12)	−0.15	(.12)
Motive (self-interest)			−0.71***	(.12)	−0.58***	(.12)
Agency			−0.25*	(.12)	−0.09	(.12)
Historical animosity					−0.19***	(.03)
Hungary	−0.48*	(.22)	−0.58*	(.24)	−0.97***	(.24)
Poland	−1.06***	(.21)	−1.11***	(.24)	−1.51**	(.26)
(Constant)	5.19	(.23)	7.29	(.43)	7.68	(.46)
R^2	.114		.143		.171	
Adj. R^2	.112		.139		.166	
N	2,426		1,989		1,910	

Source: David, Lustration Systems, Trust in Government, and Reconciliation.

Note: The table displays OLS linear regression models. The trust in government scale (range 0 to 16) was regressed on experimental variables (coded 0; 1) and control variables. Hungary and Poland are contrasted against the Czech Republic.

* $p < .05$ ** $p < .01$ *** $p < .001$

systems. We have therefore created dummy variables for Hungary and Poland. Model 1 regresses trust in government against our experimental and country variables. In line with our preliminary analysis, the effect of dismissal on trust in government is about 2.87 points, other things being equal, and the result is highly significant. Confession of tainted officials increases trust in government by 0.93 points, other things being equal. The effect of confession is about three times smaller but still highly significant. On the other hand, the effect of exposure fails to reach a statistically significant level ($p = .122$). The model also reveals some differences among the three countries. The Hungarians seem to trust their government significantly less than the Czechs, other things being equal. Similarly, the Poles seem to trust their government significantly less than the Czechs, other things being equal. Differences among the three countries may be the result of various factors, one of which may be a lustration system. Although these findings contribute to our understanding of trust in government, we shall deal with country-level differences later. Now we shall turn to our second model.

We have hypothesized that trust in government may be affected by the position of the wrongdoer in the previous regime, his motives, and his agency. Our second model has therefore controlled for these three variables. As we can see from model 2 in Table 6.3, the effect of each of our experimental variables has not changed much. The effect of dismissal remains highly significant. It even slightly increases, exceeding 3 points on the scale, other things being equal. The effect of confession drops slightly to 0.79 points, other things being equal, but remains highly significant ($p < .001$). In line with our expectations, the three control variables produce negative effects. A one-point increase in the perception that the wrongdoer held a high position in the previous regime decreases trust in government by 0.28 points ($p < .05$), other things being equal. A one-point increase in the perception that he was motivated by his self-interest decreases trust in government by 0.71 points ($p < .001$), other things being equal. A one-point increase in the perception that he was acting as a social agent at his own will decreased trust in government by 0.25 points ($p < .05$), other things being equal. These results suggest that retaining a tainted official who previously held a high position in the previous regime or was motivated by his own personal interests or was not forced into his wrongdoing would significantly decrease trust in the government.

However, we conducted research in divided societies where each side may retain its own view of government and its role in the human rights abuses of the past. The lack of reconciliation may therefore undermine trust in government. For this reason, model 3 controls for the degree of historical animosities. The results of this model are very similar. They suggest the following:

- We have found strong and consistent evidence that supports our first hypothesis about the positive effect of dismissal on trust in government. Other things being equal, dismissal remains a highly significant predictor of trust in government regardless of historical animosities.
- We have found no evidence to support our second hypothesis about the effect of exposure on trust in government.
- We have found strong and consistent evidence to support our third hypothesis about the positive effect of confession on trust in government. Thus, confession established itself as a plausible, although considerably less efficient, alternative to dismissal.

After controlling for historical animosities, the effects of a high position of the tainted official and his social agency on trust in government become insignificant. Both of them affect the moral judgments about the wrong-doer in the first place, and only through these judgments do they seem to affect trust in government. On the other hand, the perception of the official as motivated by his self-interest decreases trust in government by 0.58 points, other things being equal. Nonetheless, after controlling for animosities, even this perception dramatically decreases in comparison with model 2. Indeed, historical animosities are negatively correlated with trust in government: a one-point increase on the animosities scale decreases the trust in government scale by 0.19 points, other things being equal.[53]

There are no significant country differences between the Czech Republic and Hungary in model 3, other things being equal, although the Poles tend to trust their government significantly less than the Czechs, other things being equal. Country differences are the subject of our next analysis.

The Effects of Dismissal, Exposure, and Confession on Trust in Government in the Czech Republic, Hungary, and Poland

The Czech Republic, Hungary, and Poland developed different lustration systems. This means that there were three different political cultures that gave rise to these systems. The question we are asking here is whether dismissal, exposure, and confession can promote trust in government within these different political contexts. Table 6.4 and Figure 6.2 summarize the mean scores of trust in government for the experimental treatments in each country.

The preliminary analyses indicate that dismissal produced the strongest effect on trust in government in all three countries. Among the three countries, dismissal generated the largest effect in the Czech Republic. The mean scores of trust in government were 9.62 for Czech respondents who heard the vignette versions containing dismissal and 5.79 for those who heard the continuance of employment of tainted officials. The difference of 3.83 points is highly significant ($p < .001$) and may have been stimulated by the persistent practice of the exclusive system in the Czech Republic: the Czechs may see dismissal as a natural solution to the presence of tainted officials in government. In Hungary, the mean scores of trust in government were 8.72 and 5.70 for those hearing dismissal and continuance, respectively. The difference of over 3 points was still fairly large and highly significant

Table 6.4. Mean Scores of Trust in Government Scale for Dismissal, Exposure, and Confession in the Czech Republic, Hungary, and Poland

	Czech Republic		Hungary		Poland	
	Mean	S.D.	Mean	S.D.	Mean	S.D.
Dismissal	9.62***	(4.16)	8.72***	(4.31)	7.54***	(4.54)
Continuation	5.79	(4.17)	5.70	(4.66)	5.73	(4.32)
Exposure	8.01^	(4.68)	7.23	(4.93)	6.74	(4.43)
No exposure	7.37	(4.47)	7.10	(4.54)	6.57	(4.61)
Confession	8.29***	(4.59)	7.69***	(4.74)	6.94^	(4.52)
Denial	7.12	(4.50)	6.64	(4.71)	6.37	(4.52)
Sequence 1	7.76	(4.44)	7.18	(4.67)	6.53	(4.65)
Sequence 2	7.59	(4.72)	7.15	(4.82)	6.77	(4.39)

Source: David, Lustration Systems, Trust in Government, and Reconciliation.

Note: The table presents the mean scores of trust in government for each experimental treatment and their absence in each country and the results of Anova tests that determine whether the difference between the means of experimental treatments and their orthogonal version is significant within each country.

^$p < .1$ ***$p < .001$

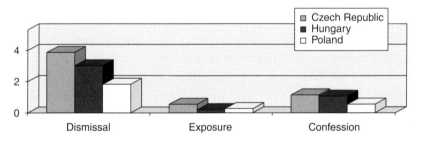

Figure 6.2. Mean differences in the trust in government scale between dismissal and continuation, exposure and no exposure, and confession and denial in the Czech Republic, Hungary, and Poland. The trust in government scale ranged from 0 to 16. Source: David, Lustration Systems, Trust in Government, and Reconciliation.

($p < .001$). It is a surprising result for a country that fostered a culture of consensus and that practiced an inclusive system in which dismissals almost never occurred. Dismissal had its smallest effect in Poland. The mean scores for trust in government were 7.54 and 5.73 among those who heard the vignette versions containing dismissals and continuance of employment, respectively. These scores indicated that dismissal increases trust in government by 1.81 points but the result is still highly significant ($p < .001$). These preliminary results indicate that the Czechs found the continuation of the old personnel more problematic than the Hungarians and especially more than the Poles did. But overall dismissal is a means to establish trust in government in all countries.

Exposure seemed to generate a small positive effect on trust in government in all three countries. The mean score of trust in government was 8.01 among Czechs whose vignettes were based on the exposure of the identity of wrongdoers versus 7.37 among those whose vignettes were based on non-exposure. In Hungary, the mean scores of trust in government for these two sets of experimental vignettes were 7.23 and 7.10, respectively. In Poland, the mean scores of trust in government were 6.74 and 6.57, respectively. Thus, the effect of exposure was a 0.64-point increase in trust in government in the Czech Republic, a mere 0.13-point increase in Hungary, and a 0.17-point increase in Poland. It failed to reach an acceptable level of significance in Hungary and Poland; it was marginally insignificant in the Czech Republic ($p = .061$).

Confession seemed to affect trust in government more than exposure but less than dismissal. In the Czech Republic, the mean value of the trust in government scale for confession was 8.29, while the mean for denial was 7.12, creating a 1.17-point increase in the scale. The difference between the two means was highly significant ($p < .001$). The fact that a secular state such as the Czech Republic took the lead in accepting confession of a public official is certainly unexpected. The effect of confession on trust in government was slightly weaker in Hungary than in the Czech Republic. Hungarian respondents whose vignettes involved confession versus those whose vignettes involved denial scored 7.69 and 6.64 on average, respectively, meaning confession increased trust in government by 1.05 points. Given the country's experience with the reconciliatory system, the impact of confession on trust in government seems surprisingly small in Poland. Poles whose vignettes involved a confession scored on average 6.94 on the trust in government scale, while their counterparts, whose vignettes involved denial, scored an average of 6.37 in the same scale. Thus, confession of tainted officials increased the general public's trust in the government by a mere 0.57 points and the difference marginally fails to reach the acceptable level of significance in the country ($p = .078$).

Table 6.5   Predictors of Trust in Government in the Czech Republic, Hungary, and Poland

	Czech Republic		Hungary		Poland	
	B	SE	B	SE	B	SE
Dismissal	3.97***	(.33)	3.13***	(.31)	2.19***	(.38)
Exposure	0.43	(.33)	− 0.09	(.31)	0.13	(.38)
Confession	0.91**	(.33)	0.86**	(.31)	0.31	(.38)
Sequence	0.43	(.33)	0.11	(.31)	− 0.29	(.38)
High position	− 0.33	(.20)	0.03	(.18)	− 0.16	(.24)
Motive (self-interest)	− 0.53*	(.21)	− 0.57	(.20)	− 0.80**	(.24)
Agency	− 0.20	(.21)	− 0.09	(.19)	0.02	(.26)
Historical animosity	− 0.12*	(.05)	0.29***	(.04)	− 0.10*	(.05)
(Constant)	7.05	(.74)	6.47	(.70)	7.29	(.84)
R^2	0.233		0.200		0.088	
Adj. R^2	0.223		0.192		0.084	
N	593		760		557	

Source: David, Lustration Systems, Trust in Government, and Reconciliation.
Note: The table displays OLS linear regression models. The trust in government scale (range 0 to 16) was regressed on experimental variables (coded 0; 1) and control variables.

$^\wedge p < .1$ $^* p < .05$ $^{**} p < .01$ $^{***} p < .001$

The preliminary analysis presented in this section has advantages and disadvantages. On the positive side, its parsimony facilitates easy comprehension of the results for each experimental treatment in each country. On the other hand, it does not take into account the effects of other factors. The following analyses therefore rectify this deficiency by using a multivariate regression model that takes into account the effects of dismissal, exposure, and confession on trust in government after other factors are controlled for.

The results from the OLS linear regression analyses confirm that dismissal is a powerful predictor of trust in government in all three countries (see Table 6.5). In comparison to other experimental variables, dismissal is the strongest predictor of trust in government. Other things being equal, dismissal produces the strongest effects in the Czech Republic ($B = 3.97$, $p < .001$), followed by Hungary ($B = 3.13, p < .001$), and then Poland ($B = 2.19, p < .001$). The effect of exposure is insignificant in all three countries. This is particularly surprising with respect to Hungary, which pursued the inclusive system to deal with tainted officials. As in our preliminary analyses, confession is a significant predictor of trust in government in the

Czech Republic and Hungary. Other things being equal, confession results in a 0.91-point increase in the trust in government scale in the Czech Republic ($p < 0.01$) and in a 0.86-point increase in Hungary ($p < 0.01$). The effect of confession on trust in government is not significant in Poland. This difference is surprising given the fact that Poland is a Catholic country that practiced the reconciliatory system.

As in the merged data set, historical animosities absorb most of the effects attributed to the position of the tainted official in the previous regime and to his agency. The results concerning position and agency are insignificant in each of the studied countries. However, the view of the tainted official as motivated by self-interest produces negative effects in all three countries. Other things being equal, a one-point increase in the self-interest of the tainted official to commit wrongdoing decreases trust in government by 0.53 points in the Czech Republic ($p < .05$), by 0.57 points in Hungary ($p < .01$) and by 0.80 points in Poland ($p < .01$). Historical animosities have generated significant negative effects on trust in government in all three countries. Other things being equal, a one-point increase in the historical animosities scale generates a 0.12-point decrease in the trust in government scale in the Czech Republic ($p < .05$), a 0.29-point decrease in Hungary ($p < .001$), and a 0.10-point decrease in Poland ($p < .05$).

Thus, most of the results are consistent in all three countries. The only major inconsistency concerns the effect of confession on trust in government, which is significant in the Czech Republic and Hungary but insignificant in Poland. This suggests that the use of the reconciliatory system may be context dependent, although in a different way from expected. Perhaps the strong Catholic background of Polish society and the practice of the reconciliatory system may put an emphasis on higher requirements for accepting confession.

Discussion

The analyses presented in this chapter shed light on the propensity of different methods of personnel systems to impact trust in government and on the roles of other factors in this process. First of all, none of the methods of personnel systems has produced any negative effects on trust in government. The absence of negative results about the effects of dismissal, exposure, and confession across the three countries, as well as in the merged

data set, implies the potential use of lustration systems as methods of reju-
venating trust in government after transition.

Dismissal

In accordance with our first hypothesis, dismissal is consistently the strongest predictor of trust in government. Dismissal produced highly significant
results in all of our models in the merged data set and in all three countries.
This indicates that dismissal unequivocally conveys a message of discontinuity with the past: the establishment of trust in a new government after a
transition requires that it be purified by the removal of tainted officials.

The role of dismissal in establishing trust in government remains highly
significant even after controlling for historical animosities. Naturally, common sense suggests that governments without tainted officials would be
more trustworthy in the eyes of the public than governments that include
tainted officials. This may hold in established democracies, but it is far less
obvious in divided societies where *wrongdoing* is a relative term interpreted
differently by each side of the historical conflict. Initially, we had concerns
that dismissal may satisfy those who had opposed the previous regime but
dissatisfy those who had supported it. However, our findings dispel these
concerns. Dismissal is an effective means of bolstering the public's trust
in the new government before as well as after controlling for historical
animosities.

Dismissals generated the most robust results in the Czech Republic,
followed by Hungary and Poland. Owing to the implementation of the
exclusive system, the Czechs may see dismissal as a natural solution to the
presence of old personnel entrenched in the government. In light of this,
the marked impact of dismissals in Hungary may be surprising given the
rare occurrence of dismissals in a country that pursued the inclusive system.
The results suggest that there was indeed a degree of dissatisfaction with
the presence of secret informers in government in Hungary, as indicated in
the previous chapter. Even in Poland, which remains deeply divided about
its past, the effect of dismissals on trust in government was highly significant.

Exposure

We hypothesized that exposure would increase trust in government because
it signifies discontinuity with the past and enhances transparency. We

found that exposure has positive effects on trust in government, although the effects failed to reach a statistically significant level in all models. Exposure of a tainted official by revealing shaming information about him does not resonate with the public in these three countries.

Confession

Confession can be credited with the most exciting findings. We hypothesized that confession would increase trust in government because it signaled a change of loyalty and the commitment of tainted officials to the new regime. First of all, our preliminary analyses found a highly significant effect of confession on trust in government in the merged data set (Tables 6.2 and 6.3). Thus, confession aspires to establish itself as a plausible alternative to dismissals. However, the effect of confession is only about one-third of the effect of dismissal.

Contrasting the effects of confession with those of exposure offers some meaningful insights. Both exposure and confession are forms of truth processes. However, the former is external to a tainted official, while the latter is a form of self-expression. Our research suggests that the effect of personal truth revelation is greater than the effect of disclosure of truth by the government. Although both exposure and confession give wrongdoers a second chance, citizens are willing to grant it only to wrongdoers who demonstrate a change of heart.

Confession does seem to be culturally dependent. The first set of findings from analyses of individual countries (Table 6.4) reveals that the largest effect of confession was in the Czech Republic, a secular state that implemented the exclusive system. The effect of confession is also highly significant in Hungary and marginally failed to reach an acceptable level of significance in Poland. This may be because of a particular sensitivity of Poles to confession: since the country is the most religious (Catholic) among the three countries and practices the reconciliatory system, Poles may be willing to accept confession only when they see it as genuine. Indeed, further analysis of the sample in Poland confirmed that confession is more effective when it is not obstructed by previous exposure.[54] Unlike in the Czech Republic and Hungary, not all confessions are accepted as confessions in Poland. In sum, confession may be employed in the macropolitical process in different countries, although countries that practice confession may demand higher standards in its implementation.

After controlling for historical animosities, the effect of confession becomes insignificant in Poland. This does not mean that confession is irrelevant or that confession is unable to reach both sides of divided societies. Instead, as we shall clearly see in the next chapter, the effect of confession is also indirect. Confession also affects reconciliation, which in turn affects trust in government. In contrast, the effects of dismissals and exposures affect trust in government directly.

The different dynamics of the effect of confession run contrary to our theorization in Chapter 2 about the top-down effects of personnel systems on reconciliation. We expected that all personnel systems would generate a spillover effect on reconciliation. While details of the eventual spillover effects of dismissal, exposure, and confession remain the subject of the following chapter, here we can see that the method of confession is different from that of exposures and dismissals. Confession by a tainted official also inspires a change at the micro level by decreasing the negative perception about the official. By confessing, the official purifies himself in the eyes of the public. In doing so, confession contributes to reconciliation, and through reconciliation may it eventually facilitate changes at the macro level and help establish trust in government.

Position, Motives, and Agency

Among our control variables, the perception of a tainted official of the previous regime as having a high position (in contrast to a low position), as being motivated by his own personal interest (in contrast to ideological motives), or as having acted on his own (in contrast to being forced to collaborate) decreased the trust in government (model 2, Table 6.3). The negative effect of the perception of the tainted official as having a high position in the previous regime on trust in government seems obvious but it is far from being self-evident in transitional societies. The public demands the prosecution of high officials whenever a small fry is caught but claims that injustices occurred among neighbors and colleagues whenever a high-profile case is resolved. The positive assessment of ideological motives may indicate a measure of tolerance toward wrongdoing of those who believed in communism. Alternatively, it may reflect disapproval of those who breached interpersonal trust to pursue their personal interests. In other words, the government is seen as more trustworthy with an official who was tainted by his wrongdoing in the pursuit of beliefs than personal gain.

Finally, it seems natural that the public judges government more strictly when it sees the tainted officials as social agents than when it sees them as victims. However, after controlling for historical animosities, the effect of position and social agency became insignificant, while the effect of motives was diluted. Although there are some country differences, these findings suggest social dynamics similar to that of confession. The position, motives, and agency seem to directly affect historical animosities, and then through them they affect trust in government.

Historical Animosities

Since we conducted research in divided societies, we have also controlled for the degree of historical animosities against the tainted official. Historical animosities—as indicated above—have been found to be a highly significant predictor of trust in government. However, we are unable to determine the causal direction, that is, whether animosities affect trust in government or trust in government affects animosities.

If any simple conclusions can be drawn from these analyses, they would indicate that the exclusive system is a means to establish trust in government; the reconciliatory system is a plausible, though less efficient, alternative to exclusions in order to achieve that goal; and there is no evidence of negative effects of lustration systems on trust in government.

7

Social Effects: Reconciliation and Collective Memory

I think you judged him too harshly. Sure, he went too far in what he said. . . . But put yourself in his shoes for a moment. You, as a man of honour. He can't remove his name from that statement . . . His black-listing. . . .

[T]hat's what we all love about your plays. Your love for mankind . . . your belief that people can change. Dreyman, no matter how often you say it in your plays. . . . People do not change!

—Florian Henckel von Donnersmarck[1]

Government policies often bring unintended social consequences. Chapter 2 theorized that personnel systems, though originally deviced to reform the state administration, carry expressive meanings that may affect historical social divisions. Chapter 5 suggested that lustration systems in the Czech Republic, Hungary, and Poland may affect the social standing of tainted officials and shape the memory of the past in different ways. This chapter examines the effects of personnel systems on social reconciliation and on the collective memory of the past. It is divided into three main sections. The first section theorizes that in the pursuit of political objectives, transitional personnel policies send ideological messages that either reproduce or transform social relationships. The second section uses the experimental vignette described in the previous chapter to examine the effects of dismissal, exposure, and confession on social reconciliation. The third section investigates the effects of different lustration systems on the collective memory of the past. It uses the non-experimental part of the vignette to assess country-level differences in people's responses to the same wrongdoing.

The Indirect Effects of Personnel Systems

The case of de-Baathification of Iraq, which was briefly referred to in the introduction to this book, has demonstrated that the political-administrative process, in addition to its exogenous causes and consequences, affected vital elements of political culture in Iraq. Although it was primarily intended to transform the government, it augmented historical divisions in society, creating deep political instability. Thus, the macropolitical process of personnel change generated microlevel consequences. Drawing on insights from cultural sociology, Chapter 2 offered a theoretical explanation, suggesting that even tangible political acts carry symbolic meanings that are communicated to the wider audience. The expressive power of political processes is particularly strong in times of transition, which are highly politicized and ritualized, and thus have repercussions for future social dynamics. Consequently, most policies of transitional justice generate profound social effects, redistribute guilt, and reassign responsibility for historical injustices. Although they concern only a limited number of perpetrators and victims, measures of transitional justice, such as criminal tribunals, truth commissions, and apologies, are frequently expected to promote reconciliation within an entire society.[2]

Similar to other policies related to transitional justice, lustrations reset value systems and redefine patterns of acceptable behavior across the whole society.[3] In Chapter 3, we saw that lustrations may be viewed as instances of social rituals, which aim to purify the public sphere. This political process inevitably communicates ideological messages about the social standing of tainted officials and about their past. Some lustration systems may transform the negative perceptions about tainted officials, while others may strengthen them. In Chapter 5, we pointed out that the Czech exclusive system created an image of former communists as intractable and unchangeable. It fostered a view that there was no "former communist" just as there is no "former Black man." In doing so, the exclusive system sent a strong ideological message that had consequences for the current standing of tainted persons and for the perception of their pasts.

First, it signaled that any positive interpersonal or formal relationship with the tainted official was forever impossible because the person could not change. His political beliefs—like the color of his skin—are biological characteristics, a matter of his *human nature*. Second, it signaled that all former communists, and other former collaborators, were of the same homogeneous social class. The exclusive system created a uniform image of them as untrustworthy, regardless of their motives for joining the party or for collaborating with the regime. This indiscriminate treatment may have created enemies among those who were not enemies in the first place. In other words, personnel systems—in addition to their political effects—may produce indirect effects: social effects on reconciliation in the society and historical effects that shape the memory of the past.

1. Social reconciliation. Personnel systems pass moral judgment on people's past actions. In their effort to purify the government, they re-create, or deal with, tainted officials. They effectively issue concessions of trustworthiness or untrustworthiness, redefining social boundaries of the new polity, indicating who is in and who is excluded.[4] Personnel systems may signal that past actions and loyalties are no longer officially rewarded because they have been replaced by new loyalties, systems of rewards, and norms of acceptable behavior. Alternatively, they may purify tainted officials by signaling that they have been reformed or by suggesting that the system, not their behavior in it, was abusive. Thus, by reassessing the social standing of wrongdoers in a particular way, personnel systems affect the prospect for reconciliation within the entire society.

2. Collective memory. Personnel systems may produce retrospective historical effects, assigning new meanings to the past. They reassess the past behavior of tainted officials and equalize their motives. Personnel systems may reinforce or alter particular historical perceptions of the past, similar to other memory-shaping exercises such as trials of former leaders and truth commissions. Transitional justice, according to Alexandra Barahona de Brito, Carmen González Enríquez, and Paloma Aguilar, affects people's understanding of the past.[5] Thus, personnel systems are likely to affect the collective memory of historical injustices.

Figure 7.1 illustrates the social and historical effects of personnel systems on the example of an exclusive system. In the past, society was divided into

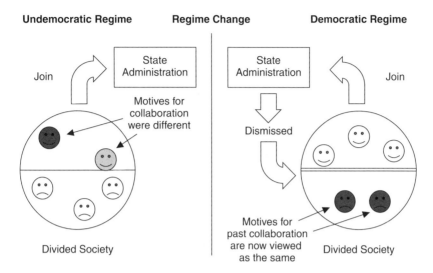

Figure 7.1. Indirect effects of personnel systems on social reconciliation and collective memory. The figure illustrates the hypotheses about the social and historical effects of an exclusive system. Dismissals may have twofold indirect effects: they may inhibit reconciliation by reproducing historical divisions in society, and they may affect the collective memory of the past by redefining motives for collaborating with the undemocratic regime.

two main groups: the first one was allowed to join the government, while the second one was excluded from participation (the gray zone between them is not necessary to illustrate the main point here). People within the group that had engaged with the apparatus of the previous regime and its illegitimate activities may have had different motives. Some may have been reformers, while others were hard-liners; some may have been forced to collaborate, while others may have collaborated willingly. Then, a change of regime occurs and the new government implements an exclusive system and dismisses the existing personnel. Owing to the application of the exclusive system, the roles of those who had previously participated in the regime and those who were excluded get switched. It means that the society has not reached reconciliation because of divisions naturally inherited from the past and because of their official certification by law. We can illustrate historical effects here as well. Owing to the application of the exclusive system, all dismissed personnel would acquire the same image. The blanket treatment of individuals as enemies irrespective of their motives for taking public employment in the previous regime may, paradoxically, transform their image from reformers to hard-liners and from bystanders to foes.

Figure 7.1 would look different in cases of other personnel systems. The inclusive and the reconciliatory system would lighten the negative image of tainted officials and enable a more flexible view of their historical motives. Figure 7.1 also omits people in the middle, between the poles of the society. Chapters 2 and 4 suggested that the pressure to identify enemies may paradoxically come from what has been called the "gray zone": people who neither actively engaged with the previous regime nor were with the opposition. In Figure 7.1, the official "in gray" is a proxy for the gray zone because in this chapter we do not study the motives of the gray zone for personnel systems but their effects on the perception of the "gray official." The gray zone is nevertheless an important conceptual tool in our examination of the origin of the exclusive system in Chapter 4.

Personnel Systems and Reconciliation

In this book, social reconciliation was defined as a process of restoring minimal civic relationships with wrongdoers. In contrast to religious, ecumenical, and other substantive concepts of reconciliation, social reconciliation is used as a purely secular concept in this book. Reconciliation signifies a renewal of a minimal civic relationship even though the parties may not have known each other before. It is assumed that they would have had a civic relationship if the wrongdoing had not occurred. We characterize social reconciliation as a multifaceted concept encompassing interpersonal trust, tolerance, and social closeness. Adversaries do not need to establish a positive relationship but they should be able "to get along" (e.g., expect that other people will act legally, respect each other's rights, and live as neighbors).

By passing judgment on wrongdoers, personnel systems may affect the standing of wrongdoers in society. Each system assesses the gravity of the wrongdoer's past behavior and sends a signal about his or her future. It may express condemnation of the wrongdoer, aggravating perceptions about his or her trustworthiness, or it may give a wrongdoer a second chance, effectively signaling that the renewal of a minimal social relationship is possible. Different personnel systems have different propensities to facilitate or inhibit social reconciliation.

One of the key characteristics that distinguish the three major personnel systems is the different assumptions each of them make about the malleability of "human nature." In this context human nature does not refer to the psychological dispositions of individuals to particular political systems. It refers to the perception about loyalty of former adversaries to the new system, perceptions about their trustworthiness during the dynamic transitional process, and other critical perceptions. Some systems may promote flexible perceptions about former adversaries, while others may inhibit it. When can a system be considered transformative? To what extent does a personnel system assume that human nature is pliable? Which system has the greatest propensity to transform inherited perceptions? To what extent does a personnel system assume that the future is, or is not, predicted by the past? More precisely, to what extent are past human actions that occurred under particular macropolitical contexts considered a reliable predictor of future behavior in other contexts? Does the system allow a way out of past roles?

There is a conceptual parallel between transition from authoritarian rule to democracy studied here, and transition from the state of nature to the state studied by classical social contract theorists. The paradigmatic teaching of these thinkers on human nature, which underpins the notion of loyalties and identities in transition and aligns them with their political-structural frameworks, may help us delineate the varied effects of different measures of transitional justice.

Hypothesis I. The Effects of Dismissal

The exclusive system assumes that past records are a reliable predictor of future behavior. The symbolic power of the exclusive system preserves an unyielding view of former adversaries. Their loyalties, identities, and characters remain firmly fixed and determined by their past behavior, actions, and associations. In order to be justified and sustainable, the system not only perpetuates but also fosters the inimical view of wrongdoers as unchangeable and intractable. For this reason, people who once associated with the former regime are not only excluded; they also continue to be barred from any position of trust.

Naturally, members of society are accountable for their past behavior in many areas of daily life: they have to submit résumés when applying for jobs or declare their criminal records when entering certain countries. This intransigent perspective resembles Hobbes's teaching on human nature:

people will act in the same negative way in the future as they did in the past if they have an opportunity to do so. It reflects mistrust of others and supports fear about a return to the "state of war." In the context of political transition, there is no guarantee that people associated with the previous undemocratic regime would genuinely renounce their past affiliations and switch their loyalties to the new democracy. They may be perceived as a threat to the new order. Thus, the only way to secure democratic transition and to avert the risk of subversion is to maintain the exclusive system.

According to Schwartz, Šiklová, Teitel, and other critics of the Czech exclusive system, inherited personnel were portrayed as corrupt, inefficient, and loyal to the previous regime in order to serve the interests of the new political elite to justify dismissals just as show trials and purges had been frequently used by the communist party to eliminate its enemies.[6] Although the socialist regimes were largely corrupt, inefficient, and ideological, and their officials may have had these characteristics, no provision in the lustration law served to determine whether this was true in a particular case. According to Eyal, dismissals have conveyed a message that "these people, who spent most of their working lives under communism, are no longer fit to work, they cannot be trusted to work, hence to participate in society."[7]

The social effect of exclusive systems can be conceptualized as that of *inversion*: the elites switch their positions and wrongdoers are replaced, but the political style and adversarial relations remain the same. Historical animosities have been effectively incorporated into the new system. In conducting dismissals, the state signals that persons associated with former regimes are politically untrustworthy and remain so in their ordinary lives as well. The label of untrustworthiness solidifies the negative perception of people associated with the former regime and further diminishes their standing in society. The political exclusion of persons associated with the former regime exacerbates their social marginalization. Thus, the exclusive method may be able to facilitate political transformation at the expense of social transformation. In the pursuit of establishing trust in government, it may solidify social mistrust. While the exclusive system may be able to unequivocally condemn the past regime and legitimize the new one in the eyes of its supporters, it may be unable to reach out to both sides of the divided society, whose perceptions remain unaltered. Dismissal therefore is hypothesized to inhibit social reconciliation.

Hypothesis II. The Effects of Exposure

There is a disagreement in the literature on transitional justice about the effects of exposure on shaping citizens' trust in tainted officials. The lack of consensus might be attributed to the dual nature of "truth" in transitional societies.[8] Proponents of revelations have suggested that truth might help clarify the past[9] and disarm unwarranted suspicions and rumors.[10] The view that truth may have a healing effect and contribute to social reconciliation with former adversaries has been not only raised by intellectual leaders such as Desmond Tutu[11] but empirically substantiated by Gibson.[12] Opponents have argued that truth revelation might open old wounds, defame and ostracize former collaborators.[13] According to Claus Offe they might lead to "witch-hunts or scapegoating,"[14] which in Šiklová's view are reminiscent of the communist-era smear campaigns.[15]

The lack of consensus may also be attributed to the dual nature of the shaming effect that truth revelation may produce. On the one hand, exposure may further embarrass the tainted official by creating a sanction of stigmatizing publicity.[16] The ritualistic dimension of exposure is emphasized in the media campaigns that reveal the cover names alongside the real names of tainted officials. We have shown that cover names may become an object of ridicule with profound shaming and stigmatizing effects. On the other hand, exposure without dismissal may be an instance of a reintegrative shaming ritual as postulated by Braithwaite and Mugford.[17] It may become a part of a restorative justice project in the political context of transition.

We may consider deriving the social effects of exposure from the instrumental purpose of the legal measures that created it. If the primary purpose of exposure is to minimize the risk of blackmail that could prejudice national security,[18] then the exposed individuals are likely to be viewed as carriers of threat, traitors in the past, and subversives in the present. If the primary purpose of exposure is to establish transparency, then the exposed individuals may be viewed as corrupt, inefficient, and untrustworthy. But their exposure in the absence of dismissal effectively signifies that their "offense" was not serious, otherwise they would not have been allowed to continue in their positions. Consequently, the effects of exposure effectively diminish the seriousness of the offense. Their meaning may be similar to the symbolic meaning of fines, which according to Kahan fail to condemn wrongdoers as unequivocally as criminal punishments: "You may do what you have done but you must pay for the privilege."[19]

Thus, redefining the gravity of wrongdoing seems central to understanding the effects of the inclusive system. What is the social construction of wrongdoers' human nature under inclusive systems? In an inclusive system wrongdoers are generally treated as victims of previous political regimes. Collaborators and other people associated with former regimes are viewed as persons who could not sustain the enormous pressure, blackmail, and threats to which they and their families were exposed under the previous regime.[20] They may have been forced to "follow orders" or act "legally" in terms of the illegitimate laws of the undemocratic regime. They were denied the opportunity to act freely under the system of structural oppression. Once external constraints fade, Rousseau, Marx, or Che all believe that *Hombre Nuevo*, a new, better person will emerge.[21] For the same reason, an agreement or contract signed under duress is not an expression of free will and is therefore invalid. Thus, one of the assumptions of the Hungarian inclusive system, according to Halmai and Scheppele, was that the new regime should provide a fresh start for all.[22]

The victim-like position of wrongdoers is strengthened by the implementation of inclusive systems. Revelations of truth pursued by these systems are external to wrongdoers who may downplay their past involvement. The process may give them opportunities to deny any wrongdoing or to make excuses and give justifications for their actions. This may condone the wrongdoing by assigning it a lesser status. Consequently, inclusive systems are hypothesized to produce transformative effects by transforming the perception of the past and the role of wrongdoers in it. In fact, all personnel systems may have propensities to generate the effect of *retroversion* of collective memory: creating different representations of the past. The wrongdoings may initially still be considered illegitimate but the responsibility of wrongdoers for their pasts is gradually lifted under the regime of inclusive systems.

Thus, in contrast to dismissal, exposure tempers the gravity of the wrongdoing. The denial of any wrongdoing by the tainted official may further strengthen their perception as harmless. By making excuses, the inclusive system suggests that the personnel associated with the past regime were its victims rather than its active social agents. Owing to the retroversion, the transformation of tainted officials may formally be considered redundant because the officials were not wrongdoers in the first place. Thus, the effect of exposure on social reconciliation is hypothesized to be positive.

Hypothesis III. The Effects of Confession

The reconciliatory system is based on the confession of persons associated with the former regime. Confession is similar to the exposure of the past conduct of public officials. However, unlike externally imposed truth revelation, confession means the individual makes his own public revelation of past collaboration. Affidavits through which confessions are expressed serve as loyalty tests that give respondents a second chance in exchange for truth. However, similar to the dual nature of truth in divided societies, confessions also carry dual characters. Opponents argue that confessions are induced by external incentives and do not communicate an internal change of wrongdoers. A government policy of public employment forgiveness does not necessarily signify social reconciliation. Confessions may represent self-debasement or contrition, penalties that might generate stigmatizing effects.[23] Indeed, Chapter 5 suggested that some on Poland's right maintain that communism has not ceased to exist; it only changed its nature.

For many, however, the reconciliatory system appears to be the most efficient personnel system for communicating that a wrongdoer has changed. The system gives wrongdoers a second chance in exchange for their own revelations of truth about the past. Such "confessions" generate the same effect as apologies. By confessing, apologizing, or showing remorse, the wrongdoer is, according to Trudy Govier, "seeking, in effect, to separate his character and future actions from his past wrongs."[24] Augustine's saying "hate the sin, but love the sinner,"[25] according to Murphy, signifies that a sinner remains psychologically identified with the sin unless he breaks the identification through repentance.[26] In confessions, wrongdoers in effect ask society and victims to be respected as human beings[27] and "recognize their status as morally human."[28] Confession, remorse, and apology may enable society to reevaluate the wrongdoer as a decent person with whom a renewed civic relationship is possible.[29] Psychological research, according to Julie Exline and Roy Baumeister, as well as studies of Czech political prisoners conducted by David and Choi, corroborate this argument by showing that victims are more likely to forgive perpetrators who apologize.[30]

We therefore argue that the reconciliatory system produces the effect of *conversion*. Confessions provide wrongdoers with an opportunity to disassociate themselves from their former roles. Although they may not necessarily facilitate the moral and political transformation of wrongdoers, their confessions make wrongdoers more acceptable to their opponents than their denials. They demonstrate that at least a minimal change in personal attitude of the wrongdoers has occurred and that the old personnel are willing to play by the rules of the new regime. In turn, the public may be willing to grant them a second chance and renew a relationship of trust with them. Confessions are therefore hypothesized to foster social reconciliation.

Hypothesis IV. The Effects of Position, Motives, and Agency

The social effects of personnel systems are inevitably contextual. They are, among other things, affected by the position of the wrongdoer under the previous regime. In the previous chapter, we cited Gibson and Gouws, who considered an actor's goals, leadership, intentionality and consequences, and hate motives as plausible factors that affect the attribution of blame for the apartheid regime in South Africa.[31] Similarly, in Eastern Europe, people may be less willing to reconcile with a wrongdoer who held a high position, acted voluntarily, and was ideologically motivated than with someone who followed orders, was forced to commit wrongdoings, and took his job because he needed to feed his family or pay his mortgage. For this reason, a wrongdoer's high position, ideological motives, and agency are considered inhibitors of social reconciliation.

Hypothesis V. The Effect of Historical Animosities

As with trust in government, the effect of personnel systems on reconciliation may be affected by historical animosities in a particular society. Reconciliation may not be affected only by dismissal, exposure, and confession but also by the people's views of the wrongdoing itself. For instance, the process of de-Baathification of Iraq only augmented historical divisions, which already existed under the regime of Saddam Hussein. However, in experimental research, we cannot randomize these animosities. Thus, for reasons described in the previous chapter, we need to control for the degree of historical animosity in society. Naturally, we expect that historical animosities will negatively affect reconciliation in society.

Measurement of Reconciliation

As with trust in government, our research could not rely on the existing operationalizations of reconciliation. There has been no consensus on the definition of reconciliation in the emerging field of transitional justice.

Taking into account empirical studies of reconciliation conducted by Gibson,[32] Phuong Pham, Harvey Weinstein, and Timothy Longman,[33] and David and Choi,[34] this book defines "social reconciliation" as the willingness to establish a minimum level of civic relationship with the wrongdoer, which encompasses trust, tolerance, and social closeness (the opposite of the concept of social distance). In transitional democracies, it is essential that people are able to overcome inimical relations and mutual distrust in order to coexist with each other as citizens, respect each other's rights, work together, and live as neighbors. The following considerations shaped our understanding of reconciliation.

Interpersonal trust has been traditionally argued to be a central pillar of social, political, and economic order.[35] However, the significance of trust for cooperation has been conceptually[36] and empirically challenged.[37] For this reason, our research goes beyond trust and includes another social category, namely tolerance. According to Gibson and Gouws, "[t]olerance is the endorphin of the democratic body politic; without tolerance, it is impossible to sustain the sort of competition over political ideas that is essential to democratic politics."[38]

However, trust and tolerance may still not mean social reconciliation. One may believe that "most people can be trusted"[39] and that people associated with the past regime have the right to express their opinions, but at the same time he or she may refuse to accept them as neighbors or coworkers. For this reason, our research also asks questions that measure "social closeness" or "social distance." Social distance has been used, though in different contexts, to determine the social consequences of labeling.[40] This may also serve the purposes of our research, which examines, among other things, the social consequences of labeling the tainted official as legally untrustworthy.

The significance of social closeness or distance raises the question of why this measure is not sufficient and why trust and tolerance have to be measured as well. The answer seems obvious: being able to work with someone does not necessarily signify trust. An interview with a headmaster of a primary school during the fieldwork for this project in the Czech Republic was particularly revealing. When asked whether he would employ in his school a teacher who was known to have been a secret informer under the previous regime, the forty-year-old member of the Civic Democratic Party (ODS) gave a positive answer: "I would be able to manage him, I would be able to coach him."[41] He apparently would not trust that person, but he would tolerate his right to be employed in his school (the Czech lustration system does not concern teachers) and work with him.

In total, eight items were used to measure willingness to be reconciled with former collaborators. The questions about trust directly corresponded with the above questions about trust in government. These included trust in the wrongdoer in general, willingness to honor his expertise, belief that he would comply with the law, and belief that he would be loyal to democracy. Questions about tolerance concerned the wrongdoer's right to demonstrate and strike. These questions captured civic and social rights that are essential parts of constitutional frameworks in the three countries. The willingness to work together with the wrongdoer and to live side by side as neighbors were used as indicators of social closeness.[42] But the preliminary interviews revealed that some people in the Czech Republic were rather dissatisfied with their work or their place of living or both. Consequently, they considered the fact that Mr. Novak would be working with them and moving to their neighborhood as a form of his punishment. A thirty-four-year-old female cashier in a supermarket chain explained: "I would welcome him [to work] here. I think that he should try work like this."[43] However, this would not capture the transformation of inimical relations. For this reason, the two questions asked about working and living with *someone like* Mr. Novak.[44]

Each item had five response categories, ranging from definitely not (coded 0) to definitely yes (coded 4), allowing for a neutral response in the middle. Scores of all eight items were summed to form the social reconciliation scale, which ranged from 0 to 32. The scale was very reliable.[45] The mean score of the social reconciliation scale was 11.14 with a standard deviation of 7.25 in the merged data set (see Table 6.1).

Results

Pursuant to our hypotheses, this section empirically tests the indirect effects of dismissals, exposures, and confessions on social reconciliation and reports the major findings. Similar to the examination of the political effects, it uses two analytical approaches: the analyses of the merged data set, that is, the analyses of the three data sets pulled together in order to receive stronger evidence of these effects, and separate country analyses to observe the social effects in different sociopolitical contexts. In both cases,

Table 7.1. Mean Scores of the Social Reconciliation Scale for Dismissal, Exposure, and Confession in the Merged Data Set

	Mean	N	S.D.
Dismissal	11.26	1,044	(7.01)
Continuation	11.01	1,051	(7.49)
Exposure	11.10	1,039	(7.19)
No exposure	11.17	1,056	(7.32)
Confession	12.27***	1,045	(7.47)
Denial	10.01	1,049	(6.86)
Sequence 1	11.20	1,062	(7.30)
Sequence 2	11.07	1,032	(7.21)

Source: David, Lustration Systems, Trust in Government, and Reconciliation.

Note: The table presents the mean scores of social reconciliation for each experimental treatment and their absence in the merged data set and the results of Anova tests that determine whether the difference between the means of experimental treatments and their orthogonal version is significant (*** $p < .001$).

we use both descriptive statistics and multivariate analyses in order to take into account the influence of other factors and effectively test our hypotheses.

The Overall Effects of Dismissal, Exposure, and Confession on Reconciliation

Table 7.1 and Figure 7.2 report the mean scores of the social reconciliation scale for our experimental variables. The preliminary analysis indicates that the difference between dismissal and continuation is very small. The mean score of the social reconciliation scale for dismissal is 11.26 points, while the mean score for continuation is 11.01 points. The difference between exposure and no exposure is also very small. The mean score for exposure is 11.10 points, while the mean score for no exposure is 11.17 points. The only noticeable difference is between confession and denial. The mean score for confession is 12.27 points, while the mean score for denial is 10.01 points. The results from the Anova tests confirm that the difference of 2.26 points is statistically highly significant and that this is the only significant result among our variables in this analysis. Thus, at the outset, we observe

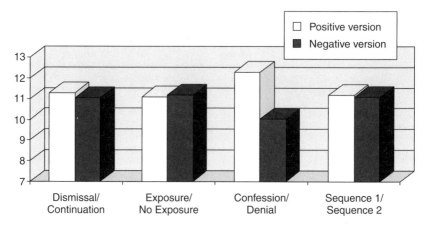

Figure 7.2. Mean scores of the social reconciliation scale for dismissal, exposure, and confession and their absence in the merged data set. The social reconciliation scale ranged from 0 to 32. Source: David, Lustration Systems, Trust in Government, and Reconciliation.

that only confession can affect social reconciliation. It may allow dissociation of the tainted official from his wrongdoing. We also note that there is no major difference between the two sequences of the experimental vignette; it is statistically irrelevant if the vignette starts with confession or with exposure.

In order to effectively test the hypothesized effects of dismissal, exposure, and confession on social reconciliation, we have to turn to our multivariate analyses. Table 7.2 presents the results of three OLS linear regression models in which the outcome variable was regressed on the predictor variables pursuant to our hypotheses.

In the first model, social reconciliation was regressed only on the experimental variables, controlling for countries. Since the data set was merged against the Czech Republic, we created dummy variables for Hungary and Poland. Overall, the model is considerably weaker than its counterpart model that tested political effects of personnel systems on trust in government in the previous chapter. But this can be explained by the meaning of this model: we are testing *indirect* effects here. The results confirm our preliminary analyses: only confession has been found to be a significant predictor of social reconciliation. Other things being equal, confession generates a 2.26-point increase on the social reconciliation scale. The result is

Table 7.2. Predictors of Social Reconciliation in the Merged Data Set

	Model 1		Model 2		Model 3	
	B	SE	B	SE	B	SE
Dismissal	0.28	(.31)	0.35	(.32)	0.40	(.27)
Exposure	−0.13	(.31)	−0.42	(.32)	−0.70*	(.27)
Confession	2.26***	(.31)	2.31***	(.32)	1.98***	(.27)
Sequence	0.14	(.31)	0.17	(.32)	0.27	(.27)
High position			−0.95***	(.19)	−0.34*	(.16)
Motive (self-interest)			−1.44***	(.20)	−0.79***	(.17)
Agency			−1.25***	(.20)	−0.42*	(.17)
Historical animosity					−0.97***	(.04)
Hungary	0.15	(.39)	−0.52	(.40)	−2.45***	(.35)
Poland	−.97*	(.37)	−1.08*	(.37)	−2.99***	(.37)
(Constant)	10.10	(.39)	16.51	(.71)	15.74	(.65)
R²	.029		.088		.359	
Adj. R²	.026		.083		.356	
N	2,095		1,777		1,721	

Source: David, Lustration Systems, Trust in Government, and Reconciliation.
Note: The table presents OLS linear regression models. The reconciliation scale (range 0 to 32) was regressed on experimental variables and control variables.

* $p < .05$ ** $p < .01$ *** $p < .001$

highly significant ($p < .001$), which suggests more than 99.9 percent proba
bility that confession will have a positive impact. On the other hand, dismissal, exposure, and the sequence of the experimental vignette fail to make
any significant impact on reconciliation in this model, other things being
equal. We also observe that Poland is significantly less reconciled about its
past than is the Czech Republic. The social reconciliation scale is 0.97 points
lower in Poland than in the Czech Republic, other things being equal. There
is no significant difference between the Czech Republic and Hungary.

The reconciliation with the tainted official may be affected by his position in the hierarchy of the past regime, his motives, and views on whether
he acted independently or was forced to commit his wrongdoing. Pursuant
to this hypothesis, we have added the position, motives, and agency of the
tainted official into the second model. We can observe that confession
remains the only significant predictor of social reconciliation among the
experimental variables. After controlling for other variables, confession
generates approximately the same effect of a 2.3-point increase on the social
reconciliation scale and the result remains highly significant. In addition,
we can observe that the effects of position, motives, and agency are highly
significant. Other things being equal, a one-point increase in the perception
that the tainted official held a high position decreases the reconciliation
scale by almost one point. Other things being equal, a one-point increase
in the perception that he was motivated by his self-interest decreases the
scale by 1.44 points. A one-point increase in the view that he acted as a
social agent generates a drop of 1.25 point on the scale, other things being
equal. It means that the perception of the past of the official is an important
factor in reconciliation. There also appear to be no significant differences
in the level of reconciliation between the Czech Republic and Hungary but
Poland remains significantly less reconciled about its past than the Czech
Republic even after controlling for the position, motives, and agency.

We have hypothesized that the impact of personnel systems on social
reconciliation may be affected by historical animosities. These animosities
are inherited from *the past* and may be different in different societies. Their
degree affects the prospect for reconciliation in the same way as the application of personnel systems during *the transition*. Our third model therefore
controlled for the degree of historical animosities. The results are telling.
Confession remains a highly significant positive predictor of social reconciliation. It generates a 1.98-point increase in the reconciliation scale, other
things being equal. However, the effect of exposure became negative and

significant in the third model. The revelation of the cover name of the tainted official decreases the reconciliation scale by 0.70 points, other things being equal. These findings run in direct contradiction to our hypothesis. It means that the inclusive system does produce a shaming effect but it is not an effect of reintegrative shaming.[46] It strengthens the image of the government official as tainted.

Each of the control variables concerning the perceptions of the tainted official, namely, his position, his motives, and his agency, retain highly significant negative effects on social reconciliation, other things being equal. The effect of historical animosities is negative, in line with our expectations. A one-point increase on the animosities scale generates a 0.97-point decrease on the reconciliation scale, other things being equal. It means that those who hold a priori a negative view of the tainted official's past are less likely to reconcile with him during transition, that is, trust him, work with him, live with him, and tolerate his actions.

The Effects of Dismissal, Exposure, and Confession on Reconciliation in the Czech Republic, Hungary, and Poland

The preliminary analyses of the three countries are in line with the preliminary analyses of the merged data set (see Table 7.3). Three of the four experimental variables—dismissal, exposure, and sequence—do not indicate any meaningful differences in the preliminary analysis. On the other hand, confession generates strong positive and highly significant effects on social reconciliation in each of the three countries. The mean score of the reconciliation scale for confession is 12.5 in the Czech Republic, 12.65 in Hungary, and 11.53 in Poland, while the mean score for denial is 10.24 in the Czech Republic, 10.39 in Hungary, and 9.29 in Poland. It seems, at the outset, that confession is able to buttress social reconciliation even in countries that are culturally as different as the secular Czech Republic and the Catholic Poland. Moreover, these preliminary findings suggest that the effect of confession in each country was almost identical. The same effect of the same experimental treatment may be explained either by the absence of specific differences among the countries or by the contradictory nature of various differences that cancelled each other out.[47] We shall therefore proceed to further analyses.

The results of the multivariate analyses of individual countries (see Table 7.4) are in line with the multivariate analyses of the merged data set, namely with the third model. Among our experimental variables,

Table 7.3. Mean Scores of Social Reconciliation Scale for Dismissal, Exposure, and Confession in the Czech Republic, Hungary, and Poland

	Czech Republic		Hungary		Poland	
	Mean	*S.D.*	*Mean*	*S.D.*	*Mean*	*S.D.*
Dismissal	11.54	*(6.81)*	11.73	*(6.90)*	10.42	*(7.25)*
Continuation	11.29	*(6.92)*	11.27	*(7.90)*	10.39	*(7.37)*
Exposure	11.43	*(6.89)*	11.47	*(7.46)*	10.25	*(6.99)*
No exposure	11.39	*(6.84)*	11.52	*(7.39)*	10.54	*(7.58)*
Confession	12.50***	*(6.98)*	12.65***	*(7.59)*	11.53***	*(7.68)*
Denial	10.24	*(6.55)*	10.39	*(7.09)*	9.29	*(6.73)*
Sequence 1	11.69	*(6.93)*	11.50	*(7.50)*	10.38	*(7.29)*
Sequence 2	11.13	*(6.79)*	11.50	*(7.35)*	10.43	*(7.33)*

Source: David, Lustration Systems, Trust in Government, and Reconciliation.

Note: The table presents the mean scores of social reconciliation scale for each experimental treatment and their absence in each country and the results of Anova tests that determine whether the difference between the means of experimental treatments and their orthogonal version is significant within each country (*** $p < .001$).

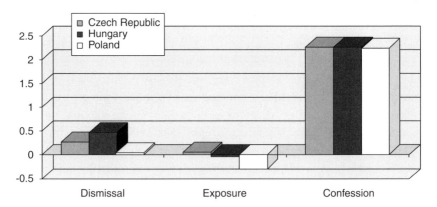

Figure 7.3. Mean differences in the social reconciliation scale between dismissal and continuation, exposure and no exposure, and confession and denial in the Czech Republic, Hungary, and Poland. The social reconciliation scale ranged from 0 to 32. Source: David, Lustration Systems, Trust in Government, and Reconciliation.

Table 7.4. Predictors of Social Reconciliation in the Czech Republic, Hungary, and Poland

	Czech Republic		Hungary		Poland	
	B	SE	B	SE	B	SE
Dismissal	0.01	(.49)	0.60	(.41)	0.39	(.54)
Exposure	−0.72	(.50)	−0.77^	(.41)	−0.48	(.54)
Confession	1.70***	(.50)	1.87***	(.41)	2.42***	(.54)
Sequence	0.68	(.49)	0.10	(.41)	0.11	(.54)
High position	−0.10	(.29)	−0.68**	(.24)	0.13	(.35)
Motive (self-interest)	−0.23	(.31)	−0.81**	(.26)	−1.47***	(.36)
Agency	−0.56^	(.31)	−0.39	(.25)	−0.46	(.37)
Historical animosity	−0.97***	(.07)	−1.01***	(.05)	−0.87***	(.07)
(Constant)	14.59	(1.08)	13.98	(.94)	13.05	(1.16)
R^2	0.334		0.406		0.324	
Adj. R^2	0.323		0.400		0.313	
N	485		736		500	

Source: David, Lustration Systems, Trust in Government, and Reconciliation.
Note: The table displays OLS linear regression models. The reconciliation scale (range 0 to 32) was regressed on experimental variables (coded 0; 1) and control variables (exogenous covariates).

^ $p < .1$ *$p < .05$ **$p < .01$ ***$p < .001$

confession is consistently the strongest positive predictor of reconciliation, although the magnitude of its effect varies across the three countries. The increase in the social reconciliation scale by 1.70 points in the Czech Republic is the smallest among the three countries but still statistically highly significant ($p < .001$), other things being equal. In Hungary, confession increases the reconciliation scale by 1.87 points, other things being equal, and in Poland by 2.42 points, other things being equal. The results in both countries are highly significant ($p < .001$). All of these findings provide consistent evidence for the positive effects of confession on reconciliation.

Unlike in our merged data set, the effect of exposure on social reconciliation is insignificant in all three countries. However, in line with the above analyses, the effect is consistently negative, creating drops in the social reconciliation scale in each country. It may mean that the effect of exposure only manifests itself in the long run.[48]

Contrary to our hypothesis, dismissal does not produce any significant negative effects. On the other hand, the perception of the wrongdoer as holding a high position in the past produces significant negative effects on social reconciliation in Hungary. The results are not significant in the Czech Republic and Poland. The perception of personal gain as a motive for the wrongdoing produces highly significant negative effects on reconciliation in Hungary and Poland, but it failed to reach a statistically significant level in the Czech Republic. The perception of a tainted official as a social agent who acted voluntarily does not significantly affect social reconciliation in any of the three countries. Finally, historical animosity is a strong significant predictor of social reconciliation in all three countries. In accordance with our hypotheses and our previous analysis in model 3 of the merged data set, historical animosity produces negative effects on social reconciliation in the Czech Republic, Hungary, and Poland.

Discussion: Personnel Systems and Reconciliation

Our experimental evidence demonstrates that personnel systems may cause social effects. The results of the multivariate analyses show that exposure and confession may affect the willingness of the public to reconcile and renew a civic relationship with the wrongdoer. However, the direction of the effects differs: exposure tends to produce negative effects, while confession produces strong positive effects. We can draw a few conclusions from our findings.

1. The final model of our analysis of the merged data set and the separate analyses in all three countries provide no evidence of negative social effects of dismissals. We have found no support for the hypothesis of the inversion effect of dismissals on social reconciliation: dismissal itself does not label the official as untrustworthy in the eyes of the public; it does not worsen his social standing. Assigning former "secret informers" or former "communists" a new legal status, officially labeling them as "former secret informers" or "former communists," can only be attributed to exposure.

2. Exposure produces negative effects on social reconciliation. Its effects are weak and are therefore manifested only in the merged data set after controlling for historical animosities. The negative effects run contrary to our hypothesis that exposure in the absence of dismissal will have positive effects on reconciliation. It means that we have found no experimental evidence of retroversion at this stage, which would suggest that exposures represent a means of rewriting history by condoning the negative social meaning of wrongdoing. Thus, shaming by means of exposures does not have a reintegrative nature as suggested by the inclusive system. The shaming ritual in the inclusive system is not constructive; it diminishes the social standing of the tainted official in the eyes of the public. The official is tainted twice: by his past record and by its official certification through exposure. This "truth" does not lead to reconciliation; it undermines it.

   As a glass can be seen as either half full or half empty, the findings can be seen from different angles. They may also suggest that the absence of exposure increases social reconciliation. However, the costs of this social reconciliation may be high. The continuation of tainted officials in public positions would eventually undermine trust in government, as demonstrated in political effects of dismissals studied in the previous chapter.

3. The analyses presented above provide evidence of the social effects of confession, which generate positive effects on social reconciliation in all models. The findings consistently support the hypothesis about the transformative effects of reconciliatory systems. Confession produces the effect of conversion: it makes tainted officials more socially acceptable to the members of the public, who may be willing to renew a relationship of trust with them and show more tolerance

than in situations in which they deny their pasts. Confession purifies the tainted official.

The multivariate analysis of our experiment also showed that confession—which is a hallmark of the reconciliatory system—is able to buttress social reconciliation in each of the three countries. To be sure, the effect of confession in Poland is the strongest among the three countries; in the Czech Republic it is the weakest. Nonetheless, confessions manifest their profound social effects in the secular Czech Republic as well as in Catholic Poland. In the end, it is not surprising that people are more likely to renew a civic relationship with someone who distances himself or herself from the past than with someone who dogmatically denies it in the face of evidence.

4. Perceptions of the tainted official's past also play a critical role in the prospect for social reconciliation. A high position, self-interest, and unforced behavior inhibit social reconciliation in the merged data set. This means that people are more likely to reconcile with someone who held a low position, followed his political beliefs, and was forced to commit the wrongdoing. This seems quite obvious. But there is an interesting parallel, or a contrast, between perceptions of the past of the tainted official and the personnel systems. The things of the past cannot be undone. The choice of an adequate personnel system may nevertheless offset some of the negative perceptions that stem from the past or worsen them. Conversely, the choice of an inadequate system may worsen these negative perceptions.

In the above analyses, we found no evidence that exposure would produce an effect of retroversion. On the other hand, we have not excluded the possibility of this effect. We shall therefore take a look at the effects of retroversion from another perspective.

Personnel Systems and Collective Memory

In his lecture on poverty and political violence, Amartya Sen maintained that the potato famine did not directly trigger Irish-British hostility. Instead, the memory of the famine as a historical injustice interacted with politics and fueled the resentment against the British among the Irish.[49] The time between the harmful event and its social construction as historical injustice may even span several centuries. The defeat of Serbs at the Kosovo Field in 1389 that was resurrected by the nationalists of "Great-Serbia" in 1989 is a frequently quoted motive to explain the war in the former Yugoslavia. It has been widely acknowledged that transitional justice measures affect people's understanding of the past. Transitional laws, according to Inga Markovits, shape what people remember about the past, what they forget, and how they reconstruct the past.[50]

In spite of its tangible political implications in stirring nationalist sentiments and fueling conflicts, the topic of historical memory has not received adequate attention in empirical research on transitional justice. Similar to other measures of transitional justice, personnel systems contribute to the creation of certain representations of the past. Personnel systems pass moral judgments that not only determine the future standing of the wrongdoer but also assess the gravity of his wrongdoing. We hypothesize that exclusive systems solidify a negative view of the past, while the alternative systems allow flexibility in forging a view of the past. Consequently, personnel systems not only deal with the past; they—at least to a certain extent—re-create the past in a particular way.

In this work it is argued that different personnel systems have different propensities to create different representations of the past, different effects of *retroversion*. In the immediate aftermath of the collapse of a former regime people as well as institutions may have their own memories, which are not yet contested by alternative interpretations of the past and not contaminated by the macropolitical sphere that forges a particular politically expedient memory of the past. After a long period of time, the effect of macropolitical factors, in particular measures that deal with the past, may become apparent. For the purposes of this research, collective memory is defined as an ideology that reassesses the present meaning of the past regime and wrongdoings committed under that regime. It is conceptualized as a two-dimensional process that includes the assessment of the wrongdoers' motives and moral judgment about the wrongdoer.

Hypotheses

The application of personnel systems may lead to rewriting the country's past or, more precisely, to shaping people's understanding of the past in different ways. Each significant lustration case and an ideological argumentation necessary for the sustenance of personnel systems may lead to the reassessment of the gravity of repression under the past regime and the individual's position in it. Pursuant to our theorization, personnel systems are hypothesized to generate the following effects:

1. The exclusive system signals that the wrongdoing was serious enough to constitute a reason for the dismissal of the wrongdoer. The continuous practice of dismissals teaches people that the wrongdoing was wrong and that the wrongdoer should be condemned. At the same time, the elimination of old personnel from positions of influence postulates absolute responsibility for individual behavior in the past, regardless of the historical context or circumstances of a particular case. The existence of an authoritarian regime with a track record of blackmail, harassment, and torture does not make a difference, does not mitigate, and does not lift the burden of citizens' responsibility. An individual's responsibility is indivisible under the exclusive system. The failure of wrongdoers to withstand the pressure under the previous regime is dismissed by heroic acts of resistance by the former opposition, proving the inalienability of internal liberty. "Every human being has always two options," said a political prisoner who spent more than fifteen years in Czechoslovak concentration camps.[51] These considerations lead to the following hypotheses: the exclusive system (a) increases the perception of wrongdoers as social agents and (b) increases the demand for their condemnation.

2. The inclusive system is hypothesized to have exactly opposite effects: external circumstances are prioritized over the responsibility of individuals. The underlying "structural approach" of the inclusive system is generous to human failures under the pressure of the past regime, and excuses for past collaboration are assigned an almost absolute, "sin-absorbing" value. It is not the wrongdoers, particularly those who were targeted by blackmail and threats, whom one should blame for the human rights violations committed in the past. It was the evil system that created evil people. By depriving people of their liberty, people could not behave along the maxim of personal responsibility. What is the value of consent that was forced under coercion? It is the anonymous structure of the oppressive political system that is held responsible for the wrongdoings. No one is a

wrongdoer; everybody is its victim. Consequently, the inclusive system is hypothesized to (a) decrease the perception of wrongdoers as social agents and (b) decrease the demand for their condemnation.

3. The ideological message of the reconciliatory system is similar to the exclusive system in one aspect and to the inclusive system in another aspect. Confessions of the wrongdoers signify disassociation of the confessors from their wrongdoing. The confessor is deemed to be a social agent, then and now: he is fully responsible for his wrongdoing in the past, but his confession demonstrates his present capability to transform. However, although the reconciliatory system signals that the past regime was illegitimate and that the tainted official was its social agent, his ability to confess would make his condemnation ultimately unfair and redundant. Consequently, the reconciliatory system is hypothesized to (a) increase the perception of wrongdoers as social agents but (b) decrease the demand for their condemnation.

Measurement

Unlike political and social effects, the effects of personnel systems on different views of the past cannot be effectively studied by the experimental design on the individual level of analysis. The creation of particular representations of the past is a long-term process that can be effectively studied only at a national level. The exclusive system was expected to generate particular historical views in the Czech Republic, which would differ from the views produced by the inclusive system in Hungary and the reconciliatory system in Poland. The research design in this section is quasi-experimental: we examine whether any difference exists in responses to the same wrongdoing given by people in the three countries. In order to ensure an effective comparison across countries, two sets of questions were asked after the first part of the vignette, which was non-experimental and was common to all respondents.

1. Questions about the *perception* of Mr. Novak's agency revolved around the perception of his position in the hierarchy of the state apparatus and his motives.[52] It contained questions about his "position," "motives," and "agency." If a wrongdoer was a social agent, he would be perceived as holding a higher position, having personal motives, and not being forced by the system. Respondents were

therefore asked whether Mr. Novak held a low position or a high position; whether he was motivated by ideology or self-interest; and whether he was forced by the previous political system or acted independently. Similar to the method discussed in the previous chapter, each of the three questions was coded from 0 to 3. However, the three items could not be computed into a scale; for this reason, they are analyzed separately (see Table 6.1).

2. Condemnation of the wrongdoer was measured by the *historical animosity scale*. The scale captured the degree of a respondent's objection vis-à-vis the wrongdoer at the end of the first part of the vignette. This research conceptualized historical animosity as a set of moral attitudes held by a respondent with respect to the wrongdoer. The question of whether a society should deal with injustices of the past was raised in the context of the "first dilemma of transitional justice," which has been outlined in the so-called torturer's problem formulated as "prosecute and punish versus forgive and forget."[53] Since "condemnation," "punishment," "forgiveness," and "forgetting" represent the plurality of attitudes that capture the degree of disapproval of the wrongdoer caused by his past, we use the same *historical animosity scale* as in Chapter 6 (see Table 7.5).

Results: Personnel Systems and Collective Memory

The analysis of historical effects was aimed at determining whether any significant differences in the views of a wrongdoer's agency and a moral attitude toward him existed among the Czech Republic, Hungary, and Poland. According to the hypotheses, the Czechs and the Poles would be more likely to consider the wrongdoer as a social agent than the Hungarians; and the Czechs would be more likely to condemn the wrongdoer than the Hungarians and the Poles.

Table 6.2 compares the mean scores for three items that capture the perceived social agency of the wrongdoer: position, motives, and agency. Although there were no apparent differences in the perception of the wrongdoer's position and his motives among the three countries, there was a clear difference concerning the perception of his agency. The mean of 1.53 for agency in the Czech Republic was very similar to the mean for agency in Poland, which stood at 1.49. In contrast to them, the mean for agency in Hungary was only 1.19 on the scale ranging from 0 to 3. Table 7.5 presents the means scores for the intensity of condemnation of the

Table 7.5. Dealing with Collaborators

	Czech Republic		Hungary		Poland	
	Mean	S.D.	Mean	S.D.	Mean	S.D.
Condemn	2.96	(1.00)	2.35	(1.25)	2.36	(1.17)
Punish	2.27	(1.12)	1.89	(1.24)	2.10	(1.18)
Forget	1.26	(1.12)	1.91	(1.31)	1.84	(1.21)
Forgive	1.35	(1.13)	2.06	(1.24)	2.14	(1.14)

Source: David, Lustration Systems, Trust in Government, and Reconciliation.

Note: The table displays mean scores of four potential solutions for dealing with the wrong-doer and the standard deviations. Answers were captured on a five-point Likert scale ranging from strongly agree (coded 4) to strongly disagree (0) and allowed a neutral answer of neither agree nor disagree (2).

wrongdoer in each country: namely the views about his moral condemnation, punishment, forgetting, and forgiving, which are the cornerstones of the dealing with the past scale.

These results are in accord with the expectations that, owing to the influence of the inclusive system, Hungarians would be more likely to see the wrongdoer as a victim than the Czechs and the Poles. Indeed, the comparison of the means in one-way Anova confirmed this: the difference between the mean for agency in the Czech Republic and Hungary was highly significant ($p < .001$). Similarly highly significant results yielded a comparison between the mean for agency in Poland and Hungary ($p < .001$).

The results also point out the apparent differences across the three countries in respondents' attitudes toward the condemnation of the wrongdoer. The highest mean of 2.73 for condemnation was detected in the Czech Republic. By a relatively large margin, this result was followed by Poland with a mean of 0.51 and Hungary with a mean of 0.26 (see Figure 7.4). Thus, these findings are also in accord with the hypothesized effects. The differences between the means in the Czech Republic and Hungary and between the Czech Republic and Poland, as analyzed by Anova, were both highly significant ($p < .001$). As expected, the difference between Poland and Hungary was rather small and failed to achieve an acceptable level of significance.

Thus, clear similarities and differences have emerged among the three Central European countries. While people in the Czech Republic and

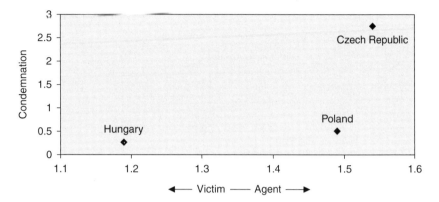

Figure 7.4. Views of secret informing in the Czech Republic, Hungary, and Poland. The figure plots the mean scores of the perception of the wrongdoer's agency for each country (*x*-axis) and the mean scores of the dealing with the past scale that represents the moral condemnation of the wrongdoer (*y*-axis). Source: David, Lustration Systems, Trust in Government, and Reconciliation.

Poland perceived Mr. Novak as a social agent who was responsible for his actions, the Hungarians saw him as a victim of the previous system. Unlike the Czechs, however, the Poles and the Hungarians were less likely to condemn the wrongdoer. The similarities and differences are captured in Figure 7.4.

Discussion: Personnel Systems and Collective Memory

Although the respondents in the three countries considered the same wrongdoing of the same person, they reached different conclusions. Significant differences existed across the three countries in the perception of Mr. Novak's agency and in attitudes toward his condemnation. The exclusive system in the Czech Republic may have generated the view of the wrongdoer as a social agent who should be condemned for his past. The inclusive system in Hungary fostered perceptions that Mr. Novak was a victim of the previous system who should not be condemned. Somewhere in between was the perception of the wrongdoer in Poland, where Mr. Novak was considered an agent but should not be condemned for his past. The findings clearly support the hypothesized effects of lustration systems.

But are these really retrospective historical effects? Were the different effects of retroversion detected in the three countries? The analysis presented above assumed that the effects that have been found in the three countries could be attributed to their lustration systems. However, the effect could have been caused by something else. The results may have been culturally determined or the situation captured in the survey may have been the same as the situation prior to the approval of the respective lustration systems. Indeed, the major drawback of cross-sectional research is its inability to deal with endogeneity and to establish clear causal relations. Consequently, the answers to the above questions cannot be found in the statistical analysis itself. However, theoretical considerations may help address these doubts.

Prior to 1989, the political regime in Czechoslovakia was the strictest among the studied countries. The pressure exercised by the regime may have narrowed the choices of individuals to make independent decisions in their lives. Indeed, Chapter 4 illustrated that some deputies who voiced their support for the removal of discredited personnel from positions of influence during the debate of the lustration bill in the Czechoslovak Federal Assembly depicted former collaborators as those who could not sustain the pressure exerted on them by the communist regime. The lack of resilience attested to their unsuitability to hold high positions of trust. The inability to determine the reasons for collaboration was reflected in the decision to keep the lustration process secret. Chapter 5 indicated that uncertainty about a person's past evaporated from the public discourse with the continuing implementation of the country's exclusive system. Uncertainty as to whether Mr. Novak was a victim or a social agent of the previous regime turned into certainty about his agency and individual responsibility for his behavior.

The case of Hungary seems to be opposite in many aspects. The communist regime of János Kádár was undoubtedly the mildest in Central Europe. The blatant repressions that followed the Soviet-led intervention in 1956 gradually evaporated during the 1960s. Collaboration with the Hungarian communist regime in the 1980s seemed more a matter of choice and less a matter of force in comparison to Czechoslovakia. The statistical analysis presented above clearly contrasts with the historical situation. In the statistical analysis, the Hungarian public considered the tainted official more a victim of the regime than its agent who should be condemned for his past. This perception, which clearly departed from the historical reality in pre-transition Hungary, could thus be attributed to constructions of the past that were related to post-transition politics, including but not necessarily exclusively related to the implementation of an inclusive lustration system, which fostered a view of wrongdoers as victims.

The intensity of the political regime in Poland toward the end of the 1980s resembled that of Hungary. Deep divisions in Polish society and the dual face of the regime that initiated political transition gave Poles reasons to consider former collaborators as social agents as well as victims. Chapter 4 showed that the decade of bickering over the approval of lustration law was marked by constant questioning of the reasons for and against lustration. Poles could not agree on whether former collaborators were social agents and whether they should be condemned. The compromise enshrined in the reconciliatory system answered the first question positively and the second negatively: the system was based on the principle of individual responsibility and the second chance. The Poles accepted that compromise. Mr. Novak was a social agent who should not be condemned for his past.

CONCLUSION

A process that had begun with wholesale incriminations turned in
the direction of wholesale exemptions and then ended in wholesale
exonerations. Denazification, in the end, meant not purge but
rehabilitation, a perversion illustrated by the change in the
meaning of the term "denazified." It was not German society that
was being "denazified" in the sense of being freed from Nazis and
Nazi influence, but Mr X, who would claim to have been
"successfully denazified" in the sense of having been certified as
being free from the taint of his previous Nazi connection.
— John Herz, *From Dictatorship to Democracy*[1]

In their efforts to establish trustworthy administration, many nascent
democracies have faced the problem of personnel inherited from anciens
régimes. Chile, South Africa, Iraq, and other countries undergoing transition from authoritarian rules have had to deal with personnel who were
entrenched in their administrative and security apparatuses, and who
remained—or were perceived to have remained—loyal to the previous
regime. However, in spite of their potential to affect democratization and
reconciliation, political science and transitional justice literature has not
considered the resolutions of the personnel problem as being as important
as those of constitutional designs, electoral systems, criminal trials, and
truth commissions. This book has attempted to draw the attention of
researchers to an overlooked topic. It has been inspired by the spread of
innovative personnel models, which developed under the banner of lustrations in Central and Eastern Europe in the 1990s and which in several
instances were alternatives to one-dimensional policies of dismissals. We
have proposed the concept of personnel systems and classified them as
exclusive, inclusive, and reconciliatory, which are based on dismissals,

exposure, and confession, respectively, and which represent the three major clusters of transitional justice: retribution, revelation, and reconciliation. We examined their operation, origin, context, and effects in the context of lustrations in the Czech Republic, Hungary, and Poland. In the conclusion, we shall summarize major findings in light of their theoretical implications and apply our findings to the Iraqi situation to explain the failure of the de-Baathification process. We argue that a reconciliatory model would better serve the interests of divided societies. We then outline the major dilemmas of personnel systems by means of a fictional narrative in Appendix A.

Summary of Major Findings

We have theorized that personnel systems have a dual nature. They are tangible political acts, which have clear administrative and security objectives. But they also carry expressive dimensions through which they communicate their political, social, and historical meanings to a wider audience. The examination of lustration processes in the Czech Republic, Hungary, and Poland has revealed the dual meanings in their etymology, political background, social contexts, application, and consequences. At the political level, personnel systems symbolize discontinuity with the past: a symbolic end of the oppressive rule and the beginning of the new system. Personnel systems may be considered instances of public rituals that deal with tainted officials in order to purify public life and society.

Given the inability of realism to explain the variety of lustration systems (all countries had non-communist majorities but only the Czechs adopted the exclusive system), we have hypothesized that their origin is a function of perceptions about the tainted and by the tainted. First, the stronger the perception of inherited personnel as tainted, the stronger the demand for dismissals and the weaker the demand for an alternative system. Officials associated with the previous regime may be seen as inefficient, corrupt, disloyal, dangerous, and unwilling to uphold human rights, and any of these perceptions may increase demands for their dismissal. This perspective is able to reconcile a number of existing theories that attempt to explain the origin of lustrations: the severity of the previous regime, its ideological rigidity, the role of the former elite during a particular mode of political transition, and its ability to adapt to democratic methods of governance are important factors that shape perceptions at the elite as well as grassroots level. In the Czech Republic, the support for dismissals was high owing to the public dissatisfaction with the continuing ideological rigidity of the communist party. The support for dismissal was low in Hungary and Poland owing to the perception of these parties as transforming. Moreover, perceptions may also explain the variation among alternative systems. We have detected that moderate perceptions were widely shared in Hungary and led to the inclusive system. Conflicting perceptions then led to the reconciliatory system in Poland.

Second, we have also considered the perceptions held by the tainted. We expected that the gray zone (people who had engaged with the former regime and who seek not to be identified as tainted) may have stronger demands for dismissals and weaker demands for any alternative personnel system. Quantitative evidence indicates that the gray zone may have played a role in the approval of the exclusive system in the Czech Republic. However, qualitative evidence suggests that people of the gray zone may not demand exclusive systems in order to escape their own responsibility for the past but because they do not see themselves as tainted in the first place. The lack of any self-reflection suggests the banality of the gray zone.

The effects of personnel systems can hardly be detected by means of standard cross-sectional surveys. Each country adopted different systems, which had different meanings, scopes, and time frames. The process of the establishment of trustworthy government in the Czech Republic, Hungary, and Poland was affected by other policies and its perception was inevitably influenced by the perception of the government of the day. We have therefore tested the effects of these policies by means of an original experimental vignette, which was devised specifically for this project. The vignette was embedded in the nationwide representative surveys conducted by means of face-to-face interviews with respondents in the Czech Republic, Hungary, and Poland in 2007. The survey experiment enabled us to establish a causal relation concerning the effects of dismissal, exposure, and confession. On the one hand, the experimental nature of our study allowed us to determine only the *potential* of these systems. On the other, it enabled us to examine the potential impact of different resolutions of the same wrongdoing in different political contexts.

All personnel systems are capable of increasing trust in government, although each uses a different method. In the process of purifying government, personnel systems send different ideological messages about the social standing of tainted officials, which affect social reconciliation. Each personnel system also shapes the collective memory of the past by producing a particular historical-mental picture of the past, which redefines the motives of tainted officials and the need for their further condemnation. Indirect social and historical effects of personnel systems may not be positive.

The *exclusive system* is based on dismissals and pursues personnel discontinuity with the past. Experimental evidence suggests that dismissals increase trust in government. The evidence is strong and consistent in all three countries. However, qualitative evidence suggests that dismissals tend to reinforce the negative image of tainted officials. The strong negative images of the tainted increase the demand for discovery of other tainted officials, which threatens the purity of public life. The strongest effect of dismissal was detected in the Czech Republic, which implemented the exclusive system. Like a puppy that chases its tail, the Czechs demand dismissals, which in turn further increase demand for dismissals. In the end, systematic dismissals transformed the image of tainted officials as "biologically tainted," certifying them as "former communists," labeling them for life, and making any prospect for dealing with the past and reconciliation nearly impossible. It put the entire "gray zone" of the tainted officials which may have originally supported the new regime back to black. Consequently, the exclusive system creates enemies out of those who were not enemies in the first place.

The *inclusive system* is based on truth revelations and pursues transparency of government. Our experimental evidence suggests that exposure does not affect trust in government but it may inhibit social reconciliation. The social effect of exposure under the inclusive system is not that of a reintegrative shaming ritual as hypothesized. This may point to the presence of two conflicting effects: a stronger shaming effect of revelation and a weaker inclusive effect of non-dismissal. While the former produces instant impacts, the latter may have long-term consequences, affecting the collective memory of the past. Indeed, the effect of retroversion—creating different representations of the past—manifested itself at the country level. In contrast to Czechs and Poles, Hungarians were more inclined to see the *same* tainted official as a victim of the previous regime who should not be condemned for past deeds. The paradox is that given the mild taste of Hungary's "goulash socialism," the collaboration was more a matter of choice, and less a matter of force, in Hungary than in the Czech Republic and Poland.

The *reconciliatory system* is based on confession, which promotes both trust in government and reconciliation. In contrast to externally pursued truth revelations, confession unequivocally signifies self-purification of the tainted official. It produces an effect of conversion through which the tainted official is able to demonstrate his willingness to play by the rules of the new regime. The reconciliatory system is the only personnel system that can lead to social reconciliation. The effect of confession on reconciliation is highly significant in countries that are as diverse as the secular Czech Republic and Catholic Poland. Hence, its effect on social reconciliation is not context dependent, although its effect on trust in government in Poland has to meet higher standards: it cannot be obscured by previous exposure. Therefore, it deserves to be called reconciliatory although its application in Poland was challenged from the left as well as the right. The system, nevertheless, survived. Unlike the inclusive system, the reconciliatory system emphasizes that past collaboration was wrong, but unlike the exclusive system, it dissolves the demand for further condemnation of the tainted official. Thus, confession cannot be disregarded as a politically impractical solution to a personnel problem. Our findings suggest that confession may be the precondition for a second chance and that citizens are willing to grant it.

Several other theoretical conclusions that go beyond the objectives of this book can be drawn from our analyses. Although they are presented here as by-products of our analyses, their meaning in related areas may be equally significant. Our findings have implications in the following areas:

> *Transitional justice.* The three personnel systems are instances of three methods of transitional justice: dismissal is a proxy for retribution, exposure for truth revelation, and confession for reconciliation. If one accepts that, then one can say that retribution and truth do not contribute to reconciliation and that confession is the only method that facilitates reconciliation. These findings may be relevant given the persistent lack of empirical research on the effect of criminal trials and truth commissions, especially when examined side-by-side within the context of countries with different political cultures. They are relevant given the lack of instances of confessional measures that were systematically practiced only in South Africa, East Timor, and Poland.
>
> *History and collective memory.* A number of theoretical assertions have been made about the propensity of transitional justice and

other social institutions to "change history." The potential of transitional laws to affect what we remember about the past and how we remember it has been theoretically established, but we are not aware of any empirical evidence of actual change in the reconstruction of the past. We have found that retributive measures shape the motives of the wrongdoers, viewing them all as social agents even if they had a little option to resist, and revelations foster their image as victims, despite the fact that they might have had the chance to resist. Another paradox stems from the comparison of retributive and reconciliatory measures. Both foster perceptions of wrongdoers as social agents but only retributive measures suggest that they should be condemned for their wrongdoing.

Political trust. Scholars have long pondered the reasons for the purported decline of trust in public institutions. Their efforts to determine the causes have led them to argue whether democracy leads to trust or trust to democracy.[2] This book makes a modest contribution to that debate. While we assume that the top-down approach has the most convincing logic in transitional societies that undergo transformation from the regimes of pervasive mistrust, we have found that different personnel systems have different effects depending on whether they are top-down or bottom-up approaches. Dismissals and exposures are top-down approaches, while confessions signify a bottom-up approach to the establishment of trust in government. Confession leads to reconciliation and then to trust in government.

Theoretical approaches to transition. We have illustrated that complex processes in transition, which have political, legal, administrative, security, and historical dimensions, can be effectively studied by using instruments of cultural sociology and political psychology. We have shown that perceptions and self-perceptions were more reliable factors in explaining the origin of lustration systems than considerations of power and rational actors. By highlighting the role of perceptions in understanding political processes, we have also set limits on social constructivism. We believe that personnel systems re-construct collaborators in a particular way, but we have also shown that wrongdoings did occur in the past and collaborators committed nefarious acts during the transition period as well. Finally, the microlevel approach that accentuated the role of perceptions in the study of effects of personnel systems produces more convincing evidence than standard comparative studies at the country level.

The findings of this book may inspire readers to further research the topic. In fact, considerably more research is needed for examining the major proposition put forward here: what personnel systems mean for democratization is as important as what election systems mean for democracy or what criminal trials and truth commissions mean for transitional justice.

Explanatory Value of the Findings and Policy Recommendations

The question is whether these findings can be generalized beyond the region. Indeed, social science operates within certain levels of probability and we cannot be entirely sure that the personnel systems studied in this book would have the same effect universally. However, the book uses highly significant experimental findings from three countries—with similar histories but with different processes of dealing with the past—to explain and predict some patterns, or constellation of effects, in the same way that we explain and predict the results of election systems. Just as scholars in democratization recommend a proportional electoral system for divided societies, so does this book recommend a reconciliatory personnel system for divided societies.

The findings of this book alongside the experience of South Africa, which systematically practiced the public ritual of confession for several years, show that there is a realistic possibility of employing the aforementioned authentic personal experiences in macropolitical schemes that buttress complicated transitions.[3] The emergence of confession as a viable alternative to dismissals suggests that the adoption of reconciliatory systems may be an optimal solution to the personnel problem in divided countries that are considered lacking in human resources. Instead of losing qualified personnel, transitional countries have the potential to boost the trustworthiness of their state administrations by adopting reconciliatory systems while simultaneously indirectly benefiting from the positive social effects of confessions.

Our theoretical arguments that dismissals augment historical divides and confessions lead to their overcoming have been substantiated by experimental evidence in three countries. Our findings may offer plausible explanations of similar phenomena beyond the region. We have mentioned that the exclusive system was associated with the breakup of Czechoslovakia, transforming Slovak leaders from federalists into separatists. We have also noted that dismissals pursued by Milošević in Serbia and Tudjman in Croatia[4] were at the start of war in the former Yugoslavia, a federation of states whose people previously lived side by side in peace. We know that de-Baathification pursued by the Coalition Provisional Authority (CPA) in Iraq has been associated with hostilities, but we do not know whether these hostilities can be attributed to these personnel policies or the personnel policies were consequences of the same phenomenon that brought those hostilities. Can our findings explain the negative effects of dismissals in Iraq?

The de-Baathification of Iraq, a politically hazardous and socially insensitive policy, clearly manifested strong adverse social effects.[5] Even if they had been feasible, wholesale dismissals, given the historical divisions in the country at that time, were impractical, but neither would their continuation have helped overcome the divisions. Dismissal was opposed by the former ruling Baath Party and its followers, while continuation was opposed by the former opposition and its followers, the Shiites, the Kurds, the Iraqi communists, and everyone else who had been excluded from public employment under Saddam's regime. Dismissals were considered by some as a process of achieving justice after transition, but others saw it as a process of creating new injustices. The problem is that, unlike confessions, personnel systems that rely exclusively on dismissals do not express any transformative potential. They assume that the human nature of former personnel is immutable, that loyalties and identities are firmly fixed in the past, and that their perceptions are unchangeable and firmly unshakeable.

Some of these perceptions about previous attitudes are likely to be inevitable in all transitional situations. Before any new perceptions can emerge, people remain in the shadow of their old identities. People are identified by their roles, positions, and affiliations of the past. However, the policy of dismissal perpetuated, and perhaps even augmented, these views rather than trying to dispel them. One year after the start of the de-Baathification of Iraq, the former "Baathists" were (still) regarded as "the former Baathists." Thus, some Western media sensationally referred to the shift in the de-Baathification policies in 2004 as a process of "re-Baathification" of

Iraq.[6] But the literal meaning of re-Baathification suggests that the Baath Party had reacquired power and staffed the administration with its loyalists. What the CPA attempted to do was to defuse the tensions surrounding the dismissal of former Baathists by showing a measure of leniency. Paradoxically, CPA's de-Baathification policy caused the label *Baathist* to acquire stronger overtones than it had under Saddam Hussein's regime. In the past, some Iraqis joined the Baath Party as a means to enhance their career prospects or to provide for their families, some may have been secularists or patriots, while others may have been forced to join, but in the past this was not uniformly viewed as a sign of their approval of the regime or their adherence to the Baathist ideology. The process of de-Baathification eradicated these nuances and gratuitously overwrote the identity of each and every Baathist as persona non grata. Thus, dismissals also generated retrospective "historical effects." De-Baathification established a new image of past motives for joining the Baath Party.

The reconciliatory system may have been, and perhaps still is, a suitable alternative to the system of dismissals pursued in Iraq. Iraqi society is deeply divided. It is traditionally diverse and heterogeneous along religious and ethnic lines. Three major groups, Sunnis, Shiites, and Kurds, are crosscut by identities of secular groups, royalists, traditional communities, and others. Under Saddam Hussein's rule, different societal factions were not given the opportunity to develop relationships and get used to each other. In fact, the past regime deepened many of these cleavages and created new political divisions. In addition, the war has magnified an anti-American sentiment among a significant part of the population. In view of the experience of Central Europe, the heterogeneity of the Iraqi society, and the complexity of its political situation, the reconciliatory system may be considered an optimal model to serve the interests of Iraqi society.[7] Its capacity to conduct a value-normative shift makes it a better option for a divided society with scattered identities than exclusive and mixed systems, which created enemies among those who may not have been enemies in the first place.

The reconciliatory system is congruent with the objectives set forth in the "Iraqi Opposition Report on the Transition to Democracy."[8] The report, foreseeing the challenge of personnel problems, recommended that the new transitional government examine the Eastern European experience with lustration.[9] The report declared three categories of objectives. It defined general objectives of transitional justice based on individual accountability, reconciliation, and forgiveness. One of its pillars was truth revelation that would disclose the atrocities of the previous regime; the government would then submit a report to recommend institutional reforms. The report specified de-Baathification objectives, which included the dissolution of some institutions and de-ideologization of the society. At the same time, in reforming the civil service, it sought to absorb people associated with the former regime in order to prevent their ostracization and resistance and to utilize their knowledge, experience, and skills. In other words, the report preferred reconciliation to retribution, inclusion to exclusion, and value-based discontinuity to personnel discontinuity as proposed here.

The individual transformation that underpins the reconciliatory system is minimal, and non-negative rather than positive. It seeks not to exclude, and accommodate, all those who are able to demonstrate a change in attitude. This may ultimately include all sorts of opportunists who switched sides when the days of the authoritarian regime were numbered or when its opposition started to win the battle for change. The reconciliatory system is not an ethical project. It may be actually perceived as unethical in a deontological sense because it is motivated by political considerations. The transformation ritual recommended here is not a process that seeks to undermine or strengthen morality in society; it is a pragmatic solution designed to initiate a decrease in the ranks of those who would oppose the new democratic regime, or at least halt an increase in their numbers.

If the tainted officials do change their behavior, governmental policies that seek to inhibit or undermine perceptions about those changes are essentially counter-democratic. In the same way that democratic society grants individuals their political rights and civil liberties, democratizing society should allow people to change their political opinions, loyalties, and affiliations as the macro-political context itself changes.[10] It is ironic when a transitional democracy, which aspires to build a culture based on human rights, incorporates measures of transitional justice that cement the rigid principles of the past into its foundations instead of contributing to their transformation. Thus, exclusive systems applied in divided societies inhibit the change of perception about wrongdoers. On the other hand, the reconciliatory system provides wrongdoers with incentives, and platforms, to demonstrate what we euphemistically call a change of heart, what cynics may see as transporkation, and what in effect means giving collaborators a chance to show their worth by collaborating with us.[11]

The Dilemmas of Personnel Systems

For many years your country suffered under the brutal regime of the Headman and his Purple Shirt Party. Coming to power through a rigged election, the Purple Shirts promised economic prosperity and "equality beyond the ballot." Instead, widespread corruption, power abuses, and the enslavement of the majority became the reality of the day. You and your fellow citizens did not have a viable chance of changing the excruciating situation. Elections were no longer contested, the opposition was outlawed, and political rights were suppressed. Any public criticism of the regime was harshly punished. The opposition leaders were imprisoned, many of them were tortured, and their families were denounced by the state-controlled media as parasites, traitors, and terrorists. Those few who dared to join occasional demonstrations were routinely teargassed, beaten up, and arrested. Your fellow citizens were even afraid to express their opinions privately, whether in a group of colleagues, neighbors, or friends, for fear of being exposed to authorities by the omnipresent network of clandestine informers. Every factory, school, and street had its "guardian angels" who gathered information and passed it on to secret services: teachers reported on their students and students reported on their teachers. You sensed that the authorities always knew about the jokes you told in your workplace, knew who had written you letters and who had visited you.

Repression and punishment were spurred on and backed by a system of incentives and rewards. The regime strived to purchase the loyalty and commitment of your countrymen. It rewarded anyone who was willing to join the party and declare his or her commitment to adhere to the official teaching of Shirtism. Most positions in the sphere of public employment, the army, and the police were reserved for members of the Purple Shirt Party, their families, sympathizers, and collaborators. Some people truly believed in the principles of Shirtism, while many others joined the party because they wanted their children to study at university or because it was a necessary condition for the advancement of their career. The party membership card was necessary to hold leading positions in any sphere of public life.

The regime of the Headman has recently been overthrown by the White Tulip Movement. Initially an underground opposition to the regime, the movement has gained mass support as the champion of freedom, democracy, and clean government. After clinging to power, it released political prisoners and launched comprehensive political reform through the promulgation of a new constitution, which guarantees human rights, civil liberties, and the fundamental principles of fair trial. Soon thereafter entrepreneurs could reopen their defunct businesses and students could read previously outlawed writers and attend concerts of bands that had previously been banned. To the appreciation of both the domestic and international communities, the movement organized the first free elections, in which all parties participated. The White Tulip Movement won the elections, although the Purple Shirt Party also gained a significant proportion of the votes. The movement established a new government but found itself isolated at the top of the state apparatus it had inherited from the Shirtist regime. The majority of operational posts in the civil service and the armed forces remained staffed with people who were associated with the Purple Shirt Party and the network of its informers.

In order to deal with this personnel problem, the new prime minister called a meeting of her cabinet to discuss feasible solutions. You were invited to attend the meeting as her advisor. The prime minister opened the meeting by stating that the problem of inherited personnel was one of the major challenges facing her administration: "Today we have to address the problem of persons who willingly participated in the repressive machinery of the Shirtist regime. They may not bear any direct criminal responsibility for gross violations of human rights but they are politically responsible for the implementation of these violations." You witnessed a heated debate during the cabinet meeting, which divided ministers into four groups.

A spokesman for the largest group passionately argued for the Deshirtization of the entire society. "In my opinion," he said, "members of the Purple Shirts are dangerous and untrustworthy. They, including so-called former party members, remain loyal to the previous regime. I say including 'the so-called former party members' because a Shirtist will always be a Shirtist regardless of his or her actual membership. Shirtism was a way of life, a way of their life; we know all about it. It is likely that these people will use the privileges of the rule of law to undermine our democratic effort or even bring back authoritarian rule, political repression, and gloom. Our country is undergoing profound political and social reforms, which may be sabotaged by them. Even if some of these old administrators formally agreed with our new program, ordinary people would not feel confident in our policies if they were implemented by them. Needless to say, most of our economic reforms will be very unpopular, given the critical state of our economy.

"The sympathizers of our government would certainly support only a thorough Deshirtization. People cannot forget that many of these state administrators and police officers were appointed under the previous regime based on the dubious ideological criteria of Shirtism. It is a matter of justice that all our citizens should have an opportunity to be employed in these positions, which were not available to them under the previous regime. Any compromise effectively means that we close our eyes to blatant injustice, while partial justice, it seems to me, remains injustice even if it is cloaked in the name of political tolerance.

"I would also like to stress that Deshirtization is also a matter of public safety. Our communities do not feel safe when the members of the Purple Shirts are part of the police force and the municipal offices. We cannot allow the Shirtist regime to effectively continue under our government. Thus, in my view, all of those who were members of the Purple Shirt Party and its secret informers should be dismissed from all public and military positions."

A minister who spoke for the second group staunchly dissented. "In my view," he said, "the policy of Deshirtization is shortsighted. I think that we are igniting a civil war here. I am afraid that Deshirtization would provoke the Purple Shirts. By conducting widespread dismissals, we shall send a signal to the members of the Purple Shirts that there is no place for them in the new system. They may perceive Deshirtization not as a measure that addresses past injustices but as one that creates new injustices. It, after all, deprives them of earning their livelihood. Let me remind you the crisis that was experienced by our northern neighbor a few decades ago: as their new government attempted to replace senior officers, it provoked the military. I think that there is a real chance that Deshirtization will trigger a rebellion and insurgency. Thus, our nascent democracy may be subverted by the very policies that we want to use to strengthen it. Instead of unifying our society, the policy may perpetuate historical divisions. I therefore suggest that we should maintain the status quo. Instead of purging the officials of the old regime from their offices, we should forget the past and provide a fresh start for all."

The prime minister tried to calm the debate. "I understand your concerns, gentlemen," she said. "Why don't we just try to find a suitable compromise between the two views? Let's face it. We do not have a sufficient number of qualified personnel who could step in and replace the old bureaucracy at this stage of our transformation. Consequently, our reform policies may not be delivered, not because they would be sabotaged but because our new civil servants would lack essential skills and training. This would exacerbate public dissatisfaction. Therefore, we should only dismiss servants and ideologists of the Shirtist regime who were the most visible offenders and keep the rest of the administration intact. This would enable the delivery of services and policies, yet satisfy the needs of our supporters for justice."

A third minister disagreed. "I think that partial Deshirtization still carries an enormous risk of subversion. Ordinary Shirtists could hardly launch a rebellion. But their disheartened leaders are certainly able to instigate fear, violence, and revolt. I think that we have to approach the personnel conundrum in a fundamentally different fashion. We need these people onboard, but at the same time we need to demonstrate to our supporters that a real regime change has taken place and that the era of corruption and covert practices has ended. For this reason, I think that all illegitimate activities of the Shirtist administrators should be publicly exposed. Our society needs to know the truth about the past. We need to know the background of all controversial decisions the previous government and other administrative units took as well as the names of those who gave the orders and those who executed them. We have to launch investigations into the cases of alleged political corruption. We need to know the names of all informers who secretly passed on information to the security services. The secrecy of the Shirtist regime has to end. But we need to engage all of these Shirtist bureaucrats and give them a second chance, not simply dismiss them."

"Such openness," he continued, "not only aims at dismantling the past, but it is also prospective. It increases the transparency of our government and gives the public the opportunity to better scrutinize steps taken by tainted public officials. The exposure will easily dispel rumors and allegations of misconduct. It will ensure that our civil servants do not have any other secret master and minimize the risk of their blackmail. We shall offer them a second chance in exchange for enhanced transparency in public life. In the pursuit of such transparency, we shall set up a commission of inquiry that will investigate the most controversial cases, open the secret archives, and publish the names of all former members of the Shirtist party as well as their secret informers. In order to prevent revenge against those exposed, officials who fear revenge will be allowed to step down and their names must remain unpublished."

The fourth minister concurred. "We should remember that the leaders of the Purple Shirts have agreed to transfer their political power to us and endorsed our democratic reforms. Therefore, we do not need to be overly cautious about their attempts to subvert our democracy. However, I am afraid that although the policy of openness may bring transparency to our administration, it may indeed spur a wave of witch hunts and revenge. All sorts of wild lists will be compiled and published by the newspapers. People are likely to settle accounts privately, and the situation may soon become out of our control. I therefore suggest reaching out to the Purple Shirts by what I believe is quite a unique proposition: we can offer them a second chance in exchange for their own voluntary revelation of their past conduct. Every official who wants to keep his or her public post will have to publicly disclose all relevant activities with which he was engaged in the past. Those who fear revenge would be allowed to step down before the process starts. The truthfulness of these confessions will be examined against confessions made by other officials and against archival records. Those who conceal any relevant facts should be dismissed. This will allow us to keep the Shirtists onboard, vacate some posts for our supporters, and satisfy the public need to know the truth about the past."

The meeting has ended and the prime minister has requested your opinion. How would you advise her?

APPENDIX B

The Experimental Vignette

Part 1

Now I would like to tell you a short story and ask you some questions about your opinions on it. In the 1980s, Mr. Novak worked as an expert in an enterprise. For several years he secretly wrote reports against his then colleagues. These reports were critical of his colleagues who criticized the political system that existed in our country before 1989.

Characteristics of Mr. Novak

Did Mr. Novak hold a high or low position in the previous system?
Was his reporting motivated by ideology or by his personal interest?
Did Mr. Novak write reports on his own initiative or was he forced to do so by the previous system?

Historical Animosity/Condemnation Scale

Today Mr. Novak should be morally condemned for his past.
Mr. Novak deserves punishment for his past.
We should forget Mr. Novak's past.
We should forgive Mr. Novak his past.

Part 2

Recently Mr. Novak was employed as an official at a Ministry. The ministry was not aware of his past, but soon afterward it received a dossier concerning Mr. Novak, including materials that he had secretly written against his former colleagues. Now let's take a look at how this case was resolved:

[Version 1] Mr. Novak publicly confessed that he wrote these materials. All information about his past, including his cover name, was published. Afterward, he was dismissed from the ministry. So, he confessed it, his cover name was published, and he was dismissed.

[Version 16] No information about Mr. Novak's past was published. He publicly denied that he wrote these materials. Afterward, he continued working in the same position at the ministry. So, he denied it, no information was published, and he continued working at the ministry.

Trust in Government Scale

Do you trust this ministry?

Do you believe that this ministry will effectively implement government programs?

Do you believe that this ministry will operate according to law?

Do you believe that this ministry will be reliable in times of a threat to our democracy?

Social Reconciliation Scale

Do you trust Mr. Novak today?

Do you trust Mr. Novak as an expert?

Do you believe that Mr. Novak will act in accordance with the law?

Do you believe that Mr. Novak is committed to democracy?

Do you think that Mr. Novak should be allowed to organize a public demonstration?

Do you think that Mr. Novak should be allowed to organize a strike?

Would you be willing to work on a common task with someone like Mr. Novak?

Would you be willing have someone like Mr. Novak as a neighbor?

Manipulation Check

Was Mr. Novak a secret informer in the past?

Did Mr. Novak personally admitt that he wrote the secret materials?

Was information about Mr. Novak's past released?

Did the ministry terminate Mr. Novak's employment?

NOTES

Introduction

1. Václav Havel, "Výročí okupace Československa vojsky Varšavského paktu," August 21, 1990, http://old.hrad.cz/president/Havel/speeches/ (accessed September 9, 2009). This speech was intended for a domestic audience and, unlike other speeches, was not translated into English. Havel could hardly have chosen a more symbolic day on which to deliver this speech. August 21 marks the anniversary of the invasion of Czechoslovakia by the Warsaw Pact armies. His listeners were aware of the historical undertones that he evoked by the parallel between political reforms in post-communist Czechoslovakia and the events of 1968, when the progressive wing of the Communist Party around Alexander Dubček had attempted to initiate the liberal reform of the socialist system. The effort of the so-called Prague Spring to build "socialism with a human face" was halted by the Soviet-led intervention, which had acted officially in response to a request from a group of hard-liners within the Czechoslovak Communist Party. The echo of betrayal, and concerns about the democratic reforms, reverberated with the same urgency in 1990.

2. L. Paul Bremer III with Malcolm McConnell, *My Year in Iraq: The Struggle to Build a Future of Hope* (New York: Threshold Editions, 2006), 341. Bremer recalls making this remark in the spring of 2004, almost a year after the launch of de-Baathification.

3. See, e.g., Manuel Antonio Garretón, "Redemocratization in Chile," *Journal of Democracy* 6, no. 1 (1995): 147.

4. Ibid.

5. *Truth and Reconciliation Commission of South Africa Report* (Cape Town: Juta, 1998), 2:709–10. But cf. Adrian Guelke, "Interpretations of Political Violence During South Africa's Transition," *Politikon* 27, no. 2 (2000): 239–54.

6. The direct involvement of the state in running hit squads and providing covert funding and training to IFP was later confirmed by a commission of inquiry, headed by Judge Richard Goldstone, which was set up to investigate the acts of violence committed during that period. Richard J. Goldstone, "Commission of Inquiry Regarding the Prevention of Public Violence and Intimidation" (Pretoria, 1992–94).

7. Richard Spitz and Matthew Chaskalson, *The Politics of Transition: A Hidden*

History of South Africa's Negotiated Settlement (Johannesburg: Witwatersrand University Press, 2000), 32.

8. Ibid., 31.

9. Ibid., 97.

10. See, e.g., Wendy Hunter, "Continuity or Change? Civil-Military Relations in Argentina, Chile, and Peru," *Political Research Quarterly* 112 (1997): 458.

11. See, e.g., BBC, "Profile: Augusto Pinochet," BBC News, December 3, 2006, http://news.bbc.co.uk/2/hi/americas/3758403.stm (accessed September 9, 2009).

12. Ruti G. Teitel, *Transitional Justice* (Oxford: Oxford University Press, 2000), 152–57.

13. The literature on the topic is briefly reviewed below.

14. "Coalition Provisional Authority Order Number 1: De-Ba'athification of Iraqi Society," May 16, 2003, http://www.iraqcoalition.org/regulations/20030516_CPAORD_1_De-Ba_athification_of_Iraqi_Society_.pdf (accessed September 9, 2009). See also "Coalition Provisional Authority Memorandum Number 1: Implementation of De-Ba'athification Order No. 1," http://www.waranddecision.com/docLib/20080420_CPAOrder1imp.pdf (accessed September 9, 2009); "Coalition Provisional Authority Order Number 5: Establishment of the Iraqi De-Baathification Council," http://www.iraqcoalition.org/regulations/CPAORD5.pdf (accessed September 9, 2009).

15. In addition to ideological reasons for fighting the invaders, there were few employment options available to them. Roman David, "From Prague to Baghdad: Lustration Systems and Their Political Effects," *Government and Opposition* 41, no. 3 (2006): 367.

16. Ibid. Bremer alleviated the policy without revoking it, reinstating "some ten thousand teachers." See Bremer, *My Year in Iraq*, 343.

17. Roman David, "Lustration Laws in Action: The Motives and Evaluation of Lustration Policy in the Czech Republic and Poland (1989–2001)," *Law & Social Inquiry* 28, no. 2 (2003): 387–439.

18. Teitel, *Transitional Justice*, 15.

19. Samuel P. Huntington, *The Third Wave: Democratization in the Late Twentieth Century* (Norman: University of Oklahoma Press, 1991).

20. E.g., Teitel characterizes the lustration law in Poland as a "self-purge," although the law effectively gives inherited personnel a second chance. Teitel, *Transitional Justice*, 71.

21. David, "From Prague to Baghdad," 349.

22. *Truth and Reconciliation Commission of South Africa Report*, 5:311; Jonathan Klaaren, "Institutional Transformation and the Choice Against Vetting in South Africa's Transition," in *Justice as Prevention: Vetting Public Employees in Transitional Societies*, ed. Alexander Mayer-Rieckh and Pablo de Greiff (New York: Social Science Research Council, 2007), 146–79.

23. Radio Prague, "Czech-Chile-President," *Radio Prague E-News*, March 19, 1999.

24. Democracy Principles Working Group, "Iraqi Opposition Report on the Transition to Democracy in Iraq," *Journal of Democracy* 14, no. 3 (2003): 26. (The article names 26 members of the group, although the group was said to have 32 members.)

25. Roman David, "Lustration Systems, Trust in Government, and Reconciliation in the Czech Republic, Hungary and Poland" (Machine-readable data files, on file with author).

26. CEU (Central European University), "The Development of Party Systems and Electoral Alignments in East Central Europe [1992–96]" (Machine-readable data files, Department of Political Science, Central European University, Budapest).

27. James N. Druckman, Donald P. Green, James H. Kuklinski, and Arthur Lupia, "The Growth and Development of Experimental Research in Political Science," *American Political Science Review* 100, no. 4 (2006): 627–36.

28. Lawrence W. Neuman, *Social Research Methods: Qualitative and Quantitative Approaches* (Boston: Allyn and Bacon, 2000).

29. Paul M. Sniderman and Douglas Grob, "Innovations in Experimental Design in General Population Attitude Surveys," *Annual Review of Sociology* 22 (1996): 377–99; James L. Gibson and Amanda Gouws, "Truth and Reconciliation in South Africa: Attributions of Blame and the Struggle over Apartheid," *American Political Science Review* 93, no. 3 (1999): 501–17.

30. Other personnel systems (the system of continuance and the mixed system) are considered in this book, but they are not examined in-depth as ideal typical categories.

Chapter 1

1. Andrew Jackson, First Annual Message to Congress, December 8, 1829, http://millercenter.org/scripps/archive/speeches/detail/3632 (accessed September 29, 2009). Except for a small number of political appointments at the top level of the state administration that often follow elections, a consensus has emerged about the inadmissibility of the so-called spoils system and other methods of political patronage. Under the spoils system, "to the winners belonged the spoils": the winners of elections staffed the state administration with their political loyalists, who in return contributed time and money to fight their patrons' political wars. In the United States during the nineteenth century, this system was most frequently associated with President Andrew Jackson (1829–37), who saw it as an expression of democratic equality, a counteraction to elitism and nobility, and an opportunity to give "common men" a chance to hold a public office. See, e.g., William D. Foulke, *Fighting the Spoilsmen: Reminiscences of the Civil Reform Movement* (New York: Knickerbocker Press, 1919); Ari Hoogenboom, *Outlawing the Spoils: A History of the Civil Service Movement, 1865–1883* (Urbana: University of Illinois Press, 1968); David H. Rosenbloom, ed., *Centenary Issues of the Pendleton Act: The Problematic Legacy of Civil Service Reform* (New York:

Marcel Dekker, 1982); Jack Rabin et al., eds., *Handbook of Public Personnel Administration* (New York: Marcel Dekker, 1995). Consensus about the inadmissibility of the spoil system may be the reason why the problem of administrative personnel has disappeared to the periphery of the administrative sciences and why the topic of personnel in transition has been entirely overlooked.

2. Even not taking any active steps against former employees represents a particular response.

3. Constitution of the Republic of Haiti, 1987, Article 291, http://pdba.george town .edu/constitutions/haiti/haiti1987.html (accessed September 29, 2009).

4. The Unification Treaty between the FRG and the GDR (Berlin, August 31, 1990).

5. David, "Lustration Laws in Action," 388.

6. Rubén Zamora and David Holiday, "The Struggle for Lasting Reform: Vetting Process in El Salvador," in *Justice as Prevention*, ed. Mayer-Rieckh and de Greiff, 86.

7. Resolution 1088 (1996), UN Security Council, 3723rd meeting, Resolution S/RES/1088, December 12, 1996.

8. "Coalition Provisional Authority Order Number 1: De-Ba'athification of Iraqi Society."

9. Roman David, "Transitional Injustice? Criteria for Conformity of Lustration to the Right to Political Expression," *Europe-Asia Studies* 56, no. 6 (2004): 789–812.

10. One of the major legal battles concerned the Czechoslovak lustration law. See Neil J. Kritz, ed., *Transitional Justice: How Emerging Democracies Reckon with Former Regimes* (Washington, D.C.: U.S. Institute of Peace Press, 1995), 3:322–45; Herman Schwartz, "Lustration in Eastern Europe," *Parker School Journal of Eastern European Law* 1, no. 2 (1994): 141–71, reprinted in *Transitional Justice*, ed. Kritz, 3:461–83; Roman Boed, "Evaluation of the Legality and Efficacy of Lustration as a Tool of Transitional Justice," *Columbia Journal of Transnational Law* 37 (1999): 357–402. The major argument raised by the critics was that lustration is based on the principle of collective guilt, or a bill of attainder as it is known in U.S. constitutional law; it discriminates on the basis of political opinions, and it is retroactive. However, many of these arguments were rejected by Mark Gillis, who argued that lustration law adopts the tort law principle *res ipsa loquitur* (the thing speaks for itself): "We know that a wrong occurred and that the persons in question were in control of the instrumentality which brought about the wrong when it occurred, but we do not have more specific evidence to prove the actual event. Nonetheless, the law in this field does not throw its hands up and declare that nothing can be done." Mark Gillis, "Lustration and Decommunisation," in *The Rule of Law in Central Europe: The Reconstruction of Legality, Constitutionalism and Civil Society in the Post-Communist Countries*, ed. Jiří Přibáň and James Young (Aldershot: Ashgate, 1999), 64. By comparing transitional justice with established principles of law, Eric Posner and Adrian Vermeule found many of the arguments of the critics of lustrations unwarranted. Eric A. Posner and Adrian

Vermeule, "Transitional Justice as Ordinary Justice," *Harvard Law Review* 117 (2004): 761–825. The recent rulings of the European Courts of Human Rights and the theoretical reflections on them by Cynthia Horne confirm that some lustration laws may be problematic in their design and implementation, but lustration laws per se do not violate human rights. Cynthia M. Horne, "International Legal Rulings on Lustration Policies in Central and Eastern Europe: Rule of Law in Historical Context," *Law & Social Inquiry* 34, no. 3 (2009): 713–44.

11. Cf. Bruce Ackerman, *The Future of Liberal Revolution* (New Haven, Conn.: Yale University Press, 1992), 81–82.

12. Aleks Szczerbiak, "Dealing with the Communist Past or the Politics of the Present? Lustration in Post-Communist Poland," *Europe-Asia Studies* 54, no. 4 (2002): 553–54. See also Gillis, "Lustration and Decommunisation."

13. "[T]he visiting Chilean President Eduardo Frei stressed the need to thoroughly cleanse state and government institutions of people implicated with former totalitarian regimes. . . . [He] took a lively interest in the Czech legislation that requires mandatory screening of state officials." See Radio Prague, "Czech-Chile-President."

14. Zamora and Holiday, "The Struggle for Lasting Reform," 88–93.

15. Alexander Mayer-Rieckh, "Vetting to Prevent Future Abuses: Reforming the Police, Courts, and Prosecutor's Offices in Bosnia and Herzegovina," in *Justice as Prevention*, ed. Mayer-Rieckh and de Greiff, 190.

16. Gillis, "Lustration and Decommunisation," 56–81.

17. See Kritz, *Transitional Justice*, vol. 1.

18. Teitel, *Transitional Justice*, 149.

19. Mayer-Rieckh and de Greiff, *Justice as Prevention*.

20. Jon Elster, *Closing the Books: Transitional Justice in Historical Perspective* (New York: Cambridge University Press, 2004), 1.

21. Laurel E. Fletcher and Harvey M. Weinstein, "Violence and Social Repair: Rethinking the Contribution of Justice to Reconciliation," *Human Rights Quarterly* 24, no. 3 (2002): 573–639.

22. Naturally, trials, amnesties, purges, and executions are not new historical phenomena. See Elster, *Closing the Books*, chapter 1. What has actually been flourishing is the variety of alternatives to these traditional methods.

23. See, e.g., Teitel, *Transitional Justice*.

24. Although they usually overlap, perpetrator-centered methods include transitional justice methods that primarily address the perpetrators of human rights violations. For the victim-centered approach to transitional justice, see Roman David and Susanne Y. P. Choi, "Victims on Transitional Justice: Reparations of Victims of Human Rights Abuses in the Czech Republic," *Human Rights Quarterly* 27, no. 2 (2005): 392–435.

25. Aryeh Neier, "What Should Be Done About the Guilty," *New York Review of Books* 37, no. 1 (February 1, 1990); José Zalaquett, "Balancing Ethical Imperatives and

Political Constraints: The Dilemma of New Democracies Confronting Past Human Rights Violations," *Hastings Law Journal* 43 (1992): 1425–38.

26. Huntington, *Third Wave*, 211.

27. See Robert I. Rotberg and Dennis Thompson, eds., *Truth v. Justice: The Morality of Truth Commissions* (Princeton, N.J.: Princeton University Press, 2000).

28. For distinctions among different kinds of truth commissions, see Priscilla B. Hayner, *Unspeakable Truths: Confronting State Terror and Atrocity* (New York: Routledge, 2001), 98.

29. It is conceptually useful to distinguish between truth commissions and reconciliation commissions. In the TRC, the Human Rights Violations Committee served as a classic truth commission, while the Amnesty Committee served as a reconciliation commission. David and Choi, "Victims on Transitional Justice," 434.

30. Hayner, *Unspeakable Truths*, 107–32.

31. Roman David, "In Exchange for Truth: The Polish Lustration and the South African Amnesty Process," *Politikon: South African Journal of Political Studies* 32, no. 1 (2006): 81–99.

32. David, "In Exchange for Truth."

33. "Thick line behind the past" was a policy announced by the first Polish non-communist prime minister, Tadeusz Mazowiecki, in summer 1989. See Timothy Garton Ash, "The Truth About the Dictatorship," *New York Review of Books*, February 18, 1998.

34. David, "In Exchange for Truth."

35. David, "From Prague to Baghdad," 354–57.

36. Neil J. Kritz, "Dealing with the Legacy of Past Abuses: An Overview of the Options and Their Relationship to the Promotion of Peace," in *Dealing with the Past: Critical Issues, Lessons Learned, and Challenges for Future Swiss Policy*, ed. Mô Bleeker and Jonathan Sisson (Swisspeace, 2004), 25, http://www.swisspeace.ch/.

37. Ibid.

38. Mayer-Rieckh, "Vetting to Prevent Future Abuses," 190.

39. Teitel, *Transitional Justice*, 149–90; Elster, *Closing the Books*, 47–76.

40. See Luc Huyse, "Justice After Transition: On the Choices Successor Elites Make in Dealing with the Past," *Law & Social Inquiry* 20, no. 1 (1995), 51–78; Peter Novick, *The Resistance Versus Vichy: The Purge of Collaborators in Liberated France* (New York: Columbia University Press, 1968); Herbert R. Lottman, *Purge: Purification of French Collaborators After World War II* (New York: William Morrow, 1986); John H. Herz, ed., *From Dictatorship to Democracy: Coping with the Legacies of Authoritarianism and Totalitarianism* (Westport, Conn.: Greenwood Press, 1982).

41. David, "From Prague to Baghdad," 350.

42. Mayer-Rieckh, "Vetting to Prevent Future Abuses," 190.

43. In some countries, the only available option to prevent officers associated with former regimes from accessing leading state posts was through blocking their

promotions to those posts by civilian governments. See Valeria Barbuto, "Strengthening Democracy: *Impugnación* Procedures in Argentina," in *Justice as Prevention*, ed. Mayer-Rieckh and de Greiff, 40–79.

44. Dimitri A. Sotiropoulos, "Swift Gradualism and Variable Outcomes: Vetting in Post-Authoritarian Greece," in *Justice as Prevention*, ed. Mayer-Rieckh and de Greiff, 122.

45. An attempt to review the act was blocked by Parliament in 2009. See, e.g., Nicholas Witchell, "Why the Monarchy Discriminates," BBC News, March 27, 2009, http://news.bbc.co.uk/2/hi/uk_news/politics/7966987.stm (accessed September 29, 2009).

46. David and Choi, "Victims on Transitional Justice," 397–402.

47. See *Stalla Costa v. Uruguay*, Comm. No. 198/1985 (July 9, 1987), U.N. Doc. Supp. No. 40 (A/42/40) at 170.

48. Act 119/1990 Sb.on Judicial Rehabilitation, April 23, 1990 (Czechoslovakia). RD:Entry deleted from the biblio

49. Employment Equity Act, No. 55 (1998) (The Republic of South Africa).

50. Teitel, *Transitional Justice*, 6.

51. Claus Offe, *The Varieties of Transition: The East European and East German Experience* (Cambridge, Mass.: MIT Press, 1997), 93–94.

52. Vojtech Cepl, "The Transformation of Hearts and Minds in Eastern Europe," *Cato Journal* 17, no. 2 (1997): 229–34.

53. Elizabeth Barrett, Péter Hack, and Ágnes Munkácsi, "Lustration as Political Competition: Vetting in Hungary," in *Justice as Prevention*, ed. Mayer-Rieckh and de Greiff, 266.

54. Directive No. 1/1992, on the Election of Interim Administrative Committee Members for Districts and Neighborhoods, March 1992, Electoral Commission of the Transitional Government of Ethiopia, excerpted in Kritz, *Transitional Justice*, 3:389.

55. Huyse, "Justice After Transition," 67. See also Novick, *The Resistance Versus Vichy*, 209–14; Kritz, *Transitional Justice*, 2:1–201, 3:291–436; István Deák, Jan T. Gross, and Tony Judt, eds., *The Politics of Retribution in Europe: World War II and Its Aftermath* (Princeton, N.J.: Princeton University Press, 2000); Tony Judt, *Postwar: A History of Europe Since 1945* (New York: Penguin, 2005), 41–62.

56. *De Becker v. Belgium*, European Court of Human Rights, Application 214/56 (1958–59). See also Huyse, "Justice After Transition," 66–78.

57. Minor Retributive Decree, 138/1945 Sb. (Czechoslovakia).

58. Law Concerning Addenda to Civil Penal Code Regarding Treason and Other Crimes Against the State, No. 259/45 (June 1, 1945), §6, translated in Kritz, *Transitional Justice*, 3:375–81.

59. The Constitution of the United States, Fourteenth Amendment, section 3.

60. Spitz and Chaskalson, *The Politics of Transition*, 31.

61. David, "Lustration Laws in Action," 406.

62. Act Dz.U.96.89.402 from July 5, 1996, Art. 28 (1) 1 (Poland).

63. Lovro Šturm, interview by the author, Constitutional Court of Slovenia (Ljubljana, 1999).

64. Herz, *From Dictatorship to Democracy*, 22.

65. David, "Transitional Injustice?" 808n35.

66. Cf. Herz, *From Dictatorship to Democracy*, 29.

67. Gábor Halmai and Kim Lane Scheppele, "Living Well Is the Best Revenge: The Hungarian Approach to Judging the Past," in *Transitional Justice and the Rule of Law in New Democracies,* ed. A. James McAdams (Notre Dame, Ind.: Notre Dame University Press, 1997), 171.

68. Herz, *From Dictatorship to Democracy*, 19.

69. David, "From Prague to Baghdad," 366–68.

70. Herz, *From Dictatorship to Democracy*, 29.

71. A. James McAdams, *Judging the Past in Unified Germany* (New York: Cambridge University Press, 2001).

72. Magali Gravier, "East-Germans in the Post-Unification German Civil Service: The Role of Political Loyalty in a Transition to Democracy" (paper presented at the IPSA 19th World Congress, Durban, June 29–July 4, 2003).

73. McAdams, *Judging the Past*, 55–87.

74. Ibid., 75–76.

75. See Katy A. Crossley-Frolick, "The Fate of Former East German Police in Reunified Germany, 1990–1996: The Dialectics of Inclusion and Exclusion," *Journal of Historical Sociology* 23, no. 2 (2010): 251–83.

76. Ibid., 265.

77. Maria Łoś, "Lustration and Truth Claims: Unfinished Revolutions in Central Europe," *Law & Social Inquiry* 20, no. 1 (1995): 148–54; Kieran Williams, "Lustration as the Securitization of Democracy in Czechoslovakia and the Czech Republic," *Journal of Communist Studies and Transition Politics* 19, no. 4 (2003): 10–11; David, "Lustration Laws in Action," 400–404.

78. Edith Oltay, "Hungary's Screening Law," RFE/RL Research Report 3, no. 15 (April 15, 1994): 13–15, excerpted in Kritz, *Transitional Justice*, 2:662–67.

79. Lavinia Stan and Lucian Turcescu, "The Devil's Confessors: Priests, Communists, Spies, and Informers," *East European Politics and Societies* 19, no. 4 (2005): 658.

80. See Accountability for Human Rights Violations Act, Official Gazette of the RS, No. 58/2003.

81. Jonathan Kandell, "Kurt Waldheim Dies at 88; Ex-UN Chief Hid Nazi Past," *International Herald Tribune*, June 14, 2007.

82. Truth Commission Digital Collection, United States Institute of Peace, http://www.usip.org/ (accessed September 30, 2009).

83. Zamora and Holiday, "The Struggle for Lasting Reform," 96, 107.

84. See Ústav paměti národa, http://www.abchistory.cz/ustav-pameti-naroda.htm (accessed September 30, 2009).

85. In Argentina, human rights organizations compiled a list of personnel responsible for human rights violations and delivered it to the National Congress in 1984. Similarly, an unauthorized list of persons whom the Argentinean National Commission on the Disappearance of Persons held accountable for the disappearances was published after its *Nunca Más* report did not include that list. See Barbuto, "Strengthening Democracy," 43–44.

86. David, "From Prague to Baghdad," 360.

87. David, "In Exchange for Truth."

88. Desmond Tutu, *No Future Without Forgiveness* (New York: Random House, 1999), 220.

89. David, "From Prague to Baghdad," 360.

90. See, e.g., Teitel, *Transitional Justice*, 149–90.

91. For El Salvador, see Zamora and Holiday, "The Struggle for Lasting Reform," 84–85.

92. *Ex Parte Garland*, 71 U.S. 333 (1866), 334–35.

93. Ibid., 335.

94. Sotiropoulos, "Swift Gradualism," 122.

95. CPA, Order 2 on Dissolution on Entities (Iraq).

96. Goldstone, "Commission of Inquiry."

97. See *Truth and Reconciliation Commission of South Africa Report*

98. Herman Schwartz, *The Struggle for Constitutional Justice in Post-Communist Europe* (Chicago: University of Chicago Press, 2000), 17–18.

99. See Venice Commission of the Council of Europe, http://www.venice.coe.int/site/dynamics/N_court_links_ef.asp (accessed September 30, 2009).

100. Klaaren, "Institutional Transformation," 151.

101. Zamora and Holiday, "The Struggle for Lasting Reform," 90.

102. Sotiropoulos, "Swift Gradualism," 130.

103. Act 451/1991 Sb. That Prescribes Certain Additional Prerequisites for the Exercise of Certain Positions Filled by Election, Appointment, or Assignment in State Organs and Organizations (Czech/Czechoslovak Lustration Act).

104. Accountability for Human Rights Violations Act (Serbia).

105. On South Africa, see Klaaren, "Institutional Transformation," 148. On Bosnia and Herzegovina, see Mayer-Rieckh, "Vetting to Prevent Future Abuses," 189.

106. Stan and Turcescu, "The Devil's Confessors," 658.

Chapter 2

1. Stephen Holmes, "The End of Decommunization," *East European Constitutional Review* 3 (Summer/Fall 1994): 33–34.

2. Even in these contexts one may find mild transitional justice measures. See generally Posner and Vermeule, "Transitional Justice as Ordinary Justice."

3. According to O'Donnell and Schmitter, transitions refer to intervals between

authoritarian rule and "something else." It can be the instauration of a political democracy or the restoration of a new form of authoritarian rule. See generally Guillermo O'Donnell, Philippe Schmitter, and Laurence Whitehead, eds., *Transitions from Authoritarian Rules: Prospects for Democracy* (Baltimore: Johns Hopkins University Press, 1986).

4. Teitel, *Transitional Justice*, 5.

5. Joseph A. Schumpeter, *Capitalism, Socialism, and Democracy* (London: George Allen & Unwin, 1979), 269–70, 284–90.

6. Huntington, *Third Wave*, 7.

7. See, e.g., Tatu Vanhanen, *Prospects of Democracy: A Study of 172 Countries* (London: Routledge, 1997), 34.

8. Juan J. Linz and Alfred Stepan, *Problems of Democratic Transition and Consolidation: Southern Europe, South America, and Post-Communist Europe* (Baltimore: Johns Hopkins University Press, 1996), 4.

9. Robert A. Dahl, *Dilemmas of Pluralist Democracy* (New Haven, Conn.: Yale University Press, 1982), 11.

10. Philippe C. Schmitter and Terry Lynn Karl, "What Democracy Is . . . and Is Not," *Journal of Democracy* 2 (Summer 1991): 81–82.

11. See generally Donald P. Kommers, *The Constitutional Jurisprudence of the Federal Republic of Germany*, 2nd ed. (Durham, N.C.: Duke University Press, 1997).

12. See ibid., 36–37. See also Judgment Pl. Ús 19/93, Constitutional Court of the Czech Republic (December 21, 1993).

13. Schmitter and Karl, "What Democracy Is," 83.

14. See Terry L. Karl and Philippe Schmitter, "Modes of Transition in Latin America: Southern and Eastern Europe," *International Social Science Journal*, no. 128 (1991): 269–84.

15. Cf. Lilian A. Baria and Steven D. Roper, "How Effective Are International Criminal Tribunals? An Analysis of the ICTY and the ICTR," *International Journal of Human Rights* 9, no. 3 (2005): 351–52.

16. Cf. Dean Ajdukovic and Dinka Corkalo, "Trust and Betrayal in War," in *My Neighbor, My Enemy: Justice and Community in the Aftermath of Mass Atrocity*, ed. Eric Stover and Harvey M. Weinstein (Cambridge: Cambridge University Press, 2004).

17. See Judgment Pl. Ús 19/93.

18. Fareed Zakaria, "The Rise of Illiberal Democracy," *Foreign Affairs* 76, no. 6 (November/December 1997): 22.

19. See generally Alexis de Tocqueville, *Democracy in America* (New York: Penguin, 2004); Gabriel A. Almond and Sidney Verba, *The Civic Culture* (Boston: Little, Brown, and Company, 1963); Robert Putnam, *Making Democracy Work: Civic Traditions in Modern Italy* (Princeton, N.J.: Princeton University Press, 1993); Robert Putnam, *Bowling Alone: The Collapse and Revival of American Community* (New York: Simon and Schuster, 2001). Cf. Francis Fukuyama, *Trust: The Social Virtues and the Creation of Prosperity* (New York: Free Press, 1995).

20. Gabriel A. Almond, "The Intellectual History of the Civic Culture Concept," in *The Civic Culture Revisited*, ed. Gabriel A. Almond and Sidney Verba (Newbury Park, Calif.: Sage, 1989), 26.

21. Ibid., 27.

22. Ibid., 16.

23. Cf. Bonny Ibhawoh, "Between Culture and Constitution: Evaluating the Cultural Legitimacy of Human Rights in the African State," *Human Rights Quarterly* 22, no. 2 (2000): 938–60.

24. James L. Gibson and Amanda Gouws, *Overcoming Intolerance in South Africa* (Cambridge: Cambridge University Press, 2003); James L. Gibson, "Truth, Reconciliation, and the Creation of Human Rights Culture in South Africa," *Law & Society Review* 38, no. 1 (2004): 5–40.

25. "National Unity and Reconciliation," Constitution of the Republic of South Africa (Act 200 of 1993).

26. See Gibson, "Truth, Reconciliation, and the Creation of Human Rights Culture," 6. Cf. Laurence Whitehead, *Democratization: Theory and Experience* (Oxford: Oxford University Press, 2002), 16–18.

27. Hennie P. P. Lötter, *Injustice, Violence, and Peace: The Case of South Africa* (Atlanta, Ga.: Rodopi, 1997).

28. Vojtech Cepl and Mark Gillis, "Making Amends After Communism," *Journal of Democracy* 7, no. 4 (1996): 123.

29. Zevedei Barbu, *Democracy and Dictatorship: Their Psychology and Patterns of Life* (repr., London: Routledge, 1998), 3.

30. Ibid., 3–4.

31. We refrain from passing any normative judgment about the social process of purification.

32. The status of victim can exonerate even those who were previously complicit with the past regime or its transgressors. A classic example on the country level was the U.S. nuclear bombing of Hiroshima and Nagasaki in 1945. The bombing was clearly one of the factors that wiped away the guilt of Japan and allowed it to portray itself as a victim rather than a major World War II aggressor.

33. Václav Havel, *Audience*, in Václav Havel, *The Garden Party and Other Plays* (New York: Grove Press, 1993), 183–211.

34. One can even imagine that, following Milošević's political trajectory, the socialist regime would change into a nationalist regime, maintaining Vaněk's position as a dissident.

35. Hannah Arendt, *The Origins of Totalitarianism* (New York: Harcourt Brace Jovanovich, 1973).

36. David and Choi, "Victims on Transitional Justice."

37. Ian Buruma, *The Wages of Guilt: Memories of War in Germany and in Japan* (New York: Farrar, Straus and Giroux, 1994).

38. Jeffrie Murphy, *Getting Even: Forgiveness and Its Limits* (Oxford: Oxford University Press, 2003).

39. *The Sorrow and the Pity*, directed by Ophüls; Fabrice Virgili, *Shorn Women: Gender and Punishment in Liberation France* (New York: Berg, 2002).

40. Murphy, *Getting Even*.

41. Erving Goffman, "Embarrassment and Social Organization," *American Journal of Sociology* 62, no. 3 (1956): 264–71.

42. Robert Parker, *Miasma: Pollution and Purification in Early Greek Religion* (Oxford: Clarendon Press, [1983] 1996), 19–23.

43. Ibid., 24.

44. Mary Douglas, *Purity and Danger: An Analysis of Concepts of Pollution and Taboo* (London: Routledge, [1966] 2003), 69.

45. Chen-Bo Zhong and Katie Liljenquist, "Washing Away Your Sins: Threatened Morality and Physical Cleansing," *Science* 313 (2006): 1451–52.

46. René Girard, *Violence and the Sacred* (Baltimore: Johns Hopkins University Press, 1979), 29.

47. Cf. Václav Žák. "Lustrace nebo Spravedlnost?" *Český rozhlas* 6, December 10, 2005, http://www.rozhlas.cz/cro6/komentare/_zprava/210146 (accessed October 16, 2009).

48. George L. Hicks, *Japan's War Memories: Amnesia or Concealment?* (Aldershot: Ashgate, 1998), 128.

49. Hannah Arendt, *Eichmann in Jerusalem: A Report on the Banality of Evil* (New York: Viking Press, 1963), 251.

50. Roman David and Susanne Choi, "Getting Even, or Getting Equal? Retributive Desires and Transitional Justice, *Political Psychology* 30, no. 2 (2009): 161–92.

51. Stefan Rossbach, *Gnostic Wars: The Cold War in the Context of a History of Western Spirituality* (Edinburgh: Edinburgh University Press, 1999), 39.

52. Cf. Hannah Arendt, *The Human Condition* (Chicago: Chicago University Press, 1958), 238–39.

53. Parker, *Miasma*, 214.

54. See Thomas J. Sheff, *Catharsis in Healing, Ritual and Drama* (Berkeley: University of California Press, 1979), 5.

55. Cited in ibid., 47.

56. See, e.g., Brad J. Bushman, "Does Venting Anger Feed or Extinguish the Flame? Catharsis, Rumination, Distraction, Anger, and Aggressive Responding," *Personality and Social Psychology Bulletin* 28, no. 6 (2002): 724–31.

57. For instance, the victim-centered approach to truth telling has long been labeled the "narratives of trauma" and the human rights violation committee "a Kleenex commission": victims who publicly narrated their personal stories often cried and were offered facial tissues. See Annelies Verdoolaege, *Reconciliation Discourse: The Case of the Truth and Reconciliation Commission* (Philadelphia: John Benjamins, 2008), 83.

Thus, the method of catharsis pursued through transitional justice qualitatively differs from the one in catharsis theory.

58. Murray Edelman, *The Symbolic Uses of Politics* (Urbana: University of Illinois Press, 1964); David I. Kertzer, *Ritual, Politics, and Power* (New Haven, Conn.: Yale University Press, 1988).

59. Helena Silverstein, "The Symbolic Life of Law: The Instrumental and the Constitutive in Scheingold's *The Politics of Rights*," *International Journal for the Semiotics of Law* 16, no. 4 (2003): 407–23.

60. Erving Goffman, *Frame Analysis: An Essay on the Organization of Experience* (Cambridge, Mass.: Harvard University Press, 1974).

61. Robert Wuthnow, *Meaning and Moral Order: Explorations in Cultural Analysis* (Berkeley: University of California Press, 1987), 14.

62. See ibid.; Edelman, *The Symbolic Uses of Politics*; Stanley Cohen, *Folk Devils and Moral Panics* (London: MacGibbon and Kee, 1972); Albert J. Bergesen, "Political Witch Hunts: The Sacred and the Subversive in Cross-National Perspective," *American Sociological Review* 42 (1977): 220–33; Nachman Ben-Yehuda and Erich Goode, *Moral Panics: The Social Construction of Deviance* (Oxford: Blackwell, [1994] 2009).

63. Edelman, *The Symbolic Uses of Politics*, 12; Kertzer, *Ritual, Politics, and Power*.

64. Naomi Roht-Arriaza, "Punishment, Redress, and Pardon: Theoretical and Psychological Approaches," in *Impunity and Human Rights in International Law and Practice*, ed. Naomi Roht-Arriaza (New York: Oxford University Press, 1995).

65. Hayner, *Unspeakable Truths*, 30–31.

66. James L. Gibson, "Does Truth Lead to Reconciliation? Testing the Causal Assumptions of the South African Truth and Reconciliation Process," *American Journal of Political Science* 48, no. 2 (2004): 201–17.

67. Whitehead, *Democratization*, 36–64.

68. Gil Eyal, "Antipolitics and the Spirit of Capitalism: Dissidents, Monetarists, and the Czech Transition to Capitalism," *Theory and Society* 29, no. 1 (2000): 49–92; Eyal, Szelényi, and Townsley, *Making Capitalism Without Capitalists*.

69. Bergesen, "Political Witch Hunts," 221; Émile Durkheim, *The Elementary Forms of the Religious Life* (Oxford: Oxford University Press, [1912] 2001).

70. Bergesen, "Political Witch Hunts," 223.

71. Stanley Cohen, "State Crimes of Previous Regimes: Knowledge, Accountability, and the Policing of the Past," *Law & Social Inquiry* 20, no. 1 (1995): 12.

72. Dan M. Kahan, "What Do Alternative Sanctions Mean?" *University of Chicago Law Review* 63 (1996): 591–653.

73. Harold Garfinkel, "Conditions of Successful Degradation Ceremonies," *American Journal of Sociology* 61, no. 5 (1956): 420–24.

74. John Braithwaite and Stephen Mugford, "Conditions of Successful Reintegration Ceremonies," *British Journal of Criminology* 34, no. 2 (1994): 139–71.

75. Kahan, "What Do Alternative Sanctions Mean?"

76. Trudy Govier, *Forgiveness and Revenge* (New York: Routledge, 2002), 46–47; Murphy, *Getting Even*, 80.

77. Cf. Erving Goffman, *Relations in Public: Microstudies of the Public Order* (New York: Basic Books, 1971), 113.

78. Mike Hepworth and Bryan S. Turner, *Confession: Studies in Deviance and Religion* (London: Routledge and Kegan Paul, 1982), 14.

79. Teitel, *Transitional Justice*, 6.

80. Almond and Verba, *The Civic Culture*; Niklas Luhmann, *Trust and Power* (Chichester: Wiley, 1979); Anthony Giddens, *The Consequences of Modernity* (Cambridge: Polity, 1990), 88; Putman, *Making Democracy Work*; Valerie Braithwaite and Margaret Levi, eds., *Trust and Governance* (New York: Russell Sage Foundation, 1998); Putnam, *Bowling Alone*; Ken Newton, "Trust and Politics," in *The Handbook of Social Capital*, ed. Dario Castiglione, Jan W. van Deth, and Guglielmo Wolleb (Oxford: Oxford University Press, 2008), 243. Trust in government has been defined as "a basic evaluative orientation toward the government founded on how well the government is operating according to people's normative expectations." See Marc J. Hetherington, "The Political Relevance of Political Trust," *American Political Science Review* 92, no. 4 (1998): 791 (see Chapter 6 for further review).

81. Fukuyama, *Trust*.

82. Eric M. Uslaner, *Moral Foundations of Trust* (Cambridge: Cambridge University Press, 2002), 225.

83. Susan Rose-Ackerman, "Trust and Honesty in Post-Socialist Societies," *Kyklos* 54, no. 2/3 (2001): 415–44; Richard Rose, William Mishler, and Christian Haerpfer, *Democracy and Its Alternatives: Understanding Post-Communist Societies* (Baltimore: Johns Hopkins University Press, 1998).

84. Robert A. Dahl, *Polyarchy: Participation and Opposition* (New Haven, Conn.: Yale University Press, 1971).

85. Gibson and Gouws, *Overcoming Intolerance in South Africa*.

86. A particular social construction of others is not inevitable. See Peter L. Berger and Thomas Luckman, *The Social Construction of Reality: A Treatise in the Sociology of Knowledge* (Garden City, N.Y.: Anchor Books, 1966), 14; Ian Hacking, *The Social Construction of What?* (Cambridge, Mass.: Harvard University Press, 1999), 6.

Chapter 3

1. Tina Rosenberg, *The Haunted Land: Facing Europe's Ghosts After Communism* (New York: Random House, 1996), 68. The book was published two years before the scandal of Bill Clinton and Monica Lewinsky was exposed.

2. See, e.g., Timothy Garton Ash, "Trials, Purges, and History Lessons," in *History of the Present: Essays, Sketches, and Dispatches from Europe in the 1990s*, ed. Timothy Garton Ash (London: Vintage, 2001); Elster, *Closing the Books*, 68.

3. See, e.g., Pablo de Greiff, "Vetting and Transitional Justice," in *Justice as Prevention*, ed. Mayer-Rieckh and de Greiff, 523–44.

4. Kritz, *Transitional Justice*, vol. 1.

5. Teitel, *Transitional Justice*, 171–73.

6. Boed, "Evaluation of the Legality and Efficacy of Lustration," 358. Cf. Eyal, "Antipolitics and the Spirit of Capitalism," 56.

7. T. Charlton Lewis and Charles Short, *A Latin Dictionary* (Oxford: Clarendon Press, 1879). See also Francis Edward Jackson Valpy, *An Etymological Dictionary of the Latin Language* (London: FEJ Valpy, 1828).

8. E.g., the search of the LexisNexis Academic database revealed only one use of *lustration* prior to 1990.

9. David, "Lustration Laws in Action," 388.

10. Kieran Williams, Brigid Fowler, and Aleks Szczerbiak, "Explaining Lustration in Central Europe: A 'Post-Communist Politics' Approach," *Democratization* 12, no. 1 (2005): 40n8.

11. ČTK, "Lustrace—lustrační zákon," *ČTK Infobanka*, revised December 9, 2005.

12. Ibid.

13. Ewa Siedlecka, "Dziennikarze, wykladowcy—do lustracji majatkowej?" *Gazeta Wyborcza* (April 11, 2007), http://wyborcza.pl/1,79418,4049805.html (accessed October 12, 2009).

14. "Lustrace vozidel OCIS," http://www.neuzil.cz/article.asp?nArticleID = 20 (accessed October 15, 2009).

15. Václav Dolejší, "Prodej dětí: obviněných přibývá," *iDnes*, November 18, 2004, http://zpravy.idnes.cz/prodej-deti-obvinenych-pribyva-dmv-/domaci.asp?c = A0411 18_223226_domaci_pol (accessed October 15, 2009).

16. David, "Lustration Laws in Action," 388.

17. Žáček, *Boje o minulost*, 41.

18. Similarly, the Czech word *perlustrace*, which is equivalent to the English word *perlustration*, has similar characteristics. It also has a Latin origin, *perlustratio*, which means to pass through, survey, examine. Lewis and Short, *A Latin Dictionary*. *Perlustrace* was used to refer to a routine check of identification documents conducted by the Czechoslovak Corps of National Security, the socialist equivalent of the regular police before 1989, to determine the identity of an arbitrarily selected person (someone walking on the street, visiting an exhibition, attending a concert, and so forth).

19. David, "Lustration Laws in Action," 388.

20. Ibid.

21. Roman David, "Zákon o protipávnosti komunistického režimu, nebo právní zásady uznávané civilizovanými národy," Bulletin no. 99 (Praha: Občanský Institut, 1999).

22. David, "Lustration Laws in Action," 388.

23. Act 451/1991Sb. (hereafter the Czech Lustration Act).

24. Act XXIII/1994 on Background Checks for Individuals Holding Certain Key

Offices as Amended by Act LXVII/1996, Act XCIII/2000, and Act LXVII/2001 (Hungarian Lustration Act).

25. Act 99.42.428 on the Revealing of Work . . . Dz.U.99.42.428 (Polish Lustration Act). For the subsequent changes, see Rzecznik Interesu Publicznego, "Podstawa Prawna," http://www.rzecznikip.gov.pl/ (accessed October 15, 2009).

26. David, "Lustration Laws in Action," 387n1.

27. The result of the Google search may need to be interpreted in light of the population of Poland, which is almost four times larger than that of the Czech Republic. The population of Hungary is about ten million, about the same size as the Czech Republic.

28. Gábor Halmai, correspondence with the author, June 3, 2009. "The term *átvilágítás* ('lustration', 'shining a light through') has been adopted in Hungarian law to signify the screening out of individuals unfit for public office due to their collaboration with the previous oppressive regime, by accessing, examining and disclosing incriminating files." Hungarian Parliamentary Commissioner for Data Protection and Freedom of Information, Annual Report (2004), http://abiweb.obh.hu/dpc/index .php?menu = reports/2004/II/A/3/7 (accessed October 15, 2009). The Hungarian Google site returned 46,100 matches for "lustration" in May 2009.

29. Halmai and Scheppele, "Living Well Is the Best Revenge"; Horne, "International Legal Rulings on Lustration Policies"; Horne and Levi, "Does Lustration Promote Trustworthy Governance?"

30. Scholars writing on the Baltic States, Georgia, the former Yugoslavia, Bulgaria, and Albania also use lustrations.

31. Lewis and Short, *A Latin Dictionary*.

32. R. M. Ogilvie, "Lustrum Condere," *Journal of Roman Studies* 51, parts 1 and 2 (1961): 39.

33. See ibid., 33–34.

34. Ibid., 35. Ogilvie discusses this view but does not share it.

35. "Censor," http://www.etymonline.com/index.php?search = censor&search mode = none (accessed July 9, 2010).

36. Ibid.

37. "Census," http://www.etymonline.com/index.php?search = census&search mode = none (accessed July 9, 2010).

38. Boed, "Evaluation of the Legality and Efficacy of Lustration," 358. See also Vojtech Cepl, "Ritual Sacrifices: Lustration in the CSFR," *East European Constitutional Review* 1 (Spring 1994): 24–26; Jirina Siklova, "Lustration or the Czech Way of Screening," *East European Constitutional Review* 5, no. 1 (1996): 57; Eyal, Szelényi, and Townsley, *Making Capitalism Without Capitalists*, 102–12; Eyal, "Antipolitics and the Spirit of Capitalism." See also Lavinia Stan, "Moral Cleansing, Romanian Style," *Problems of Post-Communism* 49, no. 4 (2002): 52–62.

39. See David, "Lustration Laws in Action," 394–97.

40. Teitel, *Transitional Justice*, 269n39. It included among others Stephen Engelberg, "The Velvet Revolution Gets Rough," *New York Times Magazine*, May 31, 1992, 30; Aryeh Neier, "Watching Rights," *The Nation*, January 13, 1992, 9; Jeri Laber, "Witch-Hunt in Prague," *New York Review of Books*, April 23, 1992, 5; Mary Battiata, "East Europe, Hunts for Reds," *Washington Post*, December 28, 1991; Lawrence Weschler, "The Velvet Purge: The Trials of Jan Kavan," *New Yorker*, October 19, 1992, 66–96; John Tagliabue, "Prague Turns on Those Who Brought the Spring," *New York Times*, February 24, 1992, A9.

41. Cohen, *Folk Devils*; Ben-Yehuda and Goode, *Moral Panics*.

42. Another position on the topic is the acknowledgment of the symbolic nature of lustration laws in contrast to "pragmatic laws." See Jiri Priban, "Oppressors and Their Victims: The Czech Lustration Law and the Rule of Law," in *Justice as Prevention*, ed. Mayer-Rieckh and de Greiff, 320. In contrast, in Chapter 2, we have argued that all laws and tangible processes have a dual meaning. Přibáň's position nevertheless supports our argument about the symbolic meaning of lustration laws.

43. Edelman, *The Symbolic Uses of Politics*, 12.

44. Bergesen, "Political Witch Hunts," 221.

45. Act 451/1991 (Czech Lustration Act).

46. Adam Michnik and Václav Havel, "Confronting the Past: Justice or Revenge?" *Journal of Democracy* 4, no. 1 (1993): 20–27. Havel's views of lustrations were quite ambiguous. He later proposed an alternative lustration bill in an attempt to deal with the criticisms but the Federal Assembly struck it down. Although Havel has recognized the difficulties with lustration law, he clearly considered that in principle the country was better-off with the law than without it. Had he vetoed the law, the de facto tricameral Federal Assembly would barely have been able to find the three majorities necessary to pass it again. Havel must have been aware of the fact that several influential Slovak federal deputies, including the chairman of the assembly, Alexander Dubček, were absent during the voting on the original lustration bill. On the tricameral nature of the assembly, see Ústavní zákon o československé federaci, 143/1968 Sb. (October 27, 1968), Art. 40–42.

47. The act had to be signed by the deputy chairman of the assembly, Rudolf Battěk (ASD). It was a historical irony that Dubček did not sign the lustration law, since he had signed the so-called baton law in 1969, which facilitated widespread purges that followed the Soviet-led invasion of Czechoslovakia in 1968. See Act 99/1969 Sb., Zákonné opatření o některých přechodných opatřeních nutných k upevnění a ochraně veřejného pořádku (August 22, 1969).

48. "Report of the Committee Set Up to Examine the Representations Made by the Trade Union Association of Bohemia, Moravia, and Slovakia and by the Czech and Slovak Confederation of Trade Unions under Art. 24 of the ILO Constitution Alleging Nonobservance by the CSFR of the Discrimination (Employment and Occupation) Convention 1958 (No. 111)," *ILO Official Bulletin* 75, supp. 1, ser. B (1992) (hereafter ILO Report).

49. See ibid. The ILO repeated its criticism in 1993 and 1999.

50. Parliamentary Assembly of the Council of Europe, "Resolution on Measures to Dismantle the Heritage of Former Communist Totalitarian Systems," doc. no. 1096 (1996), http://assembly.coe.int/main.asp?Link = /documents/adoptedtext/ta96/eres10 96.htm (accessed October 16, 2009).

51. See, e.g., U.S. Department of State, "Country Reports on Human Rights Practices for 2000: Czech Republic" (Washington, D.C., 2001), [section] 1e.

52. Memorandum on the Applicability of International Agreements to the Screening Law (1992), reprinted in *Transitional Justice*, ed. Kritz, 3:335.

53. See Chapter 1. See also Rosenberg, *The Haunted Land*. Cf. Ash, *The File*; Ash, "The Truth About Dictatorship," 35.

54. Decision Pl. Ús 1/92.

55. Parliamentary Assembly of the Council of Europe, Report on "Measures to Dismantle the Heritage of Former Communist Totalitarian Systems". (June 3, 1996), Doc. 7568, n. 11, http://assembly.coe.int/Documents/WorkingDocs/doc96/EDOC75 68.htm (accessed October 16, 2009); Sharon Fisher, "Slovakia's Lustration Law No Longer in Effect," *OMRI Daily Digest*, January 3, 1997.

56. Act 254/1995 Sb., Act 422/2000 Sb.

57. According to ČTK, "Mr President did not sign the laws in 1995 either because he did not want to justify the five-year period of waiting for the bills on the civil service." ČTK, "Havel Declines to Sign Amendments to Screening Laws," November 16, 2000.

58. IVVM, "Veřejnost k lustračnímu zákonu," *Sociologický datový archív*, May 19, 2000.

59. Constitutional Court of the Czech Republic, Decision Pl. ÚS 9/01, http://angl.concourt.cz/angl_verze/cases.php (accessed September 9, 2009).

60. David, "Lustration Laws in Action," 410.

61. Ibid., 424n84.

62. Ibid., 424n85.

63. Petr Cibulka, "Kompletní seznamy spolupracovníků StB I–III," *Rudé krávo: Necenzurované noviny*, nos. 13–15 (1992).

64. Přemysl Vachalovský and John Bok, *Kato: Příběh opravdového člověka* (Olomouc, Czech Rep.: J. W. Hill, 2000).

65. Michnik and Havel, "Confronting the Past," 20–27.

66. Jan Pergler and Jiří Kubík, "Grulich a Kavan se Hradu příliš nezamlouvají," *MFDnes*, July 11, 1998.

67. Act 107/2002 Sb. That Amends Act on the Access to Files Created by Activity of the Former State Security, Act no. 140/1996 Sb (Czech Republic).

68. Act 451/1991 (Czech Lustration Act), § 18 [2]. See also David, "Lustration Laws in Action," 409n47.

69. David, "Lustration Laws in Action," 409n47.

70. Ibid.

71. Ibid.

72. Hence the petition of the Czech unions submitted to the ILO appears to be of political rather than social concern since principal officials are not supposed to be members of unions.

73. Chapter 5 will shed more light on the application of the system.

74. There are two sections of the lustration act that concern the repressive apparatus: §§ 2 and 3. The latter is only a modification of the former. The following discussion focuses on the more important one, § 2.

75. The militias were paramilitary units of the Communist Party that helped facilitate the communist takeover in 1948 and conducted various repressive tasks during the communist regime. Jiří Bílek and Vladimír Pilát, "Závodní, Dělnické a Lidové Milice v Československu," *Historie a vojenství*, no. 3 (1995): 79.

76. Huyse, "Justice After Transition," 68.

77. David, "Lustration Laws in Action," 416n68.

78. Decision Pl. ÚS 1/92.

79. Aleš Šulc, head of the Security Department, Ministry of the Interior of the Czech Republic, to the author (providing information on issued certificates according to the lustrations laws), Č.j.: BO-83/PL-2001, March 1, 2001.

80. David, "Lustration Laws in Action," 413–14.

81. For previous estimates, see ibid.

82. Ministry of the Interior of the Czech Republic, "Statistika Provedených Lustrací," March 31, 2009, http://www.mvcr.cz/mvcren/article/lustrace-659009.aspx (accessed October 16, 2009).

83. IVVM, "Veřejnost k lustračnímu zákonu."

84. Act XXIII/1994 (Hungarian Lustration Act).

85. Halmai and Scheppele, "Living Well Is the Best Revenge," 155, 171.

86. Preamble to the Hungarian Lustration Act.

87. Heino Nyyssönen, *The Presence of the Past in Politics: 1956 After "1956" in Hungary* (Jyväskylä, Finland: SoPhi Academic Press, 2000), 219–20.

88. The Constitutional Court struck down the so-called Zétényi-Takács law. See Constitutional Court of Hungary, 2086/A/1991, http://www.trybunal.gov.pl/eng/summaries/wstep_gb.htm (accessed September 9, 2009).

89. László Sólyom and Georg Brunner, *Constitutional Judiciary in a New Democracy: The Hungarian Constitutional Court* (Ann Arbor: University of Michigan Press, 2000), 306.

90. Constitutional Court of Hungary, Decision 60/1994. See also Halmai and Scheppele, "Living Well Is the Best Revenge," 176.

91. Barrett, Hack, and Munkácsi, "Lustration as Political Competition," 270–72. The amendments were passed as Act LXVII of 1996, Act XCIII of 2000, and Act LXVII of 2001.

92. Ibid. See also Constitutional Court of Hungary, 60/1994; 18/1997 (III. 19.) AB; 23/1999 (VI. 30.) AB; 31/2003 (VI. 4.) AB; 37/2005 (X. 5.) AB.

93. Barrett, Hack, and Munkácsi, "Lustration as Political Competition," 269.

94. Halmai and Scheppele, "Living Well Is the Best Revenge," 176.

95. Ibid., 176; Barrett, Hack, and Munkácsi, "Lustration as Political Competition," 275.

96. Ibid.

97. Ibid.

98. Ibid., 276.

99. Ibid., 283.

100. Hungarian Lustration Act, § 8. See also Barrett, Hack, and Munkácsi, "Lustration as Political Competition," 282.

101. Ibid.

102. Hungarian Lustration Act, §18. The individual could resign even before the process was completed, which would lead to the immediate termination of the screening process. See ibid., §11.

103. Maria Vásárhelyi, interview by the author, Budapest, June 2006.

104. Constitutional Court of Hungary, 60/1994.

105. Barrett, Hack, and Munkácsi, "Lustration as Political Competition," 268.

106. Ibid., 271–72. The amendment was a response to the 1994 Constitutional Court ruling that declared that maintaining the secrecy of the archives was not in accordance with the constitution.

107. Ibid., 273.

108. Barrett, Hack, and Munkácsi, "Lustration as Political Competition," 273–74.

109. Ibid., 274.

110. Krisztián Ungváry, interview by the author, Budapest, June 2006.

111. Act III of 2003. The Historical Archives of the Hungarian State Security was established in 2003 as a legal successor to the Historical Archive Office. See Constitutional Court of Hungary, 37/2005 (X. 5.) AB.

112. Bill No. T./14230 (Hungary).

113. Constitutional Court of Hungary, 37/2005 (X. 5.) AB. The Court maintained that while the identification of persons holding public positions who engaged in the past regime could be justified by public interests, "[t]here is no constitutional objective the achievement of which would justify and make necessary the restriction of [their] fundamental rights resulting from full disclosure." Ibid., 14.

114. See Chapter 5.

115. Hungarian Lustration Act, § 2. In 1994 the Constitutional Court found their definition unconstitutional and requested that Parliament define, in a uniform manner, the scope of persons to be checked. The 1996 version of the law therefore stipulated that the screened posts included all officials elected by Parliament or who had taken an oath before Parliament or the president. See also Constitutional Court of Hungary, 23/1999 (VI. 30.) AB.

116. Cf. David, "Lustration Laws in Action," 426–27.

117. Constitutional Court of Hungary, 60/1994.

118. Hungarian Lustration Act, § 2 (1).

119. *Lingens v. Austria*, 8 Eur. H.R. Rep. 407 (1986).

120. Hungarian Lustration Act, §§ 19–20; Constitutional Court of Hungary, 23/1999; Barrett, Hack, and Munkácsi, "Lustration as Political Competition," 279.

121. However, such manipulations were significantly limited by binding decisions of the Constitutional Court. For instance, administrative-academic positions at state universities and the management of state-owned companies were never reintroduced, and the vague clause stipulating "indirect influence" by the media was annulled in 2003. Constitutional Court of Hungary, 31/2003 (VI. 4.) AB. Even after the cancellation, the scope of the provision of the law concerning the media remained relatively wide.

122. Nikolai Gogol, *Dead Souls* (London: Penguin, 2004).

123. For a detailed interpretation, see Constitutional Court of Hungary, 23/1999.

124. György Markó, interview by the author, Budapest, June 2006.

125. Barrett, Hack, and Munkácsi, "Lustration as Political Competition," 276–77.

126. Markó, interview.

127. Oltay, "Hungary's Screening Law," 666.

128. Sebestyén Gorka, "The Undeniable Connection Between Democracy and Lustration," Institute for Transitional Democracy and International Security, http://www.itdis.org/Portals/11/SGmnLustration12-04.pdf (accessed October 16, 2009).

129. "Constitution Watch: Poland," *East European Constitutional Review* 6, nos. 2–3 and no. 4 (1997). See Act 99.42.428 (Polish Lustration Act).

130. Constitutional Tribunal of Poland, K. 24/98, http://www.trybunal.gov.pl/eng/summaries/wstep_gb.htm (accessed September 9, 2009).

131. Ibid., K. 39/97.

132. CBOS, "Oceny procesu lustracyjnego," Komunikat 2206, October 11, 1999.

133. See Chapters 4 and 5.

134. PAP, "Ustawa lustracyjna trafiła do Trybunału Konstytucyjnego," *Dziennik Internetowy PAP*, March 5, 2002.

135. PAP, "Kwaśniewski: Podpisze nowelizację ustawy lustracyjnej," *Dziennik Internetowy PAP*, October 9, 2002.

136. David, "Lustration Laws in Action."

137. Ibid., 411.

138. David, "In Exchange for Truth," 97n10.

139. Komunikat Sądu Apelacyjnego w Warszawie—V Wydziału Lustracyjnego, *Monitor Polski* z 2000 r. Nr 1, poz. 9. (December 28, 1999).

140. "Constitution Watch: Poland" (no. 4).

141. This model demonstrated the difficulty of selecting an impartial person in transitional context, even from within the transitional judiciary. It is hard to imagine anyone who would be able to give up his or her political attitudes and forget his or her experience of living in the authoritarian regime sufficiently to satisfy everyone. An alternative approach would be nominating judges that represented both sides of the

ideological cleavage, such as was achieved in the amnesty process in South Africa. David, "In Exchange for Truth," 94–95.

142. By December 2002, the Lustration Court of Appeal only managed to close 51 cases, initiated by the spokesperson, of which 17 were declared truthful, 25 were declared dishonest, and 9 were dropped. Jerzy Lesiński, "Błędne informacje w 'Rzeczpospolitej,'" Rzecznik Interesu Publicznego, December 2, 2002, http://www.rzecznikip.gov.pl/aktualnosci/111.htm (accessed October 16, 2009). The outcomes of the process are examined in Chapter 5.

143. David, "In Exchange for Truth," 93.

144. Constitutional Tribunal of Poland, K 2/07, 2007.

145. Institute of National Remembrance, Vetting Office, http://www.ipn.gov.pl/portal.php?serwis = en&dzial = 45&id = 234 (accessed July 30, 2010).

146. "IPN nie chce ruszać lustracji," Gazeta Wyborzca, February 9, 2005, http://serwisy.gazeta.pl/kraj/1,62266,2543779.html (accessed October 16, 2009).

147. Rzecznik Interesu Publicznego, Publikacje w MP, http://www.rzecznikip.gov.pl/ (accessed October 16, 2009).

148. Piotr Grzelak, Wojna o Lustracje (Warsaw: Trio, 2005), 212.

149. Rzecznik Interesu Publicznego, Wyciąg z informacji o działalności Rzecznika 2002, http://www.rzecznikip.gov.pl/ (accessed October 16, 2009).

150. See Žáček, Boje o Minulost, 42.

Chapter 4

1. István Szabó, Sunshine (Alliance Atlantis Communications, 1999). Szabó wrote and directed the movie five years after the lustration law was approved in Hungary but several years before his alleged collaboration was revealed.

2. Jan Kavan, Speech to the Federal Assembly, October 3, 1991. See Federální Shromáždění ČSFR [Federal Assembly], 17th Session (1991), http://www.psp.cz/eknih/1990fs/slsn/stenprot/017schuz/ (accessed October 16, 2009), at s017074.htm.

3. Elster, Closing the Books, 79–84.

4. Huntington, Third Wave, 228.

5. Huyse, "Justice After Transition," 77.

6. Posner and Vermeule, "Transitional Justice as Ordinary Justice," 770.

7. Political Transformation and the Electoral Process in Post-Communist Europe, http://www.essex.ac.uk/elections/ (accessed October 16, 2009).

8. John Moran, "The Communist Torturers of Eastern Europe: Prosecute and Punish or Forgive and Forget," Communist and Post-Communist Studies 27, no. 1 (1994): 95–109.

9. Ibid., 101.

10. Helga A. Welsh, "Dealing with the Communist Past: Central and East European Experiences After 1990," Europe-Asia Studies 48, no. 3 (1996): 413–28.

11. Szczerbiak, "Dealing with the Communist Past."

12. Ibid. See also Williams, Fowler, and Szczerbiak, "Explaining Lustration in Central Europe."

13. Nadya Nedelsky, "Divergent Responses to a Common Past: Transitional Justice in the Czech Republic and Slovakia," *Theory & Society* 33 (2004): 63–115.

14. Lavinia Stan, "Explaining Country Differences," in *Transitional Justice in Eastern Europe and the Former Soviet Union: Reckoning with the Communist Past*, ed. Lavinia Stan (New York: Routledge, 2009), 268.

15. Monika Nalepa, *Skeletons in the Closet: Transitional Justice in Post-Communist Europe* (Cambridge: Cambridge University Press, 2010). An anonymous reviewer of this manuscript requested revisiting the work by Nalepa, who also used survey methods. See ibid., 99–125. Similar to Welsh, Nalepa attempts to integrate various approaches to explain lustrations. She hypothesizes that past involvement in the resistance (measured as knowledge of people in the opposition), the perceptions of threat (i.e., posed by communists, controlling for fascists), due process considerations (i.e., false acquittal and false conviction), and "demands for transitional justice" (i.e., respondent's demand for lustrations) increase "demands for transitional justice" (i.e., voting in last elections for a political party that supported lustrations).

16. Stan, "Explaining Country Differences," 268. See also Stan, "Hungary," in *Transitional Justice in Eastern Europe*, ed. Stan, 112. Indeed, in Poland in 1997, the Polish Peasant Party (PSL), the coalition partner of post-communists, defected and voted with the opposition. In Hungary ex-communists had to vote for the amendment because it was requested by the Constitutional Court.

17. Ústava ČSSR, 100/1960 Sb., art 4.

18. David, "Transitional Injustice?" 790–91.

19. Nigel Swain, *Hungary: The Rise and Fall of Feasible Socialism* (New York: Verso, 1992), 27–28.

20. Łoś and Zybertowicz, *Privatizing the Police-State*, 59, 132.

21. The subordination of the secret police to the communist party explains why perceptions about them were derived from perceptions of the successor parties. The secret police was an extended *hand* of the party. We can simplify the refinement of our hypotheses by saying that if a communist has a hand in his pocket, the Czechs would think he carries a gun; the Hungarians would think he is taking his handkerchief to wipe his tears of guilt; and the Poles would argue about it.

22. See, e.g., ibid., 111–13, 179–84; David, "Lustration Laws in Action," 412–16.

23. Anna Grzymala-Busse, *Redeeming the Communist Past: The Regeneration of Communist Parties in East Central Europe* (Cambridge: Cambridge University Press, 2002), 205–14.

24. Radio Prague, "Palach Week," http://archiv.radio.cz/palach99/eng/leden89/ (accessed October 16, 2009).

25. See, e.g., Judt, *Postwar*, 606–22.

26. See ibid. See also, e.g., Charles Gati, *Failed Illusions: Moscow, Washington, Budapest, and the 1956 Hungarian Revolt* (Washington, D.C.: Woodrow Wilson Center

Press, 2006), 225; Jeffrey Simon, *Hungary and NATO: Problems in Civil-Military Relations* (Lanham, Md.: Rowman and Littlefield, 2003), 1–2.

27. Judt, *Postwar*, 618; Simon, *Hungary and NATO*, 2; Rudolf L. Tokes, "Political Transition and Social Transformation," in *Dilemmas of Transition: The Hungarian Experience*, ed. Aurel Braun and Zoltan Barany (Lanham, Md.: Rowman and Littlefield, 1999), 117–18.

28. Huntington misclassifies the case of Czechoslovakia as a transplacement instead of replacement. See David and Choi, "Victims on Transitional Justice," 397n11.

29. Grzymala-Busse, *Redeeming the Communist Past*.

30. Ibid. The only change in the party name reflected the breakdown of Czechoslovakia.

31. Milada Vachudová, *Europe Undivided: Democracy, Leverage and Integration After Communism* (Oxford: Oxford University Press, 2005).

32. David, "Transitional Injustice?" 808n33.

33. David Luban, "A Man Lost in the Gray Zone," *Law and History Review* 19, no. 1 (2001): 47, http://www.historycooperative.org/journals/lhr/19.1/luban.html (accessed August 10, 2010).

34. Ibid.

35. Arendt, *Eichmann in Jerusalem*, 125. See also Richard Rubenstein, "Gray into Black: The Case of Mordecai Chaim Rumkowski," in *Gray Zones: Ambiguity and Compromise in the Holocaust and Its Aftermath*, ed. Jonathan Petropoulos and John K. Roth (New York: Berghahn Books, 2005), 300–301.

36. Linda Mastalir, "Jirina Siklova: A Sociologist, Though Hardly Just an Observer," *Radio Prague*, July 19, 2006, http://www.radio.cz/en/article/81246 (accessed October 18, 2009). Šiklová's definition of the gray zone is very strict. It refers to those people who retained their moral integrity but were not prosecuted or discriminated against by the communist system. It actually refers to a light gray zone, if not a white zone.

37. Elster, *Closing the Books*, 99.

38. Virgili, *Shorn Women*,1.

39. Ibid.

40. Ibid., 3. Further citation omitted.

41. CEU (Central European University), *The Development of Party Systems and Electoral Alignments in East Central Europe [1992–96]* (Machine-readable data files, Department of Political Science, Central European University, Budapest).

42. The first wave of surveys was conducted in 1992, a year when the lustration process had already been under way in the former Czechoslovakia, although it was only in the preparatory stage in Hungary and Poland. This makes it difficult to determine the extent to which the perception of KSČM affected the lustration debate in the Czech Republic or vice versa. However, although intensive lustration debates may have augmented the negative perceptions of the party, its reputation had always been

questioned. It is a well-established fact that KSČM failed to demonstrate discontinuity with the past and has retained a strong ideological position ever since the collapse of the communist regime. See Grzymala-Busse, *Redeeming the Communist Past*, 82–92.

43. Country-specific policies or policies that were mere aspirations have been left out. They included questions related to the separation of Czechoslovakia, "stop[ping] the deterioration of morals," "strengthening national feelings," and "[increasing] the role of religion." The protection of unprofitable companies from bankruptcy was also excluded because a range of other economic policies was already in place.

44. On the problem of the post-communist elites, see, e.g., Eyal, Szelényi, and Townsley, *Making Capitalism Without Capitalists*; Jacek Wasilewski, "Polish Post-Transitional Elite," in *Second Generation of Democratic Elites in Central and Eastern Europe*, ed. Janina Frentzel-Zagórska and Jacek Wasilewski (Warsaw: Polish Academy of Science, 2000); John Higley, Judith Kullberg, and Jan Pakulski, "The Persistence of Postcommunist Elites," *Journal of Democracy* 7, no. 2 (1996): 133–47; and Łoś and Zybertowicz, *Privatizing the Police-State*.

45. This policy has been often dubbed "de-communization," but the use of the epithet may be misleading to many observers. It may carry various meanings, including the removal of party members from positions of influence, disbanding the party, prosecuting its leaders, or eliminating communist ideology. Here it refers to "the removal of former party members from positions of influence" pursuant to the question that was asked in the surveys.

46. Measuring the positive support for human rights (the communist party as the most likely guarantor of human rights) is more useful than measuring the negative attitude to human rights (the communist party as the least likely guarantor of human rights). The former is prospective, while the latter is retrospective. The former captures the transformation of the communist party, while the latter captures its record.

47. Roman David, Focus group session with members of ODS. Czech Republic, July 2006.

48. Interestingly, gender is a significant predictor of the opposition to the removal of the party members in all three countries, other things being equal. Women are less likely to support the removal of party members than men. In male-dominated societies, men would more likely benefit from the removal of other men from public life. Other things being equal, the frequency of church attendance is a positive predictor in Hungary, Poland, and perhaps in the Czech Republic, where it only fails marginally to reach a statistically significant level. It is not surprising that after decades of Christian persecution, the churchgoers would not like communists to remain in government.

49. David and Choi, "Victims on Transitional Justice," 401.

50. Cf. Žák, "Lustrace nebo Spravedlnost?"

51. David, "Lustration Laws in Action," 408.

52. Ibid., 408n43; Federální Shromáždění ČSFR [Federal Assembly], 17th Session (1991), http://www.psp.cz/eknih/1990fs/slsn/stenprot/017schuz/ (accessed October 16,

2009). Hereafter speeches to the Federal Assembly refer to the 17th Session of the assembly.

53. See Constitutional Court of the Czech Republic, Judgment Pl. Ús 1/92.

54. Jiří Schneider, Federální Shromáždění, s017073.htm.

55. David and Choi, "Victims on Transitional Justice," 398–99.

56. Peter Kulan, Federální Shromáždění, s017059.htm.

57. Ján Mlynárik, Federální Shromáždění, s017062.htm.

58. David, "Lustration Laws in Action," 397n25.

59. Václav Benda, Federální Shromáždění, s017061.htm.

60. Erich Kríž, Federální Shromáždění, s017066.htm.

61. Ladislav Kvasnička, Federální Shromáždění, s0170641.htm.

62. Štefan Bačinský, Federální Shromáždění, s017077/119.htm.

63. Ibid.

64. Report of the Parliamentary Commission of November 17, in *Transitional Justice*, ed. Kritz, 3:307–11.

65. Jan Ruml, "Kdo koho kryje?" *Respekt*, April 18, 1990, 3.

66. Schwartz, "Lustration in Eastern Europe," 3:478.

67. Mlynárik, Federální Shromáždění.

68. Joylon Naegele, "Slovakia: Three Prominent Personalities Seek Presidential Position," *RFE/RL*, April 9, 1999, http://www.rferl.org/content/Article/1091051.html (accessed October 16, 2009).

69. Ibid.

70. Ivan Rynda, Federální Shromáždění, s017076.htm.

71. Miloslav Ransdorf, Federální Shromáždění, s017066.htm.

72. Jiří Černý, Federální Shromáždění, s017074.htm.

73. František Šamalík, Federální Shromáždění, s017069.html.

74. Marián Farkaš, Federální Shromáždění, s017060.htm.

75. Jana Petrová, Federální Shromáždění, s017078.htm.

76. Daniel Kroupa, Federální Shromáždění, s017069.htm.

77. David, "Lustration Laws in Action," 406.

78. Oltay, "Hungary's Screening Law," 2:663.

79. Barrett, Hack, and Munkácsi, "Lustration as Political Competition," 266.

80. Sólyom and Brunner, *Constitutional Judiciary in a New Democracy*, 214. Cf. David, "Zákon o protipávnosti."

81. Barrett, Hack, and Munkácsi, "Lustration as Political Competition," 267.

82. Ibid.

83. Ibid.

84. Ibid.

85. Ibid., 268–89.

86. But cf. Oltay, "Hungary's Screening Law," 2:662–67.

87. The final voting took place on March 8, 1994. See Országgyulési Napló [Parliamentary Diary], 1990–2002, *A plenáris ülések jegyzokönyveinek teljes szövegu adatbázisa* (Budapest: Arcanum Adatbázis Kft., 2002).

88. Horne and Levi, "Does Lustration Promote Trustworthy Governance?" 64; Oltay, "Hungary's Screening Law," 2:666.

89. See Országgyulési Napló.

90. Péter Boross, Országgyulési Napló.

91. Zoltán Kátay, Országgyulési Napló.

92. Vilmos Horváth, Országgyulési Napló.

93. Zsolt Zétényi, Országgyulési Napló.

94. Ibid.

95. Balázs Horváth, Országgyulési Napló.

96. Antal Kocsenda, Országgyulési Napló.

97. Ferenc Koszeg, Országgyulési Napló.

98. Ibid.

99. Béla Katona, Országgyulési Napló.

100. Miklós Gáspár, Országgyulési Napló.

101. David, "Lustration Laws in Action," 390.

102. Ash, "The Truth About the Dictatorship."

103. Łoś and Zybertowicz, "Is Revolution a Solution?" 285.

104. Łoś and Zybertowicz, *Privatizing the Police-State*, 111–13.

105. Wasilewski, "Polish Post-Transitional Elite," 197–205, 206–7. See also Higley, Kullberg, and Pakulski, "The Persistence of Postcommunist Elites."

106. See Grzelak, *Wojna o Lustracje*, 219–26.

107. Ibid.

108. Adam Czarnota, "The Politics of the Lustration Law in Poland, 1989–2006," in *Justice as Prevention*, ed. Mayer-Rieckh and de Greiff, 227.

109. David, "Lustration Laws in Action," 399.

110. On the case of the Wałęsa's alleged collaboration, see below.

111. Klaus Bachmann, "Cień pastora Gaucka nad Polską," *Rzeczpospolita*, January 23, 1996.

112. Lech Wałęsa, "Lustracja czy gabinet luster," *Poland Outlook*, 1997, cited in David, "Lustration Laws in Action," 399.

113. Krzysztof Olszewski, "Lustracja coraz popularniejsza," *Rzeczpospolita*, November 16, 1996.

114. Klaus Bachmann, "Strach bez końca," *Rzeczpospolita*, May 6, 2000.

115. Łoś, "Lustration and Truth Claims," 143, 146, 148.

116. Misztal, "How Not to Deal with the Past," 44. See generally Łoś, "Lustration and Truth Claims," 143.

117. Paweł Reszka and Marcin D. Zdort, "Lustracja jak Boomerang [Interview with Jan Olszewski]," *Rzeczpospolita*, July 29, 1995.

118. Łoś, "Lustration and Truth Claims," 132–38.

119. Łoś and Zybertowicz, *Privatizing the Police-State*, 14.

120. The "transformed communist party opposed lustration and claimed that, for

the sake of reconciliation, all lustration efforts should be abandoned." Czarnota, "The Politics of the Lustration Law," 227.

121. Pęk's commission accepted a proposal from the UW, UP, and PSL as a benchmark. Grzelak, *Wojna o lustracje*, 116.

122. Krzysztof Kauba, "Powołanie Rzecznika Interesu Publicznego: Historia," http://www.rzecznikip.gov.pl/ (accessed October 17, 2009).

123. Misztal, "How Not to Deal with the Past," 44.

124. "Constitution Watch: Poland" (nos. 2–3).

125. Grzelak, *Wojna o Lustracje*, 116–32.

126. David, "Lustration Laws in Action," 410–11.

127. Czarnota, "The Politics of the Lustration Law," 227. However, Czarnota does not make a connection between the transformation of the ex-communist party and the "soft" lustration law in Poland. Ibid., 247.

128. Łoś and Zybertowicz, *Privatizing the Police-State*, 203–4.

129. Leszek Miller, "Moja biografia," http://www.miller.pl/strona.php?zm = bio grafia (accessed October 17, 2009).

130. Aleksander Kwaśniewski, "Polish Presidents," http://www.president.pl/en/about-poland/polish-presidents/aleksander-kwasniewski/ (accessed October 17, 2009).

131. Ibid. See also Miller, "Moja biografia."

132. In his inauguration speech, President Kaczyński stressed the need to purge "various pathologies from our life, most prominently including crime that today has assumed great proportions, particularly criminal corruption . . . degenerating the state apparatus and preventing proper fulfilment [sic] by the state of its elementary tasks." Lech Kaczyński, "Oath: The President of the Republic of Poland," http://www.president.pl/en/news-archive/news-2005/art,72,swearing-in-ceremony-of-the-president-of-poland-lech-kaczynski-at-a-session-of-the-national-assembly.html (accessed October 17, 2009).

133. Constitutional Tribunal of Poland, K2/07.

134. See Łoś, "Lustration and Truth Claims," 122–23; Łoś and Zybertowicz, "Is Revolution a Solution?" 284; Łoś and Zybertowicz, *Privatizing the Police-State*, 179–84.

Chapter 5

1. Kwaśniewski was quoted in Jane Perlez, "Polish Leader Vexed by Final Hurdle: His Past," *New York Times*, November 29, 1995.

2. Václav Havel, *Prosím stručně* (Prague: Gallery, 2006), 54.

3. See, e.g., Teitel, *Transitional Justice*.

4. See, e.g., Oltay, "Hungary's Screening Law," 2:663.

5. Cynthia M. Horne and Margaret Levi, "Does Lustration Promote Trustworthy Governance? An Exploration of the Experience of Central and Eastern Europe," in *Building a Trustworthy State in Post-Socialist Transition*, ed. János Kornai and Susan Rose-Ackerman (New York: Palgrave Macmillan, 2004), 60.

6. Csilla Kiss, "The Misuses of Manipulation: The Failure of Transitional Justice in Post-Communist Hungary," *Europe-Asia Studies* 58, no. 6 (2006): 925–40.

7. David, Lustration Systems, Trust in Government, and Reconciliation in the Czech Republic, Hungary and Poland.

8. Teitel, *Transitional Justice.*

9. Bushman, "Does Venting Anger Feed or Extinguish the Flame?" 724–31.

10. For instance, Hungary joined the International Monetary Fund in 1982 and Poland in 1986, while Czechoslovakia joined in 1991.

11. According to Petr Toman (ODS), a lawyer and the former spokesman of the Parliamentary Committee of November 17, 1989, "entrusting people with the occupation of some leading [positions] was the way to circumvent screening law." David, "Lustration Laws in Action," 413.

12. A few of these cases were related to key privatization institutions. For more details, see ibid., 413n60 (further citation omitted).

13. Jeffrey M. Jordan, "Patronage and Corruption in the Czech Republic," part 2, *East European Perspectives* 4, no. 5 (2002): 19–52.

14. Sabina Slonková and Jiří Kubík, "Kdo radí premiérovi Miloši Zemanovi?" *iDnes*, April 12, 2000, http://zpravy.idnes.cz/kdo-radi-premierovi-milosi-zemanovi-d7e-/domaci.asp?c = A000411233740domaci_bac (accessed October 17, 2009).

15. In some cases the response of the press to Šlouf was disproportional; in some cases it was not (ibid.). The investigative journalist Sabina Slonková almost paid the highest price in what seemed to be retaliation for numerous revelations she made. Šlouf was said to have recommended the alleged secret police agent Miroslav Srba to Jan Kavan, who employed him at the Ministry of Foreign Affairs. While Kavan held his post as the president of the UN General Assembly, Srba conspired to murder Slonková. Srba was later convicted for this conspiracy. See Mladá fronta Dnes, "Kavan: Rozvědka mi v resortu rozesela lidi," http://zpravy.idnes.cz/kavan-rozvedka-mi-v-resortu-rozesela-lidi-fgo-/domaci.asp?c = A020723_141115_domaci_has (accessed October 17, 2009); Marek Dvořáček, "Slonkovou dělily od smrti hodiny," *iDnes*, July 23, 2002, http://zpravy.idnes.cz/domaci.asp?r = domaci&c = A020722_121712_krimi_kot&l = 1&t = A020722_121712_krimi_kot&r2 = domaci (accessed October 17, 2009).

16. Coilin O'Connor, "Stanislav Gross: The Youngest Prime Minister in Europe," *Radio Prague*, February 2, 2002, http://www.radio.cz/en/article/62989 (accessed October 17, 2009).

17. Přibyl was forced to resign a few weeks after his appointment. Luděk Navara, "Přibyl odstoupil: Usvědčily ho archivy," *iDnes.cz*, http://zpravy.idnes.cz/pribyl-odstoupil-usvedcily-ho-archivy-dyq-/domaci.asp?c = A040820_204757_domaci_fri (accessed October 17, 2009).

18. David, "Lustration Laws in Action," 421.

19. Ibid.

20. Ibid.

21. The conspiracy to murder Slonková could be attributed to the action of the individual rather than the action of the state. Srba hired an ordinary criminal offender to execute the killing. See note 15 above.

22. David, "Lustration Laws in Action," 416.

23. Ibid. (further citations omitted).

24. Ibid. (further citations omitted).

25. Ibid. (further citations omitted).

26. Naegele, "Slovakia."

27. When Mečiar started his second term prime minister of Slovakia after the 1992 elections, the lustration system was already in effect. Mečiar immediately began negotiations with his Czech counterpart, Klaus, on the separation of the federation, although he had not openly campaigned as a Slovak separatist.

28. David, "Lustration Laws in Action," 421 (further citation omitted).

29. Jaroslav Kmenta, "Kontrola vývozu do rizikových států selhává," *Mladá fronta Dnes*, February 28, 2000, cited in Jeffrey M. Jordan, "Patronage and Corruption in the Czech Republic," *SAIS Review* 22, no. 2 (2002): 26.

30. Jaroslav Spurný, "Kavan, Grulich, Doucha: Tři esa s pestrou minulostí," *Respekt*, July 20, 1998, 4; ČTK, "Kavan tvrdí, že nevěděl o členech StB v ČSSD," *Mladá fronta Dnes*, September 7, 1998. See Aviezer Tucker, "Paranoids May Be Persecuted: Post-Totalitarian Retroactive Justice," *Archives Européennes de Sociologie* 40, no. 1 (1999): 85–87. Kavan was said to have misled the British Broadcasting Complaints Commission (BCC). See Julian Manyon, "Letter: Jan Kavan: The Questions That Remain Unanswered," *The Independent*, September 27, 1992.

31. Radio Prague, "Kavan Report," July 17, 1998, http://archiv.radio.cz/english/cur-affrs/17-7-98.html (accessed October 18, 2009). In the same year, Havel allegedly hesitated to appoint Kavan as the minister of foreign affairs. See Pergler and Kubík, "Grulich a Kavan."

32. See ČTK, "Havel Asks Kavan to Resign over Attempted Murder of Journalist [by His Former Close Aide]," *Czech Happenings*, July 23, 2002.

33. Lawrence Weschler, "The Velvet Purge: The Trials of Jan Kavan," *New Yorker* 68, no. 35 (1992): 68–94; Ross Larsen, "The Trials, Trials, and More Trials of Jan Kavan," *Prague Post*, July 22, 1998; Tomáš Pecina, "Jan Kavan: Lhal jsem a jsem na to hrdý," *Britské listy*, July 28, 1998, http://www.britskelisty.cz/9807/19980728d.html (accessed October 18, 2009).

34. Membership in the communist elite was the most significant predictor of membership in the new business elite. Petr Matějů and Blanka Řeháková, "Turning Left or Class Realignment? Analysis of the Changing Relationship Between Class and Party in the Czech Republic, 1992–1996," *East-European Politics and Societies* 11, no. 3 (1997): 507–47.

35. David, "Lustration Laws in Action," 414 (further citations omitted).

36. Ibid.

37. IVVM, "Veřejnost k lustračnímu zákonu." However, these results can be

called into question. First, the act did not concern private enterprises, and the public—like the authors of the survey—may not have been aware of that fact. Second, some of those who were aware of the limited scope of the system may have given a negative response to convey their dissatisfaction with the insufficient process of lustration. Thus, the negative responses would capture both the supporters of wider lustrations and the opponents of lustrations.

38. David, "Lustration Laws in Action," 415.

39. David, "Transitional Injustice?" 808n33.

40. Zdena Salivarová-Škvorecká, who was accused of collaboration with the secret police for allegedly spying on her husband, the renowned writer Josef Škvorecký, was judicially cleared of collaboration and compiled a collection of essays describing the fate of people whose lives had been prejudiced by being accused of collaboration. Zdena Salivarová-Škvorecká, *Osočení: Pravdivé příběhy lidí z Cibulkova seznamu* (Brno, Czech Rep.: Host, 2000).

41. Iva Hosmanová, "Omlouvám se za příkoří spáchaná ve jménu komunismu, říká Soňa Marková," *iDnes.cz*, May 13, 2008. Some confessions occurred in the early 1990s when the confessors could not predict the consequences of denial. They were made during the screenings of the personnel at the Ministry of the Interior. At the later stage, after the archives were opened, denial was increasingly difficult.

42. See Žáček, *Boje o minulost*, 46–53.

43. In 1990 Jiří Dienstbier, the minister of foreign affairs, and Petr Uhl, the head of the Czechoslovak Press Agency (ČTK), used lustrations. See David, "Lustration Laws in Action," 398.

44. Žantovský, "Ladislav Jakl."

45. This ideological position can most vividly be attributed to the founder of ODS, Václav Klaus. For Klaus, "the third way" had a political dimension in resisting traditional party systems, which he attributed to his political rivals, such as President Havel, Prime Minister Petr Pithart (OH), and the former Federal minister of foreign affairs, Jiří Dientsbier (OH), and an economic dimension seen among those who sought to reform the socialist economic system in 1968. See Václav Klaus, "Před patnácti lety se u nás začal rodit kapitalismus," *Mladá fronta Dnes*, January 11, 2006.

46. Siklova, "Lustration or the Czech Way of Screening," 60.

47. David and Choi, "Victims on Transitional Justice," 414n71.

48. Václav Klaus, "17. listopad v českých dějinách," *Mladá fronta Dnes*, November 15, 2003. Cf. Jana Nosková, "'The Little Czech': The Way of Life of 'Ordinary People' in Socialist Czechoslovakia?" (paper presented at the "Memories in Post-Socialism" international conference, Newcastle, September 2008).

49. See, e.g., ČTK, "Czech Senator Wants New Government to Ban Communists," *Czech Happenings*, June 2, 2009.

50. A book with this title was published by two journalists. Adam Drda and Petr Dudek, *Kdo ve stínu čeká na moc* (Prague: Paseka, 2006).

51. That the communist crimes could have been prosecuted without the act on

the illegitimacy of the communist regime was considered "provocative" by the authors. See ibid., 132.

52. "Known Czech Pop Singer Was Communist Secret Police Agent—Newspaper," *Euroasian Secret Services Daily Review*, June 21, 2007, http://www.axisglobe.com/article.asp?article = 1334 (accessed August 4, 2010).

53. David, "Lustration Laws in Action," 425n89.

54. Ibid.

55. See Jiri Priban, "Oppressors and Their Victims: The Czech Lustration Law and the Rule of Law," in *Justice as Prevention*, ed. Mayer-Rieckh and de Greiff, 334–36.

56. ČTK, "Pražská výstava představuje tváře 28 příslušníků StB," *České Noviny*, November 14, 2008.

57. Vachalovský and Bok, *Kato*. The book contains copies of various allegedly authentic documents from his file, including an undersigned receipt of financial support that Kavan received from an official, or an officer, of the Czechoslovak Embassy in London in 1969.

58. However, not many Czechs would know that Kato referred to Cato Censorius, who censored the Greek culture that threatened Rome and who expelled its protagonists from the Senate. See Alan E. Astin, *Cato the Censor* (Oxford: Clarendon Press, [1978] 2000), 78–103.

59. Přemysl Vachalovský and Pavel Žáček, *Jan Kavan: V labyrintu služeb* (Prague: Formát, 2003).

60. E.g., ČTK, "Czech Greens Leader May Employ Communist Secret Service Agent," *Finanční noviny*, November 25, 2008.

61. Cf. Anna Seleny, "The Foundations of Post-Socialist Legitimacy," in *Dilemmas of Transition*, ed. Braun and Barany.

62. See Political Transformation and the Electoral Process. Both parties had been in the opposition to the center-right government of prime ministers József Antall and Péter Boros that ruled in Hungary between 1990 and 1994. The political partnership eventually collapsed in 2008 after SzDSz withdrew its support of government. See, e.g., Marcus Salzmann, "Hungarian Ruling Coalition Collapses," World Socialist Web Site, May 7, 2008, http://www.wsws.org/articles/2008/may2008/hung-m07.shtml (accessed October 18, 2009).

63. The coexistence of the two stimuli at the same time—the launch of the inclusive system and the formation of the coalition between former adversaries—makes it hard to ascribe a positive transformative effect on state administration and reconciliation to either of them by a standard cross-sectional survey.

64. János Kis, interview by the author, Budapest, June 2006.

65. "[C]onsider the case where politicians in office have been charged with collaboration with the secret services in the past. Even Oleksy, prime minister in Poland, and Medgyessy, prime minister in Hungary, have been charged. Oleksy resigned, Medgyessy stayed in office. . . . If you want to avoid these kinds of cases you need complete

transparency. To be sure, there are many reasons why people mistrust political leaders. But at least one reason for mistrust would be eliminated." Ibid.

66. Gorka, "Undeniable Connection."

67. Ibid.

68. Horne and Levi, "Does Lustration Promote Trustworthy Governance?"

69. Gábor Halmai, e-mail correspondence with the author, June 3, 2009.

70. Ibid.

71. Adam LeBor, "Secret Service Past Returns to Haunt Hungary's Leaders," *The Independent,* August 27, 2002.

72. Eugen Tomiuc, "Hungary: Government Proposes Further Opening of Communist Era Files," *RFE/RL Newsline,* June 27, 2002.

73. Ibid.

74. RFE/RL, "Hungarian President Calls Mecs Commission 'Unconstitutional and Illegitimate,'" *RFE/RL Newsline,* August 21, 2002.

75. Ibid.

76. RFE/RL, "Hungarian Opposition Walks Out of Commission Hearings," *RFE/RL Newsline,* August 6, 2002.

77. RFE/RL, "Hungarian Socialists Submit Separate Report on Prime Minister's Past," *RFE/RL Newsline,* August 21, 2002.

78. RFE/RL, "Hungarian Ministers Authorize Release of Information on Past Links with Communist Secret Services," *RFE/RL Newsline,* August 13, 2002; RFE/RL, "Former Hungarian Premier Denies Secret Service Involvement," *RFE/RL Newsline,* August 16, 2002; RFE/RL, "MNB Governor Says Hungarian Government Wants to Push Him Out of His Job," *RFE/RL Newsline,* August 16, 2002; RFE/RL, "Kover Joins Him in Boycotting Mecs Commission," *RFE/RL Newsline,* August 16, 2002.

79. RFE/RL, "Medgyessy Commission Ends Work in Acrimony," *RFE/RL Newsline,* August 16, 2002.

80. RFE/RL, "Former Hungarian Minister Accused of Working with Secret Services," *RFE/RL Newsline,* August 21, 2002.

81. The list included five officials who worked in the cabinet headed by Viktor Orbán during 1998–2002, namely, László Bogár, Imre Boros, Zsigmond Járai, János Martonyi, and László Nógrádi. From the József Antall government, it included Béla Kádár, Ferenc Rabár, Erno Raffay, and László Sárossy. From the Gyula Horn government, it included Szabolcs Fazakas in 1996–98 and Péter Medgyessy, finance minister (1996–98) and prime minister (2002–4). RFE/RL, "Magyar Hirlap Scores Weekend Scoop," *RFE/RL Newsline,* August 26, 2002.

82. RFE/RL, "Hungary's Fidesz Says Mecs Commission Running 'Politically Amok,'" *RFE/RL Newsline,* August 30, 2002.

83. Oltay, "Hungary's Screening Law."

84. In opinion polls conducted by the Median Market Research agency in the aftermath of the Medgyessy scandal and its aftershocks on September 11–12, 2002, 75 percent of Hungarians thought that the parliamentary commission headed by Mécs

should wind up its work; about 49 percent of the population was not interested at all in learning which politicians collaborated with the communist-era secret services; and only 15 percent cared about learning which politicians collaborated with the communist-era secret services. RFE/RL, "Poll Reiterates That Public Does Not Care," *RFE/RL Newsline*, September 24, 2002.

85. Tomiuc, "Hungary."

86. Ibid.

87. Oltay, "Hungary's Screening Law," 667.

88. Markó, interview.

89. RFE/RL, "Hungarian Premier Admits to Communist Era Past," *RFE/RL Newsline*, June 19, 2002.

90. Tomiuc, "Hungary."

91. RFE/RL, "Hungarian Premier Apologizes to Electorate," *RFE/RL Newsline*, June 24, 2002.

92. Petr Morvay, "Když všichni, tak všichni," *Respekt*, July 24, 2000, 13.

93. Eyal, Szelényi, and Townsley, *Making Capitalism Without Capitalists*, 108.

94. RFE/RL, "Former Hungarian Ministers React to *Magyar Hirlap* Revelations," *RFE/RL Newsline*, August 27, 2002.

95. "Boros Leaves Party," *Budapest Sun* 10, no. 37 (September 12, 2002).

96. Maria Vasarhelyi, "Airing the Dirty Laundry," *TOL Wire*, April 2, 2003, http://www.tol.cz/look/wire/printf.tpl?IdLanguage = 1&IdPublication = 10&NrIssue = 667& NrSection = 1&NrArticle = 9157 (accessed October 19, 2009).

97. Thomas Fuller, "Stark History/Some See a Stunt: Memory Becomes Battleground in Budapest's House of Terror Friday," *New York Times*, August 2, 2002.

98. Ibid.

99. See Political Transformation and the Electoral Process.

100. "One Million Visitors at the House of Terror Museum," April 26, 2005, http://www.terrorhaza.hu/en/news/about_us/about_us.html&sort = createTime& page = 7&archive = 1 (accessed October 19, 2009).

101. The allegations that the socialist party was representing the interests of large businesses were made by the intellectual left as well as by the right. Salzmann, "Hungarian Ruling Coalition Collapses."

102. Roman David, interviews with members of Fidesz, Budapest, June 2006.

103. BBC, "Hungarian PM Defiant over Riots," BBC News, September 20, 2006, http://news.bbc.co.uk/1/hi/world/europe/5363412.stm (accessed October 19, 2009).

104. Historians hold various views of the extent of Nagy's collaboration, while the fact of collaboration itself is not contested. See Gati, *Failed Illusions*, 33, 35–36, 225.

105. Thomas Escritt, "More 'Spies' Are Revealed," *Budapest Sun* 13, no. 7 (February 17, 2005).

106. Thomas Escritt, "List Naming Alleged Interior Ministry Informers from Before 1990 Published on Internet," *Budapest Sun* 13, no. 9 (March 3, 2005).

107. "Was Cardinal an Informant?" *Budapest Sun* 14, no. 6 (February 9, 2006); "Five Bishops Ousted," *Budapest Sun* 14, no. 10 (March 9, 2006).

108. PAP, "PiS: Projekt Dezyderatu ws. Odwolania Wiatra," *Dziennik Internetowy PAP*, September 3, 2002.

109. "Constitutional Watch: Poland," 8 (nos. 2–3).

110. Janina Paradowska, "Prawda ukarana," *Polityka*, no. 11 (2184) (March 13, 1999): 15.

111. Piotr Woyciechowski, "To nie jest lustracja," *Rreczpospolita*, April 11, 1997.

112. Łoś and Zybertowicz, *Privatizing the Police-State*, 165, 173.

113. Ibid., 20.

114. Janina Paradowska, "Loteria teczkowa," *Polityka*, no. 20 (2193) (May 15, 1999): 18.

115. "Constitutional Watch: Poland," 8 (nos. 2–3).

116. Constitutional Tribunal of Poland, K. 24/98, part 3.3.

117. Grzelak, *Wojna o Lustracje*, 213–14.

118. Paradowska, "Loteria."

119. Adam Michnik, "Lustracja błotem się toczy," *Gazeta Wyborcza*, December 23, 1999.

120. Janina Paradowska, "Czysta sympatia," *Polityka*, no. 2287 (March 3, 2001): 15.

121. Jerzy Baczyński, "Alek i Bolek," *Polityka*, no. 2257 (August 5, 2000): 15.

122. David, "Lustration Laws in Action," 417.

123. Aleksander Chećko, "Wymięta Rzeczpospolita," *Polityka,* no. 2192 (May 8, 1999): 16.

124. See, e.g. Michnik, "Lustracja blotem się toczy"; Chećko, "Wymięta Rzeczpospolita"; Cezary Michalski, "Dzika antylustracja," *Życie Warszawy*, December 30, 1999.

125. See Rzecznik Interesu Publicznego, "Aktualności."

126. According to Śpiewak, the supporters of lustrations responded to Michnik with the same virulence and hatred. Paweł Śpiewak, *Pamięć po komunizmie* (Gdansk, Poland: Słowo/obraz terytoria, 2005), 170.

127. See Rzecznik Interesu Publicznego, Aktualności: "Pismo Krzysztofa Kauby do Adama Michnika z dnia 9 grudnia 1999 r."

128. *Gazeta Wyborcza*, December 27, 1999.

129. Bronisław Wildstein, *Długi cień PRL-u* (Kraków, Poland: Arkana, 2005), 71–72.

130. Ibid., 72.

131. Robert Brier, "The Roots of the 'Fourth Republic': Solidarity's Cultural Legacy to Polish Politics," *East European Politics and Societies* 23, no. 1 (2009): 80.

132. PAP, "Platforma nie ma czasu na lustrację," *Gazeta Wyborcza*, May 7, 2008, http://wiadomosci.gazeta.pl/Wiadomosci/1,80708,5186754.html (accessed October 19, 2009).

133. For the analysis of lustration discourses in Poland, see Łoś, "Lustration and Truth Claims"; Śpiewak, *Pamięć po komunizmie*, 104–73.

134. Tomasz Sawczuk, "Ubekistan, czyli kraina agentów," *Wiadomosci24.pl,* October 3, 2006, http://www.wiadomosci24.pl/artykul/ubekistan_czyli_kraina_ agentow_8026.html (accessed October 19, 2009).

135. Łoś, "Lustration and Truth Claims"; Śpiewak, *Pamięć po komunizmie*.

136. Śpiewak, *Pamięć po komunizmie*, 162–64.

137. Autorzy Rzeczpospolitej, "Prezydent nie sklamal," *Rzeczpospolita*, August 11, 2000.

138. Rzecznik Interesu Publicznego, "Podstava Prawna."

139. Wildstein, *Długi cień PRL-u*, 29.

140. "Lista IPN—'Lista Wildsteina,' lista agentów i pokrzywdzonych," http:// www.listaipn.pl/ (accessed October 19, 2009).

141. Wojciech Czuchnowski, "Ubecka lista krąży po Polsce," *Gazeta Wyborcza*, January 29, 2005.

142. See *Rzeczpospolita*, January 8, 2009, http://lustronauki.wordpress.com/2009/ 01/09/lista-wildsteina-w-strasburgu/ (accessed October 19, 2009).

143. Zbigniew Girzyński, interview by the author, July 2006.

144. Adam Michnik, "Waiting for Freedom, Messing It Up," *New York Times*, March 25, 2007. See also Adam Michnik, "The Polish Witch-Hunt," *New York Review of Books*, June 28, 2007.

145. See Chapter 4.

146. See Biuletyn Informacji Publicznej, http://katalog.bip.ipn.gov.pl/ (accessed July 30, 2010).

147. Sławomir Cenckiewicz and Piotr Gontarczyk, *SB a Lech Wałęsa: Przyczynek do biografii* (Gdańsk, Poland: IPN, 2008).

148. "Wałęsa atakuje: 'Wnuk ubeka chce wybielić dziadziusia,'" *Gazeta Wyborcza,* February 22, 2009, http://wiadomosci.gazeta.pl/Wiadomosci/1,80708,6305098,Walesa_ atakuje___Wnuk_ubeka_chce_wybielic_dziadziusia_.html (accessed October 20, 2009).

149. Paweł Zyzak, *Lech Wałęsa: Idea i Historia* (Kraków, Poland: Arcana, 2009); Sławomir Cenckiewicz, *Sprawa Lecha Wałęsy* (Poznań, Poland: Zysk i S-ka, 2008).

150. David, Lustration Systems, Trust in Government, and Reconciliation in the Czech Republic, Hungary and Poland.

151. The "puppy effect" of lustrations may be described in terms of frequency-dependent equilibrium, in which an independent variable is a dependent variable at the same time.

Chapter 6

1. Thucydides, "Pericles' Funeral Oration," http://www1.umn.edu/humanrts/ education/thucydides.html (accessed October 19, 2009).

2. See generally Braithwaite and Levi, *Trust and Governance.*

3. Russell Hardin, "Trust in Government," in *Trust and Governance*, ed. Braithwaite and Levi, 17–19; Piotr Sztompka, *Trust: A Sociological Theory* (New York: Cambridge University Press, 1999), 148–50; Uslaner, *Moral Foundations of Trust*, 225.

4. See generally Braithwaite and Levi, *Trust and Governance.*

5. Horne and Levi, "Does Lustration Promote Trustworthy Governance?"; Rose, Mishler, and Haerpfer, *Democracy and Its Alternatives*; Rose-Ackerman, "Trust and Honesty in Post-Socialist Societies," 436.

6. See, e.g., Giddens, *The Consequences of Modernity*, 88; Putnam, *Bowling Alone*, 137; Karen S. Cook, Russell Hardin, and Margaret Levi, *Cooperation Without Trust* (New York: Russell Sage Foundation, 2005), 10–12; Newton, "Trust and Politics," 242–43.

7. See Hetherington, "The Political Relevance of Political Trust," 791.

8. Newton, "Trust and Politics," 242.

9. Russell Hardin, *Trust* (Cambridge: Polity Press, 2006), 2–3; Newton, "Trust and Politics," 247–48.

10. David, "Lustration Laws in Action," 392–97; Williams, "Lustration as the Securitization of Democracy in Czechoslovakia and the Czech Republic," 9–12.

11. Teitel, *Transitional Justice*, 164–67.

12. Havel, "Výročí okupace."

13. See, e.g., Schwartz, "Lustration in Eastern Europe"; Teitel, *Transitional Justice*, 172.

14. Horne and Levi, "Does Lustration Promote Trustworthy Governance?"

15. Łoś, "Lustration and Truth Claims," 148–54; Williams, "Lustration as the Securitization of Democracy," 10–11; David, "Lustration Laws in Action," 402–3.

16. Hayner, *Unspeakable Truths,* 107–32.

17. Kis, interview by the author.

18. Teitel, *Transitional Justice,* 172.

19. Michnik and Havel, "Justice or Revenge?" 23; but see Jefferson Adams, "Probing the East German State Security Archives," *International Journal of Intelligence and CounterIntelligence* 13, no. 1 (2000): 21–34.

20. Posner and Vermeule, "Transitional Justice as Ordinary Justice," 783.

21. Tutu, *No Future Without Forgiveness*; Michnik and Havel, "Justice or Revenge?" 22.

22. Eyal, Szelényi, and Townsley, *Making Capitalism Without Capitalists*, 108.

23. Kahan, "What Do Alternative Sanctions Mean?" 633–34.

24. David, "From Prague to Baghdad," 359–60.

25. Gibson and Gouws, "Truth and Reconciliation in South Africa."

26. Ibid., 509.

27. Druckman et al., "The Growth and Development of Experimental Research."

28. Gibson and Gouws, "Truth and Reconciliation in South Africa"; James L.

Gibson, "Truth, Justice, and Reconciliation: Judging the Fairness of Amnesty in South Africa," *American Journal of Political Science* 46, no. 3 (2002): 540–56.

29. Sniderman and Grob, "Innovations in Experimental Design." Internal validity means the ability to eliminate alternative explanations of the dependent variable. Experimental designs without random assignment pose a threat to internal validity by their inability to eliminate selection bias. See, e.g., Neuman, *Social Research Methods*, 236–41.

30. See Nalepa, *Skeletons in the Closet*. The meaning of lustrations differed from country to country depending on the particular lustration system. For instance, in the Czech Republic in 1991, the IVVM asked a question about whether lustration would help solve the personnel situation in offices and enterprises. See IVVM, "Veřejnost k lustračnímu zákonu." In Poland, on the other hand, CBOS asked whether it was "necessary to conduct lustration, i.e., determine the past of people holding public posts." CBOS, "Lustracja—Problem spoleczny czy gra polityczna," Komunikat 1708, January 23, 1998. In sum, comparative research has to avoid using not only the word lustration but also the results of country-specific surveys that may express support for a specific model of lustration.

31. Neuman, *Social Research Methods*, 222–45.

32. The selection of "secret informer" does not necessarily weaken an eventual applicability of lustration systems to different situations. Although holding a public office in authoritarian regimes is not secret, the officeholder may be involved in secret activities. Even in democratic states, public officials are not immune to the revelations of their secret activities. Consider the revelations concerning Richard Nixon, Kurt Waldheim, or Bill Clinton (see Chapter 2).

33. Gillis, "Lustration and Decommunisation."

34. Gibson, "Truth, Justice, and Reconciliation."

35. The question is widely used in the academic research. See, e.g., Citrin and Green, "Presidential Leadership and the Resurgence of Trust in Government," 434; Gary Orren, "Fall from Grace: The Public's Loss of Faith in Government," in *Why People Don't Trust Government*, ed. Joseph S. Nye, Philip Zelikow, and David C. King (Cambridge, Mass.: Harvard University Press, 1997), 87; Hetherington, "The Political Relevance of Political Trust," 804.

36. Cook, Hardin, and Levi, *Cooperation Without Trust*, 11.

37. Cf. Gibson and Gouws, *Overcoming Intolerance*, 95.

38. However, Cook, Hardin, and Levi (*Cooperation Without Trust*, 12) criticize the questions on trust because they were originally proposed as a cynicism scale. But a choice of the inappropriate nomenclature certainly should not be a reason to throw the questions out. Moreover, trust assumes a certain existence of mistrust. Newton, "Trust and Politics," 247–48. In fact, cynicism toward government and mistrust of government may overlap. Having said that, we do not support these questions, which have a number of problems. We argue that the theoretical foundation of these questions is relatively solid and that it can be used as a starting point for our considerations about trust.

39. Hetherington, "The Political Relevance of Political Trust," 791. Hetherington based this definition on Donald E. Stokes, "Popular Evaluations of Government: An Empirical Assessment," in *Ethics and Bigness: Scientific, Academic, Religious, Political, and Military*, ed. Harlan Cleveland and Harold D. Lasswell (New York: Harper and Brothers, 1962); Arthur H. Miller, "Political Issues and Trust in Government, 1964–70," *American Political Science Review* 68 (1974): 989–1001.

40. Stokes, "Popular Evaluations of Government," 64, cited in Hetherington, "The Political Relevance of Political Trust," 791.

41. See Hardin, *Trust*, 27–41.

42. Hardin defines trust as an encapsulated interest. This definition is shared by Cook, Hardin, and Levi. Hardin, *Trust*, 18–20; Cook, Hardin, and Levi, *Cooperation Without Trust*, 5–8.

43. The relational substitute of trust is "to believe." See Hardin, *Trust*, 17. For this reason, the questions started either with "Do you trust . . ." or "Do you believe . . ."

44. Interviewers also coded a "don't know" answer. Respondents who provided this indefinite answer were by default excluded from the analyses.

45. The alpha values of the scale were 0.95 in the merged data set, 0.95 in the Czech Republic, 0.94 in Hungary, and 0.96 in Poland.

46. See James L. Gibson, Gregory A. Caldeira, and Lester K. Spence, "The Role of Theory in Experimental Design: Experiments Without Randomization," *Political Analysis* 10, no. 4 (2002): 362–75.

47. See, e.g., Neuman, *Social Research Methods*, 236–41.

48. See Gibson and Gouws, *Overcoming Intolerance in South Africa*.

49. See James L. Gibson, Gregory A. Caldeira, and Lester K. Spence, "Measuring Attitudes Toward the United States Supreme Couort," *American Journal of Political Science* 47, no. 2 (2003): 354–67.

50. John L. Sullivan, James Piereson, and George E. Marcus, "An Alternative Conceptualization of Political Tolerance: Illusory Increases 1950s–1970s," *American Political Science Review* 73, no. 3 (1979): 781–94.

51. A classical example is an experimental testing of an effect of a fertilizer on grain yield. The statistical analysis of the experiment has to take into account not only the effect of the fertilizer but also other exogenous influences, such as the amount of rainfall that may be uneven across the experimental lots. In our experiment, divided society represents the rainfall; therefore it needs to be accounted for.

52. In addition to the three models presented in Table 6.3, we devised a fourth model that added all interaction terms between our four experimental variables. We recoded our experimental variables originally coded as dummy variables (0, 1) into (-1) and (1) in order to enhance the statistical power of the model. See Jacob Cohen, Patricia Cohen, Stephen G. West, and Leona S. Aiken, *Applied Multiple Regression Analysis for the Behavioral Science* (Mahwah, N.J.: Lawrence Erlbaum, 2003), 333. However, the model with the second, third, and fourth interaction terms did not improve its performance. Adjusted R^2 remained almost the same at 0.168 as in model

3. Thus, the interaction terms were not included in the analyses. Another reason for their exclusion is the principle of Occam's razor: if two explanations can account for the same phenomenon, the more parsimonious explanation should be given precedence.

53. Respondents who failed to answer all questions were by default in the statistical software excluded from the analysis. This led to the data loss. This problem can be overcome by the multiple imputation of missing data, which, however, is not universally accepted in the academic community. In spite of convincing arguments for its use, some see it as a method of tempering data. We therefore adhere to the conservative method and count only complete answers given by respondents.

54. We compared the sequence of the experimental vignette for Poland. In the sequence starting with confession, confession was significant, while in the second sequence starting with exposure, confession was insignificant.

Chapter 7

1. *The Lives of Others*, directed by Florian Henckel von Donnersmarck.

2. See the introduction and Chapter 2.

3. Ibid.

4. Cf. Stinchcombe, "Lustration as a Problem of the Social Basis of Constitutionalism."

5. See, e.g., Alexandra Barahona de Brito, Carmen González Enríquez, and Paloma Aguilar, eds., *The Politics of Memory: Transitional Justice in Democratizing Societies* (Oxford: Oxford University Press, 2001).

6. See, e.g., Schwartz "Lustration in Eastern Europe"; Siklova, "Lustration or the Czech Way of Screening"; Teitel, *Transitional Justice*, 164–67, 172.

7. Eyal, "Antipolitics and the Spirit of Capitalism," 56.

8. Łoś, "Lustration and Truth Claims."

9. Ibid., 143–46.

10. Misztal, "How Not to Deal with the Past," 51.

11. Tutu, *No Future Without Forgiveness*, 26.

12. Gibson, "Does Truth Lead to Reconciliation?"

13. Ethan Klingsberg, "The Triumph of the Therapeutic: The Quest to Cure Eastern Europe Through Secret Police Files," in *Truth and Justice: Delicate Balance* (Budapest: Central European University, 1992), 9, cited in Łoś, "Lustration and Truth Claims," 129.

14. Offe, *The Varieties of Transition*, 95.

15. Siklova, "Lustration or the Czech Way of Screening," 61.

16. See Kahan, "What Do Alternative Sanctions Mean?" 632–33.

17. Braithwaite and Mugford, "Conditions of Successful Reintegration Ceremonies."

18. Cf. Łoś, "Lustration and Truth Claims," 148–54; Williams, "Lustration as the Securitization of Democracy," 10–11; David, "Lustration Laws in Action."

19. Kahan, "What Do Alternative Sanctions Mean?" 593.

20. See David, "From Prague to Baghdad," 357.

21. Ibid.

22. Halmai and Scheppele, "Living Well Is the Best Revenge," 156.

23. Cf. Kahan, "What Do Alternative Sanctions Mean?" 633–34.

24. Govier, *Forgiveness and Revenge*, 46–47.

25. Saint Augustine, *The City of God* (New York: Random House, 1993), 14/6.

26. Murphy, *Getting Even*, 80.

27. Murphy, "Forgiveness and Resentment," 14–34.

28. Jodi Halpern and Harvey M. Weinstein, "Rehumanizing the Other: Empathy and Reconciliation," *Human Rights Quarterly* 26 (2004): 561–83.

29. Jean Hampton, "Forgiveness, Resentment and Hatred," in *Forgiveness and Mercy*, ed. Jeffrie G. Murphy and Jean Hampton (New York: Cambridge University Press, 1988), 83.

30. Julie J. Exline and Roy F. Baumeister, "Expressing Forgiveness and Repentance: Benefits and Barriers," in *Forgiveness: Theory, Research, and Practice*, ed. Michael E. McCullough, Kenneth I. Pargament, and Carl E. Thoresen (New York: Guilford, 2000), 136–39; Roman David and Susanne Choi, "Forgiveness and Transitional Justice in the Czech Republic," *Journal of Conflict Resolution* 50, no. 3 (2006): 339–67.

31. Gibson and Gouws, "Truth and Reconciliation in South Africa."

32. Gibson, "Does Truth Lead to Reconciliation?"

33. Phuong N. Pham, Harvey Weinstein, and Timothy Longman, "Trauma and PTSD Symptoms in Rwanda: Implications for Attitudes Toward Justice and Reconciliation," *Journal of the American Medical Association* 292 (2004): 602–12.

34. David and Choi, "Victims on Transitional Justice."

35. See, e.g., Putnam, *Bowling Alone*; Fukuyama, *Trust*. See also Chapter 2.

36. Cook, Hardin, and Levi argue that trust "cannot carry the weight of making complex societies function productively and effectively" (*Cooperation Without Trust*, 1).

37. See Newton, "Trust and Politics."

38. Gibson and Gouws, *Overcoming Intolerance*, 6.

39. The third question on trust that is asked in the National Election Studies surveys is, "Generally speaking, would you say that most people can be trusted, or that you can't be too careful dealing with people?"

40. Bruce G. Link, Francis T. Cullen, James Frank, and John F. Wozniak, "The Social Rejection of Former Mental Patients: Understanding Why Labels Matter," *American Journal of Sociology* 92 (1987): 1461–1500.

41. Anonymous interview by the author, Karviná, Czech Republic, June 2006.

42. Our survey included another two questions concerning tolerance: allowing the wrongdoer to run in elections and to sue the ministry. The first question was not included in the scale because lustrations concerned elected positions in Poland and Hungary but not in the Czech Republic. The question to sue the ministry was not

included because there was no reason to sue the ministry in cases of non-dismissal. Our survey also had two questions concerning social closeness: entrusting keys from home while away and willingness to accept the wrongdoer in the same association. The former was not included because it is an extreme measure of closeness, which, in addition to the low variation that it produces, may not have been taken seriously (one such incidence was recorded). The latter was dropped due to unwillingness to associate in these societies following the experience with forced associations in the past. Moreover, the factor analysis revealed that the contribution of these questions to the overall variance of the scale was minimal. Furthermore, their eventual inclusion would increase the size of missing data.

43. Anonymous interview by the author, Frýdek-Místek, Czech Republic, June 2006.

44. "Someone like" was also used in Link et al., "The Social Rejection of Former Mental Patients."

45. The scale had an alpha value of 0.89 in the merged data set, 0.88 in the Czech Republic, 0.89 in Hungary, and 0.91 in Poland.

46. Similar to the previous chapter, we also constructed a fourth model that included interaction terms. The model did not improve the adjusted R^2, which stood at 0.357. Therefore, we do not report its results here. We use the principle of Occam's razor and choose a parsimonious explanation instead of a complex explanation.

47. This paradox can be illustrated with the following example. Two companies implemented the same equal opportunity policy. One company employed a large number of women in lower-rank leading positions, while another one employed a female CEO. Consequently, the gender inequalities measured by the average income in both companies may have decreased by the same margin but for a different reason.

48. The reason why the effect of exposure has become insignificant may be attributed to the data loss in our analyses, which by default uses a listwise deletion. It means that if a respondent failed to provide an answer to any of the questions used to create a scale in the analyses, he or she was automatically excluded from the entire analysis. As we mentioned in the previous chapter, this can be overcome by the multiple imputation of missing data, which, however, is not universally accepted in the academic community. We therefore adhere to the conservative method and count only complete answers given by respondents. We nevertheless analyzed the missing data to find out any pattern of missingness. We recoded the missing data as 1 and complete data as 0. We then computed the scales in which the highest score indicated that respondents skipped all questions and zero indicated that the respondent did not skip any. The results show that exposure is a statistically significant predictor of missingness. It means that our respondents were more likely to skip a question after they heard that an exposure of the official had occurred. In other words, exposure may be associated with a scandal and a scandal may prompt respondents to avoid answers.

49. Amartya Sen, *Identity and Violence: The Illusion of Destiny* (New York: W. W. Norton, 2006).

50. Inga Markovits, "Selective Memory: How the Law Affects What We Remember and Forget About the Past: The Case of East Germany," *Law and Society Review* 35, no. 3 (2001): 513–63.

51. M. S., interview by the author, Confederation of Political Prisoners Annual Meeting, Brno, 2000.

52. Gibson and Gouws, "Truth and Reconciliation in South Africa."

53. Huntington, *Third Wave*, 211.

Conclusion

1. Herz, *From Dictatorship to Democracy*, 29.

2. Natalia Letki and Geoffrey Evans, "Endogenizing Social Trust: Democratization in East-Central Europe," *British Journal of Political Science* 35, no. 3 (2005): 515–29. Similarly, political corruption affects interpersonal trust in Eastern Europe. Christopher J. Anderson and Yulia V. Tverdova, "Corruption, Political Allegiances, and Attitudes Toward Government in Contemporary Democracies," *American Journal of Political Science* 47, no. 1 (2003): 91–109; Edward N. Muller and Mitchell A. Seligson, "Civic Culture and Democracy: The Question of Causal Relationships," *American Political Science Review* 88, no. 3 (1994): 645; Jack Citrin and Donald Green, "Presidential Leadership and the Resurgence of Trust in Government," *British Journal of Political Science* 16, no. 4 (1996): 431–53; Kathleen M. McGraw, "Managing Blame: Experimental Test of the Effects of Political Accounts," *American Political Science Review* 85, no. 4 (1991): 1133–57; Cook, Hardin, and Levi, *Cooperation Without Trust*, 184.

3. Gibson, "Truth, Justice, and Reconciliation."

4. Baria and Roper, "How Effective Are International Criminal Tribunals?" 351, 352.

5. Bremer claims that the policy was well designed but poorly implemented. See Bremer, *My Year in Iraq*, 341. However, when speaking to the press on the eve of its launch, he "was prepared to accept that the policy will result in some temporary inefficiency in the administration of government." Ibid., 45.

6. See, e.g., Wolf Blitzer, "From De-Baathification to Re-Baathification?" CNN.com, April 22, 2004, http://edition.cnn.com/2004/US/04/22/Iraq.rebaathification/ (accessed September 16, 2009).

7. David, "From Prague to Baghdad." For the application of the reconciliatory system as a method of pre-transitional justice in Burma/Myanmar, see Roman David and Ian Holliday, "Set the Junta Free: Pre-Transitional Justice in Myanmar," *Australian Journal of Political Science* 41, no. 1 (2006): 91–105.

8. "Iraqi Opposition Report on the Transition to Democracy in Iraq."

9. Ibid., 26.

10. As students of elections examine the swing voters, attention can also be paid to swing citizens during the regime change, the gray zone of collaborators and tainted officials, and the causes and consequences of the change of their allegiances.

11. The word "transporkation" seems appropriate in those cultural traditions where public office is seen as a feed trough. "Transporkation" comes from Czech "přeprasení," which literally means "pigging-over." According to Cepl, it was coined by Deputy Prime Minister Jan Kalvoda (ODA) to denote "the selfish motives of Czech deputies in the now-defunct [Czechoslovak] Federal Assembly, who devised the idea of an upper house [in the Czech Republic] because they faced unemployment as a result of the dissolution of that body." See Vojtech Cepl, "Senate, Anyone? The Real Reason behind the Czech Upper House," http://cepl.eu/senate-anyone.html (accessed October 1, 2009).

Appendix A

The narration aims to demonstrate the problem of personnel inherited in the state apparatus of a transitional state and its different resolutions. It is inspired by Lon L. Fuller's "Problem of the Grudge Informer," *The Morality of Law*, 245–54, which demonstrates the moral dilemma facing criminal justice after transition.

SELECTED BIBLIOGRAPHY

Act XXIII/1994 on Background Checks for Individuals Holding Certain Key Offices as Amended by Act LXVII/1996, Act XCIII/2000, and Act LXVII/2001 (Hungarian Lustration Act).

Act 99.42.428. On the Revealing of Work or Service in State Security Organs or of Collaboration with Them Between 1944 and 1990 by Persons Holding Public Positions, in the version of Dz.u.99.42.428, Dz.u.99.57.618, Dz.u.99.62.681, Dz.u.99.63.701, Dz.u.00.43.488, Dz.u.00.50.600 (Polish Lustration Act).

Act 451/1991 That Prescribes Certain Additional Prerequisites for the Exercise of Certain Positions Filled by Election, Appointment, or Assignment in State Organs and Organizations, in the version of Act 254/1995 and Act 422/2000 (Czech/Czechoslovak Lustration Act).

Adams, Jefferson. "Probing the East German State Security Archives." *International Journal of Intelligence and CounterIntelligence* 13, no. 1 (2000): 21–34.

Ajdukovic, Dean, and Dinka Corkalo. "Trust and Betrayal in War." In *My Neighbor, My Enemy: Justice and Community in the Aftermath of Mass Atrocity*, ed. Eric Stover and Harvey M. Weinstein. Cambridge: Cambridge University Press, 2004.

Almond, Gabriel A. "The Intellectual History of the Civic Culture Concept." In *The Civic Culture Revisited*, ed. Gabriel A. Almond and Sidney Verba. Newbury Park, Calif.: Sage, 1989.

Almond, Gabriel A., and Sidney Verba. *The Civic Culture*. Boston: Little, Brown, and Company, 1963.

Anderson, Christopher J., and Yulia V. Tverdova. "Corruption, Political Allegiances, and Attitudes Toward Government in Contemporary Democracies." *American Journal of Political Science* 47, no. 1 (2003): 91–109.

Arendt, Hannah. *Eichmann in Jerusalem: A Report on the Banality of Evil*. New York: Viking Press, 1963.

———. *The Human Condition*. Chicago: Chicago University Press, 1958.

———. *The Origins of Totalitarianism*. New York: Harcourt Brace Jovanovich, 1973.

Ash, Timothy Garton. *The File: A Personal History*. New York: Random House, 1997.

———. "Trials, Purges, and History Lessons." In *History of the Present: Essays, Sketches, and Dispatches from Europe in the 1990s*, ed. Timothy Garton Ash. London: Vintage, 2001.

———. "The Truth About the Dictatorship." *New York Review of Books*, February 18, 1998, 35–40.

Ackerman, Bruce. *The Future of Liberal Revolution*. New Haven, Conn.: Yale University Press, 1992.

Augustine, Saint. *The City of God*. New York: Random House, 1993.

Barbu, Zevedei. *Democracy and Dictatorship: Their Psychology and Patterns of Life*. Reprint, London: Routledge, 1998.

Barbuto, Valeria. "Strengthening Democracy: *Impugnación* Procedures in Argentina." In *Justice as Prevention*, ed. Mayer-Rieckh and de Greiff, 40–79.

Baria, Lilian A., and Steven D. Roper. "How Effective Are International Criminal Tribunals? An Analysis of the ICTY and the ICTR." *International Journal of Human Rights* 9, no. 3 (2005): 349–68.

Barrett, Elizabeth, Péter Hack, and Ágnes Munkácsi. "Lustration as Political Competition: Vetting in Hungary." In *Justice as Prevention*, ed. Mayer-Rieckh and de Greiff, 260–307.

Bassiouni, M. Cherif. "Searching for Peace and Achieving Justice: The Need for Accountability." *Law and Contemporary Problems* 59 (Autumn 1996): 9–28.

Ben-Yehuda, Nachman, and Erich Goode. *Moral Panics: The Social Construction of Deviance*. Oxford: Blackwell, [1994] 2009.

Berger, Peter L., and Thomas Luckman. *The Social Construction of Reality: A Treatise in the Sociology of Knowledge*. Garden City, N.Y.: Anchor Books, 1966.

Bergesen, Albert J. "Political Witch Hunts: The Sacred and the Subversive in Cross-National Perspective." *American Sociological Review* 42 (1977): 220–33.

Bílek, Jiří, and Vladimír Pilát. "Závodní, Dělnické a Lidové Milice v Československu." *Historie a vojenství*, no. 3 (1995): 79–106.

Boed, Roman. "Evaluation of the Legality and Efficacy of Lustration as a Tool of Transitional Justice." *Columbia Journal of Transnational Law* 37 (1999): 357–402.

Braithwaite, John, and Stephen Mugford. "Conditions of Successful Reintegration Ceremonies." *British Journal of Criminology* 34, no. 2 (1994): 139–71.

Braithwaite, Valerie, and Margaret Levi, eds. *Trust and Governance*. New York: Russell Sage Foundation, 1998.

Bremer, L. Paul, III with Malcolm McConnell. *My Year in Iraq: The Struggle to Build a Future of Hope*. New York: Threshold Editions, 2006.

Brier, Robert. "The Roots of the 'Fourth Republic': Solidarity's Cultural Legacy to Polish Politics." *East European Politics and Societies* 23, no. 1 (2009): 63–85.

Buruma, Ian. *The Wages of Guilt: Memories of War in Germany and in Japan*. New York: Farrar, Straus and Giroux, 1994.

Bushman, Brad J. "Does Venting Anger Feed or Extinguish the Flame? Catharsis, Rumination, Distraction, Anger, and Aggressive Responding," *Personality and Social Psychology Bulletin* 28, no. 6 (2002), 724–31

Calhoun, Noel. "The Ideological Dilemma of Lustration in Poland." *East European Politics and Societies* 16, no. 2 (2002): 494–520.

Cenckiewicz, Sławomir. *Sprawa Lecha Wałęsy*. Poznań, Poland: Zysk i S-ka, 2008.

Cenckiewicz, Sławomir, and Piotr Gontarczyk. *SB a Lech Wałęsa: Przyczynek do biografii.* Gdańsk, Poland: IPN, 2008.

CEU (Central European University). *The Development of Party Systems and Electoral Alignments in East Central Europe [1992–96].* Machine-readable data files. Department of Political Science, Central European University, Budapest.

Cepl, Vojtech. "Ritual Sacrifices: Lustration in the CSFR." *East European Constitutional Review* 1 (Spring 1994): 24–26.

Cepl, Vojtech. "The Transformation of Hearts and Minds in Eastern Europe." *Cato Journal* 17, no. 2 (1997): 229–34.

———. "Senate, Anyone? The Real Reason behind the Czech Upper House." http://cepl.eu/senate-anyone.html, accessed October 1, 2009.

Cepl, Vojtech, and Mark Gillis. "Making Amends After Communism." *Journal of Democracy* 7, no. 4 (1996): 118–24.

Citrin, Jack, and Donald Green. "Presidential Leadership and the Resurgence of Trust in Government." *British Journal of Political Science* 16, no. 4 (1996): 431–53.

Cohen, Jacob, Patricia Cohen, Stephen G. West, and Leona S. Aiken. *Applied Multiple Regression Analysis for the Behavioral Science.* Mahwah, N.J.: Lawrence Erlbaum, 2003.

Cohen, Stanley. *Folk Devils and Moral Panics.* London: MacGibbon and Kee, 1972.

———. "State Crimes of Previous Regimes: Knowledge, Accountability, and the Policing of the Past." *Law & Social Inquiry* 20, no. 1 (1995): 7–50.

Constitutional Court of the Czech Republic, Decisions, http://angl.concourt.cz/angl_verze/cases.php (accessed September 9, 2009).

Constitutional Court of Hungary Decisions, http://www.mkab.hu/en/enpage3.htm (accessed September 9, 2009).

Constitutional Tribunal of Poland Decisions, http://www.trybunal.gov.pl/eng/summaries/wstep_gb.htm (accessed September 9, 2009).

Cook, Karen S., Russell Hardin, and Margaret Levi. *Cooperation Without Trust.* New York: Russell Sage Foundation, 2005.

Crossley-Frolick, Katy A. "The Fate of Former East German Police in Reunified Germany, 1990–1996: The Dialectics of Inclusion and Exclusion." *Journal of Historical Sociology* 23, no. 2 (2010): 251–83.

Czarnota, Adam. "The Politics of the Lustration Law in Poland, 1989–2006." In *Justice as Prevention*, ed. Mayer-Rieckh and de Greiff, 222–58.

Dahl, Robert A. *Dilemmas of Pluralist Democracy.* New Haven, Conn.: Yale University Press, 1982.

———. *Polyarchy: Participation and Opposition.* New Haven, Conn.: Yale University Press, 1971.

David, Roman. "From Prague to Baghdad: Lustration Systems and Their Political Effects." *Government and Opposition* 41, no. 3 (2006): 347–72.

———. "In Exchange for Truth: The Polish Lustration and the South African

Amnesty Process." *Politikon: South African Journal of Political Studies* 32, no. 1 (2006): 81–99.

———. "Lustration Laws in Action: The Motives and Evaluation of Lustration Policy in the Czech Republic and Poland (1989–2001)." *Law & Social Inquiry* 28, no. 2 (2003): 387–439.

———. Lustration Systems, Trust in Government, and Reconciliation in the Czech Republic, Hungary and Poland. Machine-readable data files. On file with the author.

———. "Transitional Injustice? Criteria for Conformity of Lustration to the Right to Political Expression." *Europe-Asia Studies* 56, no. 6 (2004): 789–812.

David, Roman, and Susanne Y. P. Choi. "Forgiveness and Transitional Justice in the Czech Republic." *Journal of Conflict Resolution* 50, no. 3 (2006): 339–67.

———. "Getting Even, or Getting Equal? Retributive Desires and Transitional Justice." *Political Psychology* 30, no. 2 (2009): 161–92.

———. "Victims on Transitional Justice: Reparations of Victims of Human Rights Abuses in the Czech Republic." *Human Rights Quarterly* 27, no. 2 (2005): 392–435.

David, Roman, and Ian Holliday. "Set the Junta Free: Pre-Transitional Justice in Myanmar." *Australian Journal of Political Science* 41, no. 1 (2006): 91–105.

Deák, István, Jan T. Gross, and Tony Judt, eds. *The Politics of Retribution in Europe: World War II and Its Aftermath.* Princeton, N.J.: Princeton University Press, 2000.

De Becker v. Belgium. European Court of Human Rights. Application 214/56 (1958–59).

de Brito, Alexandra Barahona, Carmen González Enríquez, and Paloma Aguilar, eds. *The Politics of Memory: Transitional Justice in Democratizing Societies.* Oxford: Oxford University Press, 2001.

de Greiff, Pablo. "Vetting and Transitional Justice., In *Justice as Prevention,* ed. Mayer-Rieckh and de Greiff, 523–44.

Democracy Principles Working Group, "Iraqi Opposition Report on the Transition to Democracy in Iraq." *Journal of Democracy* 14, no. 3 (2003): 14–29.

Denhardt, Robert B., and Linda de Leon. "Great Thinkers in Personnel Management." In *Handbook of Public Personnel Administration,* ed. Rabin et al., 21–41.

Di Palma, Giuseppe. "Italy: Is There a Legacy and Is It Fascist?" In *From Dictatorship to Democracy,* ed. Herz, 107–34.

Douglas, Mary. *Purity and Danger: An Analysis of Concepts of Pollution and Taboo.* London: Routledge, [1966] 2003.

Drda, Adam, and Petr Dudek. *Kdo ve stínu čeká na moc.* Prague: Paseka, 2006.

Druckman, James N., Donald P. Green, James H. Kuklinski, and Arthur Lupia. "The Growth and Development of Experimental Research in Political Science." *American Political Science Review* 100, no. 4 (2006): 627–36.

Durkheim, Émile. *The Elementary Forms of the Religious Life.* Oxford: Oxford University Press, [1912] 2001.

Edelman, Murray. *The Symbolic Uses of Politics*. Urbana: University of Illinois Press, 1964.

Ellis, Mark S. "Purging the Past: The Current State of Lustration Laws in the Former Communist Bloc." *Law & Contemporary Problems* 59, no. 4 (1996): 181–96.

Elster, Jon. *Closing the Books: Transitional Justice in Historical Perspective*. New York: Cambridge University Press, 2004.

Exline, Julie J., and Roy F. Baumeister. "Expressing Forgiveness and Repentance: Benefits and Barriers. In *Forgiveness: Theory, Research, and Practice*, ed. Michael E. McCullough, Kenneth I. Pargament, and Carl E. Thoresen, 133–55. New York: Guilford, 2000.

Eyal, Gil. "Antipolitics and the Spirit of Capitalism: Dissidents, Monetarists, and the Czech Transition to Capitalism." *Theory and Society* 29, no. 1 (2000): 49–92.

Eyal, Gil, Iván Szelényi, and Eleanor Townsley. *Making Capitalism Without Capitalists: The New Ruling Elites in Eastern Europe*. London: Verso, 1998.

Federální Shromáždění ČSFR. 17th Session. 1991, http://www.psp.cz/eknih/1990fs/slsn/stenprot/017schuz/ (accessed October 16, 2009).

Fletcher, Laurel E., and Harvey M. Weinstein. "Violence and Social Repair: Rethinking the Contribution of Justice to Reconciliation." *Human Rights Quarterly* 24, no. 3 (2002): 573–639.

Foulke, William D. *Fighting the Spoilsmen: Reminiscences of the Civil Reform Movement*. New York: Knickerbocker Press, 1919.

Friedrich, Robert J. "In Defense of Multiplicative Terms in Multiple Regression Equations." *American Journal of Political Science* 26, no. 4 (1982): 797–833.

Fukuyama, Francis. *Trust: The Social Virtues and the Creation of Prosperity*. New York: Free Press, 1995.

Fuller, Lon L. *The Morality of Law*. New Haven, Conn.: Yale University Press, 1964.

Fuller, Thomas. "Stark History/Some See a Stunt: Memory Becomes Battleground in Budapest's House of Terror Friday." *New York Times,* August 2, 2002.

Garfinkel, Harold. "Conditions of Successful Degradation Ceremonies." *American Journal of Sociology* 61, no. 5 (1956): 420–24.

Garretón, Manuel Antonio. "Redemocratization in Chile." *Journal of Democracy* 6, no. 1 (1995): 146–58.

Gati, Charles. *Failed Illusions: Moscow, Washington, Budapest, and the 1956 Hungarian Revolt*. Washington, D.C.: Woodrow Wilson Center Press, 2006.

Gibson, James L. "Does Truth Lead to Reconciliation? Testing the Causal Assumptions of the South African Truth and Reconciliation Process." *American Journal of Political Science* 48, no. 2 (2004): 201–17.

———. "Truth, Justice, and Reconciliation: Judging the Fairness of Amnesty in South Africa." *American Journal of Political Science* 46, no. 3 (2002): 540–56.

———. "Truth, Reconciliation, and the Creation of Human Rights Culture in South Africa." *Law & Society Review* 38, no. 1 (2004): 5–40.

Gibson, James L., and Amanda Gouws. *Overcoming Intolerance in South Africa.* Cambridge: Cambridge University Press, 2003.

———. "Truth and Reconciliation in South Africa: Attributions of Blame and the Struggle over Apartheid." *American Political Science Review* 93, no. 3 (1999): 501–17.

Giddens, Anthony. *The Consequences of Modernity.* Cambridge: Polity, 1990.

Gillis, Mark. "Lustration and Decommunisation." In *The Rule of Law in Central Europe: The Reconstruction of Legality, Constitutionalism and Civil Society in the Post-Communist Countries,* ed. Jiří Přibáň and James Young, 56–81. Aldershot: Ashgate, 1999.

Girard, René. *Violence and the Sacred.* Baltimore: Johns Hopkins University Press, 1979.

Goffman, Erving. *Frame Analysis: An Essay on the Organization of Experience.* Cambridge, Mass.: Harvard University Press, 1974.

Goffman, Erving. "Embarrassment and Social Organization," *American Journal of Sociology* 62, no. 3 (1956): 264–71.

———. *Relations in Public: Microstudies of the Public Order.* New York: Basic Books, 1971.

Goldstone, Richard J. "Commission of Inquiry Regarding the Prevention of Public Violence and Intimidation." Pretoria, 1992–94.

Gorka, Sebestyén. "The Undeniable Connection Between Democracy and Lustration." Institute for Transitional Democracy and International Security, http://www.itdis .org/Portals/11/SGmnLustration12-04.pdf (accessed October 16, 2009).

Govier, Trudy. *Forgiveness and Revenge.* New York: Routledge, 2002.

Gravier, Magali. "East-Germans in the Post-Unification German Civil Service: The Role of Political Loyalty in a Transition to Democracy." Paper presented at the IPSA 19th World Congress, Durban, June 29–July 4, 2003.

Grzelak, Piotr. *Wojna o Lustracje.* Warsaw: Trio, 2005.

Grzymala-Busse, Anna. *Redeeming the Communist Past: The Regeneration of Communist Parties in East Central Europe.* Cambridge: Cambridge University Press, 2002.

Guelke, Adrian. "Interpretations of Political Violence During South Africa's Transition." *Politikon* 27, no. 2 (2000): 239–54.

Hacking, Ian. *The Social Construction of What?* Cambridge, Mass.: Harvard University Press, 1999.

Halmai, Gábor. E-mail correspondence with the author. June 3, 2009.

Halmai, Gábor, and Kim Lane Scheppele. "Living Well Is the Best Revenge: The Hungarian Approach to Judging the Past." In *Transitional Justice,* ed. McAdams, 155–84.

Halpern, Jodi, and Harvey M. Weinstein. "Rehumanizing the Other: Empathy and Reconciliation." *Human Rights Quarterly* 26 (2004): 561–83.

Hampton, Jean. "Forgiveness, Resentment and Hatred." In *Forgiveness and Mercy,* ed.

Jeffrie G. Murphy and Jean Hampton. New York: Cambridge University Press, 1988, 35–87.

Hardin, Russell. *Trust*. Cambridge: Polity Press, 2006.

———. "Trust in Government." In *Trust and Governance*, ed. Braithwaite and Levi, 9–27.

Hatch, Richard. "A Year of De-Baathification in Post-Conflict Iraq: Time for Mid-Course Corrections and a Long-Term Strategy." *Journal of Human Rights* 4, no. 1 (2005): 103–12.

Havel, Václav. *Audience*. In *The Garden Party and Other Plays*, 183–211. New York: Grove Press, 1993.

———. *Prosím stručně*. Prague: Gallery, 2006.

Hayner, Priscilla B. *Unspeakable Truths: Confronting State Terror and Atrocity*. New York: Routledge, 2001.

Hepworth, Mike, and Bryan S. Turner. *Confession: Studies in Deviance and Religion*. London: Routledge and Kegan Paul, 1982.

Herz, John H., ed. *From Dictatorship to Democracy: Coping with the Legacies of Authoritarianism and Totalitarianism*. Westport, Conn.: Greenwood Press, 1982.

Hetherington, Marc J. "The Political Relevance of Political Trust." *American Political Science Review* 92, no. 4 (1998): 791–808.

Hicks, George L. *Japan's War Memories: Amnesia or Concealment?* Aldershot: Ashgate, 1998.

Higley, John, Judith Kullberg, and Jan Pakulski. "The Persistence of Postcommunist Elites." *Journal of Democracy* 7, no. 2 (1996): 133–47.

Holmes, Stephen. "The End of Decommunization," *East European Constitutional Review* 3 (Summer/Fall 1994): 33–34.

Hoogenboom, Ari. *Outlawing the Spoils: A History of the Civil Service Movement, 1865–1883*. Urbana: University of Illinois Press, 1968.

Horne, Cynthia M. "International Legal Rulings on Lustration Policies in Central and Eastern Europe: Rule of Law in Historical Context." *Law & Social Inquiry* 34, no. 3 (2009): 713–44.

Horne, Cynthia M., and Margaret Levi. "Does Lustration Promote Trustworthy Governance? An Exploration of the Experience of Central and Eastern Europe." In *Building a Trustworthy State in Post-Socialist Transition*, ed. János Kornai and Susan Rose-Ackerman. New York: Palgrave Macmillan, 2004, 52–74.

Hunter, Wendy. "Continuity or Change? Civil-Military Relations in Argentina, Chile, and Peru." *Political Research Quarterly* 112 (1997): 453–75.

Huntington, Samuel P. *The Third Wave: Democratization in the Late Twentieth Century*. Norman: University of Oklahoma Press, 1991.

Huyse, Luc. "Justice After Transition: On the Choices Successor Elites Make in Dealing with the Past." *Law & Social Inquiry* 20, no. 1 (1995): 51–78.

Ibhawoh, Bonny. "Between Culture and Constitution: Evaluating the Cultural Legitimacy of Human Rights in the African State." *Human Rights Quarterly* 22, no. 2 (2000): 938–60.

Jordan, Jeffrey M. "Patronage and Corruption in the Czech Republic." *SAIS Review* 22, no. 2 (2002): 19–52.

Judt, Tony. *Postwar: A History of Europe Since 1945*. New York: Penguin Press, 2005.

Kahan, Dan M. "What Do Alternative Sanctions Mean?" *University of Chicago Law Review* 63 (1996): 591–653.

Karl, Terry L., and Philippe Schmitter. "Modes of Transition in Latin America: Southern and Eastern Europe." *International Social Science Journal*, no. 128 (1991): 269–84.

Kertzer, David I. *Ritual, Politics, and Power*. New Haven, Conn.: Yale University Press, 1988.

Kis, János. Interview by the author. Budapest, June 2006.

Kiss, Csilla. "The Misuses of Manipulation: The Failure of Transitional Justice in Post-Communist Hungary." *Europe-Asia Studies* 58, no. 6 (2006): 925–40.

Klaaren, Jonathan. "Institutional Transformation and the Choice Against Vetting in South Africa's Transition." In *Justice as Prevention*, ed. Mayer-Rieckh and de Greiff, 146–79.

Klingsberg, Ethan. "The Triumph of the Therapeutic: The Quest to Cure Eastern Europe Through Secret Police Files." In *Truth and Justice: Delicate Balance*. Budapest: Central European University, 1992.

Kommers, Donald P. *The Constitutional Jurisprudence of the Federal Republic of Germany*. 2nd ed. Durham, N.C.: Duke University Press, 1997.

Kritz, Neil J., ed. "Dealing with the Legacy of Past Abuses: An Overview of the Options and Their Relationship to the Promotion of Peace." In *Dealing with the Past: Critical Issues, Lessons Learned, and Challenges for Future Swiss Policy*, ed. Mô Bleeker and Jonathan Sisson. Bern: Swisspeace, 2004.

———. *Transitional Justice: How Emerging Democracies Reckon with Former Regimes*. 3 vols. Washington, D.C.: U.S. Institute of Peace Press, 1995.

Letki, Natalia. "Lustration and Democratisation in East-Central Europe." *Europe-Asia Studies* 54, no. 4 (2002): 529–52.

Letki, Natalia, and Geoffrey Evans. "Endogenizing Social Trust: Democratization in East-Central Europe." *British Journal of Political Science* 35, no. 3 (2005): 515–29.

Lewis, T. Charlton, and Charles Short. *A Latin Dictionary*. Oxford: Clarendon Press, 1879.

Link, Bruce G., Francis T. Cullen, James Frank, and John F. Wozniak. "The Social Rejection of Former Mental Patients: Understanding Why Labels Matter." *American Journal of Sociology* 92 (1987): 1461–1500.

Linz, Juan J., and Alfred Stepan. *Problems of Democratic Transition and Consolidation: Southern Europe, South America, and Post-Communist Europe*. Baltimore: Johns Hopkins University Press, 1996.

Łoś, Maria. "Lustration and Truth Claims: Unfinished Revolutions in Central Europe." *Law & Social Inquiry* 20, no. 1 (1995): 117–61.

Łoś, Maria, and Andrzej Zybertowicz. "Is Revolution a Solution?" In *The Rule of Law*

After Communism, ed. Martin Krygier and Adam Czarnota, 261–307. Aldershot: Dartmouth, 1999.

———. *Privatizing the Police-State: The Case of Poland.* New York: Palgrave, 2000.

Lötter, Hennie P. P. *Injustice, Violence, and Peace: The Case of South Africa.* Atlanta, Ga.: Rodopi, 1997.

Lottman, Herbert R. *Purge: Purification of French Collaborators After World War II.* New York: William Morrow, 1986.

Luban, David. "A Man Lost in the Gray Zone." *Law and History Review* 19, no. 1 (2001): 47. http://www.historycooperative.org/journals/lhr/19.1/luban.html (accessed August 10, 2010).

Luhmann, Niklas. *Trust and Power.* Chichester: Wiley, 1979.

Markó, György. Interview by the author. Budapest, June 2006.

Markovits, Inga. "Selective Memory: How the Law Affects What We Remember and Forget About the Past: The Case of East Germany." *Law and Society Review* 35, no. 3 (2001): 513–63.

Matějů, Petr, and Blanka Řeháková. "Turning Left or Class Realignment? Analysis of the Changing Relationship Between Class and Party in the Czech Republic, 1992–1996." *East-European Politics and Societies* 11, no. 3 (1997): 507–47.

Mayer-Rieckh, Alexander. "Vetting to Prevent Future Abuses: Reforming the Police, Courts, and Prosecutor's Offices in Bosnia and Herzegovina." In *Justice as Prevention*, ed. Mayer-Rieckh and de Greiff, 181–220.

Mayer-Rieckh, Alexander, and Pablo de Greiff, eds. *Justice as Prevention: Vetting Public Employees in Transitional Societies.* New York: Social Science Research Council, 2007.

McAdams, A. James. *Judging the Past in Unified Germany.* New York: Cambridge University Press, 2001.

———. *Transitional Justice and the Rule of Law in New Democracies.* Notre Dame, Ind.: Notre Dame University Press, 1997.

McGraw, Kathleen M. "Managing Blame: Experimental Test of the Effects of Political Accounts." *American Political Science Review* 85, no. 4 (1991): 1133–57.

Memorandum on the Applicability of International Agreements to the Screening Law (1992). Reprinted in Kritz, *Transitional Justice*, 3:335.

Michnik, Adam, and Václav Havel. "Confronting the Past: Justice or Revenge?" *Journal of Democracy* 4, no. 1 (1993): 20–27.

Miller, Arthur H. "Political Issues and Trust in Government, 1964–70." *American Political Science Review* 68 (1974): 989–1001.

Miller, Lezsek. "Moja biografia." http://www.miller.pl/strona.php?zm = biografia (accessed October 17, 2009).

Misztal, Barbara. "How Not to Deal with the Past: Lustration in Poland." *Archives Européennes de Sociologie* 40, no. 1 (1999): 31–55.

Moran, John. "The Communist Torturers of Eastern Europe: Prosecute and Punish or Forgive and Forget." *Communist and Post-Communist Studies* 27, no. 1 (1994): 95–109.

Muller, Edward N., and Mitchell A. Seligson. "Civic Culture and Democracy: The Question of Causal Relationships." *American Political Science Review* 88, no. 3 (1994): 635–52.

Murphy, Jeffrie. "Forgiveness and Resentment." In *Forgiveness and Mercy*, ed. Jeffrie G. Murphy and Jean Hampton, 14–34. New York: Cambridge University Press, 1988.

———. *Getting Even: Forgiveness and Its Limits*. Oxford: Oxford University Press, 2003.

Nalepa, Monika. *Skeletons in the Closet: Transitional Justice in Post-Communist Europe*. Cambridge: Cambridge University Press, 2010.

Nedelsky, Nadya. "Divergent Responses to a Common Past: Transitional Justice in the Czech Republic and Slovakia." *Theory & Society* 33 (2004): 63–115.

Neier, Aryeh. "What Should Be Done About the Guilty?" *New York Review of Books* 37, no. 1 (February 1, 1990).

Neuman, Lawrence W. *Social Research Methods: Qualitative and Quantitative Approaches*. Boston: Allyn and Bacon, 2000.

Newton, Ken. "Trust and Politics." In *The Handbook of Social Capital*, ed. Dario Castiglione, Jan W. van Deth, and Guglielmo Wolleb, 241–72. Oxford: Oxford University Press, 2008.

Nosková, Jana. "'The Little Czech': The Way of Life of 'Ordinary People' in Socialist Czechoslovakia?" Paper presented at the "Memories in Post-Socialism" international conference. Newcastle, September 2008.

Novick, Peter. *The Resistance Versus Vichy: The Purge of Collaborators in Liberated France*. New York: Columbia University Press, 1968.

Nyyssönen, Heino. *The Presence of the Past in Politics: "1956" After 1956 in Hungary*. Jyväskylä, Finland: SoPhi Academic Press, 2000.

O'Donnell, Guillermo, Philippe C. Schmitter, and Laurence Whitehead, eds. *Transitions from Authoritarian Rule: Comparative Perspectives*. Baltimore: Johns Hopkins University Press, 1986.

Offe, Claus. *The Varieties of Transition: The East European and East German Experience*. Cambridge, Mass.: MIT Press, 1997.

Ogilvie, R. M. "Lustrum Condere." *Journal of Roman Studies* 51, parts 1 and 2 (1961): 31–39.

Oltay, Edith. "Hungary's Screening Law." RFE/RL Research Report 3, no. 15 (April 15, 1994): 13–15. Excerpted in *Transitional Justice*, ed. Kritz, 2:662–67.

Orren, Gary. "Fall from Grace: The Public's Loss of Faith in Government." In *Why People Don't Trust Government*, ed. Joseph S. Nye, Philip Zelikow, and David C. King, 77–108. Cambridge, Mass.: Harvard University Press, 1997.

Országgyűlési Napló 1990–2002. *A plenáris ülések jegyzőkönyveinek teljes szövegu adatbázisa*. Budapest: Arcanum Adatbázis Kft., 2002.

Parker, Robert. *Miasma: Pollution and Purification in Early Greek Religion.* Oxford: Clarendon Press, (1983) 1996, 19–23.

Parliamentary Assembly of the Council of Europe. "Resolution on Measures to Dismantle the Heritage of Former Communist Totalitarian Systems." Doc. no. 1096 (1996). http://assembly.coe.int/main.asp?Link=/documents/adoptedtext/ta96/eres1096.htm (accessed October 16, 2009).

Pham, Phuong N., Harvey Weinstein, and Timothy Longman. "Trauma and PTSD Symptoms in Rwanda: Implications for Attitudes Toward Justice and Reconciliation." *Journal of the American Medical Association* 292 (2004): 602–12.

Posner, Eric A., and Adrian Vermeule. "Transitional Justice as Ordinary Justice." *Harvard Law Review* 117 (2004): 761–825.

Priban, Jiri. "Oppressors and Their Victims: The Czech Lustration Law and the Rule of Law." In *Justice as Prevention,* ed. Mayer-Rieckh and de Greiff, 309–46.

Putnam, Robert. *Bowling Alone: The Collapse and Revival of American Community.* New York: Simon and Schuster, 2000.

———. *Making Democracy Work: Civic Traditions in Modern Italy.* Princeton, N.J.: Princeton University Press, 1993.

Rabin, Jack, Thomas Vocino, W. Bartley Hildreth, and Gerald J. Miller, eds. *Handbook of Public Personnel Administration.* New York: Marcel Dekker, 1995.

"Report of the Committee Set Up to Examine the Representations Made by the Trade Union Association of Bohemia, Moravia, and Slovakia and by the Czech and Slovak Confederation of Trade Unions under Art. 24 of the ILO Constitution Alleging Nonobservance by the CSFR of the Discrimination (Employment and Occupation) Convention 1958 (No.111)." *ILO Official Bulletin* 75, supp. 1, ser. B (1992).

Roht-Arriaza, Naomi. "Punishment, Redress, and Pardon: Theoretical and Psychological Approaches." In *Impunity and Human Rights in International Law and Practice,* ed. Naomi Roht-Arriaza. New York: Oxford University Press, 1995.

Róna-Tas, Ákos. "The First Shall Be the Last? Entrepreneurship and Communist Cadres in the Transition from Socialism." *American Journal of Sociology* 100 (1994): 40–69.

Rose, Richard, William Mishler, and Christian Haerpfer. *Democracy and Its Alternatives: Understanding Post-Communist Societies.* Baltimore: Johns Hopkins University Press, 1998.

Rose-Ackerman, Susan. "Trust and Honesty in Post-Socialist Societies." *Kyklos* 54, no. 2/3 (2001): 415–44.

Rosenberg, Tina. *The Haunted Land: Facing Europe's Ghosts After Communism.* New York: Random House, 1996.

Rosenbloom, David H., ed. *Centenary Issues of the Pendleton Act: The Problematic Legacy of Civil Service Reform.* New York: Marcel Dekker, 1982.

Rossbach, Stefan. *Gnostic Wars: The Cold War in the Context of a History of Western Spirituality.* Edinburgh: Edinburgh University Press, 1999.

Rotberg, Robert I., and Dennis Thompson, eds. *Truth v. Justice: The Morality of Truth Commissions*. Princeton, N.J.: Princeton University Press, 2000.

Rubenstein, Richard. "Gray into Black: The Case of Mordecai Chaim Rumkowski." In *Gray Zones: Ambiguity and Compromise in the Holocaust and Its Aftermath*, ed. Jonathan Petropoulos and John K. Roth, 299–310. New York: Berghahn Books, 2005.

Rustow, Dankwart. "Transitions to Democracy: Toward a Dynamic Model." *Comparative Politics* 2, no. 3 (1970): 337–63.

Salivarová-Škvorecká, Zdena. *Osočení: Pravdivé příběhy lidí z_Cibulkova seznamu*. Brno: Host, 2000.

Schmitter Philippe C., and Terry Lynn Karl. "What Democracy Is . . . and Is Not." *Journal of Democracy* 2 (Summer 1991): 75–88.

Schumpeter, Joseph A. *Capitalism, Socialism, and Democracy*. London: George Allen & Unwin, 1979.

Schwartz, Herman. "Lustration in Eastern Europe." *Parker School Journal of Eastern European Law* 1, no. 2 (1994): 141–71. Reprinted in *Transitional Justice*, ed. Kritz, 3:461–83.

———. *The Struggle for Constitutional Justice in Post-Communist Europe*. Chicago: University of Chicago Press, 2000.

Seleny, Anna. "The Foundations of Post-Socialist Legitimacy." In *Dilemmas of Transition: The Hungarian Experience*, ed. Aurel Braun and Zoltan Barany. Lanham, Md.: Rowman and Littlefield, 1999.

Sen, Amartya. *Identity and Violence: The Illusion of Destiny*. New York: W. W. Norton, 2006.

Sheff, Thomas J. *Catharsis in Healing, Ritual and Drama*. Berkeley: University of California Press, 1979.

Siklova, Jirina. "Lustration or the Czech Way of Screening." *East European Constitutional Review* 5, no. 1 (1996): 57–62.

Simon, Jeffrey. *Hungary and NATO: Problems in Civil-Military Relations*. Lanham, Md.: Rowman and Littlefield, 2003.

Silverstein, Helena, "The Symbolic Life of Law: The Instrumental and the Constitutive in Scheingold's *The Politics of Rights*." *International Journal for the Semiotics of Law* 16, no. 4 (2003): 407–23.

Sniderman, Paul M., and Douglas Grob. "Innovations in Experimental Design in General Population Attitude Surveys." *Annual Review of Sociology* 22 (1996): 377–99.

Sólyom, László, and Georg Brunner. *The Constitutional Judiciary in a New Democracy: The Hungarian Constitutional Court*. Ann Arbor: University of Michigan Press, 2000.

Sotiropoulos, Dimitri A. "Swift Gradualism and Variable Outcomes: Vetting in Post-Authoritarian Greece." In *Justice as Prevention*, ed. Mayer-Rieckh and de Greiff, 120–45

Śpiewak, Paweł. *Pamięć po komunizmie*. Gdansk, Poland: Słowo/obraz terytoria, 2005.

Spitz, Richard, and Matthew Chaskalson. *The Politics of Transition: A Hidden History of South Africa's Negotiated Settlement.* Johannesburg: Witwatersrand University Press, 2000.

Stan, Lavinia. "Explaining Country Differences." In *Transitional Justice in Eastern Europe and the Former Soviet Union: Reckoning with the Communist Past*, ed. Lavinia Stan. New York: Routledge, 2009.

———. "Hungary." In *Transitional Justice in Eastern Europe and the Former Soviet Union: Reckoning with the Communist Past*, ed. Lavinia Stan. New York: Routledge, 2009.

———. "Moral Cleansing, Romanian Style." *Problems of Post-Communism* 49, no. 4 (2002): 52–62.

Stan, Lavinia, and Lucian Turcescu. "The Devil's Confessors: Priests, Communists, Spies, and Informers." *East European Politics and Societies* 19, no. 4 (2005): 655–85.

Stinchcombe, Arthur. "Lustration as a Problem of the Social Basis of Constitutionalism." *Law & Social Inquiry* 20, no. 1 (1995): 245–76.

Stokes, Donald E. "Popular Evaluations of Government: An Empirical Assessment." In *Ethics and Bigness: Scientific, Academic, Religious, Political, and Military*, ed. Harlan Cleveland and Harold D. Lasswell. New York: Harper and Brothers, 1962.

Šturm, Lovro. Interview by the author. Constitutional Court of Slovenia, Ljubljana, 1999.

Sullivan, John L., James Piereson, and George E. Marcus. "An Alternative Conceptualization of Political Tolerance: Illusory Increases, 1950s–1970s." *American Political Science Review* 73, no. 3 (1979): 781–94.

Swain, Nigel. *Hungary: The Rise and Fall of Feasible Socialism.* New York: Verso, 1992.

Szczerbiak, Aleks. "Dealing with the Communist Past or the Politics of the Present? Lustration in Post-Communist Poland." *Europe-Asia Studies* 54, no. 4 (2002): 553–72.

Sztompka, Piotr. *Trust: A Sociological Theory.* New York: Cambridge University Press, 1999.

Teitel, Ruti G. *Transitional Justice.* Oxford: Oxford University Press, 2000.

Tocqueville, Alexis de. *Democracy in America.* New York: Penguin, 2004.

Truth and Reconciliation Commission of South Africa Report. Cape Town: Juta, 1998.

Tucker, Aviezer. "Paranoids May Be Persecuted: Post-Totalitarian Retroactive Justice." *Archives Européennes de Sociologie* 40, no. 1 (1999): 56–100.

Tutu, Desmond M. *No Future Without Forgiveness.* New York: Random House, 1999.

Ungváry, Krisztián. Interview by the author. Budapest, June 2006.

Uslaner, Eric M. *Moral Foundations of Trust.* Cambridge: Cambridge University Press, 2002.

Vachalovský, Přemysl, and John Bok. *Kato: Příběh opravdového člověka.* Olomouc, Czech Rep.: J. W. Hill, 2000.

Vachalovský, Přemysl, and Pavel Žáček. *Jan Kavan: V labyrintu služeb.* Prague: Formát, 2003.

Vachudová, Milada A. *Europe Undivided: Democracy, Leverage and Integration After Communism*. Oxford: Oxford University Press, 2005.

Valpy, Francis Edward Jackson. *An Etymological Dictionary of the Latin Language*. London: FEJ Valpy, 1828.

Vanhanen, Tatu. *Prospects of Democracy: A Study of 172 Countries*. London: Routledge, 1997.

Vásárhelyi, Maria. Interview by the author. Budapest, June 2006.

Verdoolaege, Annelies. *Reconciliation Discourse: The Case of the Truth and Reconciliation Commission*. Philadelphia: John Benjamins, 2008.

Virgili, Fabrice. *Shorn Women: Gender and Punishment in Liberation France*. New York: Berg, 2002.

Wasilewski, Jacek. "Polish Post-Transitional Elite." In *Second Generation of Democratic Elites in Central and Eastern Europe*, ed. Janina Frentzel-Zagórska and Jacek Wasilewski. Warsaw: Polish Academy of Science, 2000.

Welsh, Helga A. "Dealing with the Communist Past: Central and East European Experiences After 1990." *Europe-Asia Studies* 48, no. 3 (1996): 413–28.

Whitehead, Laurence. *Democratization: Theory and Experience*. Oxford: Oxford University Press, 2002.

Wildstein, Bronisław. *Długi cień PRL-u*. Kraków, Poland: Arkana, 2005.

Williams, Kieran. "Lustration as the Securitization of Democracy in Czechoslovakia and the Czech Republic." *Journal of Communist Studies and Transition Politics* 19, no. 4 (2003): 1–24.

Williams, Kieran, and Dennis Deletant. *Security Intelligence Services in New Democracies: The Czech Republic, Slovakia and Romania*. New York: Palgrave, 2000.

Williams, Kieran, Brigid Fowler, and Aleks Szczerbiak. "Explaining Lustration in Central Europe: A 'Post-Communist Politics' Approach." *Democratization* 12, no. 1 (2005): 22–43.

Wuthnow, Robert. *Meaning and Moral Order: Explorations in Cultural Analysis*. Berkeley: University of California Press, 1987.

Žáček, Pavel. *Boje o minulost*. Brno, Czech Rep.: Barrister and Principal, 2000.

Žák, Václav. "Lustrace nebo Spravedlnost?" *Český rozhlas* 6, December 10, 2005, http://www.rozhlas.cz/cro6/komentare/_zprava/210146 (accessed October 16, 2009).

Zakaria, Fareed. "The Rise of Illiberal Democracy." *Foreign Affairs* 76, no. 6 (November/December 1997): 22–43.

Zalaquett, José. "Balancing Ethical Imperatives and Political Constraints: The Dilemma of New Democracies Confronting Past Human Rights Violations." *Hastings Law Journal* 43 (1992): 1425–38.

Zamora, Rubén, and David Holiday. "The Struggle for Lasting Reform: Vetting Process in El Salvador." In *Justice as Prevention*, ed. Mayer-Rieckh and de Greiff, 80–118.

Zhong, Chen-Bo, and Katie Liljenquist. "Washing Away Your Sins: Threatened Morality and Physical Cleansing." *Science* 313 (2006): 1451–52.

Zyzak, Paweł. *Lech Wałęsa: Idea i Historia*. Kraków, Poland: Arcana, 2009.

INDEX

ACKNOWLEDGMENTS

The experimental vignette that tested the effects of lustration systems was embedded in surveys conducted in 2007 by CVVM in the Czech Republic, Tárki in Hungary, and OBOP in Poland in 2007. The collaboration with the survey agencies that belong to the most renowned in the region would have been impossible without a grant from the United States Institute of Peace (Grant SG 100–05S). In addition, my gratitude goes to all the institutions and individuals who helped me with this project during the past decade; this research was conducted under the auspices of several institutions, namely, the University of the Witwatersrand, the City University of Hong Kong, the Chinese University of Hong Kong, Yale University, and Newcastle University. The fieldwork was conducted under the auspices of the Czech Academy of Science, Central European University, and Copernicus University.

A number of individuals both inside and outside these institutions commented on the conceptualization of personnel systems, advised me on the research design, provided me with conditions for writing the book or with research assistance, or worked as interpreters, translators, or editors. I would like to thank Anikó Balogh, Derek Bell, Tomas Berglund, Tamás Berki, Bill Case, Cheung Yuet-wah, Filip Gołębiewski, Gábor Halmai, Ian Holliday, Stathis Kalyvas, Pierre Landry, William Maloney, Zdena Mansfeldová, Markéta Moore, Zdena Pospíšilová, Piotr Prosol, Christopher Roederer, Jeremy Seekings, Andrew Skeen, Iván Szelényi, Ting Kwok-fai, Gábor Tóka, Jiří Vinopal, Glenda Webster, Katarzyna Wilk, Agata Zadrożna, Andrzej Zybertowicz, the anonymous reviewers of my work, and other individuals who helped me or advised me with respect to about the project. I would also like to thank to Peter Agree, Erica Ginsburg, Jennifer Backer, and other members of the team at the University of Pennsylvania Press. My special thanks go to Susanne Y. P. Choi for her support and insightful comments on the first version of the manuscript. Any errors or omissions are my sole responsibility.

I started to study the processes of dealing with the past in 1998. Since 2000, I have presented numerous papers on the topic of lustration at specialized workshops as well as at major international conferences in political science, political psychology, and law and society. Sections of this book have been published as journal articles: "From Prague to Baghdad: Lustration Systems and Their Political Effects," *Government and Opposition* 41, no. 3 (2006): 347–72; "Lustration Laws in Action: The Motives and Evaluation of Lustration Policy in the Czech Republic and Poland (1989–2001)," *Law & Social Inquiry* 28, no. 2 (2003): 387–439; and "In Exchange for Truth: The Polish Lustration and the South African Amnesty Process," *Politikon: South African Journal of Political Studies* 32, no. 1 (2006): 81–99.